The Other Girls

by
A. D. T. Whitney

The Other Girls
by A. D. T. Whitney

Copyright © 2023

All Rights reserved.

No part of this publication may be reproduced, stored in a retrieval system, or transmitted in any form or by any means, electronic, mechanical, photocopying or Otherwise, without the written permission of the publisher.
The author/editor asserts the moral right to be identified as the author/editor of this work.

ISBN: 978-93-59950-34-1

Published by
DOUBLE 9 BOOKS
2/13-B, Ansari Road
Daryaganj, New Delhi – 110002
info@double9books.com
www.double9books.com
Tel. 011-40042856

This book is under public domain

ABOUT THE AUTHOR

The Adeline Dutton Train Whitney was an American poet and writer who wrote a lot. She had more than 20 books for girls and used the pen name A. D. T. Whitney. She was born September 15, 1824, and died March 20, 1906. Her books, which had standard ideas about women's roles, were very popular all through her life. A Book of Rhymes was her first project. After that came Mother Goose for Grown Folks, Boys at Chequassett, Faith Gartney's Girlhood, hitherto-a Story of Yesterday, Prince Strong's Outings, The Gayworthys, Leslie Goldthwaite, We Girls, Holy Tides, Real Folks, The Other Girls, Sights and Insights, Odd and Even, Bannyborough Whiten Memories, Daffodils, Pansies, Homespun Yarns, Ascutney Street, A Golden Gossip, Bird Talk, and Just How. She was born in Boston, Massachusetts, on September 15, 1824. Her name was Adeline Dutton Train. Eleanor Train and Enoch Train had a daughter named Eleanor. Enoch ran a large trade business with his cousin Samuel Train of Medford. They owned ships and sent goods to Russia and South America. In later years, he started his own line of packet ships that ran between Boston and Liverpool. This line became known as the "Warren Line." Her cousin was George Francis Train, who helped to start the Union Pacific Railroad.

CONTENTS

PREFACE 9

CHAPTER I
   SPILLED OUT 11

CHAPTER II
   UP-STAIRS 16

CHAPTER III
   TWO TRIPS IN THE TRAIN 22

CHAPTER IV
   NINETY-NINE FAHRENHEIT 38

CHAPTER V
   SPILLED OUT AGAIN 50

CHAPTER VI
   A LONG CHAPTER OF A WHOLE YEAR 62

CHAPTER VII
   BEL AND BARTHOLOMEW 83

CHAPTER VIII
   TO HELP: SOMEWHERE 95

CHAPTER IX
   INHERITANCE 102

CHAPTER X
   FILLMER AND BYLLES 108

CHAPTER XI
   CRISTOFERO 117

CHAPTER XII
   LETTERS AND LINKS 122

CHAPTER XIII
 RACHEL FROKE'S TROUBLE 129

CHAPTER XIV
 MAVIS PLACE CHAPEL 133

CHAPTER XV
 BONNY BOWLS 138

CHAPTER XVI
 RECOMPENSE 150

CHAPTER XVII
 ERRANDS OF HOPE 157

CHAPTER XVIII
 BRICKFIELD FARMS 165

CHAPTER XIX
 BLOSSOMING FERNS... 182

CHAPTER XX
 "WANTED"... 187

CHAPTER XXI
 VOICES AND VISIONS.. 195

CHAPTER XXII
 BOX FIFTY-TWO 206

CHAPTER XXIII
 EVENING AND MORNING: THE SECOND DAY 218

CHAPTER XXIV
 TEMPTATION 223

CHAPTER XXV
 BEL BREE'S CRUSADE: THE PREACHING 230

CHAPTER XXVI
 TROUBLE AT THE SCHERMANS' 237

CHAPTER XXVII
 BEL BREE'S CRUSADE: THE TAKING OF JERUSALEM.................. 243

CHAPTER XXVIII
 "LIVING IN" 252

CHAPTER XXIX
    WINTERGREEN 261

CHAPTER XXX
    NEIGHBOR STREET AND GRAVES ALLEY 269

CHAPTER XXXI
    CHOSEN: AND CALLED 277

CHAPTER XXXII
    EASTER LILIES 287

CHAPTER XXXIII
    KITCHEN CRAMBO 293

CHAPTER XXXIV
    WHAT NOBODY COULD HELP 307

CHAPTER XXXV
    HILL-HOPE 317

PREFACE

"Wait until you are helped, my dear! Don't touch the pie until it is cut!"

The old Mother, Life, keeps saying that to us all.

As individuals, it is well for us to remember it; that we may not have things until we are helped; at any rate, until the full and proper time comes, for courageously and with right assurance helping ourselves.

Yet it is good for *people,* as people, to get a morsel—a flavor—in advance. It is well that they should be impatient for the King's supper, to which we shall all sit down, if we will, one day.

So I have not waited for everything to happen and become a usage, that I have told you of in this little story. I confess that there are good things in it which have not yet, literally, come to pass. I have picked something out of the pie beforehand.

I meant, therefore, to have laid all dates aside; especially as I found myself a little cramped by them, in re-introducing among these "Other Girls" the girls whom we have before, and rather lately, known. Lest, possibly, in anything which they have here grown to, or experienced, or accomplished, the sharply exact reader should seem to detect the requirement of a longer interval than the almanacs could actually give, I meant to have asked that it should be remembered, that we story-tellers write chiefly in the Potential Mood, and that tenses do not very essentially signify. It will all have had opportunity to be true in eighteen-seventy-five, if it have not had in eighteen-seventy-three. Well enough, indeed, if the prophecies be justified as speedily as the prochronisms will.

The Great Fire, you see, came in and dated it. I could not help that; neither could I leave the great fact out.

Not any more could I possibly tell what sort of April days we should have, when I found myself fixed to the very coming April and Easter, for the closing chapters of my tale. If persistent snow-storms fling a falsehood in my face, it will be what I have not heretofore believed possible,—a *white* one; and we can all think of balmy Aprils that have been, and that are yet to be.

With these appeals for trifling allowance,—leaving the larger need to the obvious accounting for in a largeness of subject which no slight fiction can adequately handle,—I give you leave to turn the page.

A. D. T. W.

BOSTON, *March*, 1873.

CHAPTER I
SPILLED OUT

Sylvie Argenter was driving about in her mother's little basket-phæton.

There was a story about this little basket-phæton, a story, and a bit of domestic diplomacy.

The story would branch away, back and forward; which I cannot, right here in this first page, let it do. It would tell—taking the little carriage for a text and key—ever so much about aims and ways and principles, and the drift of a household life, which was one of the busy little currents in the world that help to make up its great universal character and atmosphere, at this present age of things, as the drifts and sweeps of ocean make up the climates and atmospheres that wrap and influence the planet.

But the diplomacy had been this:—

"There is one thing, Argie, I should really like Sylvie to have. It is getting to be almost a necessity, living out of town as we do."

Mr. Argenter's other names were "Increase Muchmore;" but his wife passed over all that, and called him in the grace of conjugal intimacy, "Argie."

Increase Muchmore Argenter.

A curious combination; but you need not say it could not have happened. I have read half a dozen as funny combinations in a single advertising page of a newspaper, or in a single transit of the city in a horse-car.

It did not happen altogether without a purpose, either. Mr. Argenter's father had been fond of money; had made and saved a considerable sum himself; and always meant that his son should make and save a good deal more. So he signified this in his cradle and gave him what he called a lucky name, to begin with. The wife of the elder Mr. Argenter had been a Muchmore; her only brother had been named Increase, either out of oddity, such as influenced a certain Mr. Crabtree whom I have heard of, to call his son Agreen, or because the old Puritan name had been in the family, or with a like original inspiration of luck and thrift to that which influenced the later christening, if you can call it such; and now, therefore, resulted Increase

Muchmore Argenter. The father hung, as it were, a charm around his son's neck, as Catholics do, giving saints' names to their children. But young Increase found it, in his earlier years, rather of the nature of a millstone. It was a good while, for instance, before Miss Maria Thorndike could make up her mind to take upon herself such a title. She did not much mind it now. "I.M. Argenter" was such a good signature at the bottom of a check; and the surname was quite musical and elegant. "Mrs. Argenter" was all she had put upon her cards. There was no other Mrs. Argenter to be confounded with. The name stood by itself in the Directory. All the rest of the Argenters were away down in Maine in Poggowantimoc.

"Living out of town as we do." Mrs. Argenter always put that in. It was the nut that fastened all her screws of argument.

"Away out here as we are, we *must* keep an expert cook, you know; we can't send out for bread and cake, and salads and soups, on an emergency, as we did in town." "We *must* have a seamstress in the house the year round; it is such a bother driving about a ten-mile circuit after one in a hurry;" and now,—"Sylvie *ought* to have a little vehicle of her own, she is so far away from all her friends; no running in and out and making little daily plans, as girls do in a neighborhood. All the girls of her class have their own pony-chaises now; it is a part of the plan of living."

"It isn't any part of *my* plan," said Mr. Argenter, who had his little spasms of returning to old-fashioned ideas he was brought up in, but had long ago practically deserted; and these spasms mostly took him, it must be said, in response to new propositions of Mrs. Argenter's. His own plans evolved gradually; he came to them by imperceptible steps of mental process, or outward constraint; Mrs. Argenter's "jumped" at him, took him at unawares, and by sudden impinging upon solid shield of permanent judgment struck out sparks of opposition. She could not very well help that. He never had time to share her little experiences, and interests, and perplexities, and so sympathize with her as she went along, and up to the agreeing and consenting point.

"I won't set her up with any such absurdities," said Mr. Argenter. "It's confounded ruinous shoddy nonsense. Makes little fools of them all. Sylvie's got airs enough now. It won't do for her to think she can have everything the Highfords do."

"It isn't that," said Mrs. Argenter, sweetly. Her position, and the soft "g" in her name, giving her a sense of something elegant and gentle-bred to be always sustained and acted up to, had really helped and strengthened Mrs. Argenter in very much of her established amiability. We don't know, always, where our ties and braces really are. We are graciously allowed many a little temporary stay whose hold cannot be quite directly raced to the everlasting foundations.

"It isn't *that*; I don't care for the Highfords, particularly. Though I do like to have Sylvie enjoy things as she sees them enjoyed all around her, in her own circle. But it's the convenience; and then, it's a real means of showing kindness. She can so often ask other girls, you know, to drive with her; girls who haven't pony-chaises."

"*Showing* kindness, yes; you've just hit it there. But it isn't always *fun to the frogs*, Mrs. A.!"

Now if Mrs. Argenter disliked one thing more than another, that her husband ever did, it was his calling her "Mrs. A.;" and I am very much afraid, I was going to say, that he knew it; but of course he did when she had mildly told him so, over and over,—I am afraid he *recollected* it, at this very moment, and others similar.

"I don't know what you mean, Mr. Argenter," she said, with some quiet coldness.

"I mean, I know how she takes *other* girls to ride; she *sets them down at the small gray house,—the house without any piazza or bay window, Michael!*" and Mr. Argenter laughed. That was the order he had heard Sylvie give one day when he had come up with his own carriage at the post-office in the village, whither he had walked over for exercise and the evening papers. Sylvie had Aggie Townsend with her, and she put her head out at the window on one side just as her father passed on the other, and directed Michael, with a very elegant nonchalance, to "set this little girl down" as aforesaid. Mr. Argenter had been half amused and half angry. The anger passed off, but he had kept up the joke.

"O, do let that old story alone," exclaimed Mrs. Argenter. "Sylvie will soon outgrow all that. If you want to make her a real lady, there is nothing like letting her get thoroughly used to having things."

"I don't intend her to get used to having a pony-chaise," Mr. Argenter said very quietly and shortly. "If she wants to 'show a kindness,' and take 'other' girls to ride, there's the slide-top buggy and old Scrub. She may have that as often as she pleases."

And Mrs. Argenter knew that this ended—or had better end—the conversation.

For that time. Sylvie Argenter did get used to having a pony-chaise, after all. Her mother waited six months, until the pleasant summer weather, when her friends began to come out from the city to spend days with her, or to take early teas, and Michael had to be sent continually to meet and leave them at the trains. Then she began again, and asked for a pony-chaise for herself. To "save the cost of it in Michael's time, and the wear and tear of the heavy carriages. Those little sunset drives would be such a pleasure to her, just when Michael had to be milking and putting up for the night." Mr. Argenter had forgotten all about the other talk, Sylvie's name now being not once mentioned; and the end of it was that a pretty little low phæton was added to the Argenter equipages, and that Sylvie's mother was always lending it to her.

So Sylvie was driving about in it this afternoon. She had been over to West Dorbury to see the Highfords, and was coming round by Ingraham's Corner, to stop there and buy one of his fresh big loaves of real brown bread for her father's tea. It was a little unspoken, politic understanding between Sylvie and her mother, that some small, acceptable errand like this was to be accomplished whenever the former had the basket-phæton of an afternoon. By quiet, unspoken demonstration, Mr. Argenter was made to feel in his own little comforts what a handy thing it was to have a daughter flitting about so easily with a pony-carriage.

But there was something else to be accomplished this time that Sylvie had not thought of, and that when it happened, she felt with some dismay might not be quite offset and compensated for by the Ingraham brown bread.

Rod Sherrett was out too, from Roxeter, Young-Americafying with his tandem; trying, to-day, one of his father's horses with his own Red Squirrel, to make out the team; for which, if he should come to any grief, Rodgers, the coachman, would have to bear responsibility for being persuaded to let Duke out in such manner.

Just as Sylvie Argenter drew up her pony at the baker's door, Rod Sherrett came spinning round the corner in grand style. But Duke was not used to tandem harness, and Red Squirrel, put ahead, took flying side-leaps now and then on his own account; and Duke, between his comrade's escapades and his driver's checks and admonitions, was to that degree perplexed in his mind and excited off his well-bred balance, that he was by this time becoming scarcely more reliable in the shafts. Rod found he had his hands full. He found this out, however, only just in time to realize it, as they were suddenly relieved and emptied of their charge; for, before his call and the touch of his long whip could bring back Red Squirrel into line at this turn, he had sprung so far to the left as to bring Duke and the "trap" down upon the little phæton. There was a lock and a crash; a wheel was off the phæton, the tandem was overturned, Sylvie Argenter, in the act of alighting, was thrown forward over the threshold of the open shop-door, Rod Sherrett was lying in the road, a man had seized the pony, and Duke and Red Squirrel were shattering away through the scared Corner Village, with the wreck at their heels.

Sylvie's arm was bruised, and her dress torn; that was all. She felt a little jarred and dizzy at first, when Mr. Ingraham lifted her up, and Rodney Sherrett, picking himself out of the dust with a shake and a stamp, found his own bones unbroken, and hurried over to ask anxiously—for he was a kind-hearted fellow—how much harm he had done, and to express his vehement regret at the "horrid spill."

Rod Sherrett and Sylvie Argenter had danced together at the Roxeter Assemblies, and the little Dorbury "Germans;" they had boated, and picknicked, and skated in company, but to be tumbled together into a baker's shop, torn and frightened, and dusty,—each feeling, also, in a great scrape,—this was an odd and startling partnership. Sylvie was pale; Rod was sorry; both were very much demolished as to dress: Sylvie's hat had got a queer crush, and a tip that was never intended over her eyes; Rodney's was lying in the street, and his hair was rumpled and curiously powdered. When they had stood and looked at each other an instant after the first inquiry and reply, they both laughed. Then Rodney shrugged his shoulders, and walked over and picked up his hat.

"It might have been worse," he said, coming back, as Mr. Ingraham and the man who had held Sylvie's pony took the latter out of the shafts and led him to a post to fasten him, and then proceeded together, as well as they could, to lift the disabled phæton and roll it over to the blacksmith's shop to be set right.

"You'll be all straight directly," he said, "and I'm only thankful you're not much hurt. But I *am* in a mess. Whew! What the old gentleman will say if Duke don't come out of it comfortable, is something I'd rather not look ahead to. I must go on and see. I'll be back again, and if there's anything—anything *more*," he added with a droll twinkle, "that I can do for you, I shall be happy, and will try to do it a little better."

The feminine Ingrahams were all around Sylvie by this time: Mrs. Ingraham, and Ray, and Dot. They bemoaned and exclaimed, and were "thankful she'd come off as she had;" and "she'd better step right in and come up-stairs." The village boys were crowding round,—all those who had not been in time to run after the "smash,"—and Sylvie gladly withdrew to the offered shelter. Rod Sherrett gave his hair a toss or two with his hands, struck the dust off his wide-awake, put it on, and walked off down the hill, through the staring and admiring crowd.

CHAPTER II
UP-STAIRS

The two Ingraham girls had been sitting in their own room over the shop when the accident occurred, and it was there they now took Sylvie Argenter, to have her dress tacked together again, and to wash her face and hands and settle her hair and hat. Mrs. Ingraham came bustling after with "arnicky" for the bruised arm. They were all very delighted and important, having the great Mr. Argenter's daughter quite to themselves in the intimacy of "up-stairs," to wait upon and take care of. Mrs. Ingraham fussed and "my-deared" a good deal; her daughters took it with more outward calmness. Although baker's daughters, they belonged to the present youthful generation, born to best education at the public schools, sewing-machines, and universal double-skirted full-fashions; and had read novels of society out of the Roxeter town library.

There was a good deal of time after the bathing and mending and re-arranging were all done. The axle of the phæton had been split, and must be temporarily patched up and banded. There was nothing for Sylvie to do but to sit quietly there in the old-fashioned, dimity-covered easy-chair which they gave her by the front window, and wait. Meanwhile, she observed and wondered much.

She had never got out of the Argenter and Highford atmosphere before. She didn't know—as we don't about the moon—whether there might *be* atmosphere for the lesser and subsidiary world. But here she found herself in the bedroom of two girls who lived over a bake-shop, and, really, it seemed they actually *did* live, much after the fashion of other people. There were towels on the stand, a worked pincushion on the toilet, white shades and red tassels to the windows, this comfortable easy-chair beside one and a low splint rocker in the other,—with queer, antique-looking soft footstools of dark cloth, tamboured in bright colors before each,—white quilted covers on table and bureau, and positively, a striped, knitted foot-spread in scarlet and white yarn, folded across the lower end of the bed.

She had never thought of there being anything at Ingraham's Corner but a shop on a dusty street, with, she supposed,—only she never really supposed about it,—some sort of places, behind and above it, under the same roof, for the people to get away into when they weren't selling bread, to cook, and eat, and sleep, she had never exactly imagined how, but of course not as they did in real houses that were not shops. And when Mrs. Ingraham, who had bustled off down-stairs, came shuffling up again as well as she could with both hands full and her petticoats in her way, and appeared bearing a cup of hot tea and a plate of spiced gingerbread,—the latter *not* out of the shop, but home-made, and out of her own best parlor cupboard,—she perceived almost with bewilderment, that cup and plate were of spotless china, and the spoon was of real, worn, bright silver. She might absolutely put these things to her own lips without distaste or harm.

"It'll do you good after your start," said kindly Mrs. Ingraham.

The difference came in with the phraseology. A silver spoon is a silver spoon, but speech cannot be rubbed up for occasion. Sylvie thought she must mean *before* her start, about which she was growing anxious.

"O, I'm sorry you should have taken so much trouble," she exclaimed. "I wonder if the phæton will be ready soon?"

"Mr. Ingraham he's got back," replied the lady. "He says Rylocks'll be through with it in about half an hour. Don't you be a mite concerned. Jest set here and drink your tea, and rest. Dot, I guess you'd as good's come down-stairs. I shall be wantin' you with them fly nets. Your father's fetched home the frames."

Ray Ingraham sat in the side window, and crocheted thread edging,— of which she had already yards rolled up and pinned together in a white ball upon her lap,—while Sylvie sipped her tea.

The side window looked out into a shady little garden-spot, in the front corner of which grew a grand old elm, which reached around with beneficent, beautiful branches, and screened also a part of the street aspect. Seen from within, and from under these great, green, swaying limbs,—the same here in the village as out in free field or forest,—the street itself seemed less dusty, less common, less impossible to pause upon for anything but to buy bread, or mend a wheel, or get a horse shod.

"How different it is, in behind!" said Sylvie, speaking out involuntarily.

Ray shot a quick look at her from her bright dark eyes.

"I suppose it is,—almost everywheres," she answered. "I've got turned round so, sometimes, with people and places, until they never seemed the same again."

If Ray had not said "everywheres," Sylvie would not have been reminded; but that word sent her, in recollection, out to the house-front and the shop-sign again. Ray knew better; she was a good scholar, but she heard her mother and others like her talk vernacular every day. It was a wonder she shaded off from it as delicately as she did.

Ray Ingraham, or Rachel,—for that was her name, and her sister's was Dorothy, though these had been shortened into two as charming, pet little appellatives as could have been devised by the most elegant intention,—was a pretty girl, with her long-lashed, quick-glancing dark eyes, her hair, that crimped naturally and fell off in a deep, soft shadow from her temples, her little mouth, neatly dimpled in, and the gypsy glow of her clear, bright skin. Dot was different: she was dark too, not *so* dark; her eyes were full, brilliant gray, with thick, short lashes; she was round and comfortable: nose, cheeks, chin, neck, waist, hands; her mouth was large, with white teeth that showed easily and broadly, instead of, like Ray's, with just a quiver and a glimmer. She was like her mother. She looked the smart, buxom, common-sense village girl to perfection. Ray had the hint of something higher and more delicate about her, though she had the trigness, and readiness, and every-day-ness too.

Sylvie sat silent after this, and looked at her, wondering, more than she had wondered about the furniture. Thinking, "how many girls there were in the world! All sorts—everywhere! What did they all do, and find to care for?" These were not the "other" girls of whom her mother had blandly said that she could show kindnesses by taking them to drive. Those were such as Aggie Townsend, the navy captain's widow's daughter,—nice, but poor; girls whom everybody noticed, of course, but who hadn't it in their power to notice anybody. That made such a difference! These were *otherer* yet! And for all that they were girls,—girls! Ever so much of young life, and glow, and companionship, ever so much of dream, and hope, and possible story, is in just that little plural of five letters. A company of girls! Heaven only knows what there is *not* represented, and suggested, and foreshadowed there!

Sylvie Argenter, with all her nonsense, had a way of putting herself, imaginatively, into other people's places. She used to tell her mother, when she was a little child and said her hymns,—which Mrs. Argenter, not having any very fresh, instant spiritual life, I am afraid, out of which to feed her child, chose for her in dim remembrance of what had been thought good for herself when she was little,—that she "didn't know exactly as she *did* 'thank the goodness and the grace that on her birth had smiled.'" She "should like pretty well to have been a little—Lapland girl with a sledge; or—a Chinese; or—a kitchen girl; a little while, I mean!"

She had a way of intimacy with the servants which Mrs. Argenter found it hard to check. She liked to get into Jane's room when she was "doing herself up" of an afternoon, and look over her cheap little treasures in her band-box and chest-drawer. She made especial love to a carnelian heart, and a twisted gold ring with two clasped hands on it.

"I think it's real nice to have only *two* or *three* things, and to 'clean yourself up,' and to have a 'Sunday out!'" she said.

Mrs. Argenter was anxiously alarmed at the child's low tastes. Yet these were very practicably compatible with the alternations of importance in being driven about in her father's barouche, taking Aggie Townsend up on the road, and "setting her down at the small gray house."

Sylvie thought, this afternoon, looking at Ray Ingraham, in her striped lilac and white calico, with its plaited waist and cross-banded, machine-stitched double skirt, sitting by her shady window, beyond which, behind the garden angle, rose up the red brick wall of the bakehouse, whence came a warm, sweet smell of many new-drawn loaves,—looking around within, at the snug tidiness of the simple room, and even out at the street close by, with its stir and curious interest, yet seen from just as real a shelter as she had in her own chamber at home,—that it might really be nice to be a baker's daughter and live in the village,—"when it wasn't your own fault, and you couldn't help it."

Ray nodded to some one out of her window.

Sylvie saw a bright color come up in her cheeks, and a sparkle into her eyes as she did so, while a little smile, that she seemed to think was all to herself, crept about her mouth and lingered at the dimpled corners. There was an expression as if she hid herself quite away in some consciousness of her own, from any recollection of the strange girl sitting by.

The strange girl glanced from *her* window, and saw a young carpenter with his box of tools go past under the elm, with some sort of light subsiding also in like manner from his face. He was in his shirt sleeves,—but the sleeves were white,—and his straw hat was pushed back from his forehead, about which brown curls lay damp with heat. Sylvie did not believe he had even touched his hat, when he had looked up through the friendly elm boughs and bowed to the village girl in her shady corner. His hands were full, of course. Such people's hands were almost always full. That was the reason they did not learn such things. But how cute it had been of Ray Ingraham *not* to sit in the front window! He was certain to come by, too, she supposed. To be sure; that was the street. Ray Ingraham would not have cared to live up a long avenue, to wait for people to come on purpose, in carriages.

She got as far as this in her thinkings, at the same moment that she came to the bottom of her cup of tea. And then she caught a glimpse of Rylocks, rolling the phæton across from the smithy.

"What a funny time I have had! And how kind you have all been!" she said, getting up. "I am ever so much obliged, Miss Ingraham. I wonder"— and then, suddenly, she thought it might not be quite civil to wonder.

Ray Ingraham laughed.

"So do I!" she said quickly, with a bright look. She knew well enough what Sylvie stopped at.

Each of these two girls wondered if there would ever be any more "getting in behind" for them, as regarded each other, in their two different lives.

As Sylvie Argenter came out at the shop-door, Rodney Sherrett appeared at the same point, safely mounted on the runaway Duke. The team had been stopped below at the river; he had found a stable and a saddle, had left Red Squirrel and the broken vehicle to be sent for, and was going home, much relieved and assured by being able to present himself upon his father's favorite roadster, whole in bones and with ungrazed skin.

The street boys stood round again, as he dismounted to make fresh certainty of Sylvie's welfare, handed her into her phæton, and then, springing to the saddle, rode away beside her, down the East Dorbury road.

Mrs. Argenter was sitting with her worsted work in the high, many-columned terrace piazza which gave grandeur to the great show-house that Mr. Argenter had built some five years since, when Sylvie, with Rod Sherrett beside her, came driving up the long avenue, or, as Mrs. Argenter liked to call it, out of the English novels, the *approach*. She laid back her canvas and wools into the graceful Fayal basket-stand, and came down the first flight of stone steps to meet them.

"How late you are, Sylvie! I had begun to be quite worried," she said, when Sylvie dropped the reins around the dasher and stood up in the low carriage, nodding at her mother. She felt quite brave and confident about the accident, now that Rodney Sherrett had come all the way with her to the very door, to account for it and to help her out with the story.

Rodney lifted his hat to the lady.

"We've had a great spill, Mrs. Argenter. All my fault, and Red Squirrel's. Miss Argenter has brought home more than I have from the *mêlée*. I started with a tandem, and here I am with only Gray Duke and a borrowed saddle. It was out at Ingraham's Corner,—a quick turn, you know,—and Miss

Argenter had just stopped when Squirrel sprang round upon her. My trap is pretty much into kindlings, but there are no bones broken. You must let me send Rodgers round on his way to town to-morrow, to take the phæton to the builder's. It wants a new axle. I'm awful sorry; but after all" — with a bright smile, — "I can't think it altogether an ill wind, — for *me*, at any rate. I couldn't help enjoying the ride home."

"I don't believe you could help enjoying the whole of it, except the very minute of the tip-out itself, before you knew," said Sylvie, laughing.

"Well, it *was* a lark; but the worst is coming. I've got to go home all alone. I wish you'd come and tell the tale for *me*, Miss Sylvie. I shouldn't be half so afraid!"

CHAPTER III
TWO TRIPS IN THE TRAIN

The seven o'clock morning train was starting from Dorbury Upper Village.

Early business men, mechanics, clerks, shop-girls, sewing-girls, office-boys,—these made up the list of passengers. Except, perhaps, some travellers now and then, bound for a first express from Boston, or an excursion party to take a harbor steamer for a day's trip to Nantasket or Nahant.

Did you ever contrast one of these trains—when perhaps you were such traveller or excursionist—with the after, leisurely, comfortable one at ten or eleven; when gentlemen who only need to be in the city through banking hours, and ladies bent on calls or elegant shopping, come chatting and rustling to their seats, and hold a little drawing-room exchange in the twenty-five minutes' trip?

If you have,—and if you have a little sympathetic imagination that fills out hints,—you have had a glimpse of some of these "other girls" and the thing that daily living is to them, with which my story means to concern itself.

Have you noticed the hats, with the rose or the feather behind or at top, scrupulously according to the same dictate of style that rules alike for seven and ten o'clock, but which has often to be worn through wet and dry till the rose has been washed by too many a shower, and the feather blown by too many a dusty wind, to stand for anything but a sign that she knows what should be where, if she only had it to put there? Have you seen the cheap alpacas, in two shades, sure to fade in different ways and out of kindred with each other, painfully looped in creasing folds, very much sat upon, but which would not by any means resign themselves to simple smoothed straightness, while silks were hitched and crisp Hernanis puffed?

Yet the alpacas, and all their innumerable cousinhood, have also their first mornings of fresh gloss, when the newness of the counter is still upon them; there is a youth for all things; a first time, a charm that seems as if it might last, though we know it neither will nor was meant to; if it would, or were, the counters might be taken down. And people who wear gowns that are creased and faded, have each, one at a time, their days of glory, when they begin again. The farther apart they come, perhaps the more of the spring-time there is in them.

Marion Kent bloomed out this clear, sweet, clean summer morning in a span new tea-colored zephyrine polonaise with three little frills edged with tiny brown braid, which set it off trimly with the due contrasting depth of color, and cost nearly nothing except the stitches and the kerosene she burned late in the hot July nights in her only time for finishing it. She had covered her little old curled leaf of a hat with a tea-colored corner that had been left, and puffed it up high and light to the point of the new style, with brown veil tissue that also floated off in an abundant cloudy grace behind; and she had such an air of breezy and ecstatic elegance as she came beaming and hastening into the early car, that nobody really looked down to see that the underskirt was the identical black brilliantine that had done service all the spring in the dismal mornings of waterproofs and india-rubbers and general damp woolen smells and blue nips and shivers.

Marion Kent always made you think of things that never at all belonged to her. She gave you an impression of something that she seemed to stand for, which she could not wholly be. Her zephyrine, with its silky shine, hinted at the real lustres of far more costly fabrics; her hat, perked up with puffs of grenadine (how all these things do rhyme and repeat their little Frenchy tags of endings!) put you in mind of lace and feathers, and a general float and flutter of gay millinery; her step and expression, as she came airily into this second-rate old car, put on for the "journeymen" train, brought up a notion, almost, of some ball-room advent, flushed and conscious and glad with the turning of all admiring eyes upon it; her face, even, without being absolutely beautiful, sparkled out at you a certain will and force and intent of beauty that shot an idea or suggestion of brilliant prettiness instantly through your unresisting imagination, compelling you to fill out whatever was wanting; and what more, can you explain, do feature and bearing that come nearest to perfect fulfillment effect?

The middle-aged cabinet-maker looked over his newspaper at her as she came in; he had little daughters of his own growing up to girlhood, and there might have been some thought in his head not purely admiring; but still he looked up. The knot of office-boys, crowding and skylarking across a couple of seats, stopped their shuffle and noise for a second, and one said, "My! ain't she stunning?" A young fellow, rather spruce in his own way also, with precise necktie, deep paper cuffs and dollar-store studs and initial sleeve-buttons, touched his hat with an air of taking credit to himself, as she glanced at him; and another, in a sober old gray suit, with only a black ribbon knotted under his linen collar, turned slightly the other way as she approached, and with something like a frown between his brows, looked out of the window at a wood-pile.

Marion's cheeks were a tint brighter, and her white teeth seemed to flash out a yet more determined smile, as, passing him by, she seated herself with friendly bustle among some girls a little behind him.

"In again, Marion?" said one. "I thought you'd left."

"Only in for a transient," said Marion, with a certain clear tone that reminded one of the stage-trainer's direction to "speak to the galleries." "Nellie Burton is sick, and Lufton sent for me. I'll do for a month or so, and like it pretty well; then I shall have a tiff, I suppose, and fling it up again; I can't stand being ordered round longer than that."

"Or longer than the *new* lasts," said the other slyly, touching the drapery sleeve of the zephyrine. "It *is* awful pretty, Marry!"

"Yes, and while the new lasts Lufton'll be awful polite," returned Marion. "He likes to see his girls look stylish, I can tell you. When things begin to shab out, then the snubbing begins. And how they're going to help shabbing out I should like to know, dragging round amongst the goods and polishing against the counters? and who's going to afford ready-made, or pay for sewing, out of six dollars a week and cars and dinners, let alone regular board, that some of 'em have to take off? Why there isn't enough left for shoes! No wonder Lufton's always changing. Well—there's one good of it! You can always get a temporary there. Save up a month and then put into port and refit. That's the way I do."

"But what does it come to, after all's said and done? and what if you hadn't the port?" asked Hannah Upshaw, the girl with the shawl on, who never wore suits.

Marion Kent shrugged her shoulders.

"I don't know, yet. I take things as they come to me. I don't pretend to calculate for anybody else. I know one thing, though, there is other things to be done,—and it isn't sewing-machines either, if you can once get started. And when I can see my way clear, I mean to start. See if I don't!"

The train stopped at the Pomantic station. The young man in the gray clothes rose up, took something from under the car-seat and went out. What he had with him was a carpenter's box. It was the same youth who had greeted Ray Ingraham from beneath the elm branches. As the train got slowly under way again, Marion looked straight out at her window into Frank Sunderline's face, and bowed,—very modestly and sweetly bowed. He was waiting for that instant on the platform, until the track should be clear and he could cross.

What he caught in Marion's look, as she turned it full upon him, nobody could see; but there was a quieter earnest in it, certainly, when she turned back; and the young man had responded to her salutation with a relaxing glance of friendly pleasantness that seemed more native to his face than the frown of a few minutes before.

Marion Kent had several selves; several relations, at any rate, into which she could put herself with others. I think she showed young Sunderline, for that instant, out of gentler, questioning, almost beseeching eyes, a something she could not show to the whole car-full with whom at the moment of her entrance she had been in rapport, through frills and puffs and flutters, into which she had allowed her consciousness to pass. Behind the little window he could only see a face; a face quieted down from its gay flippancy; a face that showed itself purposely and simply to him; eyes that said, "What was that you thought of me just now? *Don't* think it!"

They were old neighbors and child-friends. They had grown up together; had they been growing away from each other in some things since they had been older? Often it appeared so; but it was Marion chiefly who seemed to change; then, all at once, in some unspoken and intangible way, for a moment like this, she seemed to come suddenly back again, or he seemed to catch a glimpse of that in her, hidden, not altered, which *might* come back one of these days. Was it a glimpse, perhaps, like the sight the Lord has of each one of us, always?

Meanwhile, what of Ray Ingraham?

Ray Ingraham was sweet, and proper, and still; just what Frank Sunderline thought was prettiest and nicest for a woman to be. He was always reminded by her ways of what it would be so pretty and nice for Marion Kent to be. But Marion *would* sparkle; and it is so hard to be still and sparkle too. He liked the brightness and the airiness; a little of it, near to; he did not like a whole car-full, or room-full, or street full,—he did not like to see a woman sparkle all round.

Mr. Ingraham had come into Dorbury Upper Village some half dozen years since; had leased the bakery, house, and shop; and two years afterward, Rachel had come home to stay. She had been left in Boston with her grandmother when the family had moved out of the city, that she might keep on a while with the school that she was used to and stood so well in; with her Chapel classes, also, where she heard literature and history lectures, each once a week. Ray could not bear to leave them, nor to give up her Sunday lessons in the dear old Mission Rooms. Dot was three years younger; she could begin again anywhere, and their mother could not spare both. Besides, "what Ray got she could always be giving to Dot afterwards."

That is not so easy, and by no means always follows. Dot turned out the mother's girl,—the girl of the village, as was said; practical, comfortable, pleasant, capable, sensible. Ray was something of all these, with a touch of more; alive in a higher nature, awakened to receive through upper channels, sensitive to some things that neither pleased nor troubled Mrs. Ingraham and Dot.

It took a good while to come to know a girl like Ray Ingraham; most of her young acquaintance felt the *step up* that they must take to stand fairly beside her, or come intimately near. Frank Sunderline felt it too, in certain ways, and did not suppose that she could see in him more than he saw in himself: a plain fellow, good at his trade, or going to be; bright enough to know brightness in other people when he came across it, and with enough of what, independent of circumstances, goes to the essential making of a gentleman, to perceive and be attracted by the delicate gentleness that makes a lady.

That was just what Ray Ingraham did see; only he hardly set it down in his self-estimate at its full value.

Do you perceive, story-reader, story-raveller, that Frank Sunderline was not quite in love with either of these girls? Do you see that it is not a matter of course that he should be?

I can tell you, you girls who make a romance out of the first word, and who can tell from the first chapter how it will all end, that you will make great mistakes if you go to interpreting life so,—your own, or anybody's else.

I can tell you that men—those who are good for very much—come often more slowly to their life-conclusions than you think; that woman-*nature* is a good deal to a man, and is meant to be, in gradual bearing and influence, in the shaping of his perception, the working of comparison, the coming to an understanding of his own want, and the forming of his ideal,—yes, even in the mere general pleasantness and gentle use of intercourse—before the *individual* woman reveals herself, slowly or suddenly, as the one only central need, and motive, and reward, and satisfying, that the world holds and has kept for him. For him to gain or to lose: either way, to have mightily to do with that soul-forging and shaping that the Lord, in his handling of every man, is about.

That night they all came out together in the last train. Ray Ingraham had gone in after dinner to make some purchases for her mother, and had been to see some Chapel friends. Marion, as she came in through the gate at the station, saw her far before, walking up the long platform to the cars. She watched her enter the second in the line, and hastened on, making up her mind instantly, like a field general, to her own best manœuvre. It was not exactly what every girl would have done; and therein showed her generalship. She would get into the same carriage, and take a seat with her. She knew very well that Frank Sunderline would jump on at Pomantic, his day's work just done. If he came and spoke to Ray he should speak also to her. She did not risk trying *which* he would come and speak to. It should be, that joining them, and finding it pleasant, he should not quite know which, after all, had most made it so. Different as they were, she and Ray Ingraham toned and flavored each other, and Marion knew it. They were like rose-color and gray; or like spice and salt: you did not stop to think which ruled the taste, or which your eye separately rested on. Something charming, delicious, resulted of their being together; they set each other off, and helped each other out. Then it was something that Frank Sunderline should see that Ray would let her be her friend; that she was not altogether too loud and pronounced for her. Ray did not turn aside and look at wood-piles, and get rid of her.

Furthermore, the way home from the Dorbury depot, for Frank and Marion both, lay *past* the bakery, on down the under-hill road.

Marion did not *think out* a syllable of all this; she grasped the situation, and she acted in an instant. I told you she acted like a general in the field: perhaps neither she nor the general would be as skillful, always, with the maps and compasses, and time to plan beforehand. I do not think Marion *was* ever very wise in her fore-thoughts.

Beyond Pomantic, the next one or two stations took off a good many passengers, so that they had their part of the car almost to themselves. Frank Sunderline had come in and taken a place upon the other side; now he moved over into the seat behind them, accosting them pleasantly, but not interrupting the conversation which had been busily going on between them all the way. Ray was really interested in some things Marion had brought up to notice; her face was intent and thoughtful; perhaps she was not quite so pretty when she was set thinking; her dimples were hidden; but Marion was beaming, exhilarated partly by her own talk, somewhat by an honest, if half mischievous earnestness in her subject, and very much also by the consciousness of the young mechanic opposite, within observing and listening distance. Marion could not help talking over her shoulders, more or less, always.

"Men take the world in the rough, and do the work; women help, and come in for the finishing off," said Rachel, just as Frank Sunderline changed his place and joined them. "*We* could not handle those, for instance," she said, with a shy, quiet sign toward the carpenter's tools, and lowering her already gentle voice.

"Men break in the fields, and plough, and sow, and mow; and women ride home on the loads,—is that it?" said Marion, laughing, and snatching her simile from a hay-field with toppling wagons, that the train was at that moment skimming by. "Well, may be! All is, I shall look out for my ride. After things *are* broken in, I don't see why we shouldn't get the good of it."

"Value is what things stand for, or might procure, isn't it?" said Ray, turning to Sunderline, and taking him frankly and friendlily into the conversation.

"No fair!" cried Marion. "He doesn't understand the drift of it. Do you, see, Mr. Sunderline, why a man should be paid any more than a woman, for standing behind a counter and measuring off the same goods, or at a desk and keeping the same accounts? I don't! That's what I'm complaining of."

"That's the complaint of the day, I know," said Sunderline. "And no doubt there's a good deal of special unfairness that needs righting, and will get it. But things don't come to be as they are quite without a reason, either. There's a principle in it, you've got to look back to that."

"Well?" said Marion, gleefully interrogatory, and settling herself with an air of attention, and of demurely giving up the floor. She was satisfied to listen, if only Frank Sunderline would talk.

"I believe I see what you meant," he said to Ray. "About the values that things stand for. A man represents a certain amount of power in the world."

"O, does he?" put in Marion, with an indescribable inflection. "I'm glad to know."

"He *could* be doing some things that a woman could not do at all—was never meant to do. He stands for so much force. You may apply things as you please, but if you don't use them according to their relative capacity, the unused value has to be paid for—somewhere."

"That's a nice principle!" said Marion. "I like that I should like to be paid for what I *might* be good for!"

Frank Sunderline laughed.

"It's a good principle; because by it things settle themselves, in the long run. You may take mahogany or pine to make a table, and one will answer the common convenience of a table as well as the other; but you will learn not to take mahogany when the pine will serve the purpose. You will keep it for what the pine wouldn't be fit for; which wouldn't come to pass if the pine weren't cheapest. Women wouldn't get those places to tend counters and keep books, if the world hadn't found out that it was poor economy, as a general rule, to take men for it."

"But what do you say about mental power? About pay for teaching, for instance?" asked Ray.

"Why, you're coming round to *my* side!" exclaimed Marion. "I should really like to know *where* you are?"

"I am wherever I can get nearest to the truth of things," said Ray, smiling.

"That," said Sunderline, "is one of the specialties that is getting righted. Women *are* being paid more, in proportion, for intellectual service, and the nearer you come to the pure mental power, the nearer you come to equality in recompense. A woman who writes a clever book, or paints a good picture, or sculptures a good statue, can get as much for her work as a man. But where *time* is paid for,—where it is personal service,—the old principle at the root of things comes in. Men open up the wildernesses, men sail the seas, work the mines, forge the iron, build the cities, defend the nations while they grow, do the physical work of the world, *make way* for all the finishings of education and opportunity that come afterward, and that put women where they are to-day. And men must be counted for such things. It is man's work that has made these women's platforms. They have the capital of strength, and capital draws interest. The right of the strongest isn't necessarily *oppression* by the strongest. That's the way I look at it. And I think that what women lose in claim they gain in privilege."

"Only when women come to knock about the world without any claims, they don't seem to get much privilege," said Marion.

"I don't know. It seems rude to say so, perhaps, but they find a world ready made to knock round *in*, don't they? And it is because there's so much done that they couldn't have done themselves, that they find the chances waiting for them that they do. And the chances are multiplying with civilization, all the time. You see the question really goes back to first conditions, and lies upon the fact that first conditions may come back any day,—do come back, here and there, continually. Put man and woman together on the primitive earth, and it is the man that has got to subdue it; the woman is what Scripture calls her,—the helpmeet. And my notion is that if everything was right, a woman never should have to 'knock round alone.' It isn't the real order of Providence. I think Providence has been very much interfered with."

"There are widows," said Rachel, gently.

"Yes; and the 'fatherless and the widows' are everybody's charge to care for. I said—if things were right. I wish the energy was spent in bringing round the right that is used up in fitting things to the wrong."

"They say there are too many women in the world altogether!" said Marion, squarely.

"I guess not—for all the little children," said Frank Sunderline; and his tone sounded suddenly sweet and tender.

He was helping them out of the car, now, at the village station, and they went up the long steps to the street. All three walked on without more remark, for a little way. Then Marion broke out in her odd fashion,—

"Ray Ingraham! you've got a home and everything sure and comfortable. Just tell me what you'd do, if you were a widow and fatherless or anything, and nobody took you in charge."

"The thing I knew best, I suppose," said Rachel, quietly. "I think very likely I could be—a baker. But I'm certain of this much," she added lightly. "I never would make a brick loaf; that always seemed to me a man's perversion of the idea of bread."

A small boy was coming down the street toward them as she spoke, from the bake-shop door; a brick loaf sticking out at the two ends of an insufficient wrap of yellow brown paper under his arm.

As Ray glanced on beyond him, she caught sight of that which put the brick loaf, and their talk, instantly out of her mind. The doctor's chaise,—the horse fastened by the well-known strap and weight,—was standing before the house. She quickened her steps, without speaking.

"I say," called out the urchin at the same moment, looking up at her as he passed by with a queer expression of mixed curiosity and knowing eagerness,—"Yer know yer father's sick? Fit—or sunthin'!"

But Ray made no sign—to anybody. She had already hurried in toward the side door, through the yard, under the elm.

A neighborly looking woman—such a woman as always "steps in" on an emergency—met her at the entrance. "He's dreadful sick, I'm afraid, dear," she said, reaching out and putting her hand on Ray's shoulder. "The doctor's up-stairs; ben there an hour. And I believe my soul every identical child in the village's ben sent in for a brick loaf."

Marion and Sunderline kept on down the Underhill road. The conversation was broken off. It was a startling occurrence that had interrupted it; but it does not need startling occurrences to turn aside the chance of talk just when one would have said something that one was most anxious to say. A very little straw will do it. It is like a game at croquet. The ball you want to hit lies close; but it is not quite your turn; a play intervenes; and before you can be allowed your strike the whole attitude and aspect are changed. Nothing lies where it did a minute before. You yourself are driven off, and forced into different combinations.

Marion wanted to try Sunderline with certain new notions—certain half-purposes of her own, in the latter part of this walk they would have together. Everything had led nicely up to it; when here, just at the moment of her opportunity, it became impossible to go on from where they were. An event had thrust itself in. It was not seemly to disregard it. They could not help thinking of the Ingrahams. And yet, "if it would have done," Marion Kent could have put off her sympathies, made her own little point, and then gone back to the sympathies again, just as really and truly, ten minutes afterward. They would have kept. Why are things jostled up so?

"I am sorry for Ray," she said, presently.

Frank Sunderline, with a grave look, nodded his head thoughtfully, twice.

"If anything happens to Mr. Ingraham, won't it be strange that I should have asked her what I did, just that minute?"

"What? O, yes!"

It had fairly been jostled out of the young man's mind. They walked on silently again. But Marion could not give it up.

"I don't doubt she *would* be a baker; carry on the whole concern,—if there was money. She keeps all her father's accounts, now."

"Does she?"

"She wouldn't have had the chance if there had been a boy. That's what I say isn't fair."

"I think you are mistaken. You can't change the way of the world. There isn't anything to hinder a woman's doing work like that,—even going on with it, as you say,—when it is set for her by special circumstances. It's natural, and a duty; and the world will treat her well and think the more of her. Things are so that it is getting easier every day for it to be done. The facilities of the times can't help serving women as much as men. But people won't generally bring up their daughters to the work or the prospects that they do their sons, simply because they can't depend upon them in the same way afterwards. If a girl marries,—and she ought to if she can *right*,"—

"And what if she *has* to, if she can, wrong?"

"Then she interferes with Providence again. She hasn't patience. She takes what wasn't meant for her, and she misses what was; whether it's work, or—somebody to work for her."

They were coming near Mrs. Kent's little white gate.

"I've a great mind to tell you," said Marion, "I don't have anybody to help me judge."

Sunderline was a little disconcerted. It is a difficult position for a young man to find himself in: that of suddenly elected confidant and judge concerning a young woman's personal affairs; unless, indeed, he be quite ready to seek and assume the permanent privilege. It is a hazardous appeal for a young woman to make. It may win or lose, strengthen or disturb, much.

"Your mother"—began Sunderline.

"O, mother doesn't see; she doesn't understand. How can she, living as she does? I could make her advise me to suit myself. She never goes about. The world has run ahead of her. She says I must conclude as I think best."

Sunderline was silent.

"I've a chance," said Marion, "if I will take it. A chance to do something that I like, something that I think I *could* do. I can't stand the shops; there's a plenty of girls that are crazy for the places; let them have 'em. And I can't stay at home and iron lace curtains for other folks, or go round to rip up and make over other folks' old dirty carpets. I don't mean mother shall do it much longer. This is what I can do: I can get on to the lecture list, for reading and reciting. The Leverings,—you remember Virginia Levering, who gave a reading here last winter; her father was with her,—Hamilton Levering, the elocutionist? Well, I know them very well; I've got acquainted with them since; they say they'll help me, and put me forward. Mr. Levering will give me lessons and get me some evenings. He thinks I would do well. And next year they mean to go out West, and want me to go with them. Would you?"

Marion looked eagerly and anxiously in Sunderline's face as she asked the question. He could not help seeing that she cared what he might think. And on his part, he could not help caring a good deal what she might do. He did not like to see this girl, whom he had known and been friends with from childhood, spoilt. There was good, honest stuff in her, in spite of her second-rate vanities and half-bred ambitions. If she would only grow out of these, what a womanly woman she might be! That fair, grand-featured face of hers, what might it not come to hold and be beautiful with, if it could once let go its little airs and consciousnesses that cramped it? It had a finer look in it now than she thought of, as she waited with real ingenuous solicitude, his answer.

He gave it gravely and conscientiously.

"I don't think I have any business to advise. But I don't exactly believe in that sort of thing. It isn't a genuine trade."

"Why not? People like it. Virginia Levering makes fifty dollars a night, even when they have to hire a hall."

"And how often do the nights come? And how long is it likely to last?"

"Long enough to make money, I guess," said Marion, laughing. She was a little reassured at Sunderline's toleration of the idea, even so far as to make calm and definite objection. "And it's pleasant at the time. I like going about. I like to please people. I like to be somebody. It may be silly, but that's the truth."

"And what would you be afterward, when you had had your day? For none of these days last long, especially with women."

"O!" exclaimed Marion, with remonstrative astonishment. "Mrs. Kemble! Charlotte Cushman!"

"It won't do to quote them, I'm afraid. I suppose you'd hardly expect to come up into that row?" said Sunderline, smiling.

"They began, some time," returned Marion.

"Yes; but for one thing, it wasn't a time when everybody else was beginning. Shall I tell you plainly how it seems to me?"

"I wish you would."

They had walked slowly for the last three or four minutes, till they had come to the beginning of the paling in which, a little further on, was the white gate. They paused here; Frank Sunderline rested his box of tools on the low wall that ran up and joined the fence, and Marion turned and stood with her face toward him in the western light, and her little pink-lined linen sunshade up between her and the low sun,—between her and the roadway also, down which might come any curious passers-by.

"It seems to me," said Frank Sunderline, "that women are getting on to the platforms nowadays, not so much for any real errand they have there, as just for the sake of saying, I'm here! I think it is very much the 'to be seen of men' motive,—the poorest part of women's characters,—that plays itself out in this way, as it always has done in dancing and dressing and acting, and what not. It isn't that a woman might not be on a platform, if she were called there, as well as anywhere else. There never was a woman came out before the world in any grand, true way, that she wasn't all the more honored and attended to because she *was* a woman. There are some things too good to be made common; things that ought to be saved up for a special time, so that they may *be* special. If it falls to a woman to be a Queen, and to open and dismiss her Parliament, nobody in all the kingdom but thinks the words come nobler and sweeter for a woman's saying them. But that's because she is *put* there, not because she climbs up some other way. If a woman honestly has something that she must say—some great word from the Lord, or for her country, or for suffering people,—then let her say it; and every real woman's husband, and every real mother's son, will hear her with his very heart. Or if even she has some sure wonderful gift,—if she can sing, or read, or recite; if she can stir people up to good and beautiful things as *one in a thousand*, that's her errand; let her do it, and let the thousand come to hear. But she ought to be certain sure, or else she's leaving her real errand behind. Don't let everybody, just because the door is open, rush in without any sort of a pass or countersign. That's what it's coming to. A *sham trade*, like hundreds of other sham trades; and the shammer and the shamefuller, because women demean themselves to it. I can't bear to see women changing so, away from themselves. We shan't get them back again, this generation. The *homes* are going. Young men of these days have got to lose their wives—that they ought to have—and their homes that they looked forward to, such as their mothers made. It's hard upon them; it takes away their hopes and their motives; it's as bad for them as for the women. It's the abomination of desolation standing in the holy place. There's no end to the mischief; but it works first and worst with exactly girls of your class— *our* class, Marion. Girls that are all upset out of their natural places, and not really fit for the new things they undertake to do. As I said,—how long will it last? How long will the Mr. Hamilton Leverings put you forward and find chances for you? Just as long as you are young and pretty and new. And then, what have you got left? What are you going to turn round to?"

Sunderline stopped. The color flushed up in his face. He had spoken faster and freer and longer than he had thought of; the feeling that he had in him about this thing, and the interest he had in Marion Kent, all rushed to words together, so that he almost forgot that Marion Kent in bodily presence stood listening before him, he was dealing so much more with his abstract thought of her, and his notion of real womanhood.

But Marion Kent did stand there. She flushed up too, when he said, "We are going to lose our wives by it." What did he mean? Would he lose anything, if she took to this that she thought of, and went abroad into the world, and before it? Why didn't he say so, then? Why didn't he give her the choice?

But what difference need it make, in any such way? Why shouldn't a girl be doing her part beforehand, as a man does? He was getting ahead in his trade, and saving money. By and by, he would think he had got enough, and then he would ask somebody to be his wife. What should the wife have been doing in the mean time—before she was sure that she should ever be a wife? Why shouldn't she look out for herself?

She said so.

"I don't see exactly, Mr. Sunderline."

She called him "Mr. Sunderline," though she remembered very well that in the earnestness of his talk he had called her "Marion." They had grown to that time of life when a young man and a girl who have known each other always, are apt to drop the familiar Christian name, and not take up anything else if they can help it. The time when they carefully secure attention before they speak, and then use nothing but pronouns in addressing each other. A girl, however, says "Mr." a little more easily than a man says "Miss." The girl has always been "Miss" to the world in general; the boy grows up to his manly title, and it is not a special personal matter to give it to him. There is something, even, in the use of it, which delicately marks an attitude—not of distance, but of a certain maidenly and bewitching consciousness—in a girl friend grown into a woman, and recognizing the man.

"I don't see, exactly, Mr. Sunderline," said Marion. "Why shouldn't a girl do the best she can? Will she be any the worse for it afterwards? Why should the wives be all spoilt, any more than the husbands?"

"Real work wouldn't spoil; only the sham and the show. Don't do it, Marion. I wouldn't want my sister to, if I had one—there!"

He had not meant so directly to answer her question. He came to this end involuntarily.

Marion felt herself tingle from head to foot with the suddenness of the negative that she had asked for and brought down upon herself. Now, if she acted, she must act in defiance of it. She felt angrily ashamed, too, of the position in which his words put her; that of a girl seeking notoriety, for mere show's sake; desiring to do a sham work; to make a pretension without a claim. How did he know what her claim might be? She had a mind to find out, and let him see. Sister! what did he say that for? He needn't have talked about sisters, or wives either, after that fashion. Spoilt! Well, what should she save herself for? It was pretty clear it wouldn't be much to him.

The color died down, and she grew quiet, or thought she did. She meant to be very quiet; very indifferent and calm. She lifted up her eyes, and there was a sort of still flash in them. Now that her cheek was cool, they burned,—burned their own color, blue-gray that deepened almost into black.

"I've a good will, however," she said slowly, "to find out what I *can* do. Perhaps neither you nor I know that, yet. Then I can make up my mind. I rather believe in taking what comes. A bird in the hand is worth two in the bush. Very likely nobody will ever care particularly whether I'm spoilt or not. And if I'm spoilt for one thing, I may be made for another. There have got to be all sorts of people in the world, you know."

She was very handsome, with her white chin up, haughtily; her nose making its straight, high line, as she turned her face half away; her eyes so dark with will, and the curve of hurt pride in her lips that yet might turn easily to a quiver. She spoke low and smooth; her words dropped cool and clear, without a tone of temper in them; if there was passionate force, it was from a fire far down.

If she could do so upon a stage; if she could look like that saying other people's words—words out of a book: if she could feel into the passions of a world, and interpret them; then, indeed! But Marion Kent had never entered into heights and depths of thought and of experience; she knew only Marion Kent's little passions as they came to her, and spoke themselves in homely, unchoice words. Mrs. Kemble or Charlotte Cushman might have made a study from that face that would have served for a Queen Katharine; but Queen Katharine's grand utterances would never have thrilled Marion Kent to wear the look as she wore it now, piqued by the plain-speaking—and the *not* speaking—of the young village carpenter.

"I hope you don't feel hurt with me; I've only been honest, and I meant to be kind," said Frank Sunderline.

"No, indeed; I dare say you did," returned Marion. "After all, everybody has got to judge for themselves. I was silly to think anybody could help me."

"Perhaps you could help yourself better," said the young man, loth to leave her in this mood, "if you thought how you would judge for somebody you cared for. If your own little sister"—

Now the quiver came. Now all the hurt, and pique, and shame, and jealous disappointment rushed together to mingle and disguise themselves with a swell and pang that always rose in her at the name of her little dead sister,—dead six years ago, when she was nine and Marion twelve.

The tears sprang to the darkened eyes, and quenched down their burning; the color swept into her face, like the color after a blow; the lips gave way; and with words that came like a cry she exclaimed passionately,—

"Don't speak of little Sue! I can't bear it! I never could! I don't know what I say now. Good-night, good-by."

And she left him there with his box upon the wall; turned and hurried along the path, and in through the little white gate.

CHAPTER IV
NINETY-NINE FAHRENHEIT

Rodney Sherrett got up from the breakfast table, where he had eaten half an hour later than the rest of the family, threw aside the newspaper that had served to accompany his meal as it had previously done his father's, and walked out through the conservatory upon the slope of lawn scattered over with bright little flower-beds, among which his sister, with a large shade hat on, and a pair of garden scissors and a basket in her hands, was moving about, cutting carnations and tea-roses and bouvardia and geranium leaves and bits of vines, for her baskets and shells and vases.

"I say, Amy, why haven't you been over to the Argenters' this long while? Why don't you get Sylvie here?"

"Why, I did go, Rod! Just when you asked me to. And she has been here; she called three weeks ago."

"O, poh! After the spill! Of course you did. Just called; and she called. Why need that be the end of it? Why don't you make much of her? I can tell you she's a girl you *might* make much of. She behaved like a lady, that day; and a *woman*,—that's more. She was neither scared nor mad; didn't scream, nor pout; nor even stand round to keep up the excitement. She was just cool and quiet, and took herself off properly. I don't know another girl that would have done so. She saved me out of the scrape as far as she was concerned; she might have made it ten times the muss it was. I'd rather run down a whole flock of sheep than graze the varnish off a woman's wheel, as a general principle. There's real backbone to Sylvie Argenter, besides her prettiness. My father would like her, I know. Why don't you bring her here; get intimate with her? I can't do it,—too fierce, you know."

Amy Sherrett laughed.

"What a nice little cat's-paw a sister makes! Doesn't she, Rod?"

"I wonder if cats don't like chestnuts too, sometimes," said Rod; and then he whistled.

"What a worry you are, Rod!" said Amy, with a little frown that some pretty girls have a way of making; half real and half got up for the occasion;

a very becoming little pucker of a frown that seems to put a lovely sort of perplexed trouble into the beautiful eyes, only to show how much too sweet and tender they really are ever to be permitted a perplexity, and what a touching and appealing thing it would be if a trouble should get into them in any earnest. "In term time I'm always wishing it well over, for fear of what dreadful thing you may do next; and when it is vacation, it gets to be so much worse, here and there and everywhere, that I'm longing for you to be safe back in Cambridge."

"Coming home Saturday nights? Well, you do get about the best of me so. And we fellows get just the right little sprinkle of family influence, too. It loses its affect when you have it all the time. That's what I tell Truesdaile, when he goes on about home, and what a thing it is to have a sister,—he doesn't exactly say *my* sister; I suppose he believes in the tenth commandment. By the way, he's knocking round at the seashore some where using up the time. I've half a mind to hunt him up and get him back here for the last week or so. I think he'd like it."

"Nonsense, Rod! You can't. When Aunt Euphrasia's away."

"She would come back, if you asked her; wouldn't she? I think it would be a charity. Put it to her as an opportunity. She'd drop anything she might be about for an opportunity. I wonder if she ever goes back upon her tracks and finishes up? She's something like a mowing machine: a grand good thing, but needs a scythe to follow round and pick out the stumps and corners."

Amy shook her head.

"I don't believe I'll ask her, Rod. She's perfectly happy up there in New Ipswich, painting wild flowers and pressing ferns, and swinging those five children in her hammock, and carrying them all to drive in her pony-wagon, and getting up hampers of fish and baskets of fruit, and beef sirloins by express, and feeding them all up, and paying poor dear cousin Nan ten dollars a week for letting her do it. I guess it's my opportunity to get along here without her, and let her stay."

"Incorruptible! Well—you're a good girl, Amy. I must come down to plain soft-sawder. Put some of those things together prettily, as you know how, and drive over and take them to Sylvie Argenter this afternoon, will you?"

"Fish and fruit and sirloins!"

"Amy, you're an aggravator!"

"No. I'm only grammatical. I'm sure those were the antecedents."

"If you don't, I will."

"If you will, I will too, Rod! Drive me over, that's a good boy, and I'll go."

Amy seized with delicate craft her opportunity for getting her brother off from one of his solitary, roaming expeditions with Red Squirrel that ended too often in not being solitary, but in bringing him into company with people who knew about horses, or had them to show, and were planning for races, and who were likely to lead Rodney, in spite of his innate gentlemanhood, into more of mere jockeyism than either she or her father liked.

"But the flowers, I fancy, Rod, would be coals to Newcastle. They have a greenhouse."

"And have never had a decent man to manage it. It came to nothing this year. She told me so. You see it just is a literal *new* castle. Mr. Argenter is too busy in town to look after it; and they've been cheated and disappointed right and left. They're not to blame for being new," he continued, seeing the least possible little *lifted* look about Amy's delicate lips and eyebrows. "I hate *that* kind of shoddiness."

"'Don't fire—I'll come down,'" said Amy, laughing. "And I don't think I ever get *very* far up, beyond what's safe and reasonable for a"—

"Nice, well-bred little coon," said Rodney, patting her on the shoulder, in an exuberance of gracious approval and beamingly serene content. "I'll take you in my gig with Red Squirrel," he added, by way of reward of merit.

Now Amy in her secret heart was mortally afraid of Red Squirrel, but she would have been upset ten times over—by Rodney—sooner than say so.

When Sylvie Argenter, that afternoon, from her window with its cool, deep awning, saw Rodney Sherrett and his sister coming up the drive, there flashed across her, by a curious association, the thought of the young carpenter who had gone up the village street and bowed to Ray Ingraham, the baker's daughter.

After all, the gentleman's "place," apart and retired, and the long "approach," were not so very much worse, when the "people in the carriages,"—the right people,—really came: and "on purpose" was not such a bad qualification of the coming, either.

And when Mrs. Argenter, hearing the bell, and the movement of an arrival, and not being herself summoned in consequence, rung in her own room for the maid, and received for answer to her inquiry,—"Miss Sherrett and young Mr. Sherrett, ma'am, to see Miss Sylvie,"—she turned back to her volume of "London Society," much and mixedly reconciled in her thoughts to two things that occurred to her at once,—one of them adding itself to the other as manifestly in the same remarkable order of providence; "that tip-out" from the basket-phæton, and the new white frill-trimmed polonaise that Miss Sylvie would put on, so needlessly, this afternoon, in spite of her remonstrance that the laundress had just left without warning, and there was no knowing when they should ever find another.

"There is certainly a fate in these matters," she said to herself, complacently. "*One* thing always follows another."

Mrs. Argenter was apt to make to herself a "House that Jack built" out of her providences. She had always a little string of them to rehearse in every history; from the malt that lay in the house, and the rat that ate the malt, up to the priest all shaven and shorn, that married the man that kissed the maid—and so on, all the way back again. She counted them up as they went along. "There was the overturn," she would say, by and by "and there was Rodney Sherrett's call because of that, and then his sister's because no doubt he asked her, and then their both coming together; and there was your pretty white polonaise, you know, the day they did come; and there was"—Mrs. Argenter has not counted up to that yet. Perhaps it may be a long while before she will so readily count it in.

It had turned out a hot day; one of those days in the nineties, when if you once hear from the thermometer, or in any way have the fact forcibly brought home to you, you relinquish all idea of exertion yourself, and look upon the world outside as one great pause, out of which no movement can possibly come, unless there first come the beneficence of an east wind, which the dwellers on Massachusetts Bay have always for a reserve of hope. Yet it may quite well occur to here and there an individual with a resolute purpose in the day, to actually live through it and pursue the intended plan, without realizing the extra degrees of Fahrenheit at all, and to learn with surprise at set of sun when the deeds are done, of the excelsior performances of the mercury. With what secret amazement and dismay is one's valor recognized, however, when it has led one to render one's self at four in the afternoon on such a day, near one's friend who *has* been vividly conscious of the torrid atmosphere! Did you ever make or receive such an afternoon call?

Mrs. Argenter, comfortable in her thin wrapper, reading her thin romance, did not trouble herself to be astonished. "They were young people; young people could do anything," she dimly thought; and putting the white polonaise into the structure of the House that Jack built, she interrupted herself no farther than presently to ring her bell again, and tell the maid on no account to admit any one to see herself, and to be sure that there were plenty of raspberries brought in for tea.

Meanwhile, away in the cities, the thermometer had climbed and climbed. Pavements were blistering hot; watering carts went lumbering round only to send up a reek of noisome mist and to leave the streets whitening again a few yards behind them. Blinds were closed up and down the avenues, where people had either long left their houses vacant or were sheltering themselves in depths of gloom in the tomb-like coolness of their double walls. Builders' trowels and hammers had a sound that made you think of sparks struck out, as if the world were a great forge and all its matter at a white heat. Down in the poor, crowded places, where the gutters fumed with filth, and doors stood open upon horrible passages and staircases, little children, barefooted, with one miserable garment on, sat on grimy stone steps, or played wretchedly about the sidewalks, impeding the passers of a better class who hastened with bated breath, amidst the fever-breeding nuisances, along to railway stations whence they would escape to country and sea-side homes.

On the wharves was the smell of tarred seams and cordage, — sweltering in the sun; in the counting-rooms the clerks could barely keep the drops of moisture from their faces from falling down to blot their toilsome lines of figures on the faultless pages of the ledgers; on the Common, common men surreptitiously stretched themselves in shady corners on the grass, regardless of the police, until they should be found and ordered off; little babies in second-rate boarding-houses, where their fathers and mothers had to stay for cheapness the summer through wailed the helpless, pitiful cry of a slowly murdered infancy; and out on the blazing thoroughfares where business had to be busy, strong men were dropping down, and reporters were hovering about upon the skirts of little crowds, gathering their items; making *their* hay while this terrible sun was shining.

What did Mrs. Argenter care?

The sun would be going down now, in a little while; then the cool piazzas, and the raspberries and cream, and the iced milk, — yellow Alderney milk, — would be delightful. Once or twice she did think of "Argie" in New York, — gone thither on some perplexing, hurried errand, which he had only half told her, and the half telling of which she had only half heard, — and remembered that the heat must be "awful" there. But to-night he would be on board the splendid Sound steamer, coming home; and to-morrow, if this lasted, she would surely speak to him about getting off for a while to Rye, or Mount Desert.

She came by and by to the end of her volume, and found that the serial she was following ran on into the next.

"Provoking," she said, tossing it down to the end of the sofa, "and neither Sylvie nor I can get into town in this heat, and Argie thinks it such a bother to be asked to go to Loring's."

Just then Sylvie's step came lightly up the stairs. She looked into the large cool dressing-room where her mother lay.

"I'm only up for my 'Confession Album'," she said. "But O Mater Amata! if you'd just come down and help me through! I know they'd stay to tea and go home in the cool, if I only knew how to ask them; but if I said a word I should be sure to drive them away. *You* can do it; and they would if you came. Please do!"

"You silly child! Won't you ever be able to do anything yourself? When you were a little girl, you wouldn't carry a message, because you could get into a house, but didn't know how to get out! And now you are grown up, you can get people into the house to see you, but you don't know how to ask them to stay to tea! What *shall* I ever do with you?"

"I don't know. I'm awfully afraid of—*nice* girls!"

"Sylvie, I'm ashamed of you! As if you had any other kind of acquaintance, or weren't as nice as any of them! I wouldn't suggest it, even to myself, if I were you."

"And I don't," said Sylvie boldly—"when I'm *by* myself. But there's a kind of a little misgiving somehow, when they come, or when I go, as if—well, as if there *might* be something to it that I didn't know of, or behind it that I hadn't got; or else, that there were things that they had nothing to do with that I know too much of. A kind of a—Poggowantimoc feeling, mother! Amy Sherrett is so *fearfully* refined,—all the way through! It doesn't seem as if she ever had any common things to say or do. Don't you think it *takes* common things to get people really near to each other? It doesn't seem to me I could ever be intimate—or very easy—with Amy Sherrett."

"You seemed to get on well enough with her brother, the other day."

"Boys aren't half so bad. There isn't any such wax-work about boys. Besides,"—and Sylvie laughed a low, gay little laugh,—"we got spilt out together, you know."

"Well, don't stand talking. You mustn't keep them waiting. It isn't time to speak about tea, yet. Look over the album, and get at some music. *Keep* them without saying anything about it. When people think every minute they are just going, is just when they are having the very pleasantest time."

"I know it. But you'll come, won't you, and make it all right? Put on something loose and cool; that lovely black lace jacket with the violet lining, and your gray silk skirt. It won't take you a minute. Your hair's perfectly sweet now." And Sylvie hurried away.

Mrs. Argenter came down, twenty minutes afterwards, into the great summer drawing-room, where the finest Indian matting, and dark, rich Persian rugs, and inner window blinds folded behind lace curtains that fell like the foam of waterfalls from ceiling to floor, made a pleasantness out of the very heat against which such furnishings might be provided.

In her silken skirt of silver gray, and the llama sack, violet lined, to need no tight corsage beneath, her fair wrists and arms showing white and cool in the wide drapery sleeves, she looked a very lovely lady. Sylvie was proud of her handsome, elegant mother. She grew a great deal braver always when Mrs. Argenter came in. She borrowed a second consciousness from her in which she took courage, assured that all was right. Chairs and rugs gave her no such confidence, though she knew that the Sherretts themselves had no more faultless surroundings. Anybody could have rugs and chairs. It was the presence among them that was wanted; and poor Sylvie seemed to herself to melt quite away, as it were, before such a girl as Amy Sherrett, and not to be able to be a presence at all.

It was all right now, as Sylvie had said. They could not leave immediately upon Mrs. Argenter joining them and her joining them was of itself a welcome and an invitation. So Sylvie called upon her mother to admire the lovely basket, wherein on damp, tender, bright green moss, clustered the most exquisite blossoms, and the most delicate trails of stem and leafage wandered and started up lightly, and at last fell like a veil over rim and handle, and dropped below the edge of the tiny round table with Siena marble top, on which Sylvie had placed it between the curtains of the recess that led through to their conservatory, which had been "a failure this year."

"I would not tell you of it, Amata. I wanted you just to see it," she said. And Mrs. Argenter admired and thanked, and then lamented their own ill-success in greenhouse and garden culture.

"I am not strong enough to look after it much myself, and Mr. Argenter never has time," she said; "and our first man was a tipsifier, and the last was a rogue. He sold off quantities of the best young plants, we found, just before they came to show for anything."

"Our man has been with us for eight years," said Rodney Sherrett. "I dare say he could recommend some one to you, if you liked; and he wouldn't send anybody that wasn't right. Shall I ask him?"

Mrs. Argenter would be delighted if he would; and then Mr. Sherrett must come into the conservatory, where a few ragged palm ferns, their great leaves browning and crumbling at the edges,—some daphnes struggling into green tips, having lost their last growth of leaf and dropped all their flower buds, and several calmly enduring orange and lemon trees, gave all the suggestion of foliage that the place afforded, and served, much like the painter's inscription at the bottom of his canvas merely to signify by the scant glimpse through the drawing-room draperies,—"This is a conservatory."

Mrs. Argenter asked Rodney something about the best arrangement for the open beds, and wanted to know what would be surest to do well for the rockery, and whether it was in a good part of the house,—sufficiently shaded? Meanwhile, Amy and Sylvie were turning over music, and when they all gathered together again the call had extended to a two hours' visit.

"It is really unpardonable," Amy Sherrett was saying, and picking up the pretty little hat which she had thrown down upon a chair,—"it had been so warm to wear anything a minute that one need not." And then Mrs. Argenter said so easily and of course, that they "certainly would not think of going now, when it would soon be really pleasant for a twilight drive; tea would be ready early, for she and Sylvie were alone, and all they had cared for to-day had been a cold lunch at one. They would have it on the north veranda;" and she touched a bell to give the order.

Perhaps Amy Sherrett would hardly have consented, but that Rodney gave her a look, comical in its appeal, over Sylvie's shoulder, as she stood showing him a great scarlet Euphorbia in a portfolio of water-colors, and said with a beseeching significance,—

"Consider Red Squirrel, Amy. He really did have a pretty hard pull; and what with the heat and the flies, I dare say he would take it with more equanimity after sundown,—since Mrs. Argenter is so very kind."

And so they stayed; and Mrs. Argenter laid another little brick in her "House that Jack built."

At this same time,—how should she know it?—something very different was going on in one of the rooms of a great hotel in New York. Somebody else who had meant before now to have left for home, had been delayed till after sundown. Somebody else would go over the road by dark instead of by daylight. By dark,—though there should be broad, beating sunshine over the world again when the journey should be made.

While Mrs. Argenter's maid was bringing out the tray with delicate black-etched china cups, and costly fruit plates illuminated with color, and dainty biscuits, and large, rare, red berries, and cream that would hardly pour for richness in a gleaming crystal flagon,—and ranging them all on the rustic veranda table,—something very different,—very grim,—at which the occupants of rooms near by shuddered as it passed their open doors,—was borne down the long, wide corridor to Number Five, in the Metropolitan; and at the same moment, again, a gentleman, very grave, was standing at the counter of the Merchants' Union Telegraph Company's Office, writing with rapid hand, a brief dispatch, addressed to "Mrs. I.M. Argenter, Dorbury, Mass.," and signed "Philip Burkmayer, M.D."

Nobody knew of any one else to send to; at that hour, especially, when the office in State Street would be closed. Closed, with that name outside the door that stood for nobody now.

The news must go bare and unbroken to her.

Something occurred to Doctor Burkmayer, however, as he was just handing the slip to the attendant.

"Stop; give me that again, a minute," he said; and tearing it in two, he wrote another, and then another.

"Send this on at once, and the second in an hour," he said; as if they might have been prescriptions to be administered. "They may both be delivered together after all," he continued to himself, as he turned away. "But it is all I can do. When a weight is let drop, it has got to fall. You can't ease it up much with a string measured out for all the way down!"

The young woman operator at the little telegraph station at Dorbury Upper Village heard the call-click as she unlocked the room and came in after her half-hour supper time. She set the wires and responded, and laid the paper slip under the wonderful pins.

"Tick-tick-tick; tick-tick; tick-tick-tick-tick," and so on. The girl's face looked startled, as she spelled the signs along. She answered back when it was ended; then wrote out the message rapidly upon a blank, folded, directed it, and went to the open street door.

"Sim! Here—quick!" she called to a youth opposite, in a stable-yard.

"This has got to go down to the Argenter Place. And mind how you give it. It's bad news."

"How can *I* mind?" said Sim, gruffly. "I spose I must give it to who comes."

"You might see somebody on the way, and speak a word; a neighbor, or the minister, or somebody. 'Tain't fit for it to go right to her, *I* know. Telegraphs might as well be something else when they can, besides lightning!"

"Donno's I can go travellin' round after 'em, if that's what you mean," said Sim, putting the envelope in his rough breast pocket, and turning off.

Sylvie was standing on the stone steps, bidding the Sherretts good-by; Amy was just seated in the gig, and Rodney about to spring in beside her, when Sim Atwill drove up the avenue in the rusty covered wagon that did telegraph errands. Red Squirrel did not quite like the sudden coming face to face, as Sim reined up in a hurry just below the door, and Rodney had to pause and hold him in.

"A tellagrim for Mrs. Argenter," said Sim, seizing his opportunity, and speaking to whom it might concern. "Eighty cents to pay, and I 'believe it's bad news."

"O, Mr. Sherrett, stop, please!" cried Sylvie, turning white in the dim light. "What shall I do? Won't you wait a minute, Miss Sherrett, until I see? Won't you come in again? Mother will be frightened to death, and I'm all alone."

"Jump out, Amy; I'll take Squirrel round," was Rodney's answer. "Go right up; I'll come."

And as Sylvie took the thin envelope that held so much, and the two girls silently passed up into the piazza again, he paid Sim the eighty cents which nobody thought of at that moment or ever again, and sent him off.

Sylvie and Amy stopped under the softly bright hall lantern. Mrs. Argenter was up-stairs in her dressing room, quite at the end of the long upper hall, changing her lace sack for a cashmere, before coming out into the evening air again.

"I think I shall open it myself," whispered Sylvie, tremulously; "it would seem worse to mother, whatever it is, coming this way. She has such a horror of a telegram." She looked at it on both sides, drew a little shivering breath, and paused again.

"Is it wicked, do you think, to wish it may be—only grandma, perhaps? Do you suppose it could *possibly* be—my *father*?"

And by this time there was a hysterical sound in poor little Sylvie's voice.

"Wait a minute," said Amy, kindly. "Here's Rod."

"Office of Western Union Telegraph Co., New York, *July* 24*th*, 187-.

"To Mrs. I. M. Argenter, Dorbury, Mass.

"Mr. Argenter has had a sunstroke. Insensible. Very serious. Will telegraph again.

"Philip Burkmayer, M.D."

Sylvie's eyes, so roundly innocent, so star-like in their usual bright uplifting, were raised now with a wide terror in them, first to Rodney, then to Amy; and "O—O!" broke in short, subdued gasps from her lips.

Then they heard Mrs. Argenter's step up-stairs.

"What is the matter, Sylvie? What are you doing? Who is with you down there?" she said, over the baluster, from the hall above.

"O, mother!" cried Sylvie, "they aren't gone! Something has *come*! Go up and tell her, Amy, please!" And forgetting all about Amy as "Miss Sherrett," and all her fear of "nice girls," she dropped down on the lower step of the staircase after Amy had passed her upon her errand, put her face between her hands and caught her breath with frightened sobs.

Rodney, leaning against the newel post, looked down at her, and said, after the manner of men,—"Don't cry. It mayn't be very bad, after all. You'll hear again in an hour or two. Can't I do something? I'll go to the telegraph office. I'll get somebody for your mother. Whom shall I go for?"

"O, you are very kind. I don't know. Wait a minute. They didn't say any place! We ought to go right to New York, and we don't know where! O, dear!" She had lifted her head a little, just to say these broken sentences, and then it went down again.

Rodney did not answer instantly. It occurred to him all at once what this "not saying any place" might mean.

Just as he began,—"You couldn't go until to-morrow,"—came Mrs. Argenter's sharp cry from her room above. Amy had walked right on into the open, lighted apartment, Mrs. Argenter following, not daring to ask what she came and did this strange thing for, till Amy made her sit down in her own easy chair, and taking her hands, said gently,—

"It is a telegram from New York. Mr. Argenter—is very ill." Then Mrs. Argenter cried out, "That's not all! I know how people bring news! Tell me the whole." And Sylvie sprang to her feet, hearing the quick, excited words, and leaving Rodney Sherrett standing there, rushed up into the dressing-room.

This was the way the same sort of news came to Sylvie Argenter as had come to the baker's daughter. Did it really make any difference—the different surrounding of the two? The great house—the lights—the servants—the friends; and the open bake-shop door, the village street, the blunt, common-spoken neighbor-woman, and the boy with the brick loaf?

These two were to be fatherless: their mothers were both to be widows: that was all.

Did it happen strangely with the two—in this same story? Who know, always, when they are in the same story? These things are happening every day, and one great story holds us all. If one could see wide enough, one could tell the whole.

These things happen: and then the question comes,—alike in high and low places,—alike with money and without it,—what the women and the girls are to do?

Rodney Sherrett took his sister home; drove three miles round and brought Mrs. Argenter's sister to her from River Point, and then turned toward Dorbury Upper Village and the telegraph office. But he met Sim Atwill on the way, received the telegram from him, and hurried back.

It was the dispatch of the hour later, and this was it:—

> "Mr. Argenter died at five o'clock. His remains will be sent home to-morrow, carefully attended.
>
> "Philip Burkmayer."

CHAPTER V
SPILLED OUT AGAIN

There were paragraphs in the papers; there were resolutions at meetings of the Board of Trade, and of the Directors of the Trimountain Bank; there was a funeral from the "late residence," largely attended; there were letters and calls of condolence; there was making of crape and bombazine and silk into "mourning;" there were friends and neighbors asking each other, after mention of the sad suddenness, "how it would be;" "how much he had left;" "was there a will?"

And there was a will; made three years before. One hundred thousand dollars, outright, to Increase M. Argenter's beloved wife; also the use of the homestead; fifty thousand dollars to his daughter Sylvia on her reaching the age of twenty-five, or on her marriage; all else to be Mrs. Argenter's for her life-time, reverting afterward to Sylvia or her heirs.

There was just time for this to be ascertained and told of; just time for Sylvie to be named as an heiress, and then all at once something else came to light and was told of.

There was a mining speculation out in Colorado; there was Mr. Argenter's signature for heavy security; there were memoranda of good safe stocks that had stood in his name a little while ago, and no certificates; there had been sales and sacrifices; going in deeper and to more certain loss, because of risk and danger already run.

Mr. Sherrett, senior, came home to dinner one day with news from the street.

"I've been very sorry to hear this morning that Argenter left things in a bad way, after all. There won't be much of anything forthcoming. All swallowed up in mines and lands that have gone under. That explains the sunstroke. Half the cases are mere worry and drive. In the old, calm times it was scarcely heard of. Now, of a hot summer's day in New York, a hundred or two men drop down. And then they talk of unprecedented heat. It is the heat and the ferment that have got into life."

"Except ye repent, ye shall all likewise perish," said the quiet voice of Aunt Euphrasia. "How strange it is that men have never interpreted yet!"

"Ah, well! I'm not sure about sins and judgments. I don't undertake to blame," said Mr. Sherrett. "People are born into a whirl, nowadays,—the mass of them. How can they help it?"

"I don't know. But we begin to see how true the words were, and in what pity they must have been spoken," said Aunt Euphrasia. "Tremendous physical forces have been grasped and set to work for mere material ends. Spiritual uses and living haven't kept pace. And so there is a terrible unbalance, and the tower falls upon men's heads."

"Well, poor Argenter wasn't a sinner above all that dwelt in Jerusalem. And now, there are his wife and daughter. I'm sorry for them. They'll find it a hard time."

"I'm sorry, too," said Aunt Euphrasia, with heart-gentleness. She could not help seeing the eternal laws; she read the world and the Word with the inner illumining; but she was tender over all the poor souls who were not to blame for the whirl of fever and falseness they were born into; who could not or dared not fling themselves out of it upon the simple, steadfast, everlasting verities, and—be broken; upon whom, therefore, these must fall, and grind them to powder.

"How will it be with them?" she asked.

"Do you mean there isn't anything left, sir? Nothing to carry out the will?"

Rodney had dropped his spoon and left his soup untasted, since his father first spoke: he had lifted up his eyes quickly, and listened with his whole face, but he had kept silence until now.

Amy had looked up also; startled by the news, and waiting to hear more. The young people were both too really interested, from their intimate knowledge of the first misfortune, to reply with any common "Is it possible?" to this.

"The will, I am afraid, is only a magnificent 'might have been,'" said Mr. Sherrett. "There may be something secured; there ought to be. Mrs. Argenter had a small property, I believe. Otherwise, as such things turn out, I should suppose there would be less than nothing."

"What will they do?" The question came from Aunt Euphrasia, again. "Can't somebody help them? There is so much money in the world."

"Yes, Effie. And there is gold in the mines. And there are plenty of kind affections in the world, too; but there's loneliness and broken heartedness, for all that. The difficulty always is to bring things together."

"I suppose that is just what *people* were made for."

"It will be one more family of precisely that sort whom nobody can help, directly, and who scarcely know how to help themselves. The hardest kind of cases."

"It's an awful spill-out, this time," Rodney said to Amy, as she followed him, after her usual fashion, to the piazza, when dinner was over. "And no mistake!"

Rodney had brought a cigar with him, but he had forgotten his match, and he stood crumbling the end of it, frowning his brows together in a way they were not often used to.

"Will they have to go away?" asked Amy.

"Out of that house? Of course. They'll be just tipped out of everything."

"How dreadful it will be for Sylvie!"

"She won't stand round lamenting. I've seen her tipped out before. Amy, I'll tell you what; you ought to stick by. Maybe she won't want you, at first; but you ought to do it. Father,"—as Mr. Sherrett came out with his evening paper to his cane reclining chair,—"you'll go and see Mrs. Argenter, shall you not?"

"Why, yes, if I could be of any service. But one wouldn't like to intrude. There are executors to the will. I don't know that it is quite my place."

"I don't believe there will be much intruding—of *your* sort. And the executors have got nothing to do now. Who are they?"

"Jobling and Cardwell, I believe. Men down town. Perhaps she might like to see a neighbor. Yes, I think I will go. You can drive me round, Rodney, some evening soon. Whom has she, of her own people, I wonder?"

"Only her sister, Mrs. Lowndes, you know. The brother-in-law isn't much, I imagine."

"Stephen A. Lowndes? No. Broken-down and out of the world. He couldn't advise to any purpose. I fancy Argenter has been holding *him* up."

"I think they'll be very glad to see you, sir."

Rodney drove his father over the next night. Mr. Sherrett went in alone. Rodney sat in the chaise outside.

Mr. Sherrett waited some minutes after he had sent up his card, and then Sylvie came down to him, looking pale in her black dress, and with the trouble really in her young eyes, over which the brows bent with a strange heaviness.

"I could not persuade mother to come down," she said. "She does not feel able to see anybody. But I wanted to thank you for coming, Mr. Sherrett."

"I thought an old neighbor might venture to ask if he could be of use. A lady needs some one to talk things over with. I know your mother must have much to think of, and she cannot have been used to business. I should not come for a mere call at such a time. I should be glad to be of some service."

"Would you be kind enough to sit down a few minutes and talk with me, Mr. Sherrett?"

There was a difference already between the Sylvie of to-day and the Sylvie of a few weeks ago. It was no longer a question of little nothings,—of how she should get people in and how she could get them out,—of what she should do and say to seem "nice all through," like Amy Sherrett. Mr. Sherrett had not come for a "mere call," as he said; and there was no mere "receiving." The llama lace and the gray silk and the small *savoir faire* could not help her now. Mrs. Argenter was up-stairs in a black tamise wrapper with a large plain black shawl folded about her, as she lay in the chill of a suddenly cool August evening, on the sofa in her dressing-room, which for the last week or two she had rarely left. All at once, Sylvie found that she must think and speak both for her mother and herself.

Mrs. Argenter could run smoothly in one polished groove; she was thrown out now, and to her the whole world was off its axis. Her House that Jack built had tumbled down; she thought so, not accepting this strange block that had come to be wrought in. She had been counting little brick after little brick that she had watched idly in the piling; now there was this great weight that she could not deal with, laid upon her hands for bearing and for using; she let it crush her down, not knowing that, fitting it bravely into her life that was building, it might stand there the very threshold over which she should pass into perfect shelter of content.

"Mother has been entirely bewildered by all this trouble," said Sylvie, quietly, to Mr. Sherrett. "I don't think she really understands. She has lived so long with things as they are, that she cannot imagine them different. I think it is easier with me, because, you know, I haven't been used to *anything* such a *very* long while."

Sylvie even smiled a tremulous little smile as she said this; and Mr. Sherrett looked at her with one upon his own face that had as much pitiful tenderness in it as could have shown through tears.

"You see we shall have to do something right off,—go somewhere; and mother can't change the least thing. She can't spare Sabina, who has heard of a good place, and must go soon at any rate, because nobody else would know where things belonged or are put away, or fetch her anything she wanted. And the very things, I suppose, don't belong to us. How shall we break through and begin again?" Sylvie looked up earnestly at Mr. Sherrett, asking this question. This was what she really wanted to know.

"You will remove, I suppose?" said Mr. Sherrett "If you could hear of a house,—if you could propose something definite,—if you and Sabina could begin to pack up,—how would that be?"

He met her inquiry with primary, practical suggestions, just what she needed, wasting no words. He saw it was the best service he could do this little girl who had suddenly become the real head of the household.

"I have thought, and thought," said Sylvie; "and after all, mother must decide. Perhaps she wouldn't want to keep house. I don't know whether we could. She spoke once about boarding. But boarding costs a great deal, doesn't it?"

"To live as you would need to,—yes."

"I should hate to have to manage small, and change round, in boarding. I know some people who live so. It would give me a very mean feeling. It would be like trying to get a bite of everybody's bread and butter. I'd rather have my own little loaf."

"You are a brave, true little woman," said Mr. Sherrett, warmly. "All you want is to be set in the right direction, and see your way. You'll be sure to go on."

"I *think* I should. If mother can only be contented. I think I should rather like it. I could *understand* living better. There would only be a little at a time. A great deal, and a great many things, make it a puzzle."

"Have you any knowledge about the property?"

"Mr. Cardwell has been here two or three times. He says there are twelve thousand dollars secured to mother by a note and mortgage on this place. It was money of hers that was put into it. We shall have the income of that; and there might be things, perhaps, that we should have the right to sell, or keep to furnish with. Seven and a half per cent, on twelve thousand dollars would be nine hundred dollars a year. If we had to pay sixteen dollars a week to board, it would take eight hundred and thirty-two; almost the whole of it. But perhaps we could find a place for less; and our clothes would last a good while, I suppose."

Sylvie went through her little calculation, just as she had made it over and over before, all by herself; she did not stop to think that she was doing the small sum now for the enlightenment of the great Mr. Sherrett, who calculated in millions for himself and others, every day.

"You would hardly be comfortable in a house which you could rent for less than—say, four hundred dollars, and that would leave very little for your living. Perhaps I should advise you to board."

"But we could *do* things, maybe, if we lived by ourselves, amongst other people in small houses. We can't be *two* things, Mr. Sherrett, rich and poor; and it seems to me that is what we should be trying for, if we got into a boarding-house. We should have to be idle and ashamed. I want to take right hold. I'd like to earn something and make it do."

Sylvie's eyes really shone. The spirit that had worked in her as a little child, to make her think it would be nice to be a "kitchen girl, and have a few things in boxes, and Sundays out," threw a charm of independence and enterprise and cosy thrift over her changed position, and the chance it gave her. Mr. Sherrett wondered at the child, and admired her very much.

"Could you teach something? Could you keep a little school?"

"I've thought about it. But a person must know ever to much, nowadays, to keep even the least little school. They want Kindergartens, and all the new plans, that I haven't learnt. And it's just so about music. You must be scientific; and all I really know is a few little songs. But I can *dance* well, Mr. Sherrett. I could teach that."

There was something pathetically amusing in this bringing to market of her one exquisite accomplishment, learned for pleasure, and the suggestion of it at this moment, as she sat in her strange black dress, with the pale, worn look on her face, in the home so shadowed by heavy trouble, and about to pass away from their possession.

"You will be sure to do something, I see," said Mr. Sherrett. "Yes, I think you had better have a quiet little home. It will be a centre to work from, and something to work for. You can easily furnish it from this house. Whatever has to be done, you could certainly be allowed such things as you might make a schedule of. Would you like me to talk for you with Mr. Cardwell, and have something arranged?"

"O, if you would! Mother dreads the very sound of Mr. Cardwell's name, and the thought of business. She cannot bear it now. But your advice would be so different!"

Sylvie knew that it would go far with Mrs. Argenter that Mr. Howland Sherrett, in the relation of neighbor and friend, should plan and suggest for them, rather than Mr. Richard Cardwell, a stranger and mere man of business, should come and tell them things that must be.

"I'm afraid you'll think I don't realize things, I've planned and imagined so much," Sylvie began again, "but I couldn't help thinking. It is all I have had to do. There's a little house in Upper Dorbury that always seemed to me so pretty and pleasant; and nobody lives there now. At least, it was all shut up the last time I drove by. The house with the corner piazza and the green side yard, and the dark red roof sloping down, just off the road in the shady turn beside the bank that only leads to two other little houses beyond. Do you know?"

Mr. Sherrett did know. They were three houses built by members of the same family, some years ago, upon an old village homestead property. Two of them had passed into other hands; one—this one—remained in its original ownership, but had been rented of late; since the war, in which the proprietor had made money, and with it had bought a city residence in Chester Park.

"You see we must go where things will be convenient. We can't ride round after them any more. And we could get a girl up there, as other people do, for general housework. I'm afraid mother wouldn't quite like being in the village, but of course there can't be anything that she *would quite* like, now. And we aren't really separate people any longer; at least, we don't belong to the separate kind of people, and I couldn't bear to be *lonesomely* separate. It's good to belong to *some* kind of people; isn't it?"

"I think it is very good to belong to *your* kind, where-ever they are, Miss Sylvie. Tell your mother I say she may be glad of her daughter. I'll find out about the house for you, at any rate. And I'll see Mr. Cardwell; and I'll call again. Good-night, my dear. God bless you!"

And the grand Mr. Howland Sherrett pressed Sylvie Argenter's hand in both of his, as a father might have pressed it, and went out with the feeling of a warm rush from his heart toward his eyes.

"That's a girl like a—whatever there is that means the noblest sort of woman, and I'm not sure it *is* a queen!" he said to Rodney, as he seated himself in the chaise, and took the reins from his son's hands.

Mr. Sherrett was apt to say to Rodney, "You may drive me to this or that place," but he was very apt, also, to do the driving himself, after all; especially if he was somewhat preoccupied, and forgot, as he did now.

The way Mr. Howland Sherrett inquired about the red-roofed house, was this:

He went down to Mr. John Horner's store, in Opal Street, and asked him what was the rent of it.

"Six hundred and fifty dollars."

"Rather high, isn't it, for the situation?"

"Not for the situation of the *land*, I guess," said Mr. Horner. "I'm paying annexation taxes."

"What will you sell the property for as it stands?"

"Eighty-five hundred dollars."

"I'll give you eight thousand, Mr. Horner, in cash, upon condition that you will not mention its having changed hands. I have some friends whom I wish should live there," he added, lest some deep speculating move should be surmised.

Mr. Horner thought for the space of thirty seconds, after the rapid, Opal Street fashion, and said, —

"You may have it. When will you take the deed?"

"To-morrow morning, at eleven o'clock. Will that be convenient?"

"All right. Yes, sir."

And the next morning at eleven o'clock, the two gentlemen exchanged papers; Mr. Horner received a check on the First National Bank for eight thousand dollars, and Mr. Sherrett the title-deed to house and land on North Centre Street, Dorbury, known as part of the John Horner estate, and bordering so and so, and so on.

The same afternoon, Mr. Sherrett called at Mrs. Argenter's, and told her of the quiet, pleasant, retired, yet central house and garden in Upper Dorbury, which he found she could have on a lease of two or three years, for a rent of three hundred and fifty dollars. It was in the hands of a lawyer in the village, who would make out the lease and receive the payments. He had inquired it out, and would conclude the arrangements for her, if she desired.

"I don't know that I desire anything, Mr. Sherrett. I suppose I must do what I can, since it seems I am not to be left in my own home which I put my own money into. If it appears suitable to you, I have no doubt it is right. I am very much obliged to you, I am sure. Sylvie knows the house, and has an idea she likes it. She is childish, and likes changing. She will have enough of it, I am afraid."

She did not even care to go over and inspect the house. Sylvie was glad of that, for she knew it could be made to seem more homelike, if she and Sabina could get the parlor and her mother's rooms ready before Mrs. Argenter saw it. During the removal, it was settled that they should go and stay with Mrs. Lowndes, at River Point. This practically resulted in Mrs. Argenter's remaining with her sister, while Sylvie and Sabina spent their time, night as well as day, often, between Argenter Place and the new house.

Rodney Sherrett rode through the village one day, when they were busy there with their arrangements.

Sylvie stood on a high flight of steps in the bay-window, putting up some white muslin curtains, with little frills on the edges. They had been in a sleeping-room at Argenter Place. All the furniture of the house had been appraised, and an allowance made of two thousand dollars, to which amount Mrs. Argenter might reserve such articles as she wished, at the valuation. So much, and two thousand dollars in cash, were given her in exchange for her homestead and her right of dower in the unincumbered portion of the estate, upon which was one other smaller mortgage. No other real property appeared in the list of assets. Mr. Argenter had, unfortunately, invested almost wholly in bonds, stocks, and those last ruinous mining ventures. The land out in Colorado was useless, and besides, being wild land, did not come under the law of dower.

Mrs. Argenter thought it was all very strange, especially that a sum of money,—eighteen hundred dollars, which was in her husband's desk, the proceeds of some little mortgage that he had just sold,—was not hers to keep. She came very near stealing it from the estate, quietly appropriating it, without meaning to be dishonest; regarding it as simply money in the house, which her husband "would have given her, if she had wanted it, the very day before he died."

Possibly he might; but the day after he died, it was no longer his nor hers.

To go back to Sylvie in the bay-window. Rodney rode by, then wheeled about and came back as far as the stone sidewalk before the Bank entrance. He jumped off, hitched Red Squirrel to one of the posts that sentineled the curbstone, and passed quietly round into the "shady turn."

The front door was open, and boxes stood in the passage; he walked in as far as the parlor door; then he tapped with his riding-whip against the frame of it. Sylvie started on her perch, and began to come down.

"Don't stop. I couldn't help coming in, seeing you as I went by," said Rodney.

Sylvie sat down on one of the middle steps. She would rather keep still than exhibit herself in any further movement. Rodney ought to have known better than go in then; if indeed he did *not* know better than Sylvie herself did, how very pretty and graceful she looked, all out of regular and ordinary gear.

She had taken off her hoops, for her climbing; her soft, long black dress fell droopingly about her figure and rested in folds around and below her feet as she sat upon the step-ladder; one thick braid of her sunshiny hair had dropped from the fastening which had looped it up to her head, and hung, raveling into threads of light, down over her shoulder and into her lap; her cheeks were bright with exercise; her eyes, that trouble and thought had sobered lately to dove-gray, were deep, brilliant blue again. She was excited with her work, and flushed now with the surprise of Rodney's coming in.

"How pretty you are going to look here," said Rodney, glancing about.

The carpet Sylvie had chosen to keep for the parlor—for though Mrs. Argenter had feebly discussed and ostensibly dictated the list as Sylvie wrote it down, she had really given up all choosing to her with a reiterated, helpless, "As you please," at every question that came up—was a small figured Brussels of a soft, shadowy water-gray, with a border in an arabesque pattern. This had been upon a guest chamber; the winter carpet of the drawing-room was an Axminster, and Sylvie's ideas did not base themselves on Axminsters now, even if they might have done so with a two thousand dollar allowance. She only hoped her mother would not feel as if there were no drawing room at all, but the whole house had been put up-stairs.

The window draperies were as I have said; there was a large, plain library table in the middle of the room, with books and baskets and little easels with pictures, and paper weights and folders, and other such like small articles of use and grace and cosy expression lying about upon it, as if people had been there quite a while and grown at home. There were bronze candelabra on the mantel and upon brackets each side the bay window. Pictures were already hung,—portraits, and gifts, not included in the schedule,—a few nice engravings, and one glowing piece of color, by Mrs. Murray, which Sylvie said was like a fire in the room.

"I am only afraid it is too fine," said she, replying to Rodney. "I really want to be like our neighbors,—to *be* a neighbor. We belong here now. People should not drop out of the world, between the ranks, when changes happen; they can't change out of humanity. Do you know, Mr. Sherrett,—if it wasn't for the thought of my poor father, and my mother not caring about anything any more,—I know I should enjoy the chance of being a village girl?"

"You'll be a village girl, I imagine, as your parlor is a village parlor. All in good faith, but wearing the rue with a difference."

"I don't mean to. I've been thinking,—*ever* so much, and I've found out a good many things. It's this not falling *on* to anything that keeps people in the misery of falling. I mean to come to land, right here. I guess I preexisted as a barefoot maiden. There's a kind of homeishness about it, that there never was in being elegant. I wonder if I *have* got anything in here that has no business?"

"Not a scrap. I've no doubt the blacksmith's wife's parlor is finer. But you can't put the *character* out."

"I mean to have plants, now; in this bay window. I guess I can, now that we have no conservatory. Village people always have plants in their windows, and mother won't want to see the street staring in."

"Have you brought some?"

"How could I? Those great oranges and daphnes? No: I shall have little window plants and raise them."

"But meanwhile, won't the street be staring in?"

"Well, we can keep the blinds shut, for the warm weather."

"Amy will come and see you, when you are settled; Amy and Aunt Euphrasia; you'll let them, won't you? You don't mean to be such a violent village girl as to cut all your old friends?"

"Old friends?" Sylvie repeated, thoughtfully "Well, it does seem almost old. But I didn't think I knew any of you *very* well, only a little while ago."

"Until the overturns," said Rodney. "It takes a shaking up, I suppose, sometimes, to set things right. That's what the Shaker people believe has got to be generally. Do you know, the Scotch—Aunt Euphrasia is Scotch—have a way of using the word 'upset' to mean 'set up.' I think that is what you make it mean, Miss Sylvie. I understand the philosophy of it now. I got my first illustration when I tipped you out there at the baker's door."

"You tipped me out into one of the nicest places I ever was in. I've no doubt it was a piece of the preparation. I mean to have Ray Ingraham for my intimate friend."

Rodney Sherrett did not say anything immediately to this. He sat on the low cricket upon which he had placed himself near the door, turning his soft felt hat over and over between his hands. He was not quite ready to perceive as yet, that the baker's daughter was just the person for Sylvie Argenter's intimate friend; and he had a dim suspicion, likewise, that there was something in the girl constitution that prevented the being able to have more than one intimate friend.

He repeated presently his assurance that Amy and Aunt Euphrasia would come over to see them, and took himself off, saying that he knew he must have been horribly in the way all the time.

The next morning, a light covered wagon, driven by Mr. Sherrett's man, Rodgers, came up the Turn. There was nobody at the red-roofed house so early, and he set down in the front porch what he took carefully, one at a time, from the vehicle,—some two dozen lovely greenhouse plants, newly potted from the choicest and most flourishing growth of the season.

When Sylvie and Sabina came round from the ten o'clock street car, they stumbled suddenly upon this beauty that incumbered the entrance. To a branch of glossy green, luxuriant ivy was tied a card,—

"Rodney Sherrett,
With friendly compliments."

Sylvie really sung at her work to-day, placing and replacing till she had grouped the whole in her wire frames in the bay window so as to show every leaf and spray in light and line aright.

"Why, it is prettier than it ever was at the old place; isn't it Sabina? It's full and perfect; and that was always a great barrenness of glass. The street can't stare in now. I think mother will be able to forget that there is even a street at all."

"It's real nobby," said Sabina.

The room was all soft green and gray: green rep chairs and sofa, green topped library table; green piano cover; green inside blinds; a green velvet grape leaf border around the gray papered walls.

Sabina, though a very elegant housemaid, patronized and approved cheerfully. She was satisfied with the new home. There had not been a word of leaving since it was decided upon. She had her reasons. Sabina was "promised to be married" next spring. Dignity in her profession was not so much of an object meantime, nor even wages; she had laid up money and secured her standing, living always in the first families; she could afford to take it in a quiet way; "it wouldn't be so bothering nor so dressy;" Sabina had a saving turn with her best things, that spared both trouble and money. Besides, her kitchen windows and the back door suited her; they looked across a bit of unoccupied land to the back street where the cabinet-shop buildings were. Sabina was going to marry into the veneering profession.

CHAPTER VI
A LONG CHAPTER OF A WHOLE YEAR

Mr. Ingraham, the baker, did not die that day when the doctor's chaise stood at the door, and all the children in the village were sent in for brick loaves. He was only struck down helpless; to lie there and be waited on; to linger, and wonder why he lingered; to feel himself in the way, and a burden; to get used to all this, and submit to it, and before he died to see that it had been all right.

The bakery lease had yet two years to run. It might have been sold out, but that would have involved a breaking up and a move, which Ingraham himself was not fit to bear, and his wife and daughters were not willing to think of yet.

Rachel quietly said,—as soon as her father was so far restored and comfortable that he could think and speak of things with them,—

"I can go on with the bakehouse. I know how. The men will all stay. I spoke to them Saturday night."

Ray kept the accounts, and when Saturday night came, the first after the misfortune fell upon them, she called all the journeymen into the little bakery office, where she sat upon the high stool at her father's desk. She gave each his week's wages, asking each one, as he signed his name in receipt, to wait a minute. Then she told them all, that she meant, if her father consented, to keep on with the business.

"He may get well," she said. "Will you all stand by and help me?"

"'Deed and we wull," said Irish Martin, the newest, the smallest, and the stupidest—if a quick heart and a willing will can be stupid—of them all. Some stupidity is only brightness not properly hitched on.

Ray found that she had to go on making brick loaves, however. She must keep her men; she could not expect to train them all to new ways; she must not make radical experiments in this trust-work, done for her father, to hold things as they were for him. Brick loaves, family loaves, rolls, brown bread, crackers, cookies, these had to be made as the journeymen knew how; as bakers' men had made them ever since and before Mother Goose wrote the dear old pat-a-cake rhyme.

Ray wondered why, when everybody liked home bread and home cake,—if they could stop to make them and knew how,—home bread and cake could not be made in big bakehouse ovens also, and by the quantity. She thought this was one of the things women might be able to do better than men; one of the bits of world business that women forced to work outside of homes might accomplish. Once, men had been necessary for the big, heavy, multiplied labor; now, there was machinery to help, for kneading, for rolling; there was steam for baking, even; there were no longer the great caverns to be filled with fire-wood, and cleared by brawny, seasoned arms, when the breath of them was like the breath of the furnace seven times heated, in which walked Shadrach, Meshach, and Abednego.

Ray had often thoughts to herself; thoughts here and there, that touched from fresh sides the great agitations of the day, which she felt instinctively were beginning wrong and foremost. "I *will* work; I *will* speak," cry the women. Very well; what hinders, if you have anything really to do, really to say? Opportunities are widening in the very nature and development of things; they are showing themselves at many a turn; but they give definite business, here and there; they quiet down those who take real hold. Outcry is no business; that is why the idle women take to it, and will do nothing else. It is not they who are moving the world forward to the clear sun-rising of the good day that must shine. People whose shoulders are at steady, small, unnoticed wheels are doing that.

Dot stayed in the house and helped her mother. She had a sewing-machine also, and she took in work from the neighbors, and from ladies like Miss Euphrasia Kirkbright, and Mrs. Greenleaf, and Mrs. Farland, who drove over to bring it from Roxeter, and East Mills, and River Point.

"Why don't you call and see me?" Sylvie Argenter asked one day, when she had walked over to the shop with a small basket, in which to put brown bread, little fine rolls for her mother, and some sugar cookies. Ray and Dot were both there. Dot was sitting with her sewing, putting in finishing stitches, button-holes, and the like. She was behind the counter, ready to mind the calls. Ray had come in to see what was wanting of fresh supplies from the bakehouse.

"I've been expecting you ever since we moved into the Turn. Ain't I to have any neighbors?"

The little court-way behind the Bank had come to be called the Turn; Sylvie took the name as she found it; as it named itself to her also in the first place, before she knew that others called it so. She liked it; it was one of those names that tell just what a thing is; that have made English nomenclature of places, in the old, original land above all, so quaint and full of pleasant home expression.

Dot looked up in surprise. It had never entered her head that the Argenters would expect them to call; and truly, the Argenters, in the plural, were very far indeed from any such imagination.

Ray took it more quietly and coolly.

"We are always very busy, since my father has been sick," she said. "We hardly go to see our old friends. But if you would like it, we will try and come, some day."

"I want you to," said Sylvie. "But I don't want you to *call*, though I said so. I want you to come right in and *see* me. I never could bear calls, and I don't mean ever to begin with them again."

The Highfords had come and "called," in the carriage, with pearl-kid gloves and long-tailed carriage dresses; called in such a way that Sylvie knew they would probably never call again. It was a last shading off of the old acquaintance; a decent remembrance of them in their low estate, just not to be snobbish on the vulgar face of it; a visit that had sent her mother to bed with a mortified and exasperated headache, and taken away her slight appetite for the delicate little "tea" that Sylvie brought up to her on a tray.

The Ingrahams saw she really meant it, and they came in one evening at first, when they were walking by, and Sylvie sat alone, with a book, in the twilight, on the corner piazza. Her mother had been there; her easy-chair stood beside the open window, but she had gone in and lain down upon the sofa. Mrs. Argenter had drooped, physically, ever since the grief and change. It depends upon what one's life is, and where is the spring of it, and what it feeds upon, how one rallies from a shock of any sort. The ozone had been taken out of her atmosphere. There was nothing in all the sweet sunshine of generous days, or the rest of calm-brooding nights, to restore her, or to belong to her any more. She had nothing to breathe. She had nothing to grow to, or to put herself in rapport with. She was out of relation with all the great, full world.

"Whom did you have there?" she asked Sylvie, when Ray and Dot were gone, and she came in to see if her mother would like anything.

"The Ingrahams, mother; our neighbors, you know; they are nice girls; I like them. And they were very kind to me the day of my accident, you remember. I called first, you see! And besides," she added, loving the whole truth, "I told them the other morning I should like them to come."

"I don't suppose it makes any difference," Mrs. Argenter answered, listlessly, turning her head away upon the sofa cushion.

"It makes the difference, Amata," said Sylvie, with a bright gentleness, and touching her mother's pretty hair with a tender finger, "that I shall be a great deal happier and better to know such girls; people we have got to live amongst, and ought to live a little like. You can't think how pleasant it was to talk with them. All my life it has seemed as if I never really got hold of people."

"You certainly forget the Sherretts."

"No, I don't. But I never got hold of them much while I was just edging alongside. I think some people grasp hands the better for a little space to reach across. You mayn't be born quite in the purple, as Susan Nipper would say, but it isn't any reason you should try to pinch yourself black and blue. I've got all over it, and I like the russet a great deal better. I wish you could."

"I can't begin again," said Mrs. Argenter. "My life is torn up by the roots, and there is the end of it."

It was true. Sylvie felt that it was so, as her mother spoke, and she reproached herself for her own light content. How could her mother make intimacy with Mrs. Knoxwell, the old blacksmith's wife, or Mrs. Pevear, the carriage-painter's? Or even good, homely Mrs. Ingraham, over the bake-shop? It is so much easier for girls to come together; girls of this day, especially, who in all classes get so much more of the same things than their mothers did.

Sylvie, authorized by this feeble acquiescence in what made "no difference," went on with her intention of having Ray Ingraham for her intimate friend. She spent many an hour, as the summer wore away, at the time in the afternoon when Mrs. Argenter was always lying down, in the pleasant bedroom over the shop, that looked out under the elm-tree. This was Ray Ingraham's leisure also; the bread carts did not come in till tea time, with their returns and orders; the day's second baking was in the oven; she had an hour or two of quiet between the noon business and the night; then she was always glad to see Sylvie Argenter come down the street with her little purple straw work-basket swinging from her forefinger, or a book in her hand. Sylvie and Ray read new books together from the Dorbury library, and old ones from Mrs. Argenter's book-shelves. Dot was not so often with them; her leisure was given more to her flower beds, where all sorts of blooms,—bright petunias and verbenas, delicate sweet peas and golden lantanas, scarlet bouvardias and snowy deutzias, fairy, fragrant jessamines, white and crimson and rose-tinted fuchsias with their purple hearts, and pansies, poised on their light stems, in every rich color, like beautiful winged things half alighted in a great fluttering flock,—made a glory and a sweetness in the modest patch of ground between the grape-trellised wall of the house-end and the bricks of the bakery, against which grew, appropriately enough, some strings of hop vines.

"I think it is just the nicest place in the world," said Sylvie, in her girlish, unqualified speech, as they all stood there one evening, while Dot was cutting a bouquet for Sylvie's mother. "People that set out to have everything beautiful, get the same things over and over; graveled drives and a smooth lawn, and trees put into groups tidily, and circles and baskets of flowers, and a view, perhaps, of a village away off, or a piece of the harbor, or a peep at the hills. But you are right down *amongst* such niceness! There's the river, close by; you can hear it all night, tumbling along behind the mills and the houses; there are the woods just down the lane beside the bakehouse; and here is the door-stone and the shady trellis, and the yard crowded full of flowers, as if they had all come because they wanted to, and knew they should have a good time, like a real country party, instead of standing off in separate properness, as people do who 'go into society.' And the new bread smells so sweet! I think it's what-for and because that make it so much better. Somebody came here to *do* something; and the rest was, and happened, and grew. I can't bear things fixed up to be exquisite!"

"That is the real doctrine of the kingdom of heaven," said a sweet, cheery voice behind them. They all turned round; Miss Euphrasia Kirkbright stood upon the door-stone.

"Being and doing. Then the surrounding is born out of the living. The Lord, up there, lets the saints make their own glory."

"Then you don't think the golden streets are all paved hard, beforehand?" said Sylvie. She understood Miss Euphrasia, and chimed quickly into her key. She had had talks with her before this, and she liked them.

"No more than that," said Miss Kirkbright, pointing to the golden flush under the soft, piling clouds in the west, that showed in glimpses beneath the arches of the trees and across the openings behind the village buildings. "'New every morning, and fresh every evening.' Doesn't He show us how it is, every day's work that He himself begins and ends?"

"Do you think we shall ever live like that?" asked Ray Ingraham, perceiving.

"'Then shall the righteous shine forth as the sun, in the kingdom of their Father,'" repeated Miss Euphrasia. "And the shining of the sun makes his worlds around him, doesn't it? We shall create outside of us whatever is in us. We do it now, more than we know. We shall find it all, by and by, ready,—whatever we think we have missed; the building not made with hands."

"I'm afraid we shall find ourselves in queer places, some of us," said Dot. Dot had a way of putting little round, practical periods to things. She did not do it with intent to be smart, or epigrammatic. She simply announced her own most obvious conclusion.

"'The first last, and the last first.' That is a part of the same thing. The rich man and Lazarus; knowing as we are known; being clothed upon; unclothed and not found naked; the wedding garment. You cannot touch one link of spiritual fact, without drawing a whole chain after it. Some other time, laying hold somewhere else, the same sayings will be brought to mind again, to confirm the new thought. It is all alive, breathing; spirit in atoms, given to move and crystallize to whatever central magnetism, always showing some fresh phase of what is one and everlasting."

Miss Euphrasia could no more help talking so—given the right circumstances to draw her forth—than she could help breathing. Her whole nature was fluid to the truth, as the atoms she spoke of. Talking with her, you saw, as in a divine kaleidoscope, the gleams and shiftings and combinings of heavenly and internal things; shown in simplest movings and relations of most real and every day experience and incident.

But she never went on—and "went over," exhorting. She did not believe in *discourses*, she said, even from the pulpit—very much. She believed in a *sermon*, and letting it go. And a sermon is just a word; as the Word gives itself, in some fresh manna-particle, to any soul.

So when the girls stood silent, as girls will, not knowing how to break a pause that has come upon such speaking, she broke it herself, with a very simple question; a question of mere little business that she had come to ask Dot.

"Were the little under-kerchiefs done?"

It was just the same sweet, cheery tone; she dropped nothing, she took up nothing, turning from the inward to the outside. It was all one quiet, harmonious sense of wholeness; living, and expression of living. That was what made Miss Euphrasia's "words" chord so pleasantly, always, without any jar, upon whatever string was being played; and the impulse and echo of them to run on through the music afterward, as one clear bell-stroke marking an accent, will seem to send its lingering impression through the unaccented measures following.

Dot went into the house and got the things; fine cambric neck-covers, frilled around the throat with delicate lace. She folded them small, and put them in a soft paper. Miss Kirkbright took the parcel, and paid Dot the money for her work; she gave her three dollars. Then she said to Sylvie,—

"Will you walk as far as the car corner with me? I have missed a real call that I meant to have had with you. I have been to your house."

"Did you see mother?" Sylvie asked, as they walked on, having said good-by, and passed out through the shop.

"No: Sabina said she was lying down, and I would not have her disturbed. I came partly to tell you a little news. Amy is engaged to Mr. Robert Truesdaile. They will be married in the fall, and go out to England. He has relatives there; his mother's family. There is an uncle living near Manchester; a large cotton manufacturer; he would like to take his nephew into the business; he has a great desire to get him there and make an Englishman of him."

"Does Amy like it? I mean, going to England? I am ever so glad for her being so happy."

"Yes, she likes it. At any rate she likes, as we all do, the new pleasant beginnings. We are all made to like fresh corners to turn, unless they seem very dark ones, or unless we have grown very old and tired, which *I* think there is never any need of doing."

"How busy she will be!" was Sylvie's next remark, made after a pause in which she realized to herself the news, and received also a little suggestion from it.

"Yes, pretty busy. But such preparations are made easily in these days."

"Won't there be ever so many little things of that sort to be done?" asked Sylvie, signifying the parcel which Miss Kirkbright held lightly in her fingers. "I wish I could do some of them. I mean,"—she gathered herself up bravely to say,—"I should like dearly to do *anything* for Amy; but I have thought it would be a good plan—if I could—to do something like that for the sake of earning; as Dot Ingraham does."

"Do you not have quite enough money, my dear?" asked Miss Kirkbright, in her kindly direct way that could never hurt.

"Not quite. At least, it don't seem to go very far. There are always things that we didn't expect. And things count up so at the grocer's. And a little nice meat every day,—which we *have* to have,—turns out so very expensive. And Sabina's wages—and mother's wine—and cream—and fresh eggs,—I get so worried when the bills come in!"

Sylvie's voice trembled with the effort and excitement of telling her money and housekeeping troubles.

"Sometimes I think we ought to have a cheaper girl; but I have just as much as I can do,—of those kinds of work,—and a poor girl would waste everything if I left her to go on. And I don't know much, myself. If Sabina were to go,—and she will next spring,—I am afraid it would turn out that we should have to keep two."

For all Sylvie's little "afternoons out," it was very certain that she, and Sabina also, did have their hands full at home. It is wonderful how much work one person, who *does* none of it and who must live fastidiously, can make in a small household. From Mrs. Argenter's hot water, and large bath, and late breakfast in the morning to her glass of milk at nine o'clock at night, which she never *could* remember to carry up herself from the tea-table,—she needed one person constantly to look after her individual wants. And she couldn't help it, poor lady, either; that is the worst of it; one gets so as not to be able to help things; "it was the shape of her head," Sabina said, in a phrase she had learned of the cabinet-maker.

"You shall have anything you can do; just as Dot does," said Miss Euphrasia. "And Amy will like it all the better for your doing. You can put the love into the work, as much as we shall into the pay."

Was there ever anybody who handled the bare facts of life so graciously as this Miss Euphrasia? She did it by taking right hold of them, by their honest handles,—as they were meant to be taken hold of.

"You like your home? You haven't grown tired of being a village girl?" she said, as she and Sylvie sat down on a great flat projecting rock in the shaded walk beside the railroad track. They had just missed one car; there would not be another for twenty minutes.

"O, yes. No; I haven't got tired; but I don't feel as if I had quite *been it*, yet. I don't think I am exactly that, or anything, now. That is the worst of it. People don't understand. They won't take us in,—all of them. It's just as hard to get into a village, if you weren't born in it, as it is to get into upper-ten-dom. Mrs. Knoxwell called, and looked round all the time with her nose up in a sort of a way,—well, it *was* just like a dog sniffing round for something. And she went off and told about mother's poor, dear, old, black silk dress, that I made into a cool skirt and jacket for her. 'Some folks must be always set up in silk, she *sposed*.' Everybody isn't like the Ingrahams."

"No garment of *this* life fits exactly. There was only one seamless robe. But we mustn't take thought for raiment, you see. The body is more. And at last,—somehow, sometime,—we shall be all clothed perfectly—with his righteousness."

This was too swift and light in its spiritual touching and linking for Sylvie to follow. She had to ask, as the disciples did, for a meaning.

"It isn't clothes that I am thinking of, or that trouble me; or any outside. And I know it isn't actual clothes you mean. Please tell me plainer, Miss Euphrasia."

"I mean that I think He meant by 'raiment,' not *clothes* so much as *life*; what we put on or have put on to us; what each soul wears and moves in, to feel itself by and to be manifest; history, circumstance. 'Raiment,'—'garment,'—the words always stand for this, beyond their temporary and technical sense. 'He laid aside his *garment*,'—He gave up his own life that He might have been living,—to come and wash our feet!"

"And the people cast their garments before Him, when He rode into Jerusalem," Sylvie said presently.

"Yes; that is the way He must come into his kingdom, and lead us with Him. We are to give up our old ways, and the selfish things we lived in once, and not think about our own raiment any more. He will give it to us, as He gives it to the lilies; and the glory of it will be something that we could not in any way spin for our selves. And by and by it will come to be full and right, all through; we shall be clothed with his righteousness. What is righteousness but rightness?"

"I thought it only meant goodness. That we hadn't any goodness of our own; that we mustn't trust in it, you know?"

"But that his, by faith, is to cover us? That is the old letter-doctrine, which men didn't look through to see how graciously true it is, and how it gives them all things. For it *is things* they want, all the time; realities, of experience and having. They talk about an abstract 'justification by faith,' and struggle for an abstract experience; not seeing how good God is to tell them plainly that his 'justifying' is *setting everything right* for them, and round them, and in them: his *rightness* is sufficient for them; they need not go about, worrying, to establish their own. The minute they give up their wrongness, and fall into its line, it works for them as no working of their own could do. God doesn't forgive a soul ideally, and leave it a mere clean, naked consciousness; He brings forth the best robe and puts it on; a ring for the hand, and shoes for the feet. People try painfully to achieve a ghostly sort of regeneration that strips them and leaves them half dead. The Lord heals and binds up, and puts his own garment upon us; He *knows* that we have *need*," Miss Kirkbright repeated, earnestly. "Salvation is a real having; not an escape without anything, as people run for their lives from fire or flood."

Sylvie had listened with a shining face.

"You get it all from that one word,—'raiment.' Your words—the words you find out, Miss Kirkbright—are living things."

"Yes, words *are* living things," Miss Kirkbright answered. "God does not give us anything dead. But the life of them is his spirit, and his spirit is an instant breath. You can take them as if they were dead, if you do not inspire. Men who wrote these words, inspired. We talk about their *being* inspired, as if it were a passive thing; and quarrel about it, and forget to breathe ourselves. It is all there, just as live as it ever was; it is given over again every time we go for it; when we find it so, we never need trouble any more about authority. We shall only thank God that He has kept in the world the records of his talk with men; and the more we talk with Him ourselves, the deeper we shall understand their speech."

"Isn't all that about 'inner meanings,'—that words in the Bible stand for,—Swedenborgian, Miss Kirkbright?"

"Well?" Miss Kirkbright smiled.

"Are you a Swedenborgian?" Sylvie asked the question timidly.

"I believe in the New Church," answered Miss Euphrasia. "But I don't believe in it as standing apart, locked up in a system. I believe in it as a leaven of all the churches; a life and soul that is coming into them. I think a separate body is a mistake; though I like to worship with the little family with which I find myself most kin. We should do that without any name. The Lord gave a great deal to Swedenborg: but when his time comes, He doesn't give all in any one place, or to any one soul; his coming is as the lightening from the one part to the other part under heaven. *Lightening*—not lightning; it is wrongly printed so, I think. He set the sun in the sky, once and forever, when He came in his Christ; since then, day after day dawns, everywhere, and uttereth speech; and even night after night showeth knowledge. I believe in the fuller, more inward dispensation. Swedenborg illustrated it,—received it, wonderfully; but many are receiving the same at this hour, without ever having heard of Swedenborg. For that reason, we may never be afraid about the truth. It is not here or there. This or that may fail or pass away, but the Word shall never pass away."

"What a long talk we have had! How did we get into it?"

The car was coming up the slope, half a mile off. They could see the red top of it rising, and could hear the tinkle of the bell.

"I wish we didn't need to get out!" said Sylvie. "I wish I could tell it to my mother!"

"Can't you?"

"I'm afraid it wouldn't keep alive,—with me," Sylvie answered, with a little sigh and shadow. "Not even as these flowers will that I am taking to her. I can take,—but I can't give, and I always feel so that I ought to. Mother needs the comfort of it. Why don't you come and talk to her, Miss Kirkbright?"

"Talk on purpose never does. You and I 'got into it,' as you say. Perhaps your mother and I might. But I have got over feeling about such sort of giving—in words—as a duty. Even with people whom I work among sometimes, who need the very first gift of truth, so much! We can only keep near and dear to each other, Sylvie, and near and dear to the Lord. Then there are the two lines; and things that are equal—or similarly related—to the same thing, are related to one another. He can make the mark that proves and joins, any time. Did you know there was Bible in geometry, Sylvie? I very often go to my old school Euclid for a heavenly comfort."

"I think you go to everything for it—and to everybody with it," said Sylvie, squeezing her friend's hand as he left her on the car-step.

Nothing comes much before we need it. This talk stayed by Sylvie through months afterwards, if not the word of it, always the subtle cheer and strength of it, that nestled into her heart underneath all her upper thinkings and cares of day by day, and would not quite let them settle down upon the living core of it with a hopeless pressure.

For the real stress of her new life was bearing upon her heavily. The first poetry, the first fresh touches with which she had made pleasant signs about their altered condition, were passed into established use, and dulled into wornness and commonness. The difficulties—the grapples—came thick and forceful about her. At the same time, her reliances seemed slipping away from her.

She had hardly known, any more than her mother, how much the countenance and friendliness of the Sherrett family had done in upholding her. It was a link with the old things—the very best of the old things,—that stood as a continual assurance that they themselves were not altered—lowered in any way—by their alterings. This came to Sylvie with an interior confirmation, as it did to Mrs. Argenter exteriorly. So long as Miss Kirkbright and the Sherretts indorsed anything, it could not harm them much, or fence them out altogether from what they had been. Amy Sherrett and Miss Kirkbright thought well of the Ingrahams, and maintained all their dealings with them in a friendly—even intimate—fashion. If Sylvie chose to sit with them of an afternoon, it was no more than Miss Euphrasia did. Also, the old Miss Goodwyns, who lived up the Turn behind the maples, were privileged to offer Miss Kirkbright a cup of tea when she went in there, as she would often for an hour's talk over knitting work and books that had been lent and read. Sylvie might well enough do the same, or go to them for hints and helps in her window-gardening and little ingenuities of housekeeping. Mrs. Argenter deluded herself agreeably with the notion that the relations in each case were identical. But what with the Sherretts and Miss Kirkbright were mere kindly incidents of living, apart somewhat from the crowd of daily demand and absorption, were to Sylvie the essential resource and relaxation of a living that could find little other.

Sylvie let her mother's reading pass, not knowing how far Mrs. Argenter was able actually to believe in it herself, but clearly and thankfully recognizing, on her own part the reality,—that she had these friends and resources to brighten what would else be, after all, pretty hard to endure.

The Knoxwells and the Kents and old Mrs. Sunderline were hardly neighbors, as she had meant to neighbor with them. The Knoxwells and the Kents were a little jealous and suspicious of her overtures, as she had said, and would not quite let her in. Besides, she did not draw toward Marion Kent, who came to church with French gilt bracelets on, and a violently trimmed polonaise, as she did toward Dot and Ray.

Old Mrs. Sunderline was as nice and cosy as could be but she never went out herself, and her whole family consisted of herself, her sister,— Aunt Lora, the tailoress,—and her son, the young carpenter, whom Sylvie could not help discerning was much noted and discussed among the womenkind, old and young, as a village—what shall I say, since I cannot call my honest, manly Frank Sunderline a village beau? A village *desirable* he was, at any rate. Of course, Sylvie Argenter could not go very much to his home, to make a voluntary intimacy. And all these, if she and they had cared mutually ever so much, would hare been under Mrs. Argenter's proscription as mere common work-and-trade people whom nobody knew beyond their vocations. There was this essential difference between the baker's daughters whom the Sherrett family noticed exceptionally and the blacksmith's and carpenter's households, the woman who "took in fine washing," and her forward, dressy, ambitious girl. Though the baker's daughters and the good Miss Goodwyns themselves knew all these in their turn, quite well, and belonged among them. The social "laying on of hands" does not hold out, like the apostolic benediction, all the way down.

I began these last long paragraphs with saying, that neither Sylvie nor her mother had known how far their comfort and acquiescence in their new life had depended on the "backing up" of the Sherretts. This they found out when the Sherretts went away that autumn. Amy was married in October and sailed for England; Rodney was at Cambridge, and when the country house at Roxeter was closed, Miss Euphrasia took rooms in Boston for the winter, where her winter work all lay, and Mr. Sherrett, who was a Representative to Congress, went to Washington for the session. There were no more calls; no more pleasant spending of occasional days at the Sherrett Place; no more ridings round and droppings in of Rodney at the village. All that seemed suddenly broken up and done with, almost hopelessly. Sylvie could not see how it was ever to begin again. Next year Rodney was to graduate, and his father was to take him abroad. These plans had come out in the talks over Amy's marriage and her leaving home.

Sylvie was left to her village; she could only go in to the Miss Goodwyns and down to the bakery; and now that her condescensions were unlinked from those of Miss Kirkbright, and just dropped into next-door matter of course, Mrs. Argenter fretted. Marion Kent would come calling, too, and talk about Mrs. Browning, and borrow patterns, and ask Sylvie "how she hitched up her Marguerite."

[In case this story should ever be read after the fashion I allude to shall have disappeared from the catalogues of Butterick and Demorest, to be never more mentioned or remembered, I will explain that it is a style of upper dress most eminently un-daisy-like in expression and effect, and reminding of no field simplicities whatsoever, unless possibly of a hay-load; being so very much pitch-forked up into heaps behind.]

Not that Sylvie dressed herself with a pitchfork; she had been growing more sensible than that for a long time, to say nothing of her quiet mourning; though for that matter, I have seen bombazine and crape so voluminously bundled and massed as to remind one of the slang phrase "piling on the agony." But Marion Kent came to Sylvie for the first idea of her light loops and touches: then she developed it, as her sort do, tremendously; she did grandly by the yard, what Sylvie Argenter did modestly by the quarter; she had a soul beyond mere nips and pinches. But this was small vexation, to be caricatured by Miss Kent. Sylvie's real troubles came closer and harder.

Sabina Bowen went away.

She had not meant to be married until the spring; but she and the cabinet-maker had had their eyes upon a certain half-house, — neat and pretty, with clean brown paint and a little enticing gingerbread work about the eaves and porch, — which was to be vacated at that time; and it happened that, through some unforeseen circumstances, the family occupying it became suddenly desirous to get rid of the remainder of their lease, and move this winter. John came to Sabina eagerly one evening with the news.

Sabina thought of the long winter evenings, and the bright double-burner kerosene she had saved up money for; of a little round table with a red cloth, and John one side of it and she the other; of sitting together in a pew, and going every Sunday in her bride-bonnet, instead of getting her every-other-Sunday forenoon and hurrying home to fricassee Mrs. Argenter's chicken or sweet-bread, and boil her cauliflower; and so she gave warning the next morning when she was emptying Mrs. Argenter's bath and picking up the towels. She steeled herself wisely with choice of time and person; it would have been hard to tell Miss Sylvie when she came down to dust the parlor, or into the kitchen to make the little dessert for dinner.

And now poor Sylvie fell into and floundered in that slough of despond, the lower stratum of the Irish kitchen element, which if one once meddles with, it is almost hopeless to get out of; and one very soon finds that to get out of it is the only hope, forlorn as it may be.

She had one girl who made sour bread for a fortnight, and then flounced off on a Monday morning, leaving the clothes in the tubs, because "her bread was never faulted before, an' faith, she wudn't pit up biscuits of a Sunday night no more for annybody!" The next one disposed of all the dish towels in four days, behind barrels and in the corners of the kettle closet, and complained insolently of ill furnishing; a third kindled her fire with the clothes-pins; a fourth wore Mrs. Argenter's cambric skirts on Sunday, "for a finish, jist to make 'em worth while for the washin'," and trod out the heels of three pairs of Sylvie's best stockings, for a like considerate and economical reason. Another declined peremptorily the use of a flat-iron stand, and burnt out triangular pieces from the ironing sheet and blanket; and when Sylvie remonstrated with her about the skirt-board, which she had newly covered, finding her using it as a cleaning cloth after she had heated her "flats" upon the coals, she was met with a torrent of abuse, and the assurance that she "might get somebody else to save her old rags with their apurns, an' iron five white skirts and tin pairs o' undersleeves a week for two women, at three dollars an' a half. She had heard enough about the place or iver she kim intil it, an' the bigger fool she iver to iv set her fut inside the dooers."

That was it. It came to that pass, now. They "heard about the place before iver they kim intil it." The Argenter name was up. There was no getting out of the bog-mire. Sylvie ran the gauntlet of the village refuse, and had to go to Boston to the intelligence offices. By this time she hadn't a kitchen or a bedroom fit to show a decent servant into. They came, and looked, and went away; half-dozens of them. The stove was burnt out; there was a hole through into the oven; nothing but an entire new one would do, and a new one would cost forty dollars. Poor Sylvie toiled and worried; she went to Mrs. Ingraham and the Miss Goodwyns, and Sabina Galvin, for advice; she made ash-paste and cemented up the breaches, she hired a woman by the day, put out washing, and bought bread at the bakehouse. All this time, Mrs. Argenter had her white skirts and her ruffled underclothing to be done up. "What could she do? She hadn't any plain things, and she couldn't get new, and she must be clean."

At New Year's, they owed three hundred dollars that they could not pay, beside the quarter's rent. They had to take it out of their little invested capital; they sold ten shares of railroad stock at a poor time; it brought them eight hundred and seventy-five dollars. They bought their new stove, and some other things; they hired, at last, two girls for the winter, at three dollars and two and a half, respectively; this was a saving to what they had been doing, and they must get through the cold weather somehow. Besides, Mrs. Argenter was now seriously out of health. She had had nothing to do but to fall sick under her troubles, and she had honestly and effectually done it.

But how should they manage another year, and another? How long would they have any income, if such a piece was to be taken out of the principal every six months?

In the spring, Mrs. Argenter declared it was of no use; they must give up and go to board. They ought to have done it in the first place. Plenty of people got along so with no more than they had. A cheap place in the country for the summer would save up to pay for rooms in town for the winter. She couldn't bear another hot season in that village,—nor a cold one, either. A second winter would be just madness. What could two women do, who had never had anything to provide before, with getting in coal, and wood, and vegetables, and everything, and snow to be shoveled, and ashes sifted, and fires to make, and girls going off every Monday morning?

She had just enough reason, as the case stood, for Sylvie not to be able to answer a word. But the lease,—for another year? What should they do with that? Would Mr. Frost take it off their hands?

If Sylvie had known who really stood behind Mr. Frost, and how!

The little poem of village living,—of home simpleness and frugal prettiness,—of *that*, the two first lines alone had rhymed!

They had entered upon the last quarter of their first year when they came to this united and definite conclusion. That month of May was harsh and stormy. Nothing could be done about moving until clearer and finer weather. So the rent was continued, of course, until the year expired, and in June they would pack up and go away.

Sylvie had been to the doctor, first, and told him about her mother; and he had called, in a half-friendly, half-professional way, to see her. After his call, he had had an honest talk with Sylvie.

God sometimes shows us a glimpse of a future trouble that He holds in his hand, to neutralize the trouble we are immediately under; even, it may be, to turn it into a quietness and content. When Sylvie had heard all that Doctor Sainswell had to say, she put away her money anxiety from off her mind, at once and finally. Nothing was any matter now, but that her mother should go where she would,—have what she wanted.

Then she went to see Mr. Frost.

"He would write to his employer," he said; he could not give an answer of himself.

The answer came in five days. They might relinquish the house at any moment; they need pay the rent only for the time of their occupancy. It would suit the owner quite as well; the place would let readily.

Sylvie was happy as she told her mother how nicely it had come out. She might have been less so, had she seen Mr. Sherrett's face when he read his agent's letter and replied to it in those three lines without moving from his seat.

"I might have expected it," he said to himself. "She's a child after all. But she began so bravely! And it can't help being worse by and by. Well, one can't live people's lives for them." And he turned back to his other papers,—his notes of yesterday's debate in the House.

Early in June, there came lovely days.

Sylvie was very busy. She had kept her two girls with her to the end, by dint of raising their wages a dollar a week each, for the remainder of their stay. She had the whole house to go over; even a year's accumulation is formidable, when one has to turn out and dispose of everything anew. She began with the attic; the trunks and the boxes. She had to give away a great deal that would have been of service had they continued to live quietly on. Two old proverbs asserted themselves to her experience now, and kept saying themselves over to her as she worked: "A rolling stone gathers no moss;" "Three removes are as bad as a fire."

She had come down in her progress as far as the closets of their own rooms, and the overlooking of their own clothing, when one afternoon, as, still in her wrapper, she was busy at the topmost shelves of her mother's wardrobe, with little fear of any but village calls, and scarcely those, wheels came up the Turn, and names were suddenly announced.

"Miss Harkbird and Mr. Shoot!"

Sylvie caught in a flash the idea of what the girl ought to have said. She laughed, she turned red, and the tears very nearly sprang to her eyes, with surprise, amusement, embarrassment and flurry.

"What *shall* I do? Give me your hand, Katy! And where on earth *is* my other dress? Can't you learn to get names right ever, Katy? Miss Kirkbright and Mr. Sherrett. Say I will be down presently. O, what hair!"

She was before the glass now; she caught up stray locks and thrust in hairpins here and there; then she tied a little violet-edged black ribbon through the toss and rumple, and somehow it looked all right. Anyway, her eyes were brilliant; the more brilliant for that cloudiness beneath which they shone.

Her eyes shone and her lips trembled, as she came into the room and told Miss Euphrasia how glad she was to see them. For she remembered then why she was so glad; she remembered the things she had longed to go to Miss Euphrasia with, all the hard winter and doubtful spring.

"We are going away, you see," she told her presently. "Mother must have a change. It does not suit her here in any way. We are going to Lebanon for a little while; then we shall find some quiet place, in the mountains, perhaps. In the winter, we shall have to board in the city. Mother can't be worried any longer; she must have what she wants."

Miss Kirkbright glanced round the pretty parlor, as yet undisturbed; at all that, with such labor, Sylvie had arranged into a home a year ago.

"What a care for you, dear! What will you do with everything?"

"We are going to store some of our furniture, and sell some. Dot Ingraham is to take my plants for me till we come back to Boston; then I shall have them in our rooms. I hope the gas won't kill them."

Rodney Sherrett said nothing after the first greeting for some minutes. He only sat and listened, with a sober shadow in his handsome eyes. All this was so different from anything he had anticipated.

By and by, in a little pause, he told her that he had come out to ask her for Class Day.

"I wouldn't just send a card for the spread," said he. "Aunt Euphrasia wants you to go with her. I'm in the Reward of Merit list, you see; I've earned my good time; been grinding awfully all winter. I've even got a part for Commencement. Only a translation; and it probably won't be called; but wouldn't you like to hear it, if it were?"

"O, I wish I could!" said Sylvie, replying in earnest good faith to the question he asked quizzically for a cover to his real eagerness in letting her know. "I *wish* I could! But we shall be gone."

"Not before Class Day?"

"Yes; just about then. I'm so sorry."

Rod Sherrett looked very much as if he thought he had "ground" for nothing.

Then they talked about Lebanon, and the new Vermont Springs; perhaps Mrs. Argenter would go to some of them in July. Miss Kirkbright told Sylvie of a dear little place she had found last year, in the edge of the White Mountain country; "among the great rolling hills that lead you up and up," she said, "through whole counties of wonderful wild beauty; the sacred places of simple living that can never be crowded and profaned. It is a nook to hide away in when one gets discouraged with the world. It consoles you with seeing how great and safe the world is, after all; how the cities are only dots that men have made upon it; picnicking here and there, as it were, with their gross works and pleasures, and making a little rubbish which the Lord could clean all away, if He wanted, with one breath, out of his grand, pure heights."

All the while Sylvie and Rodney had their own young disappointed thoughts. They could not say them out; the invitation had been given and been replied to as it must be; this was only a call with Aunt Euphrasia; everything that they might have in their minds could not be spoken, even if they could have seen it quite clearly enough to speak; they both felt when the half hour was over, as if they had said—had done—nothing that they ought, or wanted to. And neither knew it of the other; that was the worst.

When Rodney at last went out to untie his horse, Miss Euphrasia turned round to Sylvie with a question.

"Is this all quite safe and easy for you, dear?"

"Yes," returned Sylvie, frankly, understanding her. "I have given up all that worry. There is money enough for a good while if we don't mind using it. And it is *mother's* money; and Dr. Sainswell says she *cannot* have a long life."

Sylvie spoke the last sentence with a break; but her voice was clear and calm,—only tender.

"And after that?" Miss Kirkbright asked, looking kindly into her face.

"After that I shall do what I can; what other girls do, who haven't money. When the time comes I shall see. All that comes hard to me—after mother's feebleness—is the changing; the not staying of anything anywhere. My life seems all broken and mixed up, Miss Kirkbright. Nothing goes right on as if it belonged."

"'Lo, it is I; be not afraid,'" repeated Miss Kirkbright softly. "When things work and change, in spite of us, we may know it is the Lord working. That is the comfort,—the certainty."

The tenderness that had been in heart and voice sprang to tears in Sylvie's eyes, at that word.

"How *do* you think of such things?" she said, earnestly. "I shall never forget that now."

Aunt Euphrasia could not help telling Rodney as they drove away toward the city, how brave and good the child was. She could not help it, although, wise woman that she was, she refrained carefully, in most ways, from "putting things in his head."

"I knew it before," was Rodney's answer.

Aunt Euphrasia concluded, at that, in her own mind, that we may be as old and as wise as we please, but in some things the young people are before us; they need very little of our "putting in heads."

"Aunt Effie," said Rodney, presently, "do you think I have been a very great good-for-nothing?"

"No, indeed. Why?"

"Well, I certainly haven't been good for much; and I'm not sure whether I could be. I don't know exactly what to think of myself. I haven't had anything to do with *horses* this winter; I sent Red Squirrel off into the country. What is the reason, Auntie, that if a fellow takes to horses, they all think he is going straight to the bad? What is there so abominable about them?"

"Nothing," said Miss Kirkbright. "On the contrary, everything grand and splendid,—in *type*,—you know. Horses are powers; men are made to handle powers, and to use them; it is the very manliest instinct of a man by which he loves them. Only, he is terribly mistaken if he stops there,—playing with the signs. He might as well ride a stick, or drive a chair with worsted reins, as the little ones do, all his life."

Rodney's face lit straight up; but for a whole mile he made no answer. Then he said, as people do after a silence,—

"How quiet we are, all at once! But you have a way of finishing up things, Aunt Euphrasia. You said all I wanted in about fifty words, just now. I begin to see. It may be just because I *might* do something, that I haven't. Aunt Euphrasia, I've done being a boy, and playing with reins. I'm going to be a man, and do some real driving. Do you know, I think I'd better not go to Europe with my father?"

"I don't *know* that," returned Miss Kirkbright. "It might be; but it is a thing to consider seriously, before you give it up. You ought to be quite sure what you stay for."

"I won't stay for any nonsense. I mean to talk with him to-night."

"Talk with yourself, first, Rod; find yourself out, and then talk it all out honestly with him."

Which advice—the first clause of it—Rodney proceeded instantly to follow; he did not say another word all the way over the Mill Dam and up Beacon Hill, and Aunt Euphrasia let him blessedly alone; one of the few women, as she was, capable of doing that great and passive thing.

When he had left her at her door, and driven his horse to the livery stable, he went round to his father's rooms and took tea with him.

The meal over, he pushed back his chair, saying, "I want a talk with you, father. Can I have it now? I must be back at Cambridge by ten."

Mr. Sherrett looked in his son's face. There was nothing there of uncomfortableness,—of conscious bracing up to a difficult matter. He repressed his first instinctive inquiry of "No scrape, I hope, Rod?" The question was asked and answered between their eyes.

"Certainly, my boy," he said, rising. "Step in there; the man will be up presently to take away these things."

The door stood open to an inner apartment; a little study, beyond which were sleeping and bath-rooms.

Rodney stepped upon the threshold, leaning against the frame, while Mr. Sherrett went to the mantel, found a match and a cigar, cut the latter carefully in two, and lit one half.

"The thing is, father," said Rodney, not waiting for a formal beginning after they should be closeted and seated,—"I've been thinking that I'd better not go abroad, if you don't mind. I'm rather waking up to the idea of earning my own way first,—before I take it. It's time I was doing something. If I use up a year or more in travelling, I shall be going on to twenty-two, you see; and I ought to have got ahead a little by that time."

Mr. Sherrett turned round, surprised. This was a new phase. He wondered how deep it went, and what had occasioned it.

"Do you mean you wish to study a profession, after all?"

"No. I don't think I've much of a 'head-piece'—as Nurse Pond used to say. At least, in the learned direction. I've just about enough to do for a gentleman,—a *man*, I hope. But I *should* like to take hold of something and make it go. I'll tell you why, father. I want to see what's in me in the first place; and then, I might want something, sometime, that I should have no right to if I couldn't take care of myself—and more."

"Come in, Rodney, and shut the door."

After that, of course, we cannot listen.

They two sat together for almost two hours. In that time, Mr. Sherrett was first discomposed; then set right upon one or two little points that had puzzled and disappointed him, and to which his son could furnish the key; then thoroughly roused and anxious at this first dealing with his boy as a man, with all a man's hopes and wishes quickening him to a serious purpose; at last, touched sympathetically, as a good father must be, with the very desire of his child, and the fears and uncertainties that may environ it. What he suggested, what he proposed and promised, what was partly planned to be afterward concluded in detail, did not transpire through that heavy closed door; neither we, nor the white-jacketed serving-man, can be at this moment the wiser. It will appear hereafter. When they came out together at last, Mr. Sherrett was saying,—

"Two years, remember. Not a word of it, decisively, till then,—for both your sakes."

"Let what will happen, father? You don't remember when you were young."

"Don't I?" said his father, with emphasis, and a kindly smile. "If anything happens, come to me. Meanwhile,—you may talk, if you like, to Aunt Euphrasia. I'll trust her."

And so the Lord set this angel of his to watch over this thread of our story.

We may leave it here for a while.

CHAPTER VII
BEL AND BARTHOLOMEW

"Kroo! kroo! I've cramp in my legs,
Sitting so long atop of my eggs!
Never a minute for rest to snatch;
I wonder when they are going to hatch!

"Cluck! cluck! listen! tseep!
Down in the nest there's a stir and a peep.
Everything comes to its luck some day;
I've got chickens! What will folks say?"

Bel Bree made that rhyme. It came into her head suddenly one morning, sitting in her little bedroom window that looked right over the grass yard into the open barn-door, where the hens stalked in and out; and one, with three chickens, was at that minute airing herself and her family that had just come out of their shells into the world, and walked about already as if the great big world was only there, just as they had of course expected it to be. The hen was the most astonished. *She* was just old enough to begin to be able to be astonished. Her whole mind expressed itself in that proud cluck, and pert, excited carriage. She had done a wonderful thing, and she didn't know how she had done it. Bel "read it like coarse print,"—as her stepmother was wont to say of her own perspicacities,—and put it into jingle, as she had a trick of doing with things.

Bel Bree lived in New Hampshire; fifteen miles from a railway; in the curious region where the old times and the new touch each other and mix up; where the women use towels, and table-cloths, and bed-spreads, of their mothers' own hand-weaving, and hem their new ones with sewing-machines brought by travelling agents to their doors; where the men mow and rake their fields with modern inventions, but only get their newspapers once a week; where the "help" are neighbors' girls, who wear overskirts and high hats, and sit at the table with the family; where there are rag carpets and "painted chamber-sets;" where they feed calves and young turkeys, and string apples to dry in the summer, and make wonderful patchwork quilts, and wax flowers, and worsted work, perhaps, in the long winters; where they go to church and to sewing societies from miles about, over tremendous hills and pitches, with happy-go-lucky wagons and harnesses that never come to grief; where they have few schools and intermitted teaching, yet turn out, somehow, young men who work their way into professions, and girls who take the world by instinct, and understand a great deal perfectly well that is beyond their practical reach; where the old Puritan stiffness keeps them straight, but gets leavened in some marvelous way with the broader and more generous thought of the time, and wears a geniality that it is half unconscious of; the region where, if you are lucky enough to get into it to know it, you find yourself, as Miss Euphrasia said, encouraged and put in heart again about the world. Things are so genuine; when they make a step forward, they are really there.

But Bel Bree was not very happy in her home, though she sat at the window and made rhymes in half merry fashion; though she loved the hills, and the lights, and the shadows, the sweet-blossoming springs and the jeweled autumns, the sunsets, and the great rains, that set all the wild little waterfalls prancing and calling to each other among the ravines.

Bel had two lives; one that she lived in these things, and one within the literal and prosaic limit of the farmhouse, where her father, as farmers must, had married a smart second wife to "look after matters."

Not that Mrs. Bree ever looked *after* anything: nothing ever got ahead of her; she "whewed round;" when she was "whewing," she neither wanted Bel to hinder nor help; the child was left to herself; to her idleness and her dreams; then she neglected something that she might and ought to have done, and then there was reproach, and hard speech; partly deserved, but running over into that wherein she should not have been blamed,— the precinct of her step-mother's own busy and self-arrogated functions. She was taunted and censured for incapacity in that to which she was not admitted; "her mother made ten cheeses a week, and flung them in her face," she said. On the other hand, Mrs. Bree said "Bel hadn't got a mite of *snap* to her." One might say that, perhaps, of an electric battery, if the wrong poles were opposed. Mrs. Bree had not found out where the "snap" lay in Bel's character. She never would find out.

Bel longed, as human creatures who are discontent always do, to get away. The world was big; there must be better things somewhere.

There was a pathos of weariness, and an inspiration of hope, in her little rhyme about the hen.

Bel was named for her Aunt Belinda. Miss Belinda Bree came up for a week, sometimes, in the summer, to the farm. All the rest of the year she worked hard in the city. She put a good face upon it in her talk among her old neighbors. She spoke of the grand streets, the parades, Duke's balls,— for which she made dresses,—and jubilees, of which she heard afar off,—as if she were part and parcel of all Boston enterprise and magnificence. It was a great thing, truly, to live in the Hub. Honestly, she had not got over it since she came there, a raw country girl, and began her apprenticeship to its wonders and to her own trade. She could not turn a water faucet, nor light her gas, nor count the strokes of the electric fire alarm, without feeling the grandeur of having Cochituate turned on to wash her hands,—of making her one little spark of the grand illumination under which the Three Hills shone every night,—of dwelling within ear-shot and protection of the quietly imposing system of wires and bells that worked by lightning against a fierce element of daily danger. She was proud of policemen; she was thrilled at the sound of steam-engines thundering along the pavements; she felt as if she had a hand in it. When they fired guns upon the Common, she could only listen and look out of windows; the little boys ran and shouted for her in the streets; that is what the little boys are for. Somebody must do the running and the shouting to relieve the instincts of older and busier people, who must pretend as if they didn't care.

All this kept Miss Belinda Bree from utterly wearing out at her dull work in the great warerooms, or now and then at days' seamstressing in families. It really keeps a great many people from wearing out.

Miss Bree's work *was* dull. The days of her early "mantua making" were over. Twenty years had made things very different in Boston. The "nice families" had been more quiet then; the quietest of them now cannot manage things as they did in those days; for the same reason that you cannot buy old-fashioned "wearing" goods; they are not in the market. "Sell and wear out; wear out and sell;" that is the principle of to-day. You must do as the world does; there is no other path cut through. If you travel, you must keep on night and day, or wait twenty-four hours and start in the night again.

Nobody—or scarcely anybody—has a dress-maker now, in the old, cosy way, of the old, cosy sort, staying a week, looking over the wardrobes of the whole family, advising, cutting, altering, remaking, getting into ever so much household interest and history in the daily chat, and listening over daily work: sitting at the same table; linking herself in with things, spring and fall, as the leaves do with their goings and comings; or like the equinoxes, that in March and September shut about us with friendly curtains of rain for days, in which so much can be done in the big up-stairs room with a cheerful fire, that is devoted to the rites and mysteries of scissors and needle. We were always glad, I remember, when our dress-making week fell in with the equinoctial.

But now, all poor Miss Bree's "best places" had slipped away from her, and her life had changed. People go to great outfitting stores, buy their goods, have themselves measured, and leave the whole thing to result a week afterward in a big box sent home with everything fitted and machined and finished, with the last inventions and accumulations of frills, tucks, and reduplications; and at the bottom of the box a bill tucked and reduplicated in the same modern proportions.

Miss Bree had now to go out, like any other machine girl, to the warerooms; except when she took home particular hand-work of button holes and trimmings, or occasionally engaged herself for two or three days to some family mother who could not pay the big bills, and who ran her own machine, cut her own basques and gores, and hired help for basting and finishing. She had almost done with even this; most people liked young help; brisker with their needles, sewing without glasses, nicer and fresher looking to have about. Poor "Aunt Blin" overheard one man ask his wife in her dressing-room before dinner, "Why, if she must have a stitching-woman in the house, she couldn't find a more comfortable one to look at; somebody a little bright and cheerful to bring to the table, instead of that old callariper?"

Miss Bree behaved like a saint; it was not the lady's fault; she resisted the temptation to a sudden headache and declining her dinner, for fear of hurting the feelings of her employer, who had always been kind to her; she would not let her suspect or be afraid that the speech had come to her ears; she smoothed her thin old hair, took off her glasses, wiped her eyes a little, washed her hands, and went down when she was called; but after that day she "left off going out to work for families."

The warehouses did not pay her very well; neither there was she able to compete with the smart young seamstresses; she only got a dollar and a quarter a day, and had to lodge and feed herself; yet she kept on; it was her lot and living; she looked out at her third-story window upon the roofs and spires, listened to the fire alarms, heard the chimes of a Sunday, saw carriages roll by and well-dressed people moving to and fro, felt the thrill of the daily bustle, and was, after all, a part of this great, beautiful Boston! Strange though it seem, Miss Belinda Bree was content.

Content enough to tell charming stories of it, up in the country, to her niece Bel, when she was questioned by her.

Of her room all to herself, so warm in winter, with a red carpet (given her by the very Mrs. "Callariper" who could not help a misgiving, after all, that Miss Bree's vocation had been ended with that wretched word), and a coal stove, and a big, splendid brindled gray cat—Bartholomew—lying before it; of her snug little housekeeping, with kindlings in the closet drawer, and milk-jug out on the stone window-sill; of the music-mistress who had the room below, and who came up sometimes and sat an hour with her, and took her cat when she came away, leaving in return, in her own absences, her great English ivy with Miss Bree. Of the landlady who lived in the basement, and asked them all down, now and then, to play a game of cassino or double cribbage, and eat a Welsh rabbit: of things outside that younger people did,—the girls at the warerooms and their friends. Of Peck's cheap concerts, and the Public Library books to read on holidays and Sundays; of ten-cent trips down the harbor, to see the surf on Nantasket Beach; of the brilliant streets and shops; of the Public Garden, the flowers and the pond, the boats and the bridge; of the great bronze Washington reared up on his horse against the evening sky; of the deep, quiet old avenues of the Common; of the balloons and the fireworks on the "Fourth of Julies."

I do not think she did it to entice her; I do not think it occurred to her that she was putting anything into Bel's head; but when Bel all at once declared that she meant to go to Boston herself and seek her fortune,—do machine-work or something,—Aunt Blin felt a sudden thankful delight, and got a glimpse of a possible cheerfulness coming to herself that she had never dreamed of. If it was pleasant to tell over these scraps of her small, husbanded enjoyments to Bel, what would it be to have her there, to share and make and enlarge them? To bring young girls home sometimes for a chat, or even a cup of tea; to fetch books from the library, and read them aloud of a winter evening, while she stitched on by the gas-light with her glasses on her little homely old nose? The little old nose radiated the concentrated delight of the whole diminutive, withered face; the intense gleam of the small, pale blue eyes that bent themselves together to a short focus above it, and the eagerness of the thin, shrunken lips that pursed themselves upward with an expression that was keener than a smile. Bel laughed, and said she was "all puckered up into one little admiration point!"

After that, it was of no use to be wise and to make objections.

"I'll take you right in with me, and look after you, if you do!" said Miss Bree. "And two together, we can housekeep real comfortable!"

It was as if a new wave of youth, from the far-retreated tide, had swept back upon the beach sands of her life, to spend its sparkle and its music upon the sad, dry level. Every little pebble of circumstance took new color under its touch. Something belonging to her was still young, strong, hopeful. Bel would be a brightness in the whole old place. The middle-aged music-mistress would like her,—perhaps even give her some fragmentary instruction in the clippings of her time. Mrs. Pimminy, the landlady,—old Mr. Sparrow, the watch-maker, who went up and down stairs to and from his nest under the eaves,—the milliner in the second-floor-back,—why, she would make friends with them all, like the sunshine! There would be singing in the house! The middle-aged music-mistress did not sing,—only played. And this would be her doing,—her bringing; it would be the third-floor-front's glory! The pert girls at the wareroom would not snub the old maid any more, and shove her into the meanest corner. She had got a piece of girlhood of her own again. Let them just see Bel Bree—that was all!

Yet she did set before Bel, conscientiously, the difference between the free country home and the close, bricked up city.

"There isn't any out-doors there, you know—round the houses; *home* out-doors; you have to be dressed up and go somewhere, when you go out. The streets are splendid, and there's lots to look at; but they're only made to *get through*, you know, after all."

They were sitting, while she spoke, on a flat stone out under the old elm-trees between the "fore-yard" and the barn. Up above was great blue depth into which you could look through the delicate stems and flickering leaves of young far tips of branches. One little white cloud was shining down upon them as it floated in the sun. Away off swelled billowy tops of hills, one behind another, making you feel how big the world was. That was what Bel had been saying.

"You feel so as long as you stay here," replied Miss Blin, "as if there was room and chance for everything 'over the hills and far away.' But in the city it all crowds up together; it gets just as close as it can, and everybody is after the same chances. 'Tain't *all* Fourth-of-July; you mustn't think it. Milk's ten cents a quart, and *jest* as blue! Don't you 'spose you're better off up here, after all? Do you think Mrs. Bree could get along without you, now?"

Bel replied most irrelevantly. She sat watching the fowls scratching around the barn-door.

"How different a rooster scratches from a hen!" said she. "He just gives one kick,—out smart,—and picks up what he's after; *she* makes ever so many little scrabbles, and half the time concludes it ain't there!—What was it you were saying? About mother? O, *she* don't want me! The trouble is, Aunt Blin, we two *don't* want each other, and never did." She picked up a straw and bent it back and forth, absently, into little bits, until it broke. Her lips curled tremulously, and her bright eyes were sad.

Miss Blin knew it perfectly well without being told; but she wouldn't have pretended that she did, for all the world.

"O, tut!" said she. "You get along well enough. You like one another full as well as could be expected, only you ain't constituted similar, that's all. She's great for turning off, and going ahead, and she ain't got much patience. Such folks never has. You can't be smart and easy going too. 'Tain't possible. She's right-up-an'-a-comin', and she expects everybody else to be. But you *like* her, Bel; you know you do. You ain't goin' away for that. I won't have it that you are."

"I like her—yes;" said Bel, slowly. "I know she's smart. I *mean* to like her. I do it on purpose. But I don't *love* her, with a *can't help it*, you see. I feel as if I ought to; I want to have my heart go out to her; but it keeps coming back again. I could be happy with you, Aunt Blin, in your up-stairs room, with the blue milk out in the window-sill. There'd be room, enough for *us*, but this whole farm isn't comfortable for Ma and me!"

After that, Miss Blin only said that she would speak to Kellup; meaning her brother, Caleb Bree.

Caleb Bree was just the sort of man that by divine compensation generally marries, or gets married by a woman that is "right-up-and-a-comin'." He "had no objections," to this plan of Bel's, I mean; perhaps his favorite phrase would have expressed his strongest feeling in the crisis just referred to, also; it was a normal state of mind with him; he had gone through the world, thus far, on the principle of *not* "having objections." He had none now, "if Ma'am hadn't, and Blin saw best." He let his child go out from his house down into the great, unknown, struggling, hustling, devouring city, without much thought or inquiry. It settled *that* point in his family. "Bel had gone down to Boston to be a dress-maker, 'long of her Aunt Blindy," was what he had to say to his neighbors. It sounded natural and satisfactory. House-holds break up after the children are grown, of course; they all settle to something; that is all it comes to—the child-life out of which if they had died and gone away, there would have been wailing and heart-breaking; the loving and tending and watching through cunning ways and helpless prettiness and small knowledge-getting: they turn into men and women, and they go out into the towns, or they get married, even—and nobody thinks, then, that the little children are dead! But they are: they are dead, out of the household, and they never come back to it any more.

Caleb Bree let Bel go, never once thinking that after this she never *could* come back the same.

Mrs. Bree had her own two children,—and there might be more—that would claim all that could be done for them. She would miss Bel's telling them stories, and washing their faces, and carrying them off into the barn or the orchard, and leaving the house quiet of a Sunday or a busy baking-day. It had been "all Bel was good for;" and it had been more than Mrs. Bree had appreciated at the time. Bel cried when she kissed them and bade them good-by; but she was gone; she and her round leather trunk and her little bird in its cage that she could not leave behind, though Aunt Blin did say that "she wouldn't altogether answer for it with Bartholomew."

Bel herself,—the other little bird,—who had never tried her wings, or been shut up in strange places with fierce, prowling creatures,—she could answer for her, she thought!

It is worth telling,—the advent of Bel and her bird in the up-stairs room in Leicester Place, and what came of it with Bartholomew. Miss Blin believed very much in her cat with the apostolic name, though she had never tried his principles with a caged bird. She had tutored him to refrain from meat and milk unless they were set down for him in his especial corner upon the hearth. He took his airings on the window-ledge where the sun slanted in of a morning, beside the very brown paper parcel in which was wrapped the mutton chop for dinner; he never touched the cheese upon the table, though he knew the word "cheese" as well as if he could spell it, and would stand up tall on his hind paws to receive his morsel when he was told, even in a whisper, and without a movement, that he might come and have some. He preferred his milk condensed in this way; he got very little of it in the fluid form, and did not think very highly of it when he did. He knew what was good, Aunt Blin said.

He understood conversation; especially moral lectures and admonitions; Miss Bree had talked to him precisely as if he had a soul, for five years. He knew when she was coming back at one o'clock to dinner, or at nine in the evening, by the ringing of the bells. After she had told him so, he would be sitting at the door, watching for its opening, from the instant of their first sound until she came up-stairs.

When Aunt Blin thought over all this and told it to Bel, on their way down in the cars, she almost persuaded her niece and quite convinced herself, that Bartholomew could be dealt with on principles of honor and confidence. They would not attempt to keep the cage out of his reach; that would be almost to keep it out of their own. She would talk to Bartholomew. She would show him the bird, and make him understand that they set great store by it, that it must not be meddled with on any account. "Why, he never *offers* to touch my tame pigeon that hops in on the table to eat the crumbs!"

"But a pigeon is pretty big, Aunt Blin," Bel answered, "and may be Bartholomew suspects that it is old and tough. I *am* afraid about my tiny, tender little bird."

Bel was charmed with Aunt Blin's room, when she opened the blinds and drew up the colored shades, and let the street-light in until she could find her matches and light the gas. It was just after dark when they reached Leicester Place. The little lamp-lighter ran down out of the court with his ladder as they turned in. There were two bright lanterns whose flames flared in the wind; one just opposite their windows, and one below at the livery stable. There was a big livery stable at the bottom of the court, built right across the end; and there was litter about the doors, and horse odor in the air. But that is not the very worst kind of city smell that might be, and putting up with that, the people who lived in Leicester Court had great counterbalancing advantages. There was only one side to the place; and though the street way was very narrow, the opposite walls shut in the grounds of a public building, where there were trees and grass, and above which there was really a chance at the sky. Further along, at the corner, loomed the eight stories of an apartment hotel. All up and down this great structure, and up and down the little three-storied fronts of the Court as well, the whole place was gay with illumination, for these last were nearly all lodging houses, and at night at least, looked brilliant and grand; certainly to Bel Bree's eyes, seeing three-storied houses and gas-lights for the first time. Inside, at number eight, the one little gas jet revealed presently just what Aunt Blin had told about: the scarlet and black three-ply carpet in a really handsome pattern of raised leaves; the round table in the middle with a red cloth, and the square one in the corner with a brown linen one; the little Parlor Beauty stove, with a boiler atop and an oven in the side, — an oval braided mat before it, and a mantel shelf above with some vases and books upon it, — all the books, some dozen in number, that Aunt Blin had ever owned in the whole course of her life. One of the blue vases had a piece broken out of its edge, but that was turned round behind. The closets, one on each side of the fire-place, answered for pantry, china closet, store-room, wardrobe, and all. The *refrigerator* was out on the stone window-sill on the east side. The room had corner windows, the house standing at the head of a little paved alley that ran down to Hero Street.

"There!" says Aunt Blin turning up the gas cheerily, and dropping her shawl upon a chair. "Now I'll go and get Bartholomew, and then I'll run for some muffins, and you can make a fire. You know where all the things are, you know!"

That was the way she made Bel welcome; treating her at once as part and parcel of everything.

Down stairs ran Aunt Blin; she came up more slowly, bringing the great Bartholomew in her arms, and treading on her petticoats all the way.

Straight up to the square table she walked, where Bel had set down her bird-cage, with the newspaper pinned over it. Aunt Blin pulled the paper off with one hand, holding Bartholomew fast under the other arm. His big head stuck out before, and his big tail behind; both eager, restless, wondering, in port and aspect.

"Now, Bartholomew," said Aunt Blin, in her calmest, most confident, most deliberate tones, "see here! We've brought—home—a little *bird*, Bartholomew!"

Bartholomew's big head was electric with feline expression; his ears stood up, his eyes sent out green sparks; hair and whiskers were on end; he devoured poor little Cheeps already with his gaze; his tail grew huger, and vibrated in great sweeps.

"O see, Aunt Blin!" cried Bel. "He's just ready to spring. He don't care a bit for what you say!"

Aunt Blin gave a fresh grip with her elbow against Bartholomew's sides, and went on with unabated faith,—unhurried calmness.

"We set *everything* by that little bird, Bartholomew! We wouldn't have it touched for all the world! Don't—you—never—go—*near* it! Do you hear?"

Bartholomew heard. Miss Bree could not see his tail, fairly lashing now, behind her back, nor the fierce eyes, glowing like green fire. She stroked his head, and went on preaching.

"The little bird *sings*, Bartholomew! You can hear it, mornings, while you eat your breakfast. And you shall have CHEESE for breakfast as long as you're good, and *don't—touch—*the *bird*!"

"O, Aunt Blin! He will! He means to! Don't show it to him any more! Let me hang it way up high, where he *can't*!"

"Don't you be afraid. He understands now, that we're precious of it. Don't you, Bartholomew? I want him to get used to it."

And Aunt Blin actually set the cat down, and turned round to take up her shawl again.

Bartholomew was quiet enough for a minute; he must have his cat-pleasure of crouching and creeping; he must wait till nobody looked. He knew very well what he was about. But the tail trembled still; the green eyes were still wild and eager.

"The kindlings are in the left-hand closet, you know," said Aunt Blin, with a big pin in her mouth, and settling her shoulders into her shawl. "You'll want to get the fire going as quick as you can."

Poor Bel turned away with a fearful misgiving; not for that very minute, exactly; she hardly supposed Bartholomew would go straight from the sermon to sin; but for the resistance of evil enticements hereafter, under Miss Bree's trustful system,—though he walked off now like a deacon after a benediction,—she trembled in her poor little heart, and was sorely afraid she could not ever come to love Aunt Blin's great gray pet as she supposed she ought.

Aunt Blin had not fairly reached the passage-way, Bel had just emerged from the closet with her hands full of kindlings, and pushed the door to behind her with her foot, when—crash! bang!—what *had* happened?

A Boston earthquake? The room was full of a great noise and scramble. It seemed ever so long before Bel could comprehend and turn her face toward the centre of it; a second of time has infinitesimal divisions, all of which one feels and measures in such a crisis. Then she and Aunt Blin came together at a sharp angle of incidence in the middle of the room, the kindlings scattered about the carpet; and there was the corollary to the exhortation. The overturned cage,—the dragged-off table-cloth,—the clumsy Bartholomew, big and gray, bewildered, yet tenacious, clinging to the wires and sprawling all over them on one side with his fearful bulk, and the tiny green and golden canary flattened out against the other side within, absolutely plane and prone with the mere smite of terror.

"You awful wild beast! I *knew* you didn't mind!" shrieked Bel, snatching at the little cage from which Bartholomew dropped discomfited, and chirping to Cheepsie with a vehemence meant to be reassuring, but failing of its tender intent through frantic indignation. It is impossible to scold and chirp at once, however much one may want to do it.

"You dreadful tiger cat!" she repeated. It almost seemed as if her love for Aunt Blin let loose more desperately her denunciations. There is something in human nature which turns most passionately,—if it does turn,—upon one's very own.

"I can't bear you! I never shall! You're a horrid, monstrous, abominable, great, gray—wolf! I knew you were!"

Miss Bree fairly gasped.

When she got breath, she said slowly, mournfully, "O Bartholomew! I *thought* I could have trusted you! *Was* you a murderer in your heart all the time? Go away! I've—no—*con*—fidence *in* you! No *co-on*—fidence *in* you, Bartholomew Bree!"

It is impossible to write or print the words so as to suggest their grieved abandonment of faith, their depth of loving condemnation.

If Bartholomew had been a human being! But he was not; he was only a great gray cat. He retreated, shamefaced enough for the moment, under the table. He knew he was scolded at; he was found out and disappointed; but there was no heart-shame in him; he would do exactly the same again. As to being trusted or not, what did he care about that?

"I don't believe you do," said Aunt Blin, thinking it out to this same point, as she watched his face of greed, mortified, but persistent; not a bit changed to any real humility. Why do they say "*dogged*," except for a noble holding fast? It is a cat which is selfishly, stolidly obstinate.

"I don't know as I shall really like you any more," said Aunt Blin, with a terrible mildness. "To think you would have ate that little bird!"

Aunt Blin's ideal Bartholomew was no more. She might give the creature cheese, but she could not give him "*con*fidence."

Bel and the bird illustrated something finer, higher, sweeter to her now. Before, there had only been Bartholomew; he had had to stand for everything; there was a good deal, to be sure, in that.

But Bel was so astonished at the sudden change,—it was so funny in its meek manifestation,—that she forgot her wrath, and laughed outright.

"Why, Auntie!" she cried. "Your beautiful Bartholomew, who understood, and let alone!"

Aunt Blin shook her head.

"I don't know. I *thought* so. But—I've no—*con*-fidence in him! You'd better hang the cage up high. And I'll go out for the muffins."

Bel heard her saying it over again, as she went down the stairs.

"No, I've no—*con*-fidence in him!"

CHAPTER VIII
TO HELP: SOMEWHERE

There was an administratrix's notice tacked up on the great elm-tree by the Bank door, in Upper Dorbury Village.

All indebted to the estate of Joseph Ingraham were called upon to make payment,—and all having demands against the same to present accounts,—to Abigail S. Ingraham.

The bakery was shut up. The shop and house-blinds were closed upon the street. The bright little garden at the back was gay with summer color; roses, geraniums, balsams, candytuft; crimson and purple, and white and scarlet flashed up everywhere. But Mrs. Ingraham had on a plain muslin cap, instead of a ribboned one such as she was used to wear; and Dot was in a black calico dress; they sat in the kitchen window together, ripping up some breadths of faded cloth that they were going to send to the dye-house. Ray was in the front room, looking over papers. Mrs. Ingraham's name appeared in the notices, but Ray really did the work, all except the signing of the necessary documents.

Everything was very different here, the moment Joseph Ingraham's breath was gone from his body. Everything that had stood in his name stood now in the name of an "estate." Large or small, an estate has always to be settled. There had been a man already applying to buy out the remainder of the bakery lease,—house and all. He was ready to take it for eight years, including the one it had yet to run in the present occupancy; he would pay them a considerable bonus for relinquishing this and the goodwill.

Ray had stood at the helm and brought the vessel to port; that was different from undertaking another voyage. She did not see that she had any right to hazard her mother's and sister's little means, and incur further risks which she had not actual capital to meet, for the ambition, or even possible gain, of carrying on a business. She understood it perfectly; she could have done it; she could, perhaps, have worked out some of her own new ideas; if she and Dot had been brothers, instead of sisters, it would very likely have been what they would have done. There was enough to pay all debts and leave them upwards of a thousand dollars apiece. But Ray sat down and thought it all over. She remembered that they *were* women, and she saw how that made all the difference.

"Suppose either of us should wish to marry? Dot might, at any rate."

That was the way she said it to herself. She really thought of Dot especially and first; for it would be her doing if her sister were bound and hampered in any way; and even though Dot were willing, could she see clear to decide upon an undertaking that would involve the seven best years of the child's life, in which "who knew what might happen?"

She did not look straight in the face her own possibilities, yet she said simply in her own mind, "A woman ought to leave room for that. It might be cheating some one else, as well as herself, if she didn't." And she saw very well that a woman could not marry and assume family ties, with a seven years' lease of a bakehouse and a seven years' business on her hands. "Why—he might be a—anything," was the odd little wording with which she mentally exclaimed at this point of her considerations. And if he were anything,—anything of a man, and doing anything in the world as a man does,—what would they do with two businesses? The whole vexed question solved itself to her mind in this home-fashion. "It isn't natural; there never will be much of it in the world," she said. "Young women, with their real womanhood in them, won't; and by the time they've lived on and found out, the chances will be over. To do business as a man does, you must choose as a man does,—for your whole life, at the beginning of it."

Ray Ingraham, with all her capacity and courage, at this turning-point where choice was given her, and duty no longer showed her one inevitable way, chose deliberately to be a woman. She took up a woman's lot, with all its uncertainty and disadvantage; the lot of *working for others*.

"I can find something simply to do and to be paid for; that will be safe and faithful; that will leave room."

She said something like that to Frank Sunderline, when he sat talking with her over some building accounts one evening.

He had come in as a friend and had helped them in many little ways; beside having especial occasion in this matter, as representing his own employer who held a small demand against the estate.

"I am too young," she told him. "Dot is too young. I should feel as if I *must* have her with me if I kept on, and we should need to keep all the little money together. How can I tell what Dot—how can I tell what either of us"—she changed her word with brave honesty, "might have a wish for, before seven years were over? If I were forty years old, and could do it, I would; I would take girls for journeymen,—girls who wanted work and pay; then they would be brought up to a very good business for women, if they came to want business and they would be free, while they *were* girls, for happier things that might happen."

"That is good Woman's Rights doctrine; it doesn't leave out the best right of all."

"A woman can't shape out her life all beforehand, as a man can; she can't be sure, you see; and nobody else could feel sure about her. I suppose *that* is what has kept women out of the real business world,—the ordering and heading of things. But they can help. I'm willing to help, somehow; and I guess the world will let me."

There was something that went straight to Frank Sunderline's deepest, unspoken apprehension of most beautiful things, in Ray Ingraham's aspect as she said these words. The man in him suddenly perceived, though vaguely, something of what God meant when He made the woman. Power shone through the beauty in her face; but power ready to lay itself aside; ready to help, not lead. Made the most tender, because most perfect outcome and blossom of humanity, woman accepts her conditions, as God Himself accepts his own, when He hides Himself away under limitations, that the secret force may lie ready to the work man thinks he does upon the earth and with it. In dumb, waiting nature, his own very Self bides subject; yes, and in the things of the Spirit, He gives his Son in the likeness of a servant. He lays *help* upon him; He lays help for man upon the woman. He took her nearest to Himself when He made her to be a help meet in all things to his Adam-child. To "*help*" is to do the work of the world.

Ray's face shone with the splendor of self-forgetting, when she said that she would "help, somewhere."

What made him suddenly think of his own work? What made him say, with a flash in his eyes,—

"I've got a job of my own, Ray, at last. Did you know it?"

"I'm *very* glad," said Ray, earnestly. "What is it?"

"A house at Pomantic. Rather a shoddy kind of house,—flashy, I mean, and ridiculously grand; but it's work; and somebody has to build all sorts, you know. When I build *my* house—well, never mind! Holder has put this contract right into my hands to carry out. He'll step over and look round, once in a while, but I'm to have the care of it straight through,—stock, work, and all; and I'm to have half the profits. Isn't that high of Holder? He has his hands full, you know, at River Point. There's no end of building there, this year a whole street going up—with Mansard roofs, of course. Everything is going into this house that *can* go into a house; and to see that it gets in right will be—practice, anyhow."

Sunderline chattered on like a boy; almost like a girl, telling Ray what he was so glad of. And Ray listened, her cheek glowing; she was so glad to be told.

He had not said a word of this to Marion Kent that afternoon, when she had stopped him at her window, going by. He had stood there a few minutes, leaning against the white fence, and looking across the little dooryard, to answer the questions she asked him; about the Ingrahams, the questions were; but he did not offer to come nearer.

Marion was sewing on a rich silk dress, sea-green in color; it glistened as she shifted it with busy fingers under the light; it contrasted exquisitely with her fair, splendid hair, and the cream and rose of her full blonde complexion. It was a "platform dress," she told him, laughing; she was going with the Leverings on a reading and musical tour; they had got a little company together, and would give entertainments in the large country towns; perhaps go to some of the fashionable springs, or up among the mountain places; folks liked their amusements to come after them, from the cities; they were sure of audiences where people had nothing to do.

Marion was in high spirits. She felt as if she had the world before her. She would travel, at any rate; whether there were anything else left of it or not, she would have had that; that, and the sea-green dress. While she talked, her mother was ironing in the back room. The dress was owed for. She could not pay for it till she began to get her own pay.

What was the use of telling a girl like that—all flushed with beauty and vanity, and gay expectation—about his having a house to build? What would it seem to her,—his busy life all spring and summer among the chips and shavings, hammering, planing, fitting, chiseling, buying screws, and nails, and patent fastenings, tiles and pipes; contriving and hurrying, working out with painstaking in laborious detail an agreement, that a new rich man might get into his new rich house by October? When she had only to make herself lovely and step out among the lights before a gay assembly, to be applauded and boqueted, to be stared at and followed; to live in a dream, and call it her profession? When Frank Sunderline knew there was nothing real in it all; nothing that would stand, or remain; only her youth, and prettiness, and forwardness, and the facility of people away from home and in by-places to be amused with second-rate amusement, as they manage to feed on second-rate fare?

It was no use to say this to her, either; to warn her as he had done before. She must wear out her illusions, as she would wear out her glistening silk dress. He must leave her now, with the shimmer of them all about her imagination, bewildering it, as the lovely, lustrous heap upon her lap threw a bewilderment about her own very face and figure, and made it for the moment beautiful with all enticing, outward complement and suggestion.

He told Ray Ingraham; and he said what a pity it was; what a mistake.

Ray did not answer for a minute; she had a little struggle with herself; a little fight with that in her heart which made itself manifest to her in a single quick leap of its pulses.

Was she glad? Glad that Marion Kent was living out, perversely, this poor side of her—making a mistake? Losing, perhaps, so much?

"Marion has something better in her than that," she made herself say, when she replied. "Perhaps it will come out again, some day."

"I think she has. Perhaps it will. You have always been good and generous to her, Ray."

What did he say that for? Why did he make it impossible for her to let it go so?

"Don't!" she exclaimed. "I am not generous to her this minute! I couldn't help, when you said it, being satisfied—that you should see. I don't know whether it is mean or true in me, that I always do want people to see the truth."

She covered it up with that last sentence. The first left by itself, might have shown him more. It was certainly so; that there was a little severity in Ray Ingraham, growing out of her clear perception and her very honesty. When she could see a thing, it seemed as if everybody ought to see it; if they did not, as if she ought to show them, that they might fairly understand. A half understanding made her restless, even though the other half were less kind and comfortable.

"You show the truth of yourself, too," said Frank. "And that is grand, at any rate."

"You need not praise me," said Ray, almost coldly. "It is impossible to be *quite* true, I think. The nearer you try to come to it, the more you can't"— and then she stopped.

"How many changes there have been among us!" she began again, suddenly, at quite a different point, "All through the village there have been things happening, in this last year. Nobody is at all as they were a year ago. And another year"—

"Will tell another year's story," said Frank Sunderline. "Don't you like to think of that sometimes? That the story isn't done, ever? That there is always more to tell, on and on? And that means more to *do*. We are all making a piece of it. If we stayed right still, you see,—why, the Lord might as well shut up the book!"

He was full of life, this young man, and full of the delight of living. There was something in his calling that made him rejoice in a confident strength. He was born to handle tools; hammer and chisel were as parts of him. He builded; he believed in building; in something coming of every stroke. Real work disposes and qualifies a man to believe in a real destiny,—a real God. A carpenter can see that nails are never driven for nothing. It is the sham work, perhaps, of our day, that shakes faith in purpose and unity; a scrambling, shifty living of men's own, that makes to their sight a chance huddle and phantasm of creation.

Mrs. Ingraham came down into the room where they were, at this moment, and Dot presently followed. They began to talk of their plans. They were going, now, to live with the grandmother in Boston, in Pilgrim Street.

It was a comfortable, plain old house, in a little strip of neighborhood long since left of fashion, and not yet demanded of business; so Mrs. Rhynde could afford to occupy it. She had used, for many years, to let out a part of her rooms,—these that the Ingrahams would take,—in a tenement, as people used to say, making no ambitious distinctions; now, it might be spoken of as "a flat," or "apartments." Everything is "apartments" that is more than a foothold.

The rooms were large, but low. At the back, they were sunny and airy; they looked through, overlapping a court-way, into Providence Square. It was a real old Boston homestead, of which so few remain. There were corner beams and wainscots, some tiled chimney-pieces, even. It made you think of the pre-Revolutionary days of tea-drinkings, before the tea was thrown overboard. The step into the front passage was a step down from the street.

Ray and Dot told these things; beguiled into reminiscences of pleasant childish visiting days; Ray, of long domestication in still later years. It would be a going home, after all.

Leicester Place was only a stone's throw from Pilgrim Street. From old Mr. Sparrow's attic window, you could look across to the Pilgrim Street roofs, and see women hanging out clothes there upon the flat tops of one or two of the houses. But what of that, in a great city? Will the Ingrahams ever come across Aunt Blin and bright little Bel Bree?

In the book that binds up this story, there is but the turn of a leaf between them. A great many of us may be as near as that to each other in the telling of the world's story, who never get the leaf turned over, or between whom the chapters are divided, with never a connecting word.

The Ingrahams moved into Boston in the early summer. It was July when Bel came down from the hill-country with Aunt Blin.

CHAPTER IX
INHERITANCE

Do you remember somebody else who lives in Boston? Have you heard of the old house in Greenley Street, and Uncle Titus Oldways, and Desire Ledwith, who came home with him after her mother and sisters went off to Europe, and something had touched her young life that had left for a while an ache after it? Do you know Rachel Froke, and the little gray parlor, and the ferns, and the ivies, and the canary,—and the old, dusty library, with its tall, crowded shelves, and the square table in the midst, where Uncle Oldways sat? All is there still, except Uncle Oldways. The very year that had been so busy elsewhere, with its rushing minutes that clashed out events and changes as moving atoms clash out heat—that had brought to pass all that it has taken more than a hundred pages for me to tell,—that had drawn toward one centre and focus, whither, as into a great whirling maelstrom of life, so many human affairs and interests are continually drifting, the far-apart persons that were to be the persons of one little history,—this same year had lifted Uncle Titus up. Out of his old age, out of his old house,—out from among his books, where he thought and questioned and studied, into the youth and vigor to which, underneath the years, he had been growing; into the knowledges that lie behind and beyond all books and Scriptures; into the house not made with hands, the Innermost, the Divine. Not *away*; I do not believe that. Lifted up, in the life of the spirit, if only taken within.

Outside,—just a little outside, for she loved him, and her life had grown into his and into his home,—Desire remained, in this home that he had given her.

People talked about her, eagerly, curiously. They said she was a great heiress. Her mother and Mrs. Megilp had written letters to her overflowing with a mixture of sentiment and congratulation, condolence and delight. They wanted her to come abroad at once, now, and join them. What was there, any longer, to prevent?

Desire wrote back to them that she did not think they understood. There was no break, she said; there was to be no beginning again. She had come into Uncle Titus's living with him; he had let her do that, and he had made it so that she could stay. She was not going to leave him now. She would as soon have robbed him of his money and run away, while the handling of his money had been his own. It was but mere handling that made the difference. *Himself* was not dependent on his breath. And it was himself that she was joined with. "How can people turn their backs on people so?" She broke off with that, in her old, odd, abrupt, blindly significant fashion.

No: they could not understand. "Desire was just queerer than ever," they said. "It was such a pity, at her age. What would she be if she lived to be as old as Uncle Titus himself?" Mrs. Megilp sighed, long-sufferingly.

Mrs. Froke lived on in the gray parlor; Hazel Ripwinkley ran in and out; she hardly knew which was most home now, Greenley or Aspen Street. She and Desire were together in everything; in the bakery and laundry and industrial asylum that Luclarion Grapp's missionary work was taking shape in; in Chapel classes and teachers meetings; in a Wednesday evening Read-and-Talk, as they called it, that they had gathered some dozen girls and young women into, for which the dear old library was open weekly; in walks to and fro about the city "on errands;" in long plans and consultations, now, since so much power had been laid on their young heads and hands.

Uncle Oldways had made "the strangest will that ever was," if that were not said almost daily of men's last disposals. Out of the two sister's families, the Ripwinkleys and the Ledwiths, he had chosen these two girls,—children almost,—whom he declared his "next of kin, in a sense that the Lord and they would know;" and to them he left, in not quite equal shares, the bulk of his large property; the income of each portion to be severally theirs,—Desire's without restriction, Hazel's under her mother's guardianship, until each should come to the age of twenty-five years. If either of the two should die before that age, her share should devolve upon the other; if neither should survive it,—then followed a division among persons and charities, such, as he said, with his best knowledge, and the Lord's help, he felt himself at the moment of devising moved to direct. At twenty-five he counseled each heir to make, promptly, her own legal testament, searching, meanwhile, by the light given her in the doing of her duty, for whom or whatsoever should be shown her to be truly, and of the will of God—not man, her own "next of kin."

"For needful human form," he said, in conclusion, "I name Frances Ripwinkley executrix of this my will; but the Lord Himself shall be executor, above and through all; may He give unto you a right judgment in all things, and keep us evermore in his holy comfort!"

Some people even laughed at such a document as this, made as if the Almighty really had to do with things, and were surer than trustees and cunning law-conditions.

"Two girls!" they said, "who will marry—the Lord knows whom—and do, the Lord knows what, with it all!"

That was exactly what Titus Oldways believed. He believed the Lord *did* know. He had shown him part; enough to go by to the end of *his* beat; the rest was his. "Everything escheats to the King, at last."

And so Desire Ledwith and Hazel Ripwinkley sat in the old house together, and made their pure, young, generous plans; so they went in and out, and did their work, blessedly; and Uncle Titus's arm-chair stood there, where it always had, at the library table; and the Book of the Gospels, with its silver cross, lay in its silken cover where it always lay; and nothing had gone but the bent old form from which the strength had risen and the real presence loosened itself; and Uncle Titus's grand, beautiful life passed over to them continually; for hands on earth, he had their hands; for feet, their feet. There was no break, as Desire had said; it was the wonderful "fellowship of the mystery" which God meant, in the manifold wisdom that they know in heavenly places, when He ordained the passing over. We call it death; we *make* it death; a separation. We leave off there. We gather up the tools that loved ones drop, and use them to carve out, selfishly, our own pleasures; we let their *life* go, as if it were no matter to keep it up upon the earth. We turn our backs, and go our ways, and leave saints' hands outstretched invisibly in vain.

It was ever so bright and cheerful in this house into which death—that was such a birth—had come. These children were brimming over with happy thankfulness that Uncle Titus had loved and trusted them so. They never solemnized their looks or lengthened their accent when they spoke of him; he had come a great deal nearer to them in departing than he had ever known how to come, or they to approach him, before. Something young in his nature that had been hidden by gray hairs and slowness of years, sprang to join itself to their youth on which he had laid his bequest of the Lord's work. They ran lightly up and down where he had walked with measured gravity; they chatted and laughed, for they knew he was gladder than either; they sat in Desire's large, bright chamber at their work, or they went down to find out things in books in the library; and here, though nothing fell with any chill upon their spirits, they handled reverently the volumes he had loved,—they used tenderly the appliances that had been his daily convenience. With an unspoken consent, they never sat in the seat that had been his. The young heiresses of his place and trust made each a place for herself at opposite ends of the large writing-table, and left his chair before his desk as if he himself had just left it and might at any moment come in and sit again there with them. They always kept a vase of flowers beside the desk, at the left hand.

One day, that summer, they were up-stairs, sewing. Rachel Froke was busy below; they could hear some light movement now and then, in the stillness; or her voice came up through the open windows as she spoke to Frendely, the dear old serving woman, helping her dust and sort over glasses and jars for the yearly preserving.

I cannot tell you what an atmosphere of things and relations that had grown and sweetened and mellowed there was about this old home; what a lovely repose of stability, in the midst of the domestic ferments that are all about us in the changing households of these changing days. Frendely, who had served her maiden apprenticeship in a country family of England, said it was like the real old places there.

"Hazel," said Desire, suddenly,—(she did her *thinking* deeply and slowly, but she had never got over her old suddenness in speech; it was like the way a good old seamstress I knew used to advise with the needle,— "Take your stitch deliberate, but pull out your thread as quick as you can,")—"Hazel! I think I may go to Europe after all."

"Desire!"

"And more than that, Hazie, you are to go with me."

"Desire Ledwith!"

"Yes, those are my names. I haven't any more; so your surprise can't expend itself any further in that direction. Now, listen. It's all to be done in our Wednesday evening Read-and-Talks. See?"

"O!"

"Very well; begin on interjections; they'll last some time. What I mean is, an idea that I got from Mrs. Hautayne, when I saw her last spring at the Schermans'. She says she always travelled so much on paper; and that paper travelling is very much like paper weddings; you can get all sorts of splendid things into it. There are books, and maps, and gazetteers, and pictures, and stereoscopes. Friends' letters and art galleries. I took it right up into my mind, silently, for my class, sometime. And pretty soon, I think we'll go."

"O, Desire, how nice!"

"That's it! One new word, or two, every time, and repeat. 'Now say the five?' as Fay's Geography used to tell us."

"O, Desire Ledwith, how nice!"

"Good girl. Now, don't you think that Mrs. Geoffrey and Miss Kirkbright would lend us pictures and things?"

"How little we seem to have seen of the Geoffreys lately! I mean, all this spring, even before they went down to Beverly," said Hazel, flying off from the subject in hand at the mention of their names. "I wonder why it is fixed so, Des', that the *best* people—those you want to get nearest to—are so busy *being* the best that you don't get much chance?"

"Perhaps the chance is laid up," said Desire, thoughtfully. "I think a good many things are. But to keep on, Hazel, about my plan. You know those two beautiful girls who came in Sunday before last, and joined Miss Kirkbright's class? Not *beautiful*, I don't mean exactly,—though one of them was that, too; but real"—

"Splendid!" filled out Hazel. "Real ready-made sort of girls. As if they'd had chapel all their lives, somehow. Not like first-Sunday girls at all."

"One of them *was* a chapel girl. Miss Kirkbright told me. She grew up there till she was sixteen years old; then she went to live in the country. Now I must have those two in, you see. I don't know but Mr. Vireo would say it was making a feast for friends and neighbors, if I pick out the ready-made. But this sort of thing—you must have some reliance, you know; then there's something for the rest to come to, and grow to. I think I shall begin about it before vacation, while they're all together and alive to things. It takes so long to warm up to the same point after the break. We might have one meeting, just to organize, and make it a settled thing. O, how good it will be when Mr. Vireo comes home!"

If I had not so many things to tell before my story can be at all complete, I should like nothing better than to linger here in Desire Ledwith's room, where there was so really "a beautiful east window, and the morning had come in." I should like to just stay in the sunshine of it, and show what the stir of it was, and what it had come to with these two; what a brightness, day by day, they lived in. I should be glad to tell their piece of the story minutely; but I should not be able to get at it to tell. We may touch such lives, and feel the lovely pleasantness; but to enter in, and have the whole—that may only be done in one way; by going and doing likewise.

This talk of theirs gives one link; it shows you how easily and naturally they came to have to do with the Ingrahams; how they belonged in one sphere and drew to one centre; how simply things happen, after all, when they have any business to happen.

Somebody speaks of the ascent of a lofty church spire, as giving such a wonderful glimpse of the unity of a great city; showing its converging movements, its net-work of connection,—its human currents swayed and turned by intelligible drifts of purpose; all which, when one is down among them, seem but whirls of a confusing and distracting medley; a heaping and a rushing together of many things and much conflicting action; where the wonder is that it stays together at all, or that one part plays and fits in with any other to harmony of service. If we could climb high enough, and see deep enough, to read a spiritual panorama in like manner, we should look into the mystery of the intent that builds the worlds and works with "birth and death and infinite motion" to evolve the wonders of all human and angelic history. We should only marvel, then, at what we, with our little bit of wayward free will, hinder; not at what God gently and mightily forecasts and brings to pass.

To find another link, we must go away and look in elsewhere.

CHAPTER X
FILLMER AND BYLLES

It was a hot morning in the heart of summer. The girls, coming in to their work, after breakfasts of sour rolls, cheap, raw, bitter coffee and blue milk, with a greasy relish, perhaps, of sausage, bacon, fried potatoes, or whatever else was economical and untouchable,—with the world itself frying in the fervid blaze of a sun rampant for fifteen hours a day,—saw in the windows early peaches, cool salads, and fresh berries; yellow and red bananas in mellow, heavy clusters; morning bouquets lying daintily on wet mosses; pale, beryl-green, transparent hothouse grapes hanging their globes of sweet, refrigerant juices before toil-parched, unsatisfied, feverish lips.

Let us hope that it did them good; it is all we can do now about it.

Up in the work-room of a great dress-making establishment were heaps of delicate cambric, Victoria lawn, piqués, muslins, piles of frillings, Hamburg edgings, insertions, bands. Machines were tripping and buzzing; cutters were clipping at the tables; the forewoman was moving about, directing here, hurrying there, reproving now and then for some careless tension, rough fastening, or clumsy seam. Out of it all were resulting lovely white suits; delicate, cloud-like, flounced robes of bewitching tints; graceful morning wrappers,—perfect toilets of all kinds for girls at watering-places and in elegant summer homes.

Orders kept coming down from the mountains, up from the sea-beaches, in from the country seats, where gay, friendly circles were amusing away the time, and making themselves beautiful before each others' eyes.

For it was fearfully hot again this year.

Bel Bree did not care. It all amused her. She had not got worn down yet, and she did not live in a cheap, working-girls' boarding-house. She had had radishes that morning with her bread and butter, and a little of last year's fruit out of a tin can for supper the night before. That was the way Miss Bree managed about peaches. I believe that was the way she thought the petition in the Litany was answered,—"Preserve to our use the kindly fruits of the earth, that in due time we may enjoy them;" after the luckier people have had their fill, and begun on the new, and the cans are cheap. There are ways of managing things, even with very little money. If you pay for the *managing*, you have to do without the things. Bel and her aunt together, with their united earnings and their nice, cosy ways, were very far from being uncomfortable. Bel said she liked the pinch,—what there was of it. She liked "a little bit brought home in a paper and made much of."

Bel had been just a fortnight in the city. She had gone right to work with her aunt at Fillmer & Bylles, she was bright and quick, knew how to run a "Wilcox & Gibbs," and had "some perception," the forewoman said, grimly; with a delicate implication that some others had not. Miss Tonker's praises always pared off on one side what they put on upon another.

It had taken Bel a fortnight to feel her ground, and to get exactly the "lay of the land." Then she went to work, unhesitatingly, to set some small things right.

This morning she had hurried herself and her aunt, come early, and put Miss Bree down, resolutely, against all her disclaimers, in a corner of the very best window in the room. To do this, she moved Matilda Meane's sewing-machine a little.

When Matilda Meane came in, she looked as though she thought the world was moved. She did not exactly dare to order Miss Bree up; but she elbowed about, she pushed her machine this way and that; she behaved like a hen hustled off her nest and not quite making up her mind whether she would go back to it or not. Miss Bree's nose grew apprehensive; it drew itself up with a little, visible, trembling gasp,—her small eyes glanced timidly from under the drawn, puckered lids, it was evidently all she could do to hold her ground. But Bel had put her there, and loyalty to Bel kept her passive. It is so much harder for some poor meek things ever to take anything, than it is forever to go without. Only for love and gratefulness can they ever be made to assume their common human rights.

Presently it had to come out.

Bel was singing away, as she gathered her work together in an opposite quarter of the room, keeping a glance out at her right eye-corner, expectantly.

"Who moved this machine?" asked Matilda Meane, stopping short in her endeavors to make it take up the middle of the window without absolutely rolling it over Aunt Blin's toes.

"I did, a little," answered Bel, promptly. "There was plenty of room for two; and if there hadn't been, Aunt Blin must have a good light, and have it over her left shoulder, at that. She's the oldest person in the room, Miss Meane!"

"She was spoken to yesterday about her buttonholes," she added, in a lower tone, to Eliza Mokey, as she settled herself in her own seat next that young lady. "And it was all because she could hardly see."

"Buttonholes or not," answered Eliza, who preferred to be called "Elise," "I'm glad somebody has taken Mat Meane down at last. She needed it. I wish you could take her in hand everywhere. If *you* boarded at our house"—

"I shouldn't," interrupted Bel, decisively. "Not under any circumstances, from what you tell of it."

"That's all very well to say now; you're in clover, comparatively. 'Chaters' and real tea,—*and* a three-ply carpet!"

Miss Mokey had gone home with Bel and Aunt Blin, one evening lately, when there had been work to finish and they had made a "bee" of it.

"See if you could help yourself if you hadn't Aunt Blin."

"Why couldn't I help myself as well as she? She had a nice place all alone, before I came."

"She must have half starved herself to keep it, then. Stands to reason. Dollar and a quarter a day, and five dollars a week for your room. Where's your muffins, and your Oolong? Or else, where's your shoes?—Where's that Hamburg edging?"

"We don't have any Hamburg edging," said Bel, laughing.

"Nonsense. You know what I mean. O, here it is, under all that piqué! For mercy's sake, won't Miss Tonker blow?—Now I get my nine dollars a week, and out of it I pay six for my share of that miserable sky-parlor, and my ends of the crusts and the cheese-parings. No place to myself for a minute. Why, I feel mixed up sometimes to that degree that I'd almost like to die, and begin again, to find out who I am!"

"Well, I wouldn't live so. And Aunt Blin wouldn't. I'm afraid she *didn't* have other things quite so—corresponding—when she was by herself; but she had the home comfort. And, truly, now, I shouldn't wonder if there was real nourishment in just looking round,—at a red carpet and things,—when you've got 'em all just to your own mind. You can piece out with—peace!"

For two or three minutes, there was nothing heard after that in Bel and Elise's corner, but the regular busy click of the machines, as the tucks ran evenly through. Miss Tonker was hovering in the neighborhood. But presently, as she moved off, and Elise had a spool to change, Bel began again.

"Why don't you get up something different? Why couldn't a dozen, or twenty, take a flat, or a whole house, and have a housekeeper, and live nice? I believe I could contrive."

Bel was a born contriver. She was a born reformer, as all poets are; only she did not know yet that she was either. That had been the real trouble up in New Hampshire. She had her ideals, and she could not carry them out; so she sat and dreamed of what she would do if she could. If she might in any way have moulded her home to her own more delicate instincts, it may be that her step-mother need not have had to complain that "there was no spunk or snap to her about anything." It was not in her to "whew round" among tubs and whey,—to go slap-dash into soapmaking, or the coarse Monday's washing, when all nicer cares were evaded or forbidden, when chairs were shoved back against each other into corners, table-cloths left crooked, and dragging and crumby, drawing the flies,—mantel ornaments of uncouth odds and ends pushed all awry and one side during a dusting, and left so,—carpets rough and untidy at the corners; no touch of prettiness or pleasantness, nothing but clear, necessary *work* anywhere. She would have made home *home*; then she would have worked for it.

Aunt Blin was like her. She would rather sit behind her blinds in her neat, quiet room of a Sunday, too tired to go to church, but with a kind of sacred rest about her, and a possible hushed thought of a presence in a place that God had let her make that He might abide with her in it,—than to live as these girls did,—even to have been young like them; to have put on fine, gay things, bought with the small surplus of her weekly earnings after the wretched board was paid, and parade the streets, or sit in a pew, with a Sunday-consciousness of gloves and new bonnet upon her.

"O, faugh!" said Elise Mokey, impatiently, to Bel's "I could contrive." "I should like to see you, with girls like Matilda Meane. You've got to *get* your dozen or twenty, first, and make them agree."

Miss Mokey had very likely never heard of Mrs. Glass, or of the "catching your hare," which is the impracticable hitch at the start of most delicious things that might otherwise be done.

"I think this world is a kind of single-threaded machine, after all. There's always something either too tight or too loose the minute you double," she said, changing her tension-screw as she spoke. "No; we've just got to make it up with cracker-frolics, the best way we can; and that takes one more of somebody's nine dollars, every time. There's some fun in it, after all, especially to see Matilda Meane come to the table. I do believe that girl would sell her soul if she could have a Parker House dinner every day. When it's a little worse, or a little better than usual, when the milk gives out, or we have a yesterday's lobster for tea, — I wish you could just see her. She's so mad, or she's so eager. She *will* have claw-meat; it *is* claw-meat with her, sure enough; and if anybody else gets it first, or the dish goes round the other way and is all picked over, — she *looks*! Why, she looks as if she desired the prayers of the congregation, and nobody would pray!"

"What *are* you two laughing at?" broke in Kate Sencerbox, leaning over from her table beyond. "Bel Bree, where are your crimps?"

In the ardor of her work, or talk, or both, Bel's hair, as usual, had got pushed recklessly aside.

"O, I only have a little smile in my hair early in the morning," replies quick, cheery Bel. "It never crimps decidedly, and it all gets straightened out prim enough as the day's work comes on. It's like the grass of the field, and a good many other things; in the morning it is fresh and springeth up; in the evening it *giveth* up, and is down flat."

"I guess you'll find it so," said Elise Mokey, splenetically.

"Was *that* what you were laughing at?" asked Kate. "Seems to me you choose rather aggravating subjects."

"Aggravations are as good as anything to laugh at, if you only know how," Bel Bree said.

"They're always handy, at any rate," said Elise.

"I thought 'aggravate' meant making worse than it is," said quiet little Mary Pinfall.

"Just it, Molly!" answered Bel Bree, quick as a flash. "Take a plague, make it out seven times as bad as it is, so that it's perfectly ridiculous and impossible, and then laugh at it. Next time you put your finger on it, as the Irishman said of the flea, it isn't there."

"That's hommerpathy," said Miss Proddle. "Hommerpathy cures by aggravating."

Miss Proddle was tiresome; she always said things that had been said before, or that needed no saying. Miss Proddle was another of those old girls who, like Miss Bree among the young ones, have outlived and lost their Christian names, with their vivacity. Never mind; it is the Christian name, and the Lord knows them by it, as He did Martha and Mary.

"*Reductio ad absurdum*," put in Grace Toppings, who had been at a High School, and studied geometry.

"Grace Toppings!" called out Kate Sencerbox, shortly, "you've stitched that flounce together with a twist in it!"

Miss Tonker heard, and came round again.

"Gyurls!" she said, with elegantly severe authority, "I *will* not have this talking over the work. Miss Toppings, this whole skirt is an unmitigated muddle. Head-tucks half an inch too near the bottom! No *room* for your flounce. If you can't keep to your measures, you'd better not undertake piece-work. Take that last welt out, and put it in over the top. And make no more blunders, if you please, unless you want to be put to plain yard-stitching."

"Eight inches and a half is *some* room for a flounce, I guess, if it ain't nine inches," muttered the mathematical Grace, as she began the slow ripping of the lock-stitched tucking, that would take half an hour out of the value of her day.

"That's a comfort, ain't it?" whispered mischievous, sharp, good-natured Kate. "Look here; I'll help, if you won't talk any more Latin, or Hottentot."

It was of no use to tell those girls not to talk over their work. The more work they had in them, the more talk; it was a test, like a steam-gauge. Only the poor, pale, worn-out ones, like Emma Hollen, who coughed and breathed short, and could not spend strength even in listening, amidst the conflicting whirr of the feeds and wheels,—and the old, sobered-down, slow ones, like Miss Bree and Miss Proddle, button-holing and gather-sewing for dear life, with their spectacles over their noses, and great bald places showing on the tops of their bent heads,—kept time with silent thoughts to the beat of their treadles and the clip of their needles against the thimble-ends.

Elise Mokey stretched up her back slowly, and drew her shoulders painfully out of their steady cramp.

"There! I went round without stopping! I put a sign on it, and I've got my wish! I'd rather sweep a room, though, than do it again."

"You *might* sweep a room, instead," said Emma Hollen, in her low, faint tone, moved to speak by some echo in that inward rhythm of her thinking. "I partly wish *I* had, before now."

"O, you goose! Be a kitchen-wolloper!"

"May be I sha'n't be anything, very long. I should like to feel as if I *could* stir round."

"I wouldn't care if anybody could see what it came to, or what there was left of it at the year's end," said Elise Mokey.

"I'd sweep a room fast enough if it was my own," said Kate Sencerbox. "But you won't catch me sweeping up other folks' dust!"

"I wonder what other folks' dust really is, when you've sifted it, and how you'd pick out your own," said Bel.

"I'd have my own *place*, at any rate," responded Kate, "and the dust that got into it would go for mine, I suppose."

Bel Bree tucked away. Tucked away thoughts also, as she worked. Not one of those girls who had been talking had anything like a home. What was there for them at the year's end, after the wearing round and round of daily toil, but the diminishing dream of a happier living that might never come true? The fading away out of their health and prettiness into "old things like Miss Proddle and Aunt Blin," — to take their turn then, in being snubbed and shoved aside? Bel liked her own life here, so far; it was pleasanter than that which she had left; but she began to see how hundreds of other girls were going on in it without reward or hope; unfitting themselves, many of them utterly, by the very mode of their careless, rootless existence, — all of them, more or less, by the narrow specialty of their monotonous drudgery, — for the bright, capable, adaptive many-sidedness of a happy woman's living in the love and use and beauty of home.

Some of her thoughts prompted the fashion in which she recurred to the subject during the hour's dinner-time.

They were grouped together — the same half dozen — in a little ante-room, with a very dusty window looking down into an alley-way, or across it rather, since unless they really leaned out from their fifth story, the line of vision could not strike the base of the opposite buildings, a room used for the manifold purposes of clothes-hanging, hand-washing, brush and broom stowing, and luncheon eating.

"Girls! What would you do most for in this world? What would you have for your choice, if you could get it?"

"Stories to read, and theatre tickets every night," said Grace Toppings.

"Something decent to eat, as often as I was hungry," said Matilda Meane, speaking thick through a big mouthful of cream-cake.

"To be married to Lord Mortimer, and go and live in an Abbey," said Mary Pinfall, who sat on a box with a cracker in one hand, and the third volume of her old novel in the other.

The girls shouted.

"That means you'd like a real good husband, — a Tom, or a Dick, or a Harry," said Kate Sencerbox. "Lord Mortimers don't grow in this country. We must take the kind that do. And so we will, every one of us, when we can get 'em. Only I hope mine will keep a store of his own, and have a house up in Chester Park!"

"If I can ever see the time that I can have dresses made for me, instead of working my head and feet off making them for other people, I don't care where my house is!" said Elise Mokey.

"Or your husband either, I suppose," said Kate, sharply.

"Wouldn't I just like to walk in here some day, and order old Tonker round?" said Elise, disregarding. "I only hope she'll hold out till I can! Won't I have a black silk suit as thick as a board, with fifteen yards in the kilting? And a violet-gray, with a yard of train and Yak-flounces!"

"That isn't *my* sort," said Kate Sencerbox, emphatically. "It's played out, for me. People talk about our being in the way of temptation, always seeing what we can't have. It isn't *that* would ever tempt me; I'm sick of it. I know all the breadth-seams, and the gores, and the gathers, and the travelling round and round with the hems and trimmings and bindings and flouncings. If I could get *out* of it, and never hear of it again, and be in a place of my own, with my time to myself! Wouldn't I like to get up in the morning and *choose* what I would do?—when it wasn't Fast Day, nor Fourth of July, nor Washington's Birthday, nor any day in particular? I think, on the whole, I'd choose *not* to get up. A chance to be lazy; that's my vote, after all, Bel Bree!"

"O, dear!" cried Bel, despairingly. "Why don't some of you wish for nice, cute little things?"

"Tell us what," said Kate. "I think we *have* wished for all sorts, amongst us."

"O, a real little *home*—to take care of," said Bel. "Not fine, nor fussy; but real sweet and pleasant. Sunny windows and flowers, and a pretty carpet, and white curtains, and one of those chromos of little round, yellow chickens. A best china tea-set, and a real trig little kitchen; pies to make for Sundays and Thanksgivings; just enough work to do in the mornings, and time in the afternoons to sit and sew, and—somebody to read to you out loud in the evenings! I think I'd do anything—that wasn't wicked—to come to live just like that!"

"There isn't anybody that does live so nowadays," said Kate. "There's nothing between horrid little stivey places, and a regular scrub and squall and slop all the week round, and silk and snow and ordering other folks about. You've got to be top or bottom; and if it's all the same to you, I mean to be top if I can; even if"—

Kate was a great deal better than her pretences, after all. She did not finish the bad sentence.

"I'll tell you what I do wonder at," said Bel Bree. "So many great, beautiful homes in this city, and so few people to live in them. All the rest crowded up, and crowded out. When I go round through Hero Street, and Pilgrim Street, and past all the little crammy courts and places, out into the big avenues where all the houses stand back from each other with such a grand politeness, I want to say, Move up a little, can't you? There's such small room for people in there, behind!"

"Say it, why don't you? I'll tell you who'd listen. Washington, sitting on his big bronze horse, pawing in the air at Commonwealth Avenue!"

"Well—Washington *would* listen, if he wasn't bronze. And its grand for *everybody* to look at him there. I shouldn't really want the houses to move up, I suppose. It's good to have grandness somewhere, or else nobody would have any place to stretch in. But there must be some sort of moving up that could be, to make things evener, if we only knew!"

Poor little Bel Bree, just dropped down out of New Hampshire! What a problem the great city was already to her!

Miss Tonker put her sub-aristocratic face in at the door. It is a curious kind of reflected majesty that these important functionaries get, who take at first hand the magnificent orders, and sustain temporary relations of silk-and-velvet intimacy with Spreadsplendid Park.

The hour was up. Mary Pinfall slid her romance into the pocket of her waterproof; Matilda Meane swallowed her last mouthful of the four cream-cakes which she had valorously demolished without assistance, and hastily washed her hands at the faucet; Kate and Elise and Grace brushed by her with a sniff of generous contempt.

In two minutes, the wheels and feeds were buzzing and clicking again. What did they say, and emphasize, and repeat, in the ears that bent over them? Mechanical time-beats say something, always. They force in and in upon the soul its own pulses of thought, or memory, or purpose; of imagination or desire. They weld and consolidate our moods, our elements. Twenty miles of musing to the rhythmic throbbings of a railroad train, who does not know how it can shape and deepen and confirm whatever one has started with in mind or heart?

CHAPTER XI
CRISTOFERO

A September morning on the deck of a steamer bound into New York, two days from her port.

A fair wind; waves gleaming as they tossed landward, with the white crests and the grand swell that told of some mid-Atlantic storm, which had given them their impulse days since, and would send them breaking upon the American capes and beaches, in splendid tumult of foam, and roar, and plunge; "white horses," wearing rainbows in their manes.

The blue heaven full of sunshine; the air full of sea-tingle; a morning to feel the throb and spring of the vessel under one's feet, as an answer to the throb and spring of one's own life and eagerness; the leap of strength in the veins, and the homeward haste in the heart.

Two gentlemen, who had talked much together in the nine days of their ship-companionship, stood together at the taffrail.

One was the Reverend Hilary Vireo, minister of Mavis Place Chapel, Boston,—coming back to his work in glorious renewal from his eight weeks' holiday in Europe. The other was Christopher Kirkbright, younger partner of the house of Ferguson, Ramsay, and Kirkbright, tea and silk merchants, Hong Kong. Christopher Kirkbright had gone out to China from Glasgow, at the age of twenty-one, pledged to a ten years' stay. For five years past, he had had a share in the business for himself; for the two last, he had represented also the interest of Grahame Kirkbright, his uncle, third partner; had inherited, besides, half of his estate; the other half had come to our friend at home, his sister, Miss Euphrasia.

"I had no right to stay out there any longer, making my tools; multiplying them, without definite purpose. It was time to put them to their use; and I have come home to find it. A man may take till thirty-one to get ready, mayn't he, Mr. Vireo?"

"The man who took up the work of the world's salvation, began to be about thirty years of age when he came forth to public ministry," returned Mr. Vireo.

"I never thought of that before. I wonder I never did. It has come home to me, in many other parts of that Life, how full it is of scarcely recognized analogy to prevailing human experience. That 'driving into the Wilderness!' What an inevitable interval it is between the realizing of a special power and the finding out of its special purpose! I am in the Wilderness,—or was,—Vireo; but I knew my way lay through it. I have been pausing—thinking—striving to know. The temptations may not have been wanting, altogether, either. There are so many things one can do easily; considering one's self, largely, in the plan. My whole life has waited, in some chief respects, till the end of these ten pledged years. What was I to do with it? Where was I to look for, and find most speedily, all that a man begins to feel the desire to establish for himself at thirty years old? Home, society, sphere; I can tell you it is a strange feeling to take one's fortune in one's hand and come forth from such a business exile, and choose where one will make the first link,—decide the first condition, which may draw after all the rest. Happily, I had my sister to come home to; and I had the remembrance of the little story my mother told me—about my name. I think she looked forward for the boy who could know so little then of the destiny partly laid out for him already."

"About your name?" reminded Mr. Vireo. He always liked to hear the whole of a thing; especially a thing that touched and influenced spiritually.

"Yes. The story of Saint Cristofero. The strong man, Offero, who would serve the strongest; who served a great king, till he learned that the king feared Satan; who then sought Satan and served him, till he found that Satan feared the Cross; who sought for Jesus, then, that he might serve Him, and found a hermit who bade him fast and pray. But he would not fast, since from his food came his strength to serve with; nor pray, because it seemed to him idle; but he went forth to help those who were in danger of being swept away, as they struggled to cross the deep, wide River. He bore them through upon his shoulders,—the weak, the little, the weary. At last, he bore a little child who entreated him, and the child grew heavy, and heavier, till, when they reached the other side, Offero said,—'I feel as if I had borne the world upon my shoulders!' And he was answered,—'Thou may'st say that; for thou hast borne Him who made the world.' And then he knew that it was the Lord; and he was called no more 'Offero,' but 'Cristofero.' My mother told me that when I was a little child; and the story has grown in me. The Christ has yet to be borne on men's shoulders."

Hilary Vireo stood and listened with gleaming eyes. Of course, he knew the old saint-legend; of course, Christopher Kirkbright supposed it; but these were men who understood without the saying, that the verities are forever old and forever new. A mother's wise and tender tale,—a child's life growing into a man's, and sanctifying itself with a purpose,—these were the informing that filled afresh every sentence of the story, and made its repetition a most fair and sweet origination.

"And so,"—

"And so, I must earn my name," said Christopher Kirkbright, simply.

"Lift them up, and take them across," said Hilary Vireo, as if thinking it over to himself. The old story had quickened him. A grand perception came to him for his friend, who had begged him to think for and advise him. "Lift them up and take them across!" he repeated, looking into Mr. Kirkbright's face, and speaking the words to him with warm energy. "They are waiting—so many of them! They are sinking down—so many! They want to be lifted through. They want—and they want terribly—a place of safety on the other side. Go down into the river of temptation, and hardship, and sin, and help them up out of it, Christopher. Take them up out of their cruel conditions; make a place for some of them to begin over again in; for some of them to rest in, once in a while, and take courage. Why shouldn't there be cities of refuge, now, Kirkbright? Men are mapping out towns for their own gain, all over the land, wherever a water power or a railroad gives the chance for one to grow; why not build a Hope for the hopeless? Nowhere on earth could that be done as it could in our own land!"

"'A City of Refuge'" Kirkbright repeated the words gravely, earnestly; like those of some message of an angel of the Lord, that sounded with self-attested authority in his ears.

After a pause, in which his thought followed out the word of suggestion into a swift dream of possible fulfillment, he said to his companion,—

"I believe there was nothing in that old Jewish economy, Vireo, that was not given as a 'pattern of things' that should be. That whole Old Testament is a type and prophecy of the kingdom coming. Only it was but the first Adam. It was given right into the very conditions that illustrated its need. It would have meant nothing, given into a society of angels. Yet because men were not angels, but very mortal and sinful men, we of to-day must fling contempt upon the Myth of the Salvation of God! It will stand, for all that,—that history of God's intimacy with men. It was *lived*, not told as a vision, that it *might* stand! It was lived, to show how near, in spite of sin, God came, and stayed. The second coming shall be without sin unto salvation."

"I'm not sure, Kirkbright, but you ought to be a minister."

"Not to stand in a pulpit. God helping me, I mean to be a minister. Wouldn't a preacher be satisfied to have studied a week upon a sermon, if he knew that on Sunday, preaching it, he had sent it, live, into one living soul? Fifty-two souls a year, to reach and save,—would not that be enough? Well, then, every day a man might be giving the Lord's word out somewhere, in some fashion, I think. He needn't wait for the Sundays. Everybody has a congregation in the course of the week. I don't doubt the week-day service is often you preachers' best."

"I *know* it is," Hilary Vireo replied.

"Come down into the cabin with me," said Mr. Kirkbright. "I want to look up that old pattern. It will tell me something."

Down in the cabin they seated themselves together where they had had many a talk before, at a corner table near Mr. Kirkbright's state-room door. Out of the state-room he had brought his Bible.

He got hold of one word in that old ordination,—"unawares."

"'He that doeth it *unawares*,'" he repeated, holding the Bible with his finger between the half-shut leaves, at that thirty-fifth chapter of Numbers. "How that reminds of, and connects with, the Atoning Prayer,—'Forgive them, for they know not what they do!' 'Sins, negligences, ignorances;' how they shade and change into each other! If all the mistakes could be forgiven and set right, how much evil, virulent and unmixed, would there be left in the world, do you suppose?"

"Not more than there was before the mistakes began," replied Vireo. "Like the Arabian genie, the monster would be drawn down from its horrible expansion to a point again,—the point of a possibility; the serpent suggestion of evil choice. When God has done his work of forgiving, there is where it will be, I think; and the Son of the woman shall set his heel upon its head."

"I wish I could see what lies behind this," said Mr. Kirkbright. "'He shall abide in it unto the death of the high-priest,' and after that, 'the slayer shall return into the land of his possession.' That might almost seem to point to the old sacrificial idea; the atonement by death. I cannot rest in that. I wish I could see its whole meaning,—for meaning it must have, and a meaning of *life*."

"A temporary ministry; a limited exile; the one the measure of the other," sail Hilary Vireo, slowly thinking it out, and taking the book from the hand of his friend, to look over the words themselves, as he did so.

"The glory is in the promise: 'he shall return into the land of his possession.' His life shall be given back to him,—all that it was meant to be. It shall be kept open for him, till the time of his banishment is over. Meanwhile, over even this period is a holy providing, an anointed commission of grace."

"But hear this," he continued, turning to the Epistle to the Hebrews, "and put the suggestions alongside. All but God's final and eternal *best* is transitional. 'They truly were many priests, because they were not suffered to continue by reason of death. But this man, because He continueth ever, hath an unchangeable priesthood. Wherefore He is able also to save them to the uttermost, that come to God by Him.' Did it ever occur to you to think about that saving to the uttermost? Not a scrap of blessed possibility forfeited, lost? All gathered up, restored, put into our hands again, from the redeeming hands of Christ? Backward and forward, through all that was irretrievable to us; sought, and traced, and found, and brought back with rejoicing; the whole house swept, until not one silver piece is missing. That is the return into the land of our possession. *That* is God's salvation, and his gospel! That is what shall come to pass. Not yet; not while we are only under the lesser ministry; but when that priesthood over the time of our waiting ends, and we have believed unto the full appearing of the Lord!"

The speaker's face flushed and glowed; Hilary Vireo, always glad and strong in look and bearing, was grandly joyful when the power of the gospel he had to preach came upon him; the gospel of a full, perfect, and unstinted hope.

"Is that what you tell your simple people?" asked Christopher Kirkbright, fixing deeply eager eyes upon him.

"Yes; just that. In simplest words, changed and repeated often. It is the whole burden of my message. What other message is there, to men's souls? 'Repent, and receive the remission of your sins!' Build your city of refuge, Mr. Kirkbright, and show them a beginning of the fulfillment."

Whist and euchre tables not far off were breaking up, just before lunch, with laughter and raised voices. Ladies were coming down from the deck. In the stir, Mr. Vireo rose and went away. Christopher Kirkbright carried his Bible back into his state-room, and shut the door.

CHAPTER XII
LETTERS AND LINKS

That same September morning, Miss Euphrasia, sitting in her pretty corner room at Mrs. Georgeson's,—just returned to her city life from the rest and sweetness of a country summer,—had letters brought to her door.

The first was in a thin, strong, blue envelope, with London and Liverpool postmarks, and "per Steamer Calabria," written up in the corner, business-wise, with the date, and a dash underneath. This she opened first, for the English postmarks, associated with that handwriting, gave her a sudden thrill of bewildered surprise:—

"My dear Sister,—Within a very few days after this will reach you, I hope myself to land in America, and to see if, after all these years, you and I can do something about a home together. We learn one good of long separations, by what we get of them in this world. We can't help beginning again, if not actually where we left off, at least with the thought we left off at, 'live and fresh in our hearts. The thought, I mean, as regards each other; we have both got some thoughts uppermost by this time, doubtless, that we had not lived to then. At any rate, I have, who had ten years ago only the notions and dreams of twenty-one. I come straight to you with them, just as I went from you, dear elder sister, with your love and blessing upon me, into the great, working world.

"Send a line to meet me in New York at Frazer and Doubleday's, and let me know your exact whereabouts. I found Sherrett here, and had a run to Manchester with him to see Amy. That's the sort of thing I can't believe when I do see it,—Mary's baby married and housekeeping! I'm glad you are my elder, Effie; I shall not see much difference in you. Thirty-one and forty-three will only have come nearer together. And you are sure to be what only such fresh-souled women as you *can* be at forty-three."

With this little touch of loving compliment the letter ended.

Miss Euphrasia got up and walked over to her toilet-glass. Do you think, with all her outgoing goodness, she had not enough in her for this, of that sweet woman-feeling that desires a true beauty-blossoming for each good season of life as it comes? A pure, gentle showing, in face and voice and movement, of all that is lovely for a woman to show, and that she tells one of God's own words by showing, if only it be true, and not a putting on of falseness?

If Miss Euphrasia had not cared what she would seem like in the eyes as well as to the heart of this brother coming home, there would have been something wanting to her of genuine womanhood. Yet she had gone daily about her Lord's business, thinking of that first; not stopping to watch the graying or thinning of hairs, or the gathering of life-lines about eyes and mouth, or studying how to replace or smooth or disguise anything. She let her life write itself; she only made all fair, according to the sense of true grace that was in her; fair as she could with that which remained. She had neither neglected, nor feverishly contrived and worried; and so at forty three she was just what Christopher, with his Scotch second-sight, beheld her; what she beheld herself now as she went to look at her face in the glass, and to guess what he would think of it.

She saw a picture like this:—

Soft, large eyes, with no world-harass in them; little curves imprinted at the corners that may be as beautiful in later age as lip-dimples are in girlhood; a fair, broad forehead, that had never learned to frown; lines about mouth and chin, in sweet, honest harmony with the record of the eyes; no strain, no distortion of consciousness grown into haggard wornness; a fine, open, contented play of feature had wrought over all like a charm of sunshine, to soften and brighten continually. Her hair had been golden-brown; there was plenty of it still; it had kept so much of the gold that it was now like a tender mist through which the light flashes and smiles. Of all color-changes, this is the rarest.

Miss Euphrasia smiled at her own look. "It is the home-face, I guess; Christie will know it." Smiling, she showed white edges of perfect teeth.

"What a silly old thing I am!" she said, softly; and she blushed up and looked prettier yet.

"Why, I *will* not be such a fool!" she exclaimed, then, really indignant; and sat down to read her second letter, which she had half forgotten:—

"Brickfield Farms, (near Tillington), Maine.

"Dear Miss Euphrasia,—I have not written to you since we left Conway, because there seemed so little really to trouble you with; but your kind letter coming the other day made me feel as if I must have a talk with you, and perhaps tell you something which I did not fully tell you before. We left our address with Mr. Dill, although except you, I hardly know of anybody from whom a letter would be likely to come. Isn't it strange, how easily one may slip aside and drop out of everything? We heard of this place from some people who bad been to Sebago Lake and Pleasant Mountain, and up from there across the country to Gorham, and so round to Conway through the Glen.

"Mother was not well at Conway; indeed, dear Miss Euphrasia, she is more ill, perhaps, than I dare to think. She is very weak; I dread another move, and the winter is so near! May be the pleasant October weather will build her up; at any rate, we must stay here until she is much better. We have found such good, kind, plain people! I will tell you presently how nice it is for us, and the plans I have been able to make for the present. It has been a very expensive summer; we have moved about so much; and in all the places where we have been before, the board has been so high. At Lebanon and Sharon it was dreadful; I really had to worry mother to get away; and then Stowe was not much better, and at Jefferson the air was too bracing. At Crawford's it was lovely, but the bill was fearful! So we drifted down, till we finished August in Conway, and heard of this. I wish we had known of it at the beginning; but then I suppose it would not have suited mother for all summer.

"I had a great worry at Sharon, Miss Euphrasia, and it has grown worse since. I can't help being afraid mother has been dreadfully cheated. We got acquainted with some people there; a Mr. and Mrs. Farron Saftleigh, rich Westerners, who made a good deal of show of everything; money, and talk, and conjugal devotion, and friendship. Mrs. Saftleigh came a great deal to mother's room, and gave her all the little chat of the place,—I'm afraid I don't amuse mother myself as much as I ought, but some things do seem so tiresome to tell over, when you've seen more than enough of them yourself,—and she used to take her out to drive nearly every day.

"Well, it seemed that Mr. Saftleigh had gone out West only six years ago, and had made all his money since, in land and railroad business. Mrs. Saftleigh said that 'whatever Farron touched was sure to double.' She *meant* money; but I thought of our perplexities when she said it, and he certainly has managed to double *them*. He went to New York two or three times while we were at the Springs; he was transacting railroad business; getting stock taken up in the new piece of road laid out from Latterend to Donnowhair; and he was at the head of a company that had bought up all the land along the route. 'Sure to sell at enormous profits any time after the railroad was opened.' Poor mother got so feverish about it! She didn't see why our little money shouldn't be doubled as well as other people's. And then she cried so about being left a widow, with nobody out in the world to get a share of anything for her; and Mrs. Saftleigh used to tell her that such work was just what friends were made for, and it was so providential that she had met her here just now; and she was always calling her 'sweet Mrs. Argenter.'

"Nobody could help it; mother worried herself sick, when I begged her to wait till we could come home and consult some friend we knew. 'The chance would be lost forever,' she said; 'and who could be kinder than the Saftleighs, or could know half so much? Mr. Farron Saftleigh risked his own money in it.' And at last, she wrote home and had her Dorbury mortgage sold, and paid eight thousand dollars of it to Mr. Saftleigh, for shares in the railroad, and land in Donnowhair. And, dear Miss Euphrasia, that is all we've got now, except just a few hundred dollars on deposit in the Continental, and the other four thousand of the mortgage, that mother put into Manufacturers' Insurance stock, to pacify me. If the land *doesn't* sell out there in six months, as Mr. Saftleigh says it will, I don't know where any more income for us is to come from.

"I am saving all I can here, for the winter *must* cost. You would laugh if you knew how I am saving! I am helping Mrs. Jeffords do her work, and she doesn't charge me any board, and so I lay up the money without letting mother know it. I don't feel as if that were quite right,—or comfortable, at least; but after all, why shouldn't she be cheated a little bit the other way, if it is possible? That is why I hope we shall be here all through October.

"We are having lovely weather now; not a sign of frost. Although this place is so far north, it is sheltered by great hills, and seems to lie under the lee, both ways, of high mountain ranges, so that the cold does not really set in very early. It is a curious place. I wish I had left room to tell you more about it. There is a great level basin, around which slope the uplands, rising farther and farther on every side except the south, until you get among the real mountain regions. On these slopes are the farms; the Jeffords', and the Applebees', and the Patchons', and the Stilphins'. Aren't they quaint, comfortable old country names? I think they only have such names among farmers. The name of the place,—or rather neighborhood, for I don't know where the *place* actually is—there are three places, and they are all four or five miles off—Mill Village, and Pemunk, and Sandon; the name of the neighborhood,—Brickfield Farms, comes from there having been brickmaking done here at one time; but it was given up. The man who owned it got in debt, and failed, I believe; and nobody has taken hold of it again, because it is so far from lines of transportation; but there are some cottages about the foot of Cone Hill, where the laborers used to live; and a big queer, old red brick house, that looks as if it were walking up stairs,—built on flat, natural steps of the rock, and so climbing up, room behind room, with steps inside to correspond. I have liked so much to go through it, and imagine stories about it, though all the story there is, is that of Mr. Flavius Josephus Browne, the man of the brick enterprise, who built it in this odd way, and probably imagined a story for himself that he never lived out in it, because his money and his business came to an end. How strange it is that work doesn't always make money, and that it takes so much combination to make anything worth while! I wonder that even men know just what to do. And as for women,—why, when they take to elbowing men out, what will it all come to?

"I have written on, until I have written off some of my heavy feelings that I began with. If I could only *talk* to you, dear Miss Euphrasia, I think they would all go. But I will not trouble you any longer now; I am quite ashamed of the great packet this will make when it is folded up. But you told me to let you know all about myself, and I can't help minding such an injunction as that!

"Yours gratefully and affectionately always,
"Sylvie Argenter."

Miss Kirkbright had not read this straight through without a pause. Two or three times she had let her hands drop to her lap with the letter in them, and sat thinking. When she came to what Sylvie said about her "laughing to know how she had been saving," Miss Euphrasia stopped, not to laugh, but to wipe tears from her eyes.

"The poor, dear, brave little soul!" she said to herself. "And that blessed Mrs. Jeffords,—to let her think she is earning her board with ironing sheets, perhaps, and washing dishes! Km!"

That last unspellable sound was a half choke and half chuckle, that Miss Euphrasia surprised herself in making out of the sudden, mixed impulse to sob, and laugh, and to catch somebody in her arms and kiss that wasn't there.

"If I were an angel, I suppose I *could* wait," she went on saying to herself after that. "But even for them, it must be hard work some times. And so,—how the great Reasons Why flash upon one out of one's own little experience!—of that wonderful, blessed Day, when all shall be made right, the angels in heaven know not, neither the Son, but the Father only! The Lord cannot even trust the pure human that is in Himself to dwell, separately, upon that End which is to be, but may not be yet!"

I do not suppose anything whatever could come into Miss Euphrasia's life, or touch her with its circumstance, that she did not straightway read in it the wider truth beyond the letter. She was a Swedenborgian, not after Swedenborg, but by the living gift itself. Her insight was no separate thing, taken up and used now and then, of a purpose. It was as different from that as eyes are from spectacles. She could not help her little sermons. They preached themselves to her and in her, continually. So, if we go along with her, we must take her with her interpretations. Some friend said of her once, that she was a life with marginal notes; and the notes were the larger part of it.

But Miss Euphrasia found a postscript, presently, to Sylvie's letter, written hurriedly on the other side of the last leaf; as if she had made haste, before she should lose courage and change her mind about saying it:—

"Do you think it would be possible to find any sort of place in Boston where I could do something to help pay, this winter,—and will you try for me? I could sew, or do little things about a house, or read or write for somebody. I could help in a nursery, or teach, some hours in a day,—hours when mother likes to be quiet; and she would not know."

This was essential. "Mother must not know."

The finding of this postscript drove out of Miss Euphrasia's mind another thought that had suddenly come into it as she turned the letter over in her fingers. It was some minutes before she went back to it; minutes in which she was quite absorbed with simple suggestions and peradventures in Sylvie's behalf.

But—"Brickfield Farms? Sandon? Josephus Browne." When had she heard those names before? What hopeless piece of property was it she had heard her brother-in-law speak of long ago,—somewhere down East,—where there were old kilns and clay-pits? Something that had come into or passed through his hands for a debt?

"There is a great tangling of links here. What are they shaken into my fingers for, I wonder? What is there here to be tied, or to be unraveled?"

For she believed firmly, always, that things did not happen in a jumble, however jumbled they might seem. Though she could scarcely keep two thoughts together of the many crowded ones that had come to her, one upon another, this strange morning, she was sure the Lord knew all about it, and that He had not sent them upon her in any real confusion. She knew that there was no precipitance—no inconsequence—with Him.

"They are threads picked out for some work that He will do," she said, as she tucked her brother's letter into a low, broad basket beside the white and rose and violet wools with which she was at odd minutes crocheting a dainty footspread for an invalid friend, and put the other in her pocket.

"Now I will tie my bonnet on, and go, as I had meant, to see Desire. That, also, is a piece of this same morning."

Miss Kirkbright, likewise, watched and learned a story that told and repeated itself as it went along, of a House that was building bit by bit, and of life that lay about it. Only hers was the house the Lord builds; and the stories of it, and all the sentences of the story, were the things He daily puts together.

CHAPTER XIII
RACHEL FROKE'S TROUBLE

Desire was out. She had gone down to Neighbor Street, to see Luclarion Grapp.

Luclarion had a Home there now; a place where girls and women came and went, and always found a rest and a welcome, to stay a night, or a week, or as long as they needed, provided only, that they entered into the work and spirit of the house while they did stay.

Luclarion still sold her good, cheap white loaves and brown, her muffins and her crumpets; and she had what she called her "big baking room," where a dozen women could work at the troughs and the kneaders and the ovens; and in this bakery they learned an honest trade that would stand them in stead for self-support, whether to furnish a commodity for sale, or in homes where daily bread must be put together as well as prayed for.

"You can do something now that all the world wants done; that's as good as a gold mine, and ever so much better," said Luclarion Grapp.

Then she had a laundry. From letting her lodgers wash and iron for themselves, to put their scanty wardrobes into the best condition and repair, she went on to showing them nice work and taking it in for them to do; until now there were some dozen families who sent her weakly washing, three to five dollars' worth each; and for ten months in the year a hundred and eighty dollars were her average receipts.

Down at "The Neighbors,"—as from the name of the street and the spirit and growth of the thing it had come to be called,—they had "Evenings;" when friends of the place came in and made it pleasant; brought books and pictures, flowers and fruit, and made a little treat of it for mind and heart and body. It was some plan for one of these that had taken Desire and Hazel to Miss Grapp's to-day.

Miss Euphrasia's first feeling was disappointment. It seemed as if her morning were going a wee wrong after all. But her second thought—that it was surely all in the day's work, and had happened so by no mistake—took her in, with a cheery and really expectant face, to Rachel Froke's gray parlor, to "sit her down a five minutes, and rest." She confidently looked for her business then to be declared to her, since the business she thought she had come upon was set aside.

"I have had a great mind to come to thee," were the first words Rachel said, as her visitor seated herself in the low chair, twin to her own, which she kept for friends. Rachel Froke liked her own; but she never felt any special comfort comfortably her own, until she could hold it thus duplicated.

"I have wanted for a little while past to talk to some one, and Hapsie Craydocke would not do. Everything she knows shines so quickly out of those small kind eyes of hers. Hapsie would have looked at me in an unspeakable way, and told it all out too soon. I have a secret, Euphrasia, and it troubleth me; yet not very much for myself; and I know it need not trouble me for anything. I have a reason that may make me leave this place,—for a time at least; and I am sorry for Desire, for she will miss me. Frendely can do all that I do, and she hath the same wish for everything at heart; but then who would help Frendely? She could not get on alone for thee knows the house is large, and Desire is always very busy, with work that should not be hindered. Can thee think of any way? I cannot bear that any uncertain, trustless person should come in here. There hath never been a common servant in this house. Doesn't thee think the Lord hath some one ready since He makes my place empty? And how shall we go rightly to find out?"

"Tell me first, Rachel, of your own matter. Is it any trouble,—any grief or pain?"

Rachel had quite forgot. The real trouble of it was this perplexity that she had told. The rest of it—that she knew was all right. She would not call it trouble—that which she simply had to wait and bear; but that in which she had to do, and knew not just how to "go rightly about,"—it was that she felt as the disquiet.

She smiled, and laid her hand upon her breast.

"The doctor calls it trouble—trouble here. But it may be helped; and there is a man in Philadelphia who treats such ailments with great skill. My cousin-in-law, Lydia Froke, will receive me at her house for this winter, if I will come and try what he can do. Thee sees: I suppose I ought to go."

"And Desire knows nothing?"

"How could I tell the child, until I saw my way? Now, can thee think?"

Rachel Froke repeated her simple question with an earnestness as if nothing were between them at this moment but the one thing to care for and provide. She waited for no word of personal pity or sympathy to come first. She had grown quite used to this fact that she had faced for herself, and scarcely remembered that it must be a pain to Miss Kirkbright for her sake to hear it.

It was hard even for Miss Kirkbright to feel it at once as a fact, looking in the fair, placid, smiling face that spoke of neither complaint nor pain nor fear; though a thrill had gone through her at the first word and gesture which conveyed the terrible perception, and had made her pale and grave.

"Must it be a servant to do mere servant's work; or could some nice young person, under Frendely's direction, relieve her of the actual care that you have taken, and keep things in the kitchen as they are?"

"That is precisely the best thing, if we could be sure," said Rachel.

"Then I think perhaps I came here with an errand straight to you, though I had no knowledge of it in coming," said Miss Kirkbright.

"That looks like the Lord's leading," said Rachel Froke. "There is always some sign to believe by."

Miss Euphrasia took out Sylvie's letter, as the best way of telling the story, and put it into Rachel Froke's hand. She did not feel it any breach of confidence to do so. Breach of confidence is letting strange air in upon a tender matter. The self-same atmosphere, the self-same temperature,— these do not harm or change anything. It is only widening graciously that which the confidence came for, to let it touch a heart tuned to the celestial key, ready with the same response of understanding. There are friends one can trust with one's self so; sure that only by true and inward channels the word, the thought, shall pass. Gossip—betrayal—sends from hand to hand, from mouth to mouth; tosses about our sacredness, or the misinterpreted sign of it, on the careless surface. From heart to heart it may be given without disloyalty. That is the way God Himself works round for us.

"It is very clear to me," said Rachel Froke, folding up the sheets of the letter, and putting them back into their envelope. "Shall Desire read this?"

"I think so. It would not be a real thing, unless she understood."

So Desire had the letter to read that day when she came home; and then Rachel Froke told her how it was that she must go away for a while; and Desire went round to Miss Euphrasia's room in the twilight, and gave her back her letter, and talked it all over with her; and they two next day explained the most of it to Hazel. It was not needful that she should know the very whole about Rachel or the Argenters; only enough was said to make plain the real companionship that was coming, and the mutual help that it might be; enough of the story to make Hazel cry out joyfully,—"Why, Desire! Miss Kirkbright! She's another! She belongs!" And then, without such drawback of sadness as the other two had had to feel, she caught them each by a hand, and danced them up and down a little dance before the fire upon the hearth-rug—singing,—

> "Four of us know the Muffin-man,
> Five of us know the Muffin-man,
> All of us know the Muffin-man,
> That lives in Drury Lane."

CHAPTER XIV
MAVIS PLACE CHAPEL

It was on the corner of Merle Street and Mavis Place. The Reverend Hilary Vireo, as I have told you, was the minister.

It might have been called, if anybody had thought of it, "The Chapel of the New Song." For it was the very gospel of hope and gladness that Hilary Vireo preached there, and had preached and lived for twenty years, making lives to sing that would have moaned.

"Haven't you a song in your heart, somewhere?" was his word once, to a man of hard life, who came to him in a trouble, and telling him of it, passed to a spiritual confidence, such as Vireo drew out of people without the asking. At the end of his story, the man had said that "he supposed it was as good as he ought to expect; he hadn't any business to look for better, and he must just bear it, for *this* life. He hoped there *was* something afterwards for them that could get to it, but he didn't know."

"Aren't you *glad* of things, sometimes?" said Mr. Vireo. "Of a pleasant day, even,—or a strong, fresh feeling in the morning? Don't you touch the edge of the great gladness that is in the world, now and then, in spite of your own little single worries? Well, *that's* what God means; and the worry is the interruption. He *never* means that. There's a great song forever singing, and we're all parts and notes of it, if we will just let Him put us in tune. What we call trouble is only his key, that draws our heart-strings truer, and brings them up sweet and even to the heavenly pitch. Don't mind the strain; believe in the *note*, every time his finger touches and sounds it. If you are glad for one minute in the day, that is his minute; the minute He means, and works for."

The man was a tuner of pianofortes. He went away with that lesson in his heart, to come back to him repeatedly in his own work, day by day. He had been believing in the twists and stretches; he began from that moment to believe in the music touches, far apart though they might come. He lived from a different centre; the growth began to be according to the life.

"It's queer," he said once, long afterward, reminding Mr. Vireo of what he had spoken in the moment it was given through him, and then forgotten.

"A man can put himself a'most where he pleases. Into a hurt finger or a toothache, till it is all one great pain with him; or outside of that, into something he cares for, or can do with his well hand, till he gets rid of it and forgets it. There's generally more comfort than ache, I do suppose, if we didn't live right in the middle of the ache. But you see, that's the great secret to find out. If ever we *do* get it,—complete"—

"Ah, that's the resurrection and the life," said Mr. Vireo.

Among the crowd that waited about the open chapel doors, and through the porches, and upon the stair-ways, one clear, sunny, October morning, on which the congregation would not gather quietly to its pews, stood this man, and many another man, and woman, and little child, to whom a word from Hilary Vireo was a word right out of heaven.

They would all have a first sight of him to-day,—his first Sunday among them after the whole summer's absence in Europe. He might easily not get into his pulpit at all, but give his gift in crumbs, all the way along from the street curb-stones to the aisles in the church above,—they waylaid him so to snatch at it from hand, face, voice, as he should come in. It would not be altogether unlike Hilary Vireo, if seeing things this way, he stopped right there amongst them, to deal out heart-cheer and sympathy right and left, face to face, and hand to hand,—the Gospel appointed for that day.

"What a crowd there'll be in heaven about some people!" said a tall, good-looking man to Hilary Vireo, in an undertone, as he came up the sidewalk with him into the edge of these waiting groups.

"May be. There'll be some scattering, I fancy, that we don't look for. We shall find *all* our centres there," returned Mr. Vireo, hastily, as his people closed about him and the hand-shaking began.

Christopher Kirkbright made his way to the stairs, as the passage on one side became cleared by the drifting of the parish over to the western door, by which the minister was entering. A little way up he found his sister, sitting with a young woman in the deep window ledge at the turn, whence they could look quietly down and watch the scene. Overhead, the heavy bell swung out slow, intermitted peals, that thrilled down through all the timbers of the building, and forth upon the crisp autumn air.

"My brother—Miss Ledwith," said Miss Euphrasia, introducing them.

Desire Ledwith looked up, The intensity that was in her gray eyes turned full into Christopher Kirkbright's own. It was like the sudden shifting of a lens through which sun-rays were pouring. She had been so absorbed with watching and thinking, that her face had grown keen and earnest without her knowing, as it had been always wont to do; only it was different from the old way in this,—that while the other had been eager, asking, unsatisfied, this was simply deep, intent; a searching outward, that was answered and fed simultaneously from within and behind; it was the *transmitted* light by which the face of Moses shone, standing between the Lord and the people.

She was not beautiful now, any more than she had been as a very young girl, when we first knew her; in feature, that is, and with mere outward grace; but her earnestness had so shaped for itself, with its continual, unthwarted flow, a natural and harmonious outlet in brow and eyes; in every curve by which the face conforms itself to that which genuinely animates it, that hers was now a countenance truly radiant of life, hope, purpose. The small, thin, clear cut nose,—the lip corners dropped with untutored simplicity into a rest and decision that were better than sparkle and smile,—the coolness, the strength, that lay in the very tint and tone of her complexion,—these were all details of character that had asserted itself. It had changed utterly one thing; the old knitting and narrowing of the forehead were gone; instead, the eyes had widened their spaces with a real calm that had grown in her, and their outer curves fell in lines of largeness and content toward the contour of the cheeks, making an artistic harmony with them.

It was not a face, so much as a living soul, that turned itself toward Miss Euphrasia's brother, as Miss Kirkbright spoke his name and Desire's.

For some reason, he found himself walking into the church beside them afterward, thinking oddly of the etymology of that word,—"introduced."

"Brought within; behind the barriers; made really known. Effie gave me a glimpse of that girl,—her *self*. I don't think I was ever so really introduced before."

He did not know at all who Miss Ledwith was; she might have been one of the chapel protégées; from Hanover or Neighbor Street, or where not; they all looked nice, in their Sunday dress; those who were helped to dress were made to look as nice as anybody.

Desire Ledwith had on a dark maroon-colored serge, made very simply; bordered, I believe, with just a little roll binding of velvet around the upper skirt. Any shop-girl might have worn that; any shop-girl would perhaps have been scarcely satisfied to wear the plain black hat, with just one curly tip of ostrich feather tucked in where the velvet band was folded together around it.

Desire sat with her class; it was her family, she said; her church-family, at any rate; she had chosen her scholars from those who had no parents to come with, and sit by; they were all glad of their home-place weekly, at her side.

Miss Kirkbright and her brother went into the minister's pew. Miss Kirkbright did not usually come to the service; the school, in which she taught, met in the afternoon; but this was Mr. Vireo's first Sunday, and his friend, her brother Christopher, had just come home with him across the Atlantic.

There was singing, in which nearly every voice joined; there was praying, in which one voice spoke as to a Presence felt close beside; and all the people felt at least that *he* felt it, and that therefore it must be there. They believed in it through him, as we all believe in it through Christ, who is in the bosom of the Father. That they might some time come where he stood now, and know as he knew, many of them were simply, carefully, daily striving to "do the Will."

He spoke to them of "journeyings;" of how God was everywhere in the whole earth; of how Abraham had the Lord with him, as he travelled up through a land he knew not, as he dwelt in Padan Aram, as he crossed the desert and came down through the hill-country into Canaan. Of how the Lord met Jacob at Bethel, when he was on his way through strange places, to go and serve his uncle Laban; how he went with Joseph into Egypt, and afterwards led out the children of Israel through forty years of wandering, showing them signs, and comforting them all the way; how "He leadeth me" is still the believer's song, still the heart-meaning of every human life.

"Whether we go or stay, as to place, we all move on; from our Mondays to our Saturdays; from one experience to another; and before us and beside us, passes always and abides near that presence of *the Lord*. Do you know what 'the Lord' means? It is the bread-giver; the feeder; the provider of every little thing. That is the name of God when He comes close to humanity. In the beginning, *God* created the heavens and the earth; but *the Lord* spoke unto Adam; *the Lord* appeared unto Abraham; *the Lord* was the God of Israel.

"God is *our* Lord; our daily leader; our bread-giver, from meal to meal, from mouthful to mouthful. The Angel of his Presence saves us continually. And in these latter days, the 'Lord' is 'Christ;' the human love of Him come down into our souls, to take away our sins,—to give us bread from heaven to eat; to fulfill in the inward kingdom every type and sign of the old leading; through need and toil, through strange places, through tedious waitings, through the long wilderness, and over the river into the Land that is beautiful and very far off."

The four walked away from the church together; they stopped on the corner of Borden Street. Here Desire and Mr. Vireo would leave them,— their way lying down the hill.

"I liked your doctrine of the Lord," said Miss Euphrasia to the minister. "That is true New Church interpretation, as I receive it."

"How can any one help seeing it? It shines so through the whole," said Desire.

"Leader and Giver; it is the one revelation of Scripture, from beginning to end," said Mr. Vireo. "'Come forth into the land that I shall show thee.' 'Follow Me, and I will give unto you everlasting life.' The same call in the Old Testament and in the New."

"'One Lord, one faith, one baptism,'" repeated Miss Euphrasia.

"Leading—*by the hand*; giving—*morsel by morsel*," said Mr. Kirkbright, emphasizing the near and dear detail.

"That makes me think," said Miss Euphrasia, suddenly. "Desire," she went on, without explaining why, "we are going up to Brickfield Farms next week, Christopher and I. Why shouldn't you go too,—and bring her home, you know?"

As true as she lived, Miss Euphrasia hadn't a thought—whatever *you* may think—of this and that, or anything, when she said it.

Except the simple fact, that it was beautiful October weather, and that *she* should like it, and that Sylvie and Desire would get acquainted.

"It will do you good. You'd better," said Mr. Vireo, kindly.

Christopher Kirkbright said nothing, of course. There was nothing for him to say. He did not think very much. He only had a passing feeling that it would be pleasant to see this grave-faced girl again, and to understand her, perhaps, a little.

CHAPTER XV
BONNY BOWLS

The great show house at Pomantic was almost finished. The architect's and builder's cares were over. There was a stained glass window to go in upon the high second landing of the splendid carved oak staircase, through which gold and rose and purple light should pour down upon the panels of the soft-tinted walls and the rich inlaying of the floors. There was a little polishing of walnut work and oiling of dark pine in kitchen and laundry, and the fastening on of a few silver knobs and faucets here and there, upstairs, remaining to be done; then it would be ready for the upholsterer.

Mr. Newrich had builded better than he thought; thanks to the delicate taste and the genius of his architect, and the careful skill of his contractor. He was proud of his elegant mansion, and fancied that it expressed himself, and the glory that his life had grown to.

Frank Sunderline knew that it expressed *him*-self; for he had put himself—his hope, his ambition, his sense of right and fitness—into every stroke and line. Now that it was done, it was more his than the man's who paid the bills,—"out of his waistcoat pocket," as he exultingly said to his wife. The designer and the builder had paid for it out of brain and heart and will, and were the real men who had got a new creation and possession of their own, though they should turn their backs upon their finished labor, and never go within the walls again.

It was a kind of a Sunday feeling with which Frank Sunderline was glad, though it was the middle of the week. The sense of accomplishment is the Sunday feeling. It is the very feeling in which God Himself rested; and out of his own joy, bade all his sons rest likewise in their turn, every time that they should end a six days' toil.

Frank Sunderline had been in Boston all the afternoon, making up accounts and papers with his employer. He came round to Pilgrim Street to tea.

He had got into a way of coming in to tell the Ingrahams the story of his work as it went on, at the same time that he continued his friendly relation with their own affairs, as always ready to do any little turn for them in which a man could be of service. This Sunday rest of his,—though a busier day had not gone over his head since the week began,—must be shared and crowned by them.

There is no subtler test of an unspoken—perhaps an unexamined—relation of a man with his women friends, than this instinctive turning with his Sabbath content and rest to the companionship he feels himself most moved to when it is in his heart. All custom, however homely, grows out of some reality, more than out of any mere convenience; this is why the Sunday coming of the country lover means so much more than his common comings, and sets an established seal upon them all.

Walking down Roulstone Street, the lowering afternoon sun full in his face across the open squares, Frank Sunderline thought how pleasant it would be to have Ray Ingraham go out to Pomantic such an afternoon as this, and see what he had done; just now, while it was still his work, warm from his hand, and before it was shut away from her and him by the Newrich carpets and curtains and china and servants going in and fastening the doors upon them.

He would make a treat of it,—a holiday,—if she would go; he would come and take her with a horse and buggy. He would not ask her to go with him in the cars and be stared at.

He had never thought of asking her to go to ride, or of showing her any set "attention" before. Frank Sunderline was not one of the young fellows who begin, and begin in a hurry, at that end.

He walked faster, as it came into his head at that moment; something of the same perception that would come to her,—if she cared for this asking of his,—came to him with the sudden suggestion that it was the next, the natural thing to do; that their friendship had grown so far as that. The story comes to a man with some such beautiful, scarce-anticipated steps of revelation as it does to a woman, when he takes his life in the true, whole, patient order, and does not go about to make some pretty sham of living before he has done any real living at all.

Yes; he would ask her to ride out to Pomantic with him to-morrow; and he thought she would go.

He liked her looks, to-night; he looked at her with this plan in his thoughts, and it lighted her up; he was conscious of his own notice of her, and of what it had grown to in him, insensibly, knowing her so well and long. He analyzed, or tried to analyze, his rest and pleasure in her; the reason why all she did and wore and said had such a sweet and winning fitness to him. What was it that made her look so different from other girls, and yet so nice?

"I like the way you dress, Ray; you and Dot;" he said to her, when tea was over and taken away, and she was replacing the cloth and setting the sewing-lamp down upon the table. "You don't snarl yourselves up. I can't bear a tangle of things."

Ray colored.

"You mean skirts, I suppose," she said, laughing "We can't afford two apiece, at a time. So we have taken to aprons."

It was a very simple expedient, and yet it came near enough to custom to avoid a strait and insufficient look. They wore plain black cashmere dresses, plaited in at the waist, and belted to their pretty figures, over these, round, full aprons, tied behind with broad, hemmed bows. They were of cross-barred muslin, for every day,—cheap and pretty and fresh; black silk ones replaced them upon serious occasions. This was their house wear; in the street they contented themselves with their plain basquines; and I think if anybody missed the bunches and festoons, it was only as Frank Sunderline said, with an unexplained impression of the absence of a "snarl."

"There's one thing certin," put in Mrs. Ingraham. "Women can't be dolls and live women too. I don't ever want anything on that'll hender me from goin' right into whatever there is to be gone into. It's cloe's that makes all the diffikelty nowadays. Young women can't do housework because of their cloe's; 'tisn't because they ain't as strong as their grandmothers; their grandmothers didn't try to wear a load and move one too. Folks that live a little nicer than common, and keep girls, don't have more than five hours to their day; the rest of the time, they're dressed up; and that means *tied* up. They can't *see* to their girls; they grow helplesser all the time and the help grows sozzlier; and so it comes to sauciness and upstrupperousness, and changes; and there's an up-stairs and a down-stairs to every house, and no *home* anywhere. That's how it is, and how it must be, till women take down some of their furbelows and live real, and keep house, and take old-fashioned comfort in it. Why, the help has to get into *their* humpty-dumpties by three or four o'clock, and see *their* company. If there's sickness or anything, that they can't, they're up a tree and off. I've known of folks breakin' up and goin' to board, because they were *afraid* of sickness; they knew their girls would clear right out if there was gruel to make and waitin' up and down to do. There ain't much left to depend on but hotels and hospitals. *Home* is too big a worry. And I do believe, my soul, its cloe's that's at the bottom of it. It's been growin' wuss and wuss ever since tight waists and holler biasses came in, and that's five and twenty years ago."

Mrs. Ingraham grew more Yankee in her dialect,—as the Scotch grow more Scotch,—with warming up to the subject.

Sunderline laughed.

"Well, I must go," he said; "though you do look so bright and cosy here. Half past seven's the last train, and there's a little job at home I promised mother I'd do to-night. I've been so busy lately that I haven't had any hammer and nails of my own. Ray!"

He had come round behind her chair, where she had seated herself at her sewing.

"It's pleasant out of town these fall days; and I want you to see my house before I give it over. If I come for you to-morrow, will you ride out with me to Pomantic?"

Ray felt half a dozen things at that moment between his question and her reply. She felt her mother's eyes just lifted at her, without another movement, over the silver rims of her spectacles; she felt Dot's utter stillness; she felt her own heart spring with a single quick beat, and her cheeks grow warm, and a moisture at her fingers' ends as they held work and needle determinedly, and she set two or three stitches with instinctive resolution of not stopping. She felt, inwardly, the certainty that this would count for much in Mrs. Ingraham's plain, old-fashioned way of judging things; she was afraid of a misjudgment for Frank Sunderline, if he did not, perhaps, mean anything particular by it; she would have refused him ten times over, and let the refusal rest with her, sooner than have him blamed; for what business had she, after all,—

"Well, Ray?"

She felt his hand upon the back of her chair, close to her shoulder; she felt that he leaned down a little. She heard something in that "Well, Ray," that she could not turn aside, though in an hour afterward she would be taking herself to task that she had let it seem like "anything."

"I was thinking," she said, quietly. "Yes, I think I could go. Thank you, Frank."

Frank Sunderline was not sure, as he walked up Roulstone Street afterward, whether Ray cared much. She made it seem all matter of course, in a minute, with that calm, deliberate answer of hers. And she sat so still, and let him go out of the room with hardly another word or look. She never stopped sewing, either.

Well,—he did not see those ten stitches! He might not have been the wiser if he had. They were not carpenter-work.

But Ray knew better than to pick them out, while her mother and Dot were by.

That next day was made for them.

Days are made for separate people, though they shine or storm over so many. Or the people are drifted into the right days; what is the difference?

I must stop for the thought here, that has to do with this question of rain and shine,—with need, and asking, and giving.

Prayers and special providences! Are these thrust out of the scheme, because there is a scheme, and a steadfastness of administration in God's laws? "No use to pray for rain, or the calming of the storm, or a blessing on the medicine?" When it was all set going, was not the *prayer* provided for? It was answered a million of years beforehand, in the heart of God, who put it into your heart and nature to pray. Long before the want or the sin, the beseeching for help or for forgiveness was anticipated; provision was made for the undoing or the counteracting of the evil,—the healing of the wrong,—just as it should be longed for in the needing and repenting soul. The more law you have, the more all things come under its foresight.

So, under the dear Law,—which is Love, and cares for the sparrow,— came the fair October day, with its unflecked firmament, its golden, conquering warmth, its richness of scent and color; and they two went forth in it.

They went early, after dinner; so that the brightness might last them home again; and because the Newriches, in their afternoon drive, might be coming out from the city, perhaps, a little later, to look at their waistcoat-pocket plaything.

Mrs. Ingraham turned away from the basement window with a long breath, as they drove off.

"Well, I suppose *that's* settled," she said, with the mother-sadness, in the midst of the not wishing it by any means to be otherwise, inflecting her voice.

"I don't believe Ray thinks so," said Dot.

In some of the hundred little indirect ways that girls find the use of, Ray had managed to really impose this impression upon the sturdy mind of Dot, without discussion. If Dot had had the least bit of experience of her own, as yet, she would not have been imposed upon. But Mrs. Ingraham had great reliance on Dorothy's common sense, and she left no lee-way for uninitiation.

"Do you really mean to say, child," she asked, turning round sharply, "that Ray don't suppose,—or don't want,—or don't intend—? She's a goose if she don't, then; and they're both geese; and I shouldn't have any patience with 'em! And that's *my* mind about it!"

It is not such a very beautiful drive straight out to Pomantic over the Roxeter road. There are more attractive ones in many directions. But no drive out of Boston is destitute of beauty; and even the long turnpike stretches—they are turnpike stretches still, though the Pike is turned into an Avenue, and built all along with blocks of little houses, exactly alike, in those places where used to be the flat, unoccupied intervals between the scattered suburban residences—have their breaks of hill and orchard and garden, and their glimpses across the marshes, of the sea.

Ray enjoyed every bit of it,—even the rows of new tenements with their wooden door-steps, and their disproportionate Mansard roofs that make them all look like the picture in "Mother Goose," of the boy under a big hat that might be slid down over him and just cover him up.

The rhyme itself came into Ray's head, and she said it to her companion.

"Little lad, little lad, where were you born?
Far off in Lancashire, under a thorn,
Where they sup buttermilk from a ram's horn;
And a pumpkin scooped, with a yellow rim,
Is the bonny bowl they breakfast in."

"Those houses make me think of that," she said; "and the picture over it—do you remember?"

Everybody remembers "Mother Goose." You can't quote or remind amiss from her.

"To be sure," Frank answered, laughing. "And the histories and the lives there carry out the idea. They all came from Lancashire, or somewhere across the big sea, and they were all born under the thorn, pretty much,—of poverty and pinches. But they sup their buttermilk, and the bowl is bonny, if it is only a pumpkin rind. Isn't that rhyme just the perfection of the glorifying of common things by imagination?"

"It always seems to me that living *might* be pretty in such places. All just alike, and snug together. I should think Mrs. Fitzpatrick and Mrs. Mahoney would have beautiful little ambitions and rivalries about their tidy parlors and kitchens, setting up housekeeping side by side, as they do. I should think they might have such nice neighborliness, back and forth. It looks full of all possible pleasantness; like the cottage quarters of the army families, down at Fort Warren, that you see so white and pretty among the trees, as you go by in the steamboat."

"Only they don't make it out," said Frank Sunderline, "after all. The prettiest part of it is the going by in the steamboat. Here, I mean. The 'Mother Goose' idea is very suggestive; but if you went through that block, from beginning to end, I wonder how many 'bonny bowls' you would really find, that you'd be willing to breakfast out of?"

"I wonder how many bonny bowls there'll be, one of these days, in the cook's closet of the grand house we're going to?" said Ray.

"That's it," said Sunderline. "It's pretty to build, and it's pretty to look at; but I should like to hear what your mother would say to the 'conveniences.' One convenience wants another to take care of it, till there's such a compound interest of them that it takes a regiment just to man the pumps and pipes, and open and shut the cupboards. Living doesn't really need so much machinery. But every household seems to want a little universe of its own, nowadays."

"I suppose they make it wrong side out," said Ray. "I mean all outside."

Further on, along the bay shores, and across the long bridge, and reaching over crests of hills that gave beautiful pictures of land and waterscape, the way was pleasanter and pleasanter. Other and different homesteads were set along the route, suggesting endless imaginations of the different character and living of the dwellers. More than once, either Ray or Frank was on the point of saying, as they passed some modest, pretty structure, with its field and garden-piece, its piazza, porch, or balcony, and its sunny windows,—"There! *that* is a nice place and way to live!"

But a young man and woman are shy of sharing such imaginations, before the sharing is quite understood and openly promised. So, many times a silence fell upon their casual talk, when the same thing was in the thought of each.

For miles before they came to it, the sightly Newrich edifice gave itself, in different aspects, to the view. Mr. Newrich, himself, never saw anything else in his drives out, of sky, or hill, or water, after the first glimpse of "my house," and the way it "showed up" in the approach.

Men were busy wheeling away rubbish, as they drove in between the great stone posts that marked the entrance, where the elegant, light-wrought, gilded iron gates were not yet hung.

Other laborers were rolling the lawn and terraces, newly sown with English grass seed that was to come up in the spring, and begin to weave its green velvet carpet. Piles of bricks and boards were gathered at the back of the house and about the stables.

The plate-glass windows glittered in the sun. The tiled-roofs, with their towers and slopes, looked like those in pictures of palace buildings. It was a group,—a pile; under these roofs a family of five—Americans, republicans, with no law of primogeniture to conserve the estate beyond a single lifetime—were to live like a little royal household. And the father had made all his money in fifteen years in Opal Street. This country of ours, and the ways of it, are certainly pretty nearly the queerest under the sun, when one looks it all through and thinks it all over.

Frank Sunderline pointed out the lovely work of the pillars in the porched veranda; every pillar a triple column, of the slenderest grace, capitaled with separate devices of leaf and flower.

Then they went into the wide, high hall, and through the lower rooms, floored and ceiled and walled most richly; and up over the stately staircase, copied from some grand old English architecture; along the galleries into the wings, where were the sleeping and dressing-rooms; up-stairs, again, into other sleeping-rooms,—places for the many servants that there must be,—pressrooms, closets, trunk-rooms,—space for stowing all the ample providings for use and change from season to season. Every frame and wainscot and panel a study of color and exact workmanship and perfect finish.

It was a "show house;" that was just what it was. "And I can't imagine the least bit of home-iness in the whole of it," said Ray, coming down from the high cupola whence they had looked far out to sea, and over inland, upon blue hills and distant woods.

They stopped half way,—on the wide second landing where they had seen, as they went up, that the great window space was open; the boards that had temporarily covered it having been removed, and the costly panes and sashes that were to fill it resting against the wall at one side.

"That is the greatest piece of nonsense in the whole house," Sunderline had said. "A crack in that would be the spoiling of a thousand dollars."

"How very silly," said Ray, quietly. "It is only fit for a church or a chapel."

"It shuts out the stables," said Sunderline. "Take care of that open frame," he had added, cautioning her.

Now, coming down, he stopped right here, and stood still with his back to the opening, looking across the front hall at some imperfection he fancied he detected in the joining of a carved cornice. Ray stood on the staircase, a little way up, facing the gorgeous window, and studying its glow of color.

"It won't do. The meeting of the pattern isn't perfect. Those grape-bunches come too near together, and there's a leaf-tip taken off at the corner. What a bungle! Come and look, Ray."

Ray turned her face toward him as he spoke, and saw what thrilled her through with sudden horror. Saw him, utterly forgetful of where he stood, against the dangerous vacancy, his heel upon the very edge, beyond which would be death!

A single movement an inch further, and he would be off his balance. Behind him was a fall of thirty feet, down to those piles of brick and timber. And he would make the movement unless he were instantly snatched away. His head was thrown back,—his shoulders leaned backward, in the attitude of one who is endeavoring to judge of an effect a little distance off.

Her face turned white, and her limbs quivered under her.

One gasping breath—and then—she turned, made two steps upward, and flung herself suddenly, as by mischance, prostrate along the broad, slowly-sloping stairs.

Half a dozen thoughts, in flashing succession, shaped themselves with and into the action. She wondered, afterward, recollecting them in a distinct order, how there had been time, and how she had thought so fast.

"I must not scream. I must not move toward him. I must make him come this way."

In the two steps up—"He might not follow; he would not understand. He *must*: I must *make* him come!" And then she flung herself down, as if she had fallen.

Once down, her strength went from her as she lay; she turned really faint and helpless.

It was all over. He was beside her.

"What is the matter, Ray? Are you ill? Are you hurt?" he said, quickly, stooping down to lift her up. She sat up, then, on the stair. She could not stand.

A man's step came rapidly through the lower hall, ringing upon the solid floor, and sounding through the unfurnished house.

"Sunderline! Thank heaven, sir, you're safe! Do you know how near you were to backing out of that confounded window? I saw you from the outside. In the name of goodness, have that place boarded up again! It shouldn't be left for five minutes."

"Was *that* it?" asked Frank, still bending over Ray, while Mr. Newrich said all this as he hurried up the stairs.

"I didn't fall, I tumbled down on purpose! It was the only thing I could think of," said Ray, nervously smiling; justifying herself, instinctively, from the betrayal of a feeling that makes girls faint away in novels. "I felt weak afterward. Anybody would."

"That's a fact," said Mr. Newrich, stopping at the landing, and glancing out through the aperture. "I shall never think of it, without shivering. You were as good as gone: a hair's breadth more would have done it. God bless my soul! If my place had had such a christening as that!"

The whiteness came over Ray Ingraham's face again She was just rising to her feet, with her hand upon the rail.

"Sit still," said Frank. "Let me go and bring you some water."

"She'll feel better to be by herself a minute or two, I dare say," said Mr. Newrich, following Frank as he went down. He had the tact to think of this, but not to go without saying it.

"A quick-witted young woman," he remarked, as they passed out of her hearing. "And sensible enough to keep her wits ahead of her feelings. If she had come *at* you, as half the women in the world would have done, you'd be a dead man this minute. Your sister, Sunderline?"

"No, sir—only a friend."

"Ah! *onlier* than a sister, may be? Well!"

Sunderline replied nothing, beyond a look.

"I beg your pardon. It's none of my business."

"It's none of my business, so far as I know," said Frank. "If it were, there would be no pardon to beg."

"You're a fine fellow; and she's a fine girl. I suppose I may say that. I tell you what; if you *had* come to grief, at the very end of this job you've done so well for me, I believe I should have put the place under the hammer. I couldn't have begun with such a piece of Friday luck as that!"

There were long pauses between the talk, as Ray and Frank drove back together into the city.

"Ray!" Frank said at last, suddenly, just as they came opposite to the row of little brown big-hatted houses, where they had talked about the bonny bowls,—"My life is either worth more or less to me, after this. You are the only woman in the world I could like to owe it to. Will you take what I owe? Will you be the *onliest* woman in the world to me?"

Oddly enough, that word of Mr. Newrich's, that had half affronted him, came up to his lips involuntarily and unexpectedly, now. Words are apt to come up so—in a sort of spite of us—that have made an impression, even when it has been that of simple misuse.

Ray did not answer. She felt it quite impossible to speak.

Frank waited—three minutes perhaps. Then he said,

"Tell me, Ray. If it is to be no, let me know it."

"If it had been no. I could have said it sooner," Ray answered, softly.

"May I come back?" he asked, when he helped her down at the door in Pilgrim Street, and held her hand fast for a minute.

"O yes; come back and see mother," Ray replied, her face all beautiful with smile and color.

Mother knew all the story, that minute, as well as when it was told her afterward. She saw her child's face, and that holding of the hand, from her upper window, where a half blind had fallen to. Mothers do not miss the home-comings from such drives as that.

"There's one thing, Frank,"—said Ray. She was standing with him, three hours afterward, at the low step of the entrance, he above her on the sidewalk, looking down upon her upturned face. The happy tea and family evening were over; that first family evening, when one comes acknowledged in, who has been almost one of the family before; and they were saying the first beautiful good-by, which has the beginning of all joining and belonging in it. "There is one thing, Frank. I'm under contract for the present; for quite a while. I'm going into the bread business, after all. I've promised Miss Grapp to take her bakery, and manage it for her, for a year or so."

"Who—is—Miss Grapp?" exclaimed Frank, pausing between the words in his astonishment.

Ray laughed. "Haven't I told you? I thought everybody knew. It's too long a story for the door-step. When you come again"—

"That'll be to-morrow."

"I'll tell you all about it."

"You'll have to manage the bakery and me too, somehow, before—a 'year or so'! How long do you suppose I expect to wait?"

"Dear me! how long *have* you waited?" returned Ray, demurely.

She only meant the three hours since they had been engaged; but it is a funny fact about the nature and prerogative of a man, that he may take years in which to come to the point of asking—years in which perhaps a woman's life is waiting, with a wear and an uncertainty in it; but the point of *having* must be moved up then, to suit his sudden impatience of full purpose.

A woman shrinks from this hurry; she wants a little of the blessed time of sure anticipation, after she knows that they belong to one another; a time to dream and plan beautiful things together in; to let herself think, safely and rightly, all the thoughts she has had to keep down until now. It is the difference of attitude in the asking and answering relations; a man's thoughts have been free enough all along; he has dreamt his dream out, and stands claiming the fulfillment.

Dot had her hair all down that night, and her nightgown on, and was sitting on the bed, with her feet curled up, while Ray stood in skirts and dressing-sack, before the glass, her braids half unfastened, stock-still, looking in at herself, or through her own image, with a most intent oblivion of what she pretended to be there for.

"Well, Ray! Have you forgotten the way to the other side of your head, or are you enchanted for a hundred years? I shall want the glass to-morrow morning."

Ray roused up from her abstraction.

"I was thinking," she said.

"Yes'm. I suppose you'll be always thinking now. You had just outgrown that trick, a little. It was the affliction of my childhood; and now it's got to begin again. 'Don't talk, Dot; I'm thinking.' Good-by."

There was half a whimper in Dorothy's last word.

"Dot! You silly little thing!"

And Rachel came over to the bedside, and put her arms round Dorothy, all crumpled as she was into a little round white ball.

"I was thinking about Marion Kent."

CHAPTER XVI
RECOMPENSE

That night, Marion Kent was fifty miles off, in the great, mixed-up, manufacturing town of Loweburg.

She had three platform dresses now,—the earnings of some half-dozen "evenings." The sea-green silk would not do forever, in place after place; they would call her the mermaid. She must have a quiet, elegant black one, and one the color of her hair, like that she had seen the pretty actress, Alice Craike, so bewitching in. She could deepen it with chestnut trimmings, all toning up together to one rich, bright harmony. Her hair was *"blond cendré,"* —not the red-golden of Alice Craike's; but the same subtle rule of art was available; *"café-au-lait"* was her shade; and the darker velvet just deepened and emphasized the effect.

She was putting this dress on to-night, with some brown and golden leaves in the high, massed braids of her hair. She certainly knew how to make a picture of herself; she was just made to make a picture of.

The hotel waitress who had brought up her tea on a tray, had gone down with a report that Miss Kent was "stunning;" and two or three housemaids and a number of little boys were vibrating and loitering about the hall and doorway below, watching for her to come down to her carriage. It was just as good, so far as these things went, as if she had been Mrs. Kemble, or Christine Nilsson, or anybody.

And Marion, poor child, had really got no farther than "these things," yet. She reached, for herself, to just what she had been able to appreciate in others. She had taken in the housemaid and small-boy view of famousness, and she was having her shallow little day of living it. She had not found out, yet, how short a time that would last. "Verily," it was said for us all long ago, "ye shall have each your reward," such as ye look and labor for.

One great boy was waiting for her, *ex officio*, and without disguise,—the President of the Lyceum Club, before which she was to read to-night.

He sat serenely in the reception-room, ready to hand her to her carriage, and accompany her to the hall.

The little boys observed him with exasperation. The housemaids dropped their lower jaws with wonder, when she swept down the staircase; her *café-au-lait* silk rolling and glittering behind her, as if the breakfast for all Loweburg were pouring down the Phoenix Hotel stairs.

The President of the People's Lyceum Club heard the rustle of elegance, and met her at the stair-foot with bowing head and bended arm.

That was a beautiful, triumphant moment, in which she crossed the space between the staircase and the door, and went down over the sidewalk to the hack. What would you have? There could not have been more of it, in her mind, though all Loweburg were standing by. She was Miss Kent, going out to give her Reading. What more could Fanny Kemble do?

Around the hall doors, when they arrived, other great boys were gathered. She was passed in quickly, to the left, through some passages and committee rooms, to the other end of the building, whence she would enter, in full glory, upon the platform.

She came in gracefully; a little breezy she could not help being; it was the one movement of the universe to her at that moment, her ten steps across the platform,—her little half bow, half droop, before the applauding audience,—the taking up of the bouquet laid upon her table,—her smile, with a scarcely visible inclination again,—and the sitting down among those waves of amber that rose up shining in the gas-light, about her, as she subsided among her silken draperies.

She was imitative; she had learned the little outsides of her art well; but you see the art was not high.

It was the same with her reading. She had had drill enough to make her elocution passable; her voice was clear and sweet; she had a natural knack, as we have seen, for speaking to the galleries. When there was a sensational, dramatic point to make, she could make it after her external fashion, strongly. The deep magnetism—the electric thrill of soul-reality—these she had nothing to do with.

Yet she read some things that thrilled of themselves; the very words of which, uttered almost anyhow, were fit to bring men to their feet and women to tears, with sublimity and pathos. Somebody had helped her choose effectively, and things very cunningly adaptive to herself.

The last selection for the first part of her reading to-night was Mrs. Browning's "Court Lady."

"Wear your fawn-colored silk when you read this," Virginia Levering had counseled.

Her self-consciousness made the first lines telling.

"Her hair was tawny with gold,—her eyes with purple were dark;

Her cheeks pale opal burned with a red and restless spark."

Her head, bright with its golden-dusty waves and braids, leaned forward under the light as she uttered the words; her great, gray-blue eyes, deepening with excitement to black, lifted themselves and looked the crowd in the face; the color mounted like a crimson spark; she glowed all over. Yes, over; not up, nor through; but some things catch from the outside. A flush and rustle ran over the faces, and the benches; she felt that every eye was upon her, lit up with an admiring eagerness, that answered to her eagerness to be admired.

O, this was living! There was a pulse and a rush in this! Marion Kent *was* living, with all her nature that had yet waked up, at that bewildering and superficial moment.

But she has got to live deeper. The Lord, who gave her life, will not let her off so. It will come. It is coming.

We know not the day nor the hour; though we go on as if we knew all things and were sure.

At this very instant, there is close upon you, Marion Kent, one of those lightning shafts that run continually quivering to and fro about the earth, with their net-work of fire, in this storm of life under which we of to-day are born. All the air is tremulous with quick, converging nerves; concentrating events, bringing each soul, as it were, into a possible focus continually, under the forces that are forging to bear down upon it. There are no delays,— no respites of ignorance. Right into the midst of our most careless or most selfish doing, comes the summons that arrests us in the Name of the King.

"She rose to her feet with a spring.

That was a Piedmontese! And this is the Court of the King!"

She was upon her feet, as if the impulse of the words had lifted her; she had learned by rote and practice when and how to do it; she had been poised for the action through the reading of all those last stanzas.

She did it well. One hand rested by the finger-tips upon the open volume before her; her glistening robes fell back as she gained her full height,—she swayed forward toward the assembly that leaned itself toward her; the left hand threw itself back with a noble gesture of generous declaring; the fingers curving from the open palm as it might have been toward the pallet of the dead soldier at her side. She was utterly motionless for an instant; then, as the applause broke down the silence, she turned, and grandly passed out along the stage, and disappeared.

Within the door of the anteroom stood a messenger from the hotel. He had a telegraph envelope in his hand; he put it into hers.

She tore it open,—not thinking, scarcely noticing; the excitement of the instant just past moved her nerves,—no apprehension of what this might be.

Then the lightning reached her: struck her through and through.

"Your ma's dying: come back: no money."

Those last words were a mistake; the whole dispatch, in its absurd homeliness and its pitiless directness, was the work of old Mrs. Knoxwell, the blacksmith's wife, used to hammers and nails, and believing in good, forceful, honest ways of doing things; feeling also a righteous and neighborly indignation against this child, negligent of her worn and lonely mother; "skitin' about the country, makin' believe big and famous. She would let her know the truth, right out plain; it would be good for her."

What she had meant to write at the end was "Pneumonia;" but spelling it "Numoney," it had got transmitted as we have seen.

It struck Marion through and through; but she did not feel it at first. It met the tide of her triumph and elation full in her throbbing veins; and the two keen currents turned to a mere stillness for a moment.

Then she dropped down where she was, all into the golden mass and shine of her bright raiment, with her hands before her eyes, the paper crumpled in the clinch of one of them.

The President of the People's Lyceum Club made a little speech, and dismissed the audience. "Miss Kent had received by telegraph most painful intelligence from her family; was utterly unable to appear again."

The audience behaved as an American People's Club knows so well how to behave; dispersed quietly, without a grumble, or a recollection of the half value of the tickets lost. Miss Kent's carriage drove rapidly from a side door. In two hours, she was on board the night train down from Vermont.

That was on Friday night.

On Sunday morning Frank Sunderline came in on the service train, and went up to Pilgrim Street.

"Mrs. Kent is dead," he told Kay. "Marion is in awful trouble. Can't you come out to her?"

Ray was just leaving the house to go to church. Instead, she went with Frank to the horse-railroad station, catching the eleven o'clock car. She had been expecting him in the afternoon, to take her to drink tea with his mother, who was not able to come in to see her.

In an hour, she went in at Mrs. Kent's white gate,—Frank leaving her there. They both felt, without saying, that it would not be kind to appear together. Marion had that news, though, as she had had the other; from her Job's comforter, Mrs. Knoxwell, who was persistently "sitting with her."

"There's Frank Sunderline and Ray Ingraham at the gate. She's coming in. They're engaged. It's just out."

"What *do* I care?" cried Marion, fiercely, turning upon her, and astounding Mrs. Knoxwell by the sudden burst of angry words; for she had not spoken for more than an hour, in which the blacksmith's wife had administered occasional appropriate sentences of stinging condolence and well-meant retrospection. "I wish you would go home!"

Every monosyllable was uttered with a desperate, wrathful deliberateness and flinging away of all pretense and politeness.

"Well—'f I *never!*" gasped Mrs. Knoxwell, with a sound in her voice as if she had received a blow in the pit of her stomach.

"Jest as you please, Marion—'f I ain't no more use!" And the aggrieved matron, who had, as she said afterward in recounting it, "done *everything,*" left the scene of her labors and her animadversions, with a face perfectly emptied of all expression by her inability to "realize what she *did* feel."

Ray Ingraham came in, went straight up to Marion, and took her into her arms without a word. And Marion put her head down on Ray's shoulder, and cried her very heart out.

"You needn't try to comfort me. I can't be comforted like anybody else. It's the day of judgment come down into my life. I've sold my birthright: I've nobody belonging to me any more. I wanted the world—to be free in it; and I'm turned out into it now; and home's gone—and mother.

"I never thought of her dying. I expected one of these days to do for her, and not let her work any more. I meant to, Ray—I did, truly! But she's dead—and I let her die!"

With sentences like these, Marion broke out now and again, putting aside all Ray's consolations; going back continually to her self-upbraidings, after every pause in which Ray had let her rest or cry quietly; after every word with which she tried to prevail against her despair and soothe her with some hope or promise.

"They are none of them for me!" she cried. "It would have been better if I had never been born. Ray!" she said suddenly, in a strained, hollow voice, grasping Rachel's arm and looking with wild, swollen eyes into hers,—"I was just as bad by little Sue. I was only fourteen then, but it was the same evil, unsuitable vanity and selfishness. I was busy, while she was sick, making a white muslin burnouse to wear to a fair. I had teased mother for it. It was a silly thing for a girl like me to wear; it had a blue ribbon run in the hem of the hood, and a bow and long blue ends behind. Poor little Sue was just down with the fever. Mother had to go out, and left me to tend her. She wanted some water—Oh!"

Marion broke down, and sobbed, with her head bowed to her knees as she sat.

Ray sat perfectly still. She longed to beg her not to think about it, not to say any more; but she knew she would feel better if she did.

"I told her I'd go presently; and she waited—the patient little thing! And I was making my blue bow, and fixing it on, and fussing with the running, and I forgot! And she couldn't bear to bother me, and didn't say a word, but waited till she dropped to sleep without it; and her lips were so red and dry. It was a whole hour that I let her lie so. She never knew anything after that.

"She waked up all in a rave of light-headedness!

"I thought I should never get over it, Ray. And I never did, way down in my heart; but I got back into the same wretched nonsense, and now—here's *mother*!

"It's no use to tell me. I've done it. I've lost my right. It'll *never* be given back to me."

"Marion—I wish you could have Mr. Vireo to talk to you; or Luclarion Grapp. Won't you come home with me, and let them come to see you? They *know* about these things, dear."

"Would you take me home?" asked Marion, slowly, looking her in the face.

"Yes, indeed. Will you come?"

"O, do take me and hide me away, and let me cry!"

She dropped herself, as it were passively, into Rachel Ingraham's hands. She could not stay among the neighbors, she said. She could not stay in that house alone, one day.

Ray stayed with her, until after the funeral.

Marion would not go to the church. She had let them decide everything just as they pleased, thinking only that she could not think about any of it.

Mrs. Kent had been a faithful, humble church-member for forty years, and the minister and her fellow-members wanted her to be brought there. There was no room in the little half-house, where she had lived, for neighbors and friends to gather, and for the services properly to take place.

So it was decided.

But when the time came, and it was too late to change, Marion said,—"She belonged to them, and they have done by her. They can all go, but I can't. To sit up in the front pew as a mourner, and be looked at, and prayed for, as if I had been a real child, and had only *lost* my mother! You know I can't, Ray. I will stay here, and bear my punishment. May be if I bear it *all* now—do you believe it might make any difference?"

Ray stayed with her through the whole.

While all was still in the church, not ten rods off, a carriage came for them to the little white gate. With the silken blinds down, and the windows open behind them, it was driven to the cemetery, and in beneath the sheltering trees, to a stopping place just upon a little side turn, near the newly opened grave. No one, of those who alighted from the vehicles of the short procession, knew exactly when or how it had come.

The words of the prayer beside the grave,—most tenderly framed by the good old minister, for the ear he knew they would reach—came in soft and clear upon the pleasant air.

"And we know, Lord, as we lay these friends away, one after another, that we give them into Thy hands,—into Thy heart; that we give into Thy heart, also, all our love and our sorrow, and our penitence for whatever more we might have been or done toward them; that through Thee, our thought of them can reach them forever. We pray Thee to forgive us, as we know we do forgive each other; to keep alive and true in us the love by which we hold each other; and finally to bring us face to face in Thy glory, which is Thy loving presence among us all. We ask Thee to do this, by the pity and grace that are in Thy Christ, our Saviour."

After that, they were driven straight in, over the long Avenue, to the city, and to the quiet house in Pilgrim Street.

Ray herself, only, led Marion to the little room up-stairs which had been made ready for her; Ray brought her up some tea, and made her drink it; she saw her in bed for the night, and sat by her till she fell asleep.

CHAPTER XVII
ERRANDS OF HOPE

"It is a very small world, after all."

Mr. Dickens, who touched the springs of the whole world's life, and moved all its hearts with tears and laughter, said so; and we find it out, each in our own story, or in any story that we know of or try to tell. How things come round and join each other again,—how this that we do, brings us face to face with that which we have done, and with its work and consequence; how people find each other after years and years, and find that they have not been very far apart after all; how the old combinations return, and almost repeat themselves, when we had thought that they were done with.

"As the doves fly to their windows," where the crumbs are waiting for them, we find ourselves borne by we know not what instinct of events,—yet we do know; for it is just the purpose of God, as all instinct is,—toward these conjunctions and recurrences. We can see at the end of weeks, or months, or years, how in some Hand the lines must have all been gathered, and made to lead and draw to the coincidence. We call it fate, sometimes; stopping short, either blindly inapprehensive of the larger and surer blessedness, or too shyly reverent of what we believe to say it easily out. Yet when we read it in a written story, we call it the contrivance of the writer,—the trick of the trade. Dearly beloved, the writer only catches, in such poor fashion as he may, the trick of the Finger, whose scripture is upon the stars.

Marion Kent is received into the Ingraham home. Hilary Vireo and Luclarion Grapp preach the gospel to her.

"Christ died."

The minister uttered his evangel of mercy in those two eternal words.

"Yes,—Christ," murmured the girl, who had never questioned about such things before, and to whose lips the holy name had been strange, unsuitable, impossible; but whose soul, smitten with its sin and need, broke through the wretched outward hinderance now, and had to cry up after the only Hope.

"But He could not forgive my letting *them* die. I have been reading the New Testament, Mr. Vireo, 'Whosoever shall offend one of these little ones, it were better for him that a millstone"—

She could not finish the quotation.

"Yes,—'*offend*;' turn aside out of the right—away from Him; mislead. Hurt their *souls*, Marion."

Marion gave a grasping look into his face. Her eyes seized the comfort,—snatched it with a starving madness out of his.

"Do you think it means *that*?" she said.

"I do. I know the word 'offend' means simply to 'turn away.' We may sin against each other's outward good, grievously; we may lay up lives full of regrets to bear; we may hurt, we may kill; and then we must repent according to our sin; but we *may* repent, and they and He will pity. It is the soul-killers—the corrupters—Christ so terribly condemns."

"But listen to me, Marion," he began again. "God let his Christ die—suffer—for the whole world. Christ lets them whom he counts worthy, die—suffer—for *their* world. The Lamb is forever slain; the sacrifice of the holy is forever making. It is so that they come to walk in white with Him; because they have washed their robes in his blood—have partaken of his sacrifice. Do you not think they are glad now, with his joy, to have given themselves for you; if it brings you back? 'If I be lifted up, I will draw all men unto me.' He who knew how to lay hold of the one great heart of humanity by a divine act, knows how to give his own work to those who can draw the single cords, and save with love the single souls. They must suffer, that they may also reign with Him. It is his gift to them and to you. Will you take your part of it, and make theirs perfect? 'Let not your heart be troubled; ye believe in God, believe also in me. Ye believe in me, believe also in these.'"

"But I want to come where they are. I want to love and do for them; do something for them in heaven, Mr. Vireo, that I did not do here! Can I *ever* have my chances given back again?"

"You have them now. Go and do something for 'the least of these.' That is how we work for our Christs who have been lifted up. Do their errands; enter into the sacrifice with them; be a link yourself in the divine chain, and feel the joy and the life of it. The moment you give yourself, you shall feel that. You shall know that you are joined to them. You need not wait to go to heaven. You can be in heaven."

He left her with that to think of; left her with a new peace in her eyes. She looked round that hour for something to do.

She went up into old Mrs. Rhynde's room. She knew Ray and Dot were busy. She found the old lady's knitting work all in a snarl; stitches dropped and twisted.

Some coals had rolled out upon the hearth, and the sun had got round so as to strike across her where she sat.

The grandmother was waiting patiently, closing her eyes, and resting them, letting the warm sun lie upon her folded hands like a friend's touch. One of the girls would be up soon.

Marion came in softly, brushed up the hearth, laid the sticks and embers together, made the fire-place bright. She changed the blinds; lowered one, raised another; kept the sunshine in the room, but shielded away the dazzle that shot between face and fingers. She left the shade with careful note, just where it let the warm beam in upon those quiet hands. Some instinct told her not to come between them and that heavenly enfolding.

She took the knitting-work and straightened it; raveled down, and picked up, and with nimble stitches restored the lost rows.

Mrs. Rhynde looked up at her and smiled.

Then she offered to read. She had not read a word aloud from a printed page since that night in Loweburg.

The old lady wanted a hymn. Marion read "He leadeth me." The book opened of itself to that place. She read it as one whose soul went searching into the words to find what was in them, and bring it forth. Of Marion Kent, sitting in the chair with the book in her hand, she thought—she remembered—nothing. Her spirit went from out of her, into spiritual places. So she followed the words with her voice, as one really *reading*; interpreting as she went. All her elocution had taught her nothing like this before. It had not touched the secret of the instant receiving and giving again; it had only been the trick of *saying out*, which is no giving at all.

"Thank you, dear," said the soft toothless voice. "That's very pretty reading."

Dot came in, and she went away.

She had done a little "errand for her mother." A very little one; she did not deserve, yet, that more should be given her to do; but her heart went up saying tenderly, remorsefully,—"For your sake."

And back into her heart came the fulfillment of the promise,—"He that doeth it in the name of a disciple, shall receive a disciple's reward."

These comforts, these reprievals, came to her; then again, she went down into the blackness of the old memories, the old self-accusations.

After she had found her way to Luclarion Grapp's, she used sometimes, when these things seized her, to tie on her bonnet, pull down her thick veil, and crying and whispering behind it as she went,—"Mother! Susie! do you know how I love you now? how sorry I am?" would hurry down, through the busy streets, to the Neighbors.

"Give me something to do," she would say, when she got there.

And Luclarion would give her something to do; would keep her to tea, or to dinner; and in the quietness, when they were left by themselves, would say words that were given her to say in her own character and fashion. It is so blessed that the word is given and repeated in so many characters and fashions! That each one receives it and passes it on, "in that language into which he was born."

"I wish you could hear Luclarion Grapp's way of talking," Ray Ingraham had said to her just after she had brought her home. "The kind of comfort she finds for the most wicked and miserable,—people who have done such shocking things as you never dreamed of."

"I want to hear somebody talk to the very wickedest. If there's any chance for me, there's where I must find it. I can't listen with the pretty-good people, any longer. It doesn't belong to me, or do me any good."

"Come and hear the gospel then." And so Ray had taken her down to Neighbor Street, to Luclarion Grapp.

"But the sin stays. You can't wipe the fact out; and you've got to take the consequences," said Marion Kent to the strong, simple woman to whom she came as to a second-seer, to have her spiritual destinies revealed to her.

"Yes," said Luclarion, gravely, but very sweetly, "you have. But the consequences wear out. Everything wears out but the Lord's love. And these old worn-out consequences—why, He can turn them into blessings; and He means to, as they go along, and fade, and change; until, by and by, we may be safer and stronger, and fuller of everlasting life, than if we hadn't had them. I was vaccinated a while ago this summer; everybody was down here; and I had a pretty sick time. It took—ferocious! Well, I got over it, and then I thought about it. I'd got something out of my system forever, that might have come upon me, to destruction, all of a sudden; but now never will! It appears to me almost as if we were sent into this world, like a kind of hospital, to be vaccinated against the awful evil—in our souls; to suffer a little for it; to take it the easiest way we can take it, and so be safe. I don't know—and if you hadn't repented, I wouldn't put it into your head; but it's been put into my head, after I've repented, and I guess it's mainly true. See here!"

And she took down a big leather-bound Bible, and opened it to the fortieth chapter of Isaiah.

"Comfort ye, comfort ye, my people, saith the Lord. Speak ye comfortably to Jerusalem, and say unto her that her warfare is accomplished, that her iniquity is pardoned; for she hath received of the Lord's hand double for all her sins."

"The Old Testament is full of the New; men's wickedness,—it took wicked men to show the way of the Lord in the earth,—and God's forgiveness, and his leading it all round right, in spite of them all! Only He didn't turn the right side out all at once; it wasn't safe to let them see both sides then. But He *trusts* us now; He gave his whole heart in Jesus Christ; He tells us, without any keeping back, what He means our very sins shall do for us, and He leaves it to us, after that, to take hold and help Him!"

"If it weren't for them! If I hadn't let them suffer and die!"

"Do you think He takes all this care of you,—lets them die for you even,—and don't take as much for them? Do you think they ain't glad and happy now? Do you think you could have hurt them, if you had tried,—and you didn't try, you only let them alone a little, forgetting? It says, 'If any man sin, we have an advocate with the Father, Jesus Christ the righteous; and He is the propitiation.' If we have somebody to take part with us against our sins, how much more against our mistakes,—our forgettings! and *they* are the propitiation, too; their angels—the Christ of them—do always behold the face of the Father. Their interceding is a part of the Lord's interceding."

"If I could once more be let to do something for them—their very selves!"

"You can. You can pray, 'Lord give them some beautiful heavenly joy this day that thou knowest of, for my asking; because I cannot any more do for them on the earth.' And then you can turn round to their errands again."

Marion stood up on her feet.

"I will say that prayer for them every day! I shall believe in it, because you told me. If I had thought of it myself, I should not have dared. But He wouldn't send such a message by you if He didn't mean it; would He?"

She believed in the God of Luclarion Grapp, as the children of Israel believed in the God of Abraham.

"He never sends any message that He doesn't mean. He means the comfort, just as much as He does the blaming."

Another day, a while after, Marion came down to Neighbor Street with something very much on her mind to say, and to ask about. They had all waited for her own plans to suggest themselves, or rather for her work to be given her to do. No one had mentioned, or urged, or even asked anything as to what she should do next.

But now it came of itself.

"Couldn't I get a place in some asylum, or hospital, do you think, Miss Grapp? To be anything—an under nurse, or housemaid, or a cook to make gruels? So that I could do for poor women and little children? That would seem to come the very nearest. I'd come here, if you wanted me; but I think I should like best to take care of poor, good women, whose children had died, or gone away; who haven't any one to look after them except asylum people. I like to treat them as if they were all my mothers; and especially to wait on any little girls that might be sick."

Was this the same Marion Kent who had given her whole soul, a little while ago, to fine dressing and public appearing, and having her name on placards? Had all that life dropped off from her so easily?

Ah, you call it easily! *She* knew, how, passing through the furnace, it had been burned away; shriveled and annihilated with the fierce, hot sweep of a spiritual flame before which all old, unworthy desire vanishes:—the living, awful breath of remorse.

"I've no doubt you can," said Luclarion. "I'll make inquiries. Mrs. Sheldon comes here pretty often; and she is one of the managers of the Women and Children's Hospital. They've just got into a great, new building, and there'll be people wanted."

"I'll begin with anything, remember; only to get in, and learn how. I'll do so they'll want to keep me, and give me more; more work, I mean. If I could come to nursing, and being depended on!"

"They train nurses, regular, there. Learn them, so that they can go anywhere. Then you might some time have a chance to go to somebody that needed great care; some sick woman or child, or a sick mother, with little children round her"—

"And every day send up some good turn by them to mother and little Sue!"

So they bound up her wounds for her, and poured in the oil and wine; so they put her on their own beast of service, and set her in their own way, and brought her to a place of abiding.

Three weeks afterward, she went in as housemaid for the children's ward to the Hospital; the beautiful charity which stands, a token of the real best growth of Boston, in that new quarter of her fast enlarging borders, where the tide of her wealth and her life is reaching out southward, toward the pure country pleasantness.

We must leave her there, now; at rest from her ambitions; reaching into a peace they could never have given her; doing daily work that comes to her as a sign and pledge of acceptance and forgiveness.

She sat by a child's bed one Sunday; the bed of a little girl ten years old, whom she had singled out to do by for Susie's sake. She had taken the place of a nurse, to-day, who was ill with an ague.

She read to Maggie the Bible story of Joseph, out of a little book for children that had been Sue's.

After the child had fallen asleep, Marion fetched her Bible, to look back after something in the Scripture words.

It had come home to her,—that betrayal and desertion of the boy by his brethren; it stood with her now for a type of her own selfish unfaithfulness; it thrust a rebuke and a pain upon her, though she knew she had repented.

She wanted to see exactly how it was, when, in the Land beyond the Desert, his brethren came face to face again with Joseph.

"Now, therefore, be not grieved, nor angry with yourselves, that ye sold me hither; for God did send me before you to preserve life.... To save your lives with a great deliverance. So it was not you that sent me hither, but God.... And thou shalt dwell in the land of Goshen, and thou shalt be near unto me."

A great throb of thankfulness, of gladness, came rushing up in her; it filled her eyes with light; it flushed her cheeks with tender color. The tears sprung shining; but they did not fall. Peace stayed them. It was such an answer!

"How pretty you are!" said Maggie, awakening. "Please, give me a drink of water."

It was as if Susie thought of it, and gave her the chance! She read secret, loving meanings now, in things that had their meanings only for her. She believed in spirit-communication,—for she knew it came; but in its own beautiful, soul-to-soul ways; not by any outward spells.

She went for the water; she found a piece of ice and put in it. She came and raised the little head tenderly,—the child was hurt in the back, and could not be lifted up,—and held the goblet to the gentle lips; lips patient, like Sue's!

"O, you move me so nice! You give me the drink so handy!"

The beauty was in Marion's face still, warm with an inward joy; the child's eyes followed her as she rose from bending over her.

"Real pretty," she said again, softly, liking to look at her. And "real" was beginning to be the word, at last, for Marion Kent.

The glory of that poem she had read, thinking only of her own petty triumph, came suddenly over her thought by some association,—she could not trace out how. Its grand meaning was a meaning, all at once, for her. With a changed phrasing, like a heavenly inspiration, the last line sprang up in her mind, as if somebody stood by and spoke it:—

"These are the lambs of the sacrifice: *this* is the court of the King!"

CHAPTER XVIII
BRICKFIELD FARMS

It was a rainy, desolate day.

It had rained the day before yesterday, and yesterday, and half cleared up last night; then this morning it had sullenly and tiresomely begun again.

All the forenoon it grew worse; in the afternoon, heavy, pelting, streaming showers came down, filling the Kiln Hollow with mist, and hiding the tops of the hills about it with low, rolling, ever-gathering and resolving clouds.

It seemed as if all the autumn joy were over; as if the pleasant days were done with till another year. After this, the cold would set in.

Mrs. Jeffords had a bright fire built in Mrs. Argenter's room, another in the family sitting-room. It looked cosy; but it reminded the sojourners that they had not simply to draw themselves into winter-quarters, and be comfortable; their winter-quarters were yet to seek.

Sylvie had been cracking a plateful of butternuts; picking out meats, I mean, from the cracked nuts, to make a plateful; and that, if you know butternuts, you know is no small task. She brought them to her mother, with some grated maple sugar sprinkled among and over them.

"This is what you liked so much at the Shakers' in Lebanon," she said. "See if it isn't as nice as theirs, I think it is fresher. Here is a tiny little pickle-fork, to eat with."

Mrs. Argenter took the offered dainty.

"You are a dear child," she said. "Come and eat some too."

"O, I ate as I went along. Now, I'll read to you." And she took up "Blindpits," which her mother had laid down.

"If it only wouldn't storm so," said Mrs. Argenter. "Mrs. Jeffords says there will be a freshet. The roads will be all torn up. We shall never be able to get home."

"O yes, we shall," said Sylvie, cheerily; putting down the wonder that arose obtrusively in her own mind as to where the home would be that they should go to.

"Did Mrs. Jeffords tell you about last year's freshet? And the apples?"

"She said they had an awful flood. The brooks turned into rivers, and the rivers swallowed up everything."

"O, she didn't get to the funny part, then?" said Sylvie. "She didn't tell you about the apples?"

"No. I think she keeps the funny parts for you, Sylvie."

"May be she does. She isn't sure that you feel up to them, always. But I guess she means them to come round, when she tells them to me. You see they had just been gathering their apples, in that great lower orchard,—five acres of trees, and such a splendid crop! There they were, all piled up,—can't you imagine? A perfect picture! Red heaps, and yellow heaps; and greenings, and purple pearmains, and streaked seek-no-furthers. Like great piles of autumn leaves! Well, the flood came, and rose up over the flats, into the lower end of the orchard. They went down over night, and moved all the piles further up, The next day, they had to move them again. And the next morning after that, when they woke up, the whole orchard was under water, and every apple gone. Mr. Jeffords said he got down just in time to see the last one swim round the corner. And when the flood had fallen,—there, half a mile below, spread out over the meadow, was three hundred barrels of apple sauce!"

Mrs. Argenter laughed a feeble little *expected* laugh; her heart was not free to be amused with an apple-story. No wonder Mrs. Jeffords kept the funny parts for Sylvie. Mrs. Argenter quenched her before she could possibly get to them. But was Sylvie's heart free for amusement? What was the difference? The years between them? Mrs. Jeffords was a far older woman than Mrs. Argenter, and had had her cares and troubles; yet she and Sylvie laughed like two girls together, over their work and their stories. That was it,—the work! Sylvie was doing *all she could*. The cheerfulness of doing followed irresistibly after, into the loops and intervals of time, and kept out the fear and the repining.

"There was nothing that chippered you up so, as being real driving busy," Mrs. Jeffords said.

Mrs. Argenter sat in her low easy-chair, watched away the time, and worried about the time to come. It left no leisure for a laugh.

Perhaps the hardest thing that Sylvie did through the day, was the setting to work to "chipper" her mother up. It was lifting up a weight that continually dropped back again.

"Do they think this rain will ever be over?" asked Mrs. Argenter, turning her face toward the dripping panes again.

"Why, yes, mother; rains always *have* been over sometime. They never knew one that wasn't, and they go by experience."

There was nothing more to be said upon the rain topic, after that simple piece of logic.

"If there doesn't come Badgett up the hill in all the pour!"

Badgett drove the daily stage from Tillington up through Pemunk and Sandon. He came round by Brickfields when there was anybody to bring.

Badgett drove up over the turf door-yard, close to the porch. He jumped off, unbuttoned the dripping canvas door, and flung it up.

Mrs. Jeffords was in the entry on the instant; surprised, puzzled, but all ready to be hospitable, to she didn't know whom. Relations from Indiana, as likely as not. That is the way people arrive in the country; and a whole houseful to stay over night does not startle the hostess as an unexpected guest to dinner may a city one.

But the persons who alighted from the clumsy stage-wagon were Mr. Christopher Kirkbright, Miss Euphrasia, and Desire Ledwith.

"Didn't you get our letter?" said Miss Euphrasia, as Sylvie, from her mother's door-way, saw who she was, and sprang forward.

"Why, no, we didn't get no letter," said Mrs. Jeffords. "Father hasn't been to the office for two days, it's stormed so continual. But you're just as welcome, exactly. Step right in here." And she flung open the door of her best parlor, where the new boughten carpet was, for the damp feet and the dripping waterproof.

"No, indeed; not there; we couldn't have the conscience."

"'Tain't very comfortable either, after all," said Mrs. Jeffords, changing her own mind in a bustle. "It's been kinder shut up. Come right out to the sittin'-room-fire finally."

Mr. Kirkbright and Miss Ledwith followed her; Miss Euphrasia went right into Mrs. Argenter's room, after she had taken off her waterproof in the hall.

As she came in at the door, a great flash of sunshine streamed from under the western clouds, in at the parlor window, followed her across the hall and enveloped her in light as she entered.

"Why, the storm's over!" cried Sylvie, joyfully. "You come in on a sunbeam, like the Angel Gabriel. But you always do. How came you to come?"

"I came to answer your letter. You know I don't like to write very well. And I've brought my brother, and a dear friend of mine whom I want you to know. It did not rain in Boston when we started, but it came on again before noon, and all the afternoon it has been a splendid down-pour. Something really worth while to be out in, you know; not a little exasperating drizzle. That's the kind of rain one can't bear, and catches cold in. How the showers swept round the hills, and the cascades thundered and flashed as we came by! What a lovely region you have discovered!"

"It's so beautiful that you're here! We'll go down to the cascades to-morrow. Won't you just come and introduce me to the others, and then come back to mother?"

The others were in the family-room, which was also dining-room. In the kitchen beyond, Mrs. Jeffords' stove was roaring up for an early tea, and she was whipping griddle-cakes together.

"My brother, Mr. Kirkbright—Miss Argenter. Miss Desire Ledwith—Sylvie."

The two girls shook hands, and looked in each others faces.

"How clear, and strong, and trusty!" Sylvie thought.

"You dear little spirit!" thought Desire, seeing the delicate face, and the brave sweetness through it.

This was the second real introduction Miss Euphrasia had made within ten days. It was a great deal, of that sort, to happen in such space of time.

"If it hadn't been for the storm, we might have hurried down and missed you. Mother was beginning to dread the coming on of the cold," said Sylvie. "But the rain came and settled it, for just now. That rested me. A real good 'can't help' is such a comfort."

"The Father's No. Shutting us in with its grand, gentle forbiddance. Many a rain-storm is that. I always feel so safe when I am shut up by really impossible weather."

After the tea, they were still in time for the whole sunset, wonderful after the storm.

Desire had gone from the table to the half-glazed door which opened from the room into a broad porch, looking out directly across the hollow, along a valley-line of side-hills, to the distant blue peaks.

"O, come!" she cried back to the others, as she hastened out upon the platform. "It is marvelous!"

Heavy lines of clouds lay banked together in the west, black with the remnant and recoil of tempest; between these, through rifts and breaks, poured down the sunlight across bright spaces into the bosoms of the hills lighting them up with revelations. The sloping outlines shone golden green with lingering summer color, and discovered each separate wave and swell of upland. The searching shafts fell upon every tree and bush and spire, moving slowly over them and illuminating point after point, making each suddenly seem distinct and near. What had been a mere margin of distant woods, stood eliminated and relieved in bough and stem and leafage, with a singular pre-Raphaelitic individuality. It was the standing-out of all things in the last radiance; called up, one by one under the flash of judgment—beautiful, clear, terrible.

Then the clouds themselves, as the sun dropped down, drank in the splendor. They turned to rose and crimson; they floated, and spread, and broke, and drifted up the valley, against the hills on right and left. Rags and shreds of them, trailing gorgeous with color, clung where the ridges caught them, and streamed like fragments of heavenly banners. The sky repeated the October woods,—the woods the sky,—in vivid numberless hues.

The sunset rolled up and around the watchers as they gazed. They were *in* it; it lay at their very feet, and beside them at either hand. Below, the sheet of water in the "Clay-Pits," gleamed like burnished gold. Here and there, from among the tree-tops, came up the smoke of little cascades, reaching for baptism into the pervading glory.

It was chilly, and they had to go in; but they kept coming back to window and door, looking out through the closed sashes, and calling, "Now! now! O, was there ever anything like that?"

At last it turned into a heavenly vision of still, far, shining waters; the earth and the pools upon it darkened, and the sky gathered up into itself the glory, and disclosed its own wider and diviner beauty.

A great rampart of gray, blue, violet clouds lay jagged, grand, like rocks along a shore. Up over them rushed light, crimson surf, foaming, tossing. Beyond, a rosy sea. In it, little golden boats floated. The flamy light flung itself up into the calm zenith; there it met the still heaven-color, and the sky was tender with saffron-touched blue.

So the tempest of trouble met the tempest of love in the end of the day, and the world rolled on into the night under the glory and peace of their rushing and melting together.

After all that, they came back by a step and a word—these mortal observers,—to practical consultation such as mortals must have, and especially if they be upon their travels; to questions about bestowal, and the homely, kindly, funny little details of Mrs. Jeffords' hospitality.

"Where should she put them? Why, she was *always* ready. To be sure, the *front* upper room had had the carpets taken up since the summer company went, and the beds were down; but, la, there was room enough!"

"There's the east down-stairs bedroom, and the little west-room over the sittin'-room, and there's *my* room! I ain't never put out!"

"But you are; out of your room; and you ought not to be."

"Don't *care!*" said Mrs. Jeffords, triumphantly. "There's the kitchen bedroom, that I keep apurpose to camp down in. It's all right. Don't you worry."

"You never care; that's the reason I do worry," said Sylvie.

"I've learnt not to care," said Mrs. Jeffords. "'Tain't no use. You must take things as they are. They will be so, and you can't help it. If they fall right side up, well and good; if they're wrong side up, let 'em lay. And they ain't wrong side up yet, I can tell you. You just go and sit down and enjoy yourselves."

Mrs. Argenter was brighter this evening than she had been for a long while. "It was nice to be among people again," she said, when the evening was over.

"So it is," said Sylvie. "But somehow I didn't feel the difference the other way. I think I always *am* among people. At least it never seems to me as if they were very far off. Next door mayn't be exactly alongside, but it is next door for all that, and it is in the world. And the world wakes up all together every morning,—that is, as fast as the morning gets round."

With her "mayn't be's" and her "is'es," Sylvie was unconsciously making a habit of the trick of Susan Nipper, but with a kindlier touch to her antitheses than pertained to those of that acerb damsel.

Mrs. Argenter wanted tangible presences. She had not reached so far as her child into that inner living where all feel each other, knowing that "these same tribulations"—and joys also—are accomplished among the brotherhood that is in all the earth; knowing, too,—ah! that is the blessedness when we come to it,—that we may walk, already, in the heavenly places with all them that are alive unto each other in the Lord.

The next morning after deep rains in a hill-country is a morning of wonders; if you can go out among them, and know where to find them. Down the ravines, from the far back, greater heights, rush and plunge the streams whitened with ecstasy, turned to sweet wild harmonies as they go. It is a day of glory for the water-drops that are born to make a part of it.

Sylvie knew the way down through the glen, from fall to fall, half a mile apart. She and Bob Jeffords had come down to them, time and again; after nearly every little summer shower; for with all the heat, the night rains had been plentiful and frequent, and the water-courses had been kept full. The brick-fields, that looked so near from the farms, were really more than two miles away; and it was a constant descent, from brow to brow, over the range of uplands between the Jeffords' place and the Basin.

"The First Cataracts are in here," said Sylvie, gleefully, leading the way in by a bar-place upon a very wet path, the wetness of which nobody minded, all having come defended with rubbers and waterproofs, and tucked up their petticoats boot-high. Great bosks of ferns grew beside, and here and there a bush burning with autumn color. Everything shone and dripped; the very stones glittered.

They climbed up rocky slopes, on which the short gray moss grew, cushiony. They followed the line of maples and alders and evergreens that sentineled and hid away the shouting stream, spreading their skirts and intertwining their arms to shelter it, like the privacy of some royal child at play, and to keep back from the pilgrims the beautiful surprise. Upon a rough table-ledge, they came to it at last; the place where they could lean in between the trees, and overlook and underlook the shining tumult,—the shifting, yet enduring apparition of delight.

It came in two leaps, down a winding channel, through which it seemed to turn and spring, like some light, graceful, impetuous living creature. You *felt* it reach the first rock-landing; you were conscious of the impetus which forced it on to take the second spring which brought it down beneath your feet. And it kept coming—coming. It was an eternal moment; a swift, vanishing, yet never over-and-done movement of grace and splendor. That is the magic of a waterfall. Something exquisite by very suggestion of evanescence, caught *in transitu*, and held for the eye and mind to dwell on.

They were never tired of looking. The chance would not come,—that ought to be a pause,—for them to turn and go away.

"But there are more," Sylvie said at length, admonishing them. "And the Second Cataract is grander than this."

"You number them going down," said Mr. Kirkbright.

"Yes. People always number things as they come to them, don't they? Our first is somebody's else last, I suppose, always."

"What a little spirit that is!" said Christopher Kirkbright to Miss Euphrasia, dropping back to help his sister down a rocky plunge.

"A little spirit waked up by touch of misfortune," said Miss Euphrasia. "She would have gone through life blindfolded by purple and fine linen, if things had been left as they were with her."

Desire and Sylvie walked on together.

"Leave them alone," said Miss Kirkbright to her brother. And she stopped, and began to gather handfuls of the late ferns.

Now she had the chance given her, Desire said it straight out, as she said everything.

"I came up here after you, Miss Argenter. Did you know it?"

"No. After me? How?" asked Sylvie.

"To see if you and your mother would come and make your home with us this winter,—pretty much as you do with Mrs. Jeffords. I can say *us*, because Hazel Ripwinkley, my cousin, is with me nearly all the time; but for the rest of it, I am all the family there really is, now that Rachel Froke has gone away; unless you came to call my dear old Frendely 'family,' as I do; seeing that next to Rachel, she is root and spring of it. You could help me; you could help her; and I think you would like my work. I should be glad of you; and your mother could have Rachel Froke's gray parlor. It is a one-sided proposition, because, you see, I know all about you already, from Miss Euphrasia. You will have to take me at hazard, and find out by trying."

"Do you think the old proverb isn't as true of good words as of mischief,—that a dog who will fetch a bone will carry a bone?" said Sylvie, laughing with the same impulse by which clear drops stood suddenly in her eyes, and a quick rosiness came into her face. "Do you suppose Miss Euphrasia hasn't told me of you?"

"I never thought I was one of the people to be told about," said Desire, simply. "Do you think you could come? Miss Euphrasia believed it would be what you wanted. There is plenty of room, and plenty of work. I want you to know that I mean to keep you honestly busy, because then you will understand that things come out honestly even."

"Even! Dear Miss Ledwith!"

"Then you'll try it?"

"I don't know how to thank Miss Euphrasia or you."

"There are no thanks in the bargain," said Desire, smiling. "I want you; if you want me, it is a Q.E.D. If we *do* dispute about anything, we'll leave it out to Miss Euphrasia. She knows how to make everything right. She shall be our broker. It is a good thing to have one, in some kinds of trade."

They had come around the curve in the road now, that brought them alongside the shady gorge at the foot of Cone Hill. Here was the little group of brick-makers' houses; empty, weather-beaten, their door-yards overgrown with brakes and mulleins. Beyond, up the ledge, to which a rough drive-way, long disused, led off, was the quaint, rambling edifice that with its feet of stone and brick went "walking up" the mountain.

"You must go in and see it," Sylvie said. "But first,—this is the way to the cascade."

Another bar-place let them in again to another narrow, wild, bush-grown path around the edge of the cliff, the lower spur of the great hill; and down over shelving rocks, a long, gradual descent, to the foot of the fall.

The water foamed and rippled to their feet, as they walked along its varying edge-line on the smooth, sloping stone that stretched back against the perpendicular rampart of the cliff. The fall itself was hidden in the turn around which, above, they had followed the tangled pathway.

At the farthest projection of the platform they were now treading, they came upon it; beneath it, rather, they looked back and up at its showery silver sheet, falling in sweet, continual thunder into the dark, hollow, rock-encircled pool, thence to tumble away headlong, from point to point, lower and lower yet, by a thousand little breaks and plunges, till it came out into a broad meadow stretch miles and miles away.

"What a hurry it is in, to get down where it is wanted," said Desire.

She had seated herself beside the curling edge of the swift stream, where it seemed to trace and keep by its own will its boundary upon the nearly level rock, and was gazing up where the white radiance poured itself as if direct from out the blue above.

Mr. Kirkbright stood behind her.

"Most things come to us at last so quietly," he said. "It is good to feel and see what a rush it starts with,—out of that heart of heaven."

Desire had not said that; but it was just what she had been feeling. Eager to get to us; coming in a hurry. Was that God's impulse toward us?

"Making haste to help and satisfy the world," Mr. Kirkbright said again.

"A river of clear water of life, coming down out of the throne," said Miss Euphrasia. "What a sign it is!"

Mr. Kirkbright walked along the margin of the ledge, farther and farther down. He tried with his stick some stones that lay across the current at a narrow point where beneath the opposite cliff it bent and turned away, losing itself from their sight as they stood here. Then he sprang across; crept, stooping, along the narrow foothold under the projecting rock, until he could follow with his eye the course of the rapid water, falling continually to its lower level as it sped on and on, all its volume gathered in one deep, rocky, unchangeable bed.

"What a waiting power!" he exclaimed, springing safely back, and coming up toward them. "What a stream for mills! And it turns nothing but the farmers' grists, till it gets to Tillington."

Desire was a very little disappointed at this utilitarianism. She had been so glad and satisfied with the reading of its type; the type of its far-back impulse.

"If there had been mills here, we should not have seen that," she said; forgetting to explain what.

But Christopher Kirkbright knew.

"What was it that we did see?" he asked, coming beside her.

"The gracious hurry," she answered, with a half-vexed surprise in her eyes.

"And what is the next thing to seeing that? Isn't it to partake? To be in a gracious hurry also, if we can?"

A smile came up now in Desire's face, and effaced gently the vexation and the surprise.

"Do you know what a legible face you have?" asked Mr. Kirkbright, seating himself near her on a step of rock.

Desire was a little disturbed again by this movement. The others had begun to walk on, up the ledge, toward the old brick house; gathering as they went, ferns that had escaped the frost, others that had delicately whitened in it, and gorgeous maple-leaves, swept from topmost, inaccessible branches,—where the most glorious color always hangs,—by last night's rain and wind.

It was so foolish of her to have sat there until he came and did this. Now she could not get right up and go away. This feeling, coming simultaneously with his question about her legible face, was doubly uncomfortable. But she had to answer. She did it briefly.

"Yes. It is a great bother. I don't like coarse print."

"Nor I. But my eyes are good; and the fine print is clear. I should like very much to tell you of something that I have to do, Miss Ledwith. I should like your thoughts upon it. For, you see, I have hardly yet got acquainted with my ground. From what my sister tells me, I think your work leads naturally up to mine. I should like to find out whether it is quite ready for the join."

"I haven't much work," said Desire. "Luclarion Grapp has; and Miss Kirkbright, and Mr. Vireo. I only help,—with some money that belongs to it."

"And I have more money that belongs to it," said Mr. Kirkbright.

It was a curious way for a rich man and a rich woman to talk to each other, about their money. But I do not believe it ought to be curious.

"Don't you often come across people who cannot be helped much just where they are? Don't you feel, sometimes, that there ought to be a place to send them to, away, out of their old tracks, where they could begin again; or even hide a while, in shame and repentance, before they *dare* to begin again?"

"I *know* Luclarion does," said Desire, earnestly.

She would have it, still, that there was no work in her own name for him to ask about.

"I must see this Luclarion of yours," said Mr. Kirkbright. "Meanwhile, since I have got you to talk to, pray tell me all you can, whoever found it out. Isn't there a need for a City of Refuge? And suppose a place like this, away from the towns, where God's beautiful water is coming down in a hurry, with a cry of power in every leap,—where there is a great lake-basin full of material for work, just stored away against men's need for their earning and their building,—suppose this place taken and used for the giving of a new chance of life to those who have failed and gone wrong, or have perhaps hardly ever had any right chances. Do you think we could manage it so as to *keep* it a place of refuge and new beginning, and not let it spoil itself?"

"With the right people at each end, why not?" said Desire. "But O, Mr. Kirkbright! how can I tell you! It is such a great idea; and I don't know anything."

These words, that she happened to say, brought back to her—by one of those little lightning threads that hold things together, and flash and thrill our recollections through us—the rainy morning when she went round in the storm to her Aunt Ripwinkley's, because she could not sit in the bay-window at home, and wonder whether "it was all finished," or whether anybody had got to contrive anything more, "before they could sit behind plate-glass and let it rain." She remembered it all by those same words that she had spoken then to Rachel Froke,—"Behold, we know not anything,—Tennyson and I!"

Nonsense stays by us, often, in stickier fashion than sense does; that is the good of nonsense, perhaps; it sticks, and draws the sense along after it.

"I think one thing is certain," said Mr. Kirkbright. "Human creatures are made for 'moving on.' I believe the Swedenborgians are right in this,—that the places above, or below, are filled from the human race, or races; and that the Lord Himself couldn't do much with beings made as He has made us, without places to *move us into*. New beginnings,—evenings and mornings; the very planet cannot go on its way without making them for itself. Life bound down to poor conditions,—and all conditions are poor in the sense of being limited while the life is resistlessly expanding,—festers; fevers; breaks out in violence and disease. I believe we want new places more than anything. I came up here on purpose to see if I could not begin one."

"How happened you to come just here?" questioned Desire. "What could you know of this, beforehand?"

"My sister had Miss Argenter's letter; and at once she remembered the name of the place and its story. That is the way things come together, you know. My brother-in-law, Mr. Sherrett, owns, or did own, this whole property. A 'dead stick,' he thought it. Well, Aaron's rod was another dead stick. But he laid it up before the Lord, and it blossomed."

Desire sat silent, looking at the white water in its gracious hurry. Pouring itself away, unused,—unheeded; yet waiting there, pouring always. The tireless impulse of the divine help; vehement; eager, with a human eagerness; yet so patient, till men's hands should reach out and lay hold of it!

She dreamed out a whole dream of life that might grow up beside this help; of work that might be done there. She forgot that she was lingering, and keeping Mr. Kirkbright lingering, behind the others.

"You would have to live here yourself, I should think," she said at length, speaking out of her vision of the things that might be, and so—would have to be. She had got drawn in to the contemplation of the scheme, and had begun to weigh and arrange, involuntarily, its details, forgetting that she "knew not anything."

Mr. Kirkbright smiled.

"Yes, I see where you are," he said, "I had arrived at precisely the same point myself. But the 'right people at the other end?' Who should they be? Who shall send me my villagers,—my workers? Who shall discriminate for me, and keep things true and unconfused at the source?"

"Your sister, Mr. Vireo, Luclarion Grapp," Desire repeated, promptly.

"And yourself?"

"Yes; I and Hazel, all we can. We help them. And now there will be Miss Argenter. As Hazel said,—'We all of us know the Muffin-man.' How queer that that ridiculous play should come to mean so much with us! Luclarion Grapp is actually a muffin-woman, you know?"

"I'm afraid I don't know the Muffin-*man* literally, except what I can guess of him by your application," said Mr. Kirkbright, laughing. "I've no doubt I ought to, and that it would do me good."

"You will have to come to Greenley Street, and find him out. Hazel and Miss Craydocke manage all the introductions, as having a kind of proprietorship; 'and quite proper, I'm sure'—Why, where are Miss Kirkbright and Miss Argenter?"

Coming back to light common speech, she came back also to the present circumstance; reminded also, perhaps, by her "quite proper" quotation.

"If I may come to Greenley Street, I may learn a good deal beside the Muffin-man," said Mr. Kirkbright, giving her his hand to help her up a steep, slippery place.

Desire foolishly blushed. She knew it, and knew that her hat did not defend her in the least. She could not take it back now; she had invited him. But what would he think of her blushing about it?

"You can learn what we all learn. I am only a scholar," she said, shortly. And then she stood accused before her own truthfulness of having covered up her blush by a disclaimer that had nothing to do with it. She was conscious that she had colored like any silly girl, at she hardly knew what. She was provoked with herself, for letting the shadow of such things touch her. She hurried on, up the rough bank, before Mr. Kirkbright. When she reached the top, she turned round and faced him; this time with a determinedly cool cheek.

"I don't know why I said that. I did not suppose you thought you could learn anything of me," she said. "I was confused to think I had asked you in that offhand way to my house. I have not been very long used to being the head of a house."

She smiled one of those bits of smiles of hers; a mere relaxation of the lips that showed the white tips of her front teeth and just indicated the peculiar, pretty curve with which the others were set behind them; feeling reassured and reinstated in her own self-respect by her explanation. Then, without letting him answer, she turned swiftly round again, and sprang up the rugged stairway of the shelving rock.

But she had not uninvited him, after all.

They found Miss Kirkbright and Sylvie waiting for them at the red house. It was a quaint structure, with a kind of old, foreign look about it. It made you think either of an ancient family mansion in some provincial French town, or of a convent for nuns.

It was of dark red brick,—the quality of which Mr. Kirkbright remarked with satisfaction,—with high walls at the gable ends carried above the slope of the roof. These were met and overclasped at the corners by wide, massive eaves. A high, narrow door with a fan-light occupied the middle of the end before which the party stood. Windows above, with little balconies, were hung with old red woolen damask, fading out in stripes; perishing, doubtless, with moth and decay; in one was suspended a rusty bird-cage which had once been gilt.

What an honest neighborhood this was, in which these things had remained for years, and not even the panes of the windows had been broken by little boys! But then the villages full of little boys were miles away, and the single families at the nearer farms were well ordered Puritan folk, fathered and mothered in careful, old fashioned sort. There was some indefinite awe, also, of the lonely place, and of the rich, far-off owner who might come any day to look after his rights, and make a reckoning with them.

Up, from platform to platform of the terraced rock, as Sylvie had said, climbed the successive sections of the dwelling. The front was two and a half stories high; the last outlying projection was a single square apartment with its own low roof; towards the back, within, you went up flight after flight of short stairs from room to room, from passage to passage. Once or twice, the few broad steps between two apartments ran the whole width of the same.

"What a place for plays!"

"Or for a little children's school, ranged in rows, one above another."

"The man who built it must have dreamt it first!"

These were the exclamations that they made to each other as they passed through, exploring.

There was a great number of bedrooms, divided off here and there; the upper front was one row of them with a gallery running across the house, in whose windows toward the south hung the old red woolen draperies and the bird-cage.

Below, at the back, the last room opened by a door upon a high, flat table of the rock, around whose overhanging edge a light railing had been run. Standing here, they looked up and down the beautiful gorge, into the heart of the hill and the depth of its secret shaded places on the one hand, and on the other into the rush and whirl of the rapidly descending and broken torrent to where it flung itself off the sudden brink, and changed into white mist and an everlasting song.

"This last room ought to be a chapel," said Mr. Kirkbright. "Out here could be open-air service in the beautiful weather, to the sound of that continual organ."

"You have thought of it, too," exclaimed Desire.

"Of what?" asked Mr. Kirkbright, turning toward her.

"Of what you might make this place."

"What would you make of it?"

They were a little apart, by themselves, again. It kept happening so. Miss Kirkbright and Sylvie had a great deal to say to each other.

"I would make it a moral sanatorium. I would take people in here, and nurse them up by beautiful living, till they were ready to begin the world again; and then I would have the little new world, of work and business, waiting just outside. I would have rooms for them here, that they should feel the *own-ness* of; flowers to tend; ferneries in the windows; they could make them from these beautiful woods, and send them away to the cities; that would be a business at the very first! I would have all the lovely, natural ways of living to win them back by,—to teach them pure things; yes,—and I would have the chapel to teach them the real gospel in! That bird-cage in the gallery window made me think of it all, I believe," she ended, bringing herself back out of her enthusiasm with a recollection.

"I knew you could tell me how," said Mr. Kirkbright, quietly.

"How Hazel would rejoice in this place! It is a place to set any one dreaming, I think; because, perhaps, as Miss Kirkbright said, the man was in a dream when he planned it."

"I mean to try if one dream cannot be lived," said Christopher Kirkbright. "At any rate, let us have the *vision* out, while we are about it! What do you think of brickmaking for the hard, rough working men, with families, with those cottages and more like them to live in; and paper-making, in mills down there, for others; for the women and children, especially. Paper for hangings, say; then, some time or other, the printing works, and the designing? Might it not all grow? And then wouldn't we have a ladder all the way up, for them to climb by,—out of the clay and common toil to art and beauty?"

"You can dream delightfully, Mr. Kirkbright."

"I will see if I cannot begin to turn it into fact, and make it pay," he answered. "Pay itself, and keep itself going. I do not need to look for my fortune from it. The fortune is to be put into it. But I have no right to lose,—to throw away,—the fortune. It must come by degrees, like all things. You know some people say that God dreamed the heavens and the earth in those six wonderful days, and then took his millions of years for the everlasting making, with the Sabbath of his divine satisfaction between the two. If I cannot do the whole, there may be others,—and if there are, we shall find them,—who would help to build the city."

"I know who," said Desire, instantly. "Dakie Thayne, and Ruth! It is just what they want."

"Will 'Dakie Thayne' build a railroad,—seven miles,—across to Tillington,—for our transportation? We'll say he will. I have no question it is Dakie Thayne, or somebody, who is waiting, and that the right people are all linked together, ready to draw each other in," said Mr. Kirkbright, giving rein to the very lightness of gladness in the joy of the thought he was pursuing. "We don't know how we stand leashed and looped, all over the world, until the Lord begins to take us in hand, and bring us together toward his grand intents. We shall want another Hilary Vireo to preach that gospel here; and I don't doubt he is somewhere, though it would hardly seem possible."

"Why don't we preach it ourselves?" said Desire, with inimitable unwittingness. She was so utterly and wholly in the vision, that she left her present self standing there on the rock with Christopher Kirkbright, and never even thought of a reason why to blush before him.

"I don't know why we shouldn't. In fact, we could not help it. It would be *all* gospel, wouldn't it? I know, at least, what I should mean the whole thing to preach."

Saying this, he fell silent all at once.

"There is a great deal of wrong gospel preached in the world. If we could only stop that, and begin again,—I think!" said Desire. "Between the old, hopeless terrors and the modern smoothing away and letting go, the real living help seems to have failed men. They don't know where it is, or whether they need it, even."

"Yes, that is it," said Christopher Kirkbright, letting his silence be broken through with the whole tide of his earnest, life-long, pondered thought. "Men have put aside the old idea of the avenging and punishing God, until they think they have no longer any need of Christ. God is Love, they tell us; not recognizing that the Christ *is* that very Love of God. He will not cast us into hell, they say; there *is* no pit of burning torment. But they know there is something that follows after sin; they know that God is not weak, but abides by his own truth. Therefore, when they have made out God to be Love, and blotted away the old, literal hell, they turn back and declare pitilessly,—'There is *Law*. Law punishes; and Law is inexorable. God Himself does not suspend or contradict his Law. You have sinned; you must take the consequences.' Are you better off in the clutch of that Law, than you were in the old hell? Isn't there the same need as ever crying up from hearts of suffering men for a Saviour? Of a side of God to be shown to them,—the forgiving side, the restoring right hand? The power to grasp and curb his own law? You must have Jesus again! You must have the Christ of God to help you against the Law of God that you have put in the place of the hell you will not believe in. Without a counteracting force, law will run on forever. The impetus that sin started will bear on downward, through the eternities! This is what threatens the sinner; and you have sinned. Beyond and above and through the necessities that He seems to have made, God reveals himself supreme in love, in the Face of Jesus Christ. He comes in the very midst of the clouds, with power and great glory! 'I have *provided* a way,' He says, 'from the foundations,—for you to repent and for Me to take you back. It was a part of my *plan* to forgive. You have seen but half the revolution of my wheel of Law. Fling yourself upon it; believe; you shall be broken; but you shall *not* be ground into powder. You shall find yourselves lifted up into the eternal peace and safety; you shall feel yourself folded in the arms of my tender compassion. The bones that I have broken shall rejoice. Your life shall be set right for you, notwithstanding the Law: yea, *by* the law. *I have provided*. Only believe.'

"This is the word,—the Christ,—on God's part This is repentance and saving faith, on our part. It is the Gospel. And it came by the mouth, and the interpreting and confirming acts, of Jesus. The *power* of the acts was little matter; the *expression* of the acts was everything. He proclaimed forgiveness,—He healed disease; He reversed evil and turned it back. He changed death into life,—taking away the sting—the implantation—of it, which is sin. For evermore the might of the Redemption stands above the might of the Law that was transgressed."

"You have dedicated your chapel, Mr. Kirkbright."

Desire Ledwith said it, with that emotion which makes the voice sound restrained and deep; and as she said it, she turned to go back into the house.

CHAPTER XIX
BLOSSOMING FERNS

The minister's covered carryall was borrowed from two miles off, to take Mrs. Argenter down to Tillington.

All she knew about the winter plan was that Miss Ledwith was a friend of Miss Kirkbright's, had a large, old-fashioned house, and scarcely any household, and would be glad to have herself and Sylvie take rooms with her for several months. She had a vague idea that Miss Ledwith might be somewhat restricted in her means, and that to receive lodgers in a friendly way would be an "object" to her. She talked, indeed, with a gentle complaisance to Miss Kirkbright, about its not being exactly what they had intended,—they had thought of rooms at Hotel Pelham or Boylston, so central and so near the Libraries; but after all, what she needed most was quiet and no stairs; and she had a horror of elevators, and a dread of fire; so that this was really better, perhaps; and Miss Ledwith was a very sweet person.

Miss Euphrasia smiled; "sweet," especially in the silvery tone in which Mrs. Argenter uttered it, was the last monosyllabic epithet she would have selected as applying to grave, earnest, downright Desire.

At East Keaton, the train stopped for five minutes.

Sylvie had begged Mr. Kirkbright beforehand to get her mother's foot-warmer filled with hot water at the station, and he had just returned with it. She was busily arranging it under Mrs. Argenter's feet again, and wrapping the rug about her, kneeling beside her chair to do so, when some one entered the drawing-room car in which the party was, and came up behind her.

She thought she was in the way of some stranger, and hastily arose.

"I beg your pardon," she said, instinctively, and turned as she spoke.

"What for?" asked Rodney Sherrett, holding out both hands, and grasping hers before she was well aware.

There were morning stars in her eyes, and a beautiful sunrise crimsoned her cheek. These two had not seen each other all summer.

Aunt Euphrasia looked from one face to the other.

"Not to say anything for two years!" she thought, recalling inwardly her brother's wise injunction. "It says itself, though; and it was made to!"

"How do you do, Mrs. Argenter? I hope you are feeling better for your country summer? Aunt Effie! *You're* not surprised to see me? Did you think I would let you go down without?"

No; Aunt Effie, when she had written him that regular little Sunday afternoon note from Brickfield, telling him that they were all to come down on Tuesday, had thought no such thing. And she was at this moment, with wise forethought, packed in behind all the others, in the most inaccessible corner of the car.

"You're not going down to the city?"

But he was. Rodney's eyes sparkled as he told her.

"Your own doctrine exemplified. Things always happen, you say. One of the mills is stopped for just this very day of all others,—repairing machinery. I'm off work, for the first time in four months. There has been no low water all summer. Regular header, straight through. Don't you see I'm perfectly emaciated with the confinement? I've breathed in wool-stuffing till I feel like a pincushion."

"An emaciated wool-stuffed pincushion! Yes, I think you do look a little like it!" Aunt Euphrasia talked nonsense just as he did, because she was so pleased she could not help it.

They paired, naturally. Miss Kirkbright and Mrs. Argenter, facing each other in the corner, were eating tongue sandwiches out of the same basket; and Sylvie had poured out for her mother the sugared claret and water with which her little travelling flask had been filled. Mr. Kirkbright had monopolized Desire, sitting upon the opposite side of the car, with another long talk, about brick and tile making, and the compatibility of a paper manufactory and a House of Refuge.

"I will not have it called that, though. It shall not be stamped with any stereotyped name. It shall not even be a Home,—except *my* home; and I'll just take them in: I and Euphrasia."

There was nothing for Rodney to do, but to sit down beside Sylvie, with three hours before him, which he had earned by four months among the wheels and cranks and wool-fluff.

Of all these four months there has been no chance to tell you anything before as concerning him.

He had been at Arlesbury; learning to be a manufacturer; beginning at the beginning with the belts and rollers, spindles, shuttles, and harnesses; finding out the secrets of satinets and doeskins and kerseys; *driving*, as he had wanted to do; taking hold of something and making it go.

"It isn't exactly like trotting tandem," he told Sylvie, "but there's a something living in it, too; a creature to bit and manage; that's what I like about it. But I hate the oil, and the noise, and the dust. Why, *this* is pin-drop silence to it! I hope it won't make me deaf, — and dumb! Father will feel bad if it does," he said, with an indescribably pathetic demureness.

"Was it your father's plan?" asked Sylvie, laughing merrily.

"Well, — yes! At least I told him to take me and set me to work; or I should pretty soon be good for nothing; and so he looked round in a great fright and hurry, as you may imagine, and put me into the first thing he could think of, and that was this. I'm to stay at it for two years, before I — ask him for anything else. I think I shall have a good right then, don't you? I'm thinking all the time about my Three Wishes. I suppose I may wish three times when I begin? They always do."

What could he talk but nonsense? Earnestness had been forbidden him; he had to cover it up with the absurdity of a boy.

But what a blessing that it made no manner of difference! That in all things of light and speech, the gracious law is that the flash should go so much farther, as well as faster than the sound!

Something between them unspoken told the story that words, though they be waited for, never tell half so well. She knew that she had to do with his being in earnest. She knew that she had to do with his being at play, this moment, laughing and joking the time away beside her on this railroad trip. He had come to join Aunt Euphrasia? Yes, indeed, and there sat Aunt Euphrasia in her corner, reading the "Vicar's Daughter," and between times talking a little with Mrs. Argenter. Not ten sentences did aunt and nephew exchange, all the way from East Keaton down to Cambridge. When Mrs. Argenter grew tired as the day wore on, and a sofa was vacated, Rodney helped Sylvie to move the shawls and the foot-warmer, and the rug, and improvise cushions, and make her mother comfortable; then, as Mrs. Argenter fell asleep, they sat near her and chatted on.

And Aunt Euphrasia read her book, and considered herself escorted and attended to, which is just such a convenience as a judicious and amiably disposed female relative appreciates the opportunity for making of herself.

Down somewhere in Middlesex, boys began to come into the cars with great bunches of trailing ferns to sell; exquisite things that people have just begun to find out and clamor for, and that so a boy-supply has vigorously arisen to meet.

"O, how lovely!" cried Sylvie, at one stopping-place, where an urchin stood with his arms full; the glossy, delicate leaves wreathed round and round in long loops, and the feathery blossoms dropping like mist-tips from among them. "And we're too exclusive here, for him to be let in."

Of course the window would not open; drawing-room car windows never do. Rodney rushed to the door; held up a dollar greenback.

"Boy! Here! toss up your load!"

The long train gave its first spasm and creak at starting; up came the tangle of beauty; down fluttered the bit of paper to the platform; and Rodney came in with the rare garlands and tassels drooping all about him.

Everybody was delighted; Aunt Euphrasia dropped her book, and made her way out of her corner; Desire and Mr. Kirkbright handled and exclaimed; Mrs. Argenter opened her eyes, and held out her fingers toward them with a smile.

"Such a quantity—for everybody!" said Sylvie, as he put them into her lap, and she began to shake out the bunches. "How kind you were, Mr. Sherrett! We've longed so to find some of these, haven't we Amata? Has anybody got a newspaper, or two? We'd better keep them all together till we get home." And she coiled the sprays carefully round and round into a heap.

No matter if they should be all given away to the very last leaf; she could thank innocently "for everybody"; but she knew very well what the last leaf, falling to her to keep, would stand for.

In years and years to come, Sylvie will never see climbing ferns again, without a feeling as of all the delicate beauty and significance of the world gathered together in a heap and laid into her lap.

She had seen the dollar that Rodney paid for them, flutter down beside the window as the car moved on, and the boy spring forward to catch it. Rodney Sherrett earned his dollars now. It was one of his very, very own that he spent for her that day. A girl feels a strange thrill when she sees for the first time, a fragment of the life she cares for given, representatively, thus, for her.

It is useless to analyze and explain. Sylvie did not stop to do it, neither did Rodney; but that ride, that little giving and taking, were full of parable and heart-telegraphy between them. That October afternoon was a long, beautiful dream; a dream that must come true, some time. Yet Rodney said to his aunt, as he bade her good-by that evening, at her own door (he had to go back to the station to take the night train up),—"Why shouldn't we have *this* piece of our lives as well as the rest, Auntie? Why should two years be cribbed off? There won't be any too much of it, and there won't be any of it just like this."

Aunt Euphrasia only stooped down from the doorstep, and kissed him on his cheek, saying nothing.

But to herself she said, after he had gone,—

"I don't see why, either. They would be so happy, waiting it out together. And there never *is* any time like this time. How is anybody sure of the rest of it?"

Aunt Euphrasia knew. She had not been sure of the rest of hers.

CHAPTER XX
"WANTED"

The half of course and half critical way in which Mrs. Argenter took possession of the gray parlor would have been funny, if it had not been painful, to Sylvie, feeling almost wrong and wickedly deceitful in betraying her mother, through ignorance of the real arrangements, into a false and unsuitable attitude; and to Desire, for Sylvie's sake.

She thought it would do nicely if the windows weren't too low, and if the little stove-grate could be replaced by an open wood fire. Couldn't she have a Franklin, or couldn't the fire-place be unbricked?

"I don't think you'll mind, with cannel coal," said Sylvie. "That is so cheerful; and there won't be any smoke, for Miss Ledwith says the draught is excellent."

"But it stands out, and takes up room; and people never keep the carpet clean behind it!" said Mrs. Argenter.

"I'll take care of that," said Sylvie. "It is my business. We couldn't have these rooms, you see, except just as I have agreed for them; and you know I like making things nice myself in the morning."

Desire had delicately withdrawn by this time; and presently coming back with a cup of tea upon a little tray, which refreshment she was sure Mrs. Argenter would need at once after her journey, she found the lady sitting quite serenely in the low cushioned chair before the obnoxious grate, in which Sylvie had kindled the lump of cannel that lay all ready for the match, in a folded newspaper, with three little pitch-pine sticks.

There was something so dainty and compact about it, and the bright blaze answered so speedily to the communicating touch, the black layers falling away from each other in rich, bituminous flakiness, and letting the fire-tongues through, that she looked on in the happy complacence with which idle or disabled persons always enjoy something that does itself, yet can be followed in the doing with a certain passive sense of participancy.

In the same manner she watched Sylvie putting away wraps, unlocking trunks, laying forth dressing-gowns and night-clothes, and setting out toilet cases upon table and stand.

For the gray parlor contained now, for Mrs. Argenter's use, a pretty, low, curtained French bed, and the other appliances of a sleeping-room. A bedroom adjoining, which had been Mrs. Froke's, was to be Sylvie's; and this had a further communication directly with the kitchen, which would be just the thing for Sylvie's quiet flittings to and fro in the fulfillment of her gladly undertaken duties. All Mrs. Argenter knew about it was that she should be able to have her hot water promptly in the mornings, without being intruded upon.

Sylvie had insisted upon Desire's receiving the seven dollars a week which she was still able to pay for her mother's board. Nobody had told her of Miss Ledwith's very large wealth, and it would have made no difference if she had known it, except the exciting in her of a quick question why they had been taken in at all, and whether she were not indeed being in her turn benevolently practised upon, as she with much compunction practised upon her mother.

"I know very well that I could not earn, beyond my own board, more than the difference between that and the ten dollars she would have to pay anywhere else," she said, simply. And Miss Kirkbright as simply told Desire, privately, to let it be so.

"If you don't need the pay, she needs the payment," she said.

Desire quietly put it all aside, as she received it. "Sometime or other I shall be able to tell her all about it, and make her take it back," she said. "When she has come to understand, she will know that it is no more mine than hers; and if I do not keep it I can see very well it will all go after the rest, for whatever whims she can possibly gratify her mother in."

There began to be happy times for Sylvie now, in Frendely's kitchen, in Desire's library; all over the house, wherever there was any little care to take, any service to render. Mrs. Argenter did not miss her; she read a great deal, and slept a great deal, and Sylvie was rarely gone long at a time. She was always ready at twilight to play backgammon, or a game of what she called "skin-deep chess," for her mother was not able to bear the exertion or excitement of chess in real, deep earnest. Sylvie brought her sewing, also,—work for Neighbor Street it was, mostly,—into the gray parlor, and "sewed for two," on the principle of the fire-watching, that something busy might be going on in the room, and Mrs. Argenter might have the content of seeing it.

On the Wednesday evenings recurred the delightful "Read-and-Talk," when the Ingrahams came, and Bel Bree, and a dozen or so more of the "other girls"; when on the big table treasures of picture, map, stereoscope and story were brought forth; when they traversed far countries, studied in art-galleries and frescoed churches, traced back old historic associations; did not hurry or rush, but stayed in place after place, at point after point, looking it all thoroughly up, enjoying it like people who could take the world in the leisure of years. And as they did not have the actual miles to go over, the standing about to do, and the fatigues to sleep between, they could "work in the ground fast," like Hamlet, or any other spirit. Their hours stood for months; their two months had given them already winters and summers of enchantment.

Hazel Ripwinkley, and very often Ada Geoffrey, was here at these travelling parties. Ada had all her mother's resources of books, engravings, models, specimens, at her command; she would come with a carriage-full. Sometimes the library was Rome for an evening, with its Sistine Raphaels, its curious relics and ornaments, its Coliseum and St. Peter's in alabaster, its views of tombs, and baths, and temples. Sometimes it was Venice; again it was transformed into a dream of Switzerland, and again, there were the pyramids, the obelisks, the sphinxes, the giant walls and gateways of Egypt, with a Nile boat, and lotus flowers, and papyrus reeds, in reality or facsimile,—even a mummied finger and a scarabœus ring.

They were not restricted, even, to a regular route, when their subject took them out of it. They could have a glimpse of Memphis, or Babylon, or Alexandria, or Athens, by way of following out an allusion or synchronism.

Hazel and Ada almost came to the conclusion that this was the perfection of travelling, and the supersedure of all literal and laborious sightseeing; and Sylvie Argenter ventured the Nipperism that "tea and coffee and spices might or might not be a little different right off the bush, but if shiploads were coming in to you all the time, you might combine things with as much comfort on the whole, perhaps, as you would have in sailing round for every separate pinch to Ceylon, and Java, and Canton."

The leaf had got turned between Leicester Place and Pilgrim Street. I suppose you knew it would as well as I.

Bel Bree had met Dorothy first in silk-and-button errands for her Aunt Blin's "finishings," at the thread-store where Dot tended. (Such machine-sewing as they could obtain, Ray had done at home, since they came into the city; and Dot had taken this place at Brade and Matchett's.) Then they came across each other in their waitings at the Public Library, and so found out their near neighborhood. At last, growing intimate, Dorothy had introduced Bel to the Chapel Bible class, and thence brought her into Desire's especial little club at her own house.

After the travel-talk was over,—and they began with it early, so that all might reach home at a safe hour in the evening,—very often some one or two would linger a few moments for some little talk of confidence or advice with Desire. These girls brought their plans to her; their disappointments, their difficulties, their suggestions; not one would make a change, or take any new action, without telling her. They knew she cared for them. It was the beginning of all religion that she taught them in this faith, this friendliness. Every soul wants some one to come to; it is easy to pass from the experience of human sympathy to the thought of the Divine; without it the Divine has never been revealed.

One bright night in this October, Dot Ingraham waited, letting her sister walk on with Frank Sunderline, who had called for them, and asking Bel Bree to stop a minute and go with her. "We'll take the car, presently," she said to Ray. "We shall be at home almost as soon as you will."

"It is about the shop work," she said to Desire, who stepped back into the library with her.

"I do not think I can do it much longer. I am pretty strong for some things, but this terrible *standing*! I could *walk* all day; but cramped up behind those counters, and then reaching up and down the boxes and things,—I feel sometimes when I get through at night, as if my bones had all been racked. I haven't told them at home, for fear they would worry about me; they think now I've lost flesh, and I suppose I have; and I don't have much appetite; it seems dragged out of me. And then,—I can't say it before the others, for they're in shops, some of 'em, and places may be different; but it's such a window and counter parade, besides; and they do look out for it. People stare in at the store as they go by; Margaret Shoey has the glove counter at that end, and she knows Mr. Matchett keeps her there on purpose to attract; she sets herself up and takes airs upon it; and Sarah Cilley does everything she sees her do, and comes in for the second-hand attention. Mr. Matchett asked me the other day if I couldn't wear a panier, and do up my hair a little more stylish! I can't stay there; it isn't fit for girls!"

Dot's cheeks flamed, and there were tears in her eyes. Desire Ledwith stood with a thoughtful, troubled expression in her own.

"There ought to be other ways," she said. "There ought to be more *sheltered* work for girls!"

"There is," said little Bel Bree from the doorway "in houses. If I hadn't Aunt Blin, I'd go right into a family as seamstress or anything. I don't believe in out-doors and shops. I've only lived in the city a little while, but I've seen it. And just think of the streets and streets of nice houses, where people live, and girls have to live with 'em, to do real woman's home work! And it's all given up to foreign servants, and *our* girls go adrift, and live anyhow. 'Tain't right!"

"There is a good deal that isn't right about it," said Desire, gravely; knowing better than Bel the difficulties in the way of new domestic ideas. "And a part of it is that the houses aren't built, or the ways of living planned, for 'our girls,' exactly. Our girls aren't happy in underground kitchens and sky bedrooms."

"I don't know. They might as well be underground as in some of those close, crowded shops. And their bedrooms can't be much to compare, certain. I'm afraid they like the crowds best. If they wanted to, and would work in, and try, they might contrive. Things fix themselves accordingly, after a while. Somebody's got to begin. I can't help thinking about it."

Desire smiled.

"Your thinking may be a first sign of good times, little Bel," she said. "Think on. That is the way everything begins; with a restlessness in some one or two heads about it. Perhaps that is just what you have come down from New Hampshire for."

"I don't know," said Bel again. She began a good many of her reflective, suggestive little speeches with that hesitating feeler into the fog of social perplexity she essayed. "They're just as bad up there, now. They all get away to the towns, and the trades, and the stores They won't go into the houses; and they might have such good places!"

"You came yourself, you see?"

"Yes. I wasn't contented. And things were particular with me. And I had Aunt Blin. I don't want to go back, either. But I can see how it is."

"Things are particular with each one, in some sort or another. That is what settles it, I suppose, and ought to. The only thing is to be sure that it is a *right* particular that does it; that we don't let in any wrong particular, anywhere. For you, Dorothy, I don't believe shop-life is the thing. You have found it out. Why not change at once? There is the machine at home, and Ray is going to be busy in Neighbor Street. Won't her work naturally come to you?"

"There isn't much of it, and it is so uncertain. The shops take up all the bulk of work nowadays; everything is wholesale; and I don't want to go into the rooms, if I can help it. I don't like days' work, either. The fact is, I want a quiet place, and the same things. I like my own machine. I would go with it into a family, if I could have my own room, and be nice, and not have to eat with careless, common servants in a dirty kitchen. Mother would spare me,—to a real good situation; and I would come home Sundays."

"I see. What you want is somewhere, of course. Wouldn't you advertise?"

"Would *you*?"

"Yes, I think I would. Say exactly what you want, wages and all. And put it into some family Sunday paper,—the 'Christian Register,' for instance. Those things get read over and over; and the same paper lies about a week. In the dailies, one thing crowds out another; a new list every night and morning. See here, I'll write one now. Perhaps it wouldn't be too late for this week. Would you go out of town?"

"*Wouldn't* I? I think sometimes that's just what ails me; wanting to see soft roads and green grass and door-yards and sun between the houses! But I couldn't go far, of course."

Desire's pencil was flying over the paper.

"'Wanted; a permanent situation in a pleasant family, as seamstress, by a young girl used to all kinds of sewing, who will bring her own machine. Would like a room to herself, and to have her meals orderly and comfortable, whether with the family or otherwise. Wages'—What?"

"By the day, I could get a dollar and a quarter, at least; but for a real good home-place, I'd go for four dollars a week."

"'Wages, $4.00 per week. A little way out of town preferred.' There! There are such places, and why shouldn't one come to you? Take that down to the 'Register' office to-morrow morning, and have it put in twice, unless stopped."

"Thank you. It's all easy enough, Miss Ledwith. Why didn't I work it out myself?"

"It isn't quite worked out, yet. But things always look clearer, somehow, through two pairs of eyes. Good-night. Let me know what you hear about it."

"She'll surprise some family with such a seamstress as they read about," said Bel Bree, on the door-step. "I should like to astonish people, sometime, with a heavenly kind of general housework."

"That was a good idea of yours about the Sunday paper," said Sylvie, as she and Hazel and Desire went back into the library to put away the books. "But what when the common sort pick up the dodge, and the weeklies get full of 'Wanteds'? Nothing holds out fresh, very long."

"There *ought* to be," said Desire, "some filtered process for these things; some way of sifting and certifying. A bureau of mutual understanding between the 'real folks,'—employers and employed. I believe it might be. There ought to be for this, and for many things, a fellowship organized, between women of different outward degree. And something will happen, sooner or later, to bring it about. A money crisis, perhaps, to throw these girls out of shop-employment, and to make heads of households look into ways of more careful managing. A mutual need,—or the seeing of it. The need is now; these girls—half of them—want homes, more than anything; and the homes are suffering for the help of just such girls."

"Why don't you edit a paper, Desire? The 'Fellowship Register,' or the 'Domestic Intelligencer,' or something! And keep lists of all the nice, real housekeepers, and the nice, real, willing girls?"

"That isn't a bad notion, Hazie. Your notions never are. May be that is what is waiting for you. Just cover up that 'raised Switzerland,' will you, and bring it over here? And roll up the 'Course of the Rhine,' and set it in the corner. There; now we may put out the gas. Sylvie, has your mother had her fresh camomile tea?"

The three girls bade each other good-night at the stairs; just where Desire had stood once, and put her arms about Uncle Titus's neck for the first time. She often thought of it now, when they went up after the pleasant evenings, and came down in the bright mornings to their cheery breakfasts. She liked to stop on just that step. Nobody knew all it meant to her, when she did. There are places in every dwelling that keep such secrets for one heart and memory alone.

Yes, indeed. Sylvie was very happy now. All her pretty pictures, and little brackets, and her mother's stands and vases in the gray parlor, were hung with the lovely, wreathing, fairy stems of star-leaved, blossomy fern; and the sweet, dry scent was a perpetual subtle message. That day in the train from East Keaton was a day to pervade the winter, as this woodland breath pervaded the old city house. Sylvie could wait with what she had, sure that, sometime, more was coming. She could wait better than Rodney. Because,—she knew she was waiting, and satisfied to wait. How did Rodney know that?

It was what he kept asking his Aunt Euphrasia in his frequent, boyish, yet most manly, letters. And she kept answering, "You need not fear. I think

I understand Sylvie. I can see. If there were anything in the way, I would tell you."

But at last she had to say,—not, "I think I understand Sylvie,"—but, "I understand girls, Rodney. I am a woman, remember. I have been a girl, and I have waited. I have waited all my life. The right girls can."

And Rodney said, tossing up the letter with a shout, and catching it with a loving grasp between his hands again,—

"Good for you, you dear, brave, blessed ace of hearts in a world where hearts are trumps! If you ain't one of the right old girls, then they don't make 'em, and never did!"

CHAPTER XXI
VOICES AND VISIONS

Madame Bylles herself walked into the great work-room of Mesdames Fillmer & Bylles, one Saturday morning.

Madame Bylles was a lady of great girth and presence. If Miss Tonker were sub-aristocratic, Madame Bylles was almost super-aristocratic, so cumulative had been the effect upon her style and manner of constant professional contact with the élite. Carriages had rolled up to her door, until she had got the roll of them into her very voice. Airs and graces had swept in and out of her private audience-room, that had not been able to take all of themselves away again. As the very dust grows golden and precious where certain workmanship is carried on, the touch and step and speech of those who had come ordering, consulting, coaxing, beseeching, to her apartments, had filled them with infinitesimal particles of a sublime efflorescence, by which the air itself in which they floated became—not the air of shop or business or down-town street—but the air of drawing-room, and bon-ton, and Beacon Hill or the New Land.

And Madame Bylles breathed it all the time; she dwelt in the courtly contagion. When she came in among her work-people, it was an advent of awe. It was as if all the elegance that had ever been made up there came floating and spreading and shining in, on one portly and magnificent person.

But when Madame Bylles came in, in one of her majestic hurries! Then it was as if the globe itself had orders to move on a little faster, and make out the year in two hundred and eighty days or so, and she was appointed to see it done.

She was in one of these grand and grave accelerations this morning. Miss Pashaw's marriage was fixed for a fortnight earlier than had been intended, business calling Mr. Soldane abroad. There were dresses to be hurried; work for over-hours was to be given out. Miss Tonker was to use every exertion; temporary hands, if reliable, might be employed. All must be ready by Thursday next; Madame Bylles had given her word for it.

The manner in which she loftily transmitted this grand intelligence, warm from the high-born lips that had favored her with the confidence,—

the air of intending it for Miss Tonker's secondarily distinguished ear alone, while the carriage-roll in her accents bore it to the farthest corner in the room, where the meekest little woman sat basting,—these things are indescribable. But they are in human nature: you can call them up and scrutinize them for yourself.

Madame Bylles receded like a tidal wave, having heaved up, and changed, and overwhelmed all things.

A great buzz succeeded her departure; Miss Tonker followed her out upon the landing.

"I'll speak for that cashmere peignoir that is just cut out. I'll make it nights, and earn me an ostrich band for my hat," said Elise Mokey.

One spoke for one thing; one another; they were claimed beforehand, in this fashion, by a kind of work-women's code; as publishers advertise foreign books in press, and keep the first right by courtesy.

Miss Proddle stopped her machine at last, and caught the news in her slow fashion hind side before.

"We might some of us have overwork, I should think; shouldn't you?" she asked, blandly, of Miss Bree.

Aunt Blin smiled. "They've been squabbling over it these five minutes," she replied.

Aunt Blin was sure of some particular finishing, that none could do like her precise old self.

Kate Sencerbox jumped up impatiently, reaching over for some fringe.

"I shall have to give it up," she whispered emphatically into Bel Bree's ear. "It's no use your asking me to go to Chapel any more. I ain't sanctified a grain. I did begin to think there was a kind of work of grace begun in me,—but I *can't* stand Miss Proddle! What *are* people made to strike ten for, always, when it's eleven?"

"I think *we* are all striking *twelve*" said Bel Bree. "One's too fast, and another's too slow, but the sun goes round exactly the same."

Miss Tonker came back, and the talk hushed.

"Clock struck one, and down they run, hickory, dickory, dock," said Miss Proddle, deliberately, so that her voice brought up the subsiding rear of sound and was heard alone.

"What *under* the sun?" exclaimed Miss Tonker, with a gaze of mingled amazement, mystification, and contempt, at the poor old maiden making such unwonted noise.

"Yes'm," said Kate Sencerbox. "It is 'under the sun,' that we're talking about; the way things turn round, and clocks strike; some too fast, and some too slow; and—whether there's anything new under the sun. I think there is; Miss Proddle made a bright speech, that's all."

Miss Tonker, utterly bewildered, took refuge in solemn and supercilious disregard; as if she saw the joke, and considered it quite beneath remark.

"You will please resume your work, and remember the rules," she said, and sailed down upon the cutters' table.

There was a certain silk evening dress, of singular and indescribably lovely tint,—a tea-rose pink; just the color of the blush and creaminess that mingle themselves into such delicious anonymousness in the exquisite flower. It was all puffed and fluted till it looked as if it had really blossomed with uncounted curving petals, that showed in their tender convolutions each possible deepening and brightening of its wonderful hue.

It *looked* fragrant. It conveyed a subtle sense of flavor. It fed and provoked every perceptive sense.

It was not a dress to be hurried with; every quill and gather of its trimming must be "set just so;" and there was still one flounce to be made, and these others were only basted, as also the corsage.

After the hours were up that afternoon, Miss Tonker called Aunt Blin aside. She uncovered the large white box in which it lay, unfinished.

"You have a nice room, Miss Bree. Can you take this home and finish it,—by Wednesday? In over-hours, I mean; I shall want you here daytimes, as usual. It has been tried on; all but for the hanging of the skirt; you can take the measures from the white one. *That* I shall finish myself."

Aunt Blin's voice trembled with humble ecstasy as she answered. She thanked Miss Tonker in a tone timid with an apprehension of some possible unacceptableness which should disturb or change the favoring grace.

"Certainly, ma'am. I'll spread a sheet on the floor, and put a white cloth on the table. Thank you, ma'am. Yes; I have a nice room, and nothing gets meddled with. It'll be quite safe there. I'm sure I'm no less than happy to be allowed. You're very kind, ma'am."

Miss Tonker said nothing at all to the meekly nervous outpouring. She did not snub her, however; that was something.

Miss Bree and her niece, between them, carried home the large box.

On the way, a dream ran through the head of Bel. She could not help it.

To have this beautiful dress in the house,—perhaps to have to stand up and be tried to, for the fall of its delicate, rosy trail; with the white cloth on the floor, and the bright light all through the room,—why it would be almost like a minute of a ball; and what if the door should be open, and somebody should happen to go by, up-stairs? If she could be so, and be seen so, just one minute, in that blush-colored silk! She should like to look like that, just once, to somebody!

Ah, little Bel! behind all her cosy, practical living—all her busy work and contentedness—all her bright notions of what might be possible, for the better, in things that concerned her class,—she had her little, vague, bewildering flashes of vision, in which she saw impossible things; things that might happen in a book, things that must be so beautiful if they ever did really happen!

A step went up and down the stairs and along the passage by her aunt's room, day by day, that she had learned to notice every time it came. A face had glanced in upon her now and then, when the door stood open for coolness in the warm September weather, when they had been obliged to have a fire to make the tea, or to heat an iron to press out seams in work that they were doing. One or two days of each week, they had taken work home. On those days, they did, perhaps, their own little washing or ironing, besides; sewing between whiles, and taking turns, and continuing at their needles far on into the night. Once Mr. Hewland had come in, to help Aunt Blin with a blind that was swinging by a single hinge, and which she was trying, against a boisterous wind, to reset with the other. After that, he had always spoken to them when he met them. He had opened and shut the street-door for them, standing back, courteously, with his hat in his hand, to let them pass.

Aunt Blin,—dear old simple, kindly-hearted Aunt Blin, who believed cats and birds,—*her* cat and bird, at least,—might be thrown trustfully into each other's company, if only she impressed it sufficiently upon the quadruped's mind from the beginning, that the bird was "very, *very* precious,"—thought Mr. Hewland was "such a nice young man."

And so he was. A nice, genial, well-meaning, well-bred gentleman; above anything ignoble, or consciously culpable, or common. His danger lay in his higher tendencies. He had artistic tastes; he was a lover of all grace and natural sweetness; no line of beauty could escape him. More than that, he drew toward all that was most genuine; he cared nothing for the elegant artificialities among which his social position placed him. He had been singularly attracted by this little New Hampshire girl, fresh and pretty as a wild rose, and full of bright, quaint ways and speech, of which he had caught glimpses and fragments in their near neighborhood. Now and then, from her open window up to his had come her gay, sweet laugh; or her raised, gleeful tone, as she said some funny, quick, shrewd thing in her original fashion to her aunt.

Through the month of August, while work was slack, and the Hewland family was away travelling, and other lodgers' rooms were vacated, the Brees had been more at home, and Morris Hewland had been more in his rooms above, than had been usual at most times. The music mistress had taken a vacation, and gone into the country; only old Mr. Sparrow, lame with one weak ankle, hopped up and down; and the spare, odd-faced landlady glided about the passages with her prim profile always in the same pose, reminding one of a badly-made rag-doll, of which the nose, chin, and chest are in one invincible flat line, interrupted feebly by an unsuccessful hint of drawing in at the throat.

Mr. Hewland liked June for his travels; and July and August, when everybody was out of the way, for his quiet summer work.

The Hewlands called him odd, and let him go; he stayed at home sometimes, and he happened in and out, they knew where to find him, and there was "no harm in Morris but his artistic peculiarities."

He had secured in these out-of-the way-lodgings in Leicester Place, one of the best north lights that could be had in the city; he would not take a room among a lot of others in a Studio Building. So he worked up his studies, painted his pictures, let nobody come near him except as he chose to bring them, and when he wanted anything of the world, went out into the world and got it.

Now, something had come right in here close to him, which brought him a certain sense of such a world as he could not go out into at will, to get what he wanted. A world of simplicities, of blessed contents, of unworn, joyous impulses, of little new, unceasing spontaneities; a world that he looked into, as we used to do at Sattler's Cosmoramas, through the merest peepholes, and comprehended by the merest hints; but which the presence of this girl under the roof with himself as surely revealed to him as the wind-flower reveals the spring.

On her part, Bel Bree got a glimpse, she knew not how, of a world above and beyond her own; a world of beauty, of power, of reach and elevation, in which people like Morris Hewland dwelt. His step, his voice, his words now and then to the friend or two whom he had the habit of bringing in with him,—the mere knowledge that he "made pictures," such pictures as she looked at in the windows and in art-dealers' rooms, where any shop-girl, as freely as the most elegant connoisseur, can go in and delight her eyes, and inform her perceptions,—these, without the face even, which had turned its magnetism straight upon hers only once or twice, and whose revelation was that of a life related to things wide and full and manifold,—gave her the stimulating sense of a something to which she had not come, but to which she felt a strange belonging.

Beside,—alongside—in each mind, was the undeveloped mystery; the spell under which a man receives such intuitions through a woman's presence,—a woman through a man's. Yet these two individuals were not, therefore, going to be necessary to each other, in the plan of God. Other things might show that they were not meant, in rightness, for each other; they represented mutually, something that each life missed; but the something was in no special companionship; it was a great deal wider and higher than that. They might have to learn that it was so, nevertheless, by some briefly painful process of experience. If in this process they should fall into mistake and wrong,—ah, there would come the experience beyond the experience, the depth they were not meant to sound, yet which, if they let their game of life run that way, they could not get back from but through the uttermost. They must play it out; the move could not be taken back,— yet awhile. The possible better combinations are in God's knowledge; how He may ever reset the pieces and give his good chances again, remains the hidden hope, resting upon the Christ that is in the heart of Him.

One morning Morris Hewland had come up the stairs with a handful of tuberoses; he was living at home, then, through the pleasant September, at his father's country place, whence the household would soon remove to the city for the winter.

Miss Bree's door was open. She was just replacing her door-mat, which she had been shaking out of the entry window. She had an old green veil tied down over her head to keep the dust off; nobody could suspect any harm of a wish or a willingness to have a word with her; Morris Hewland could not have suspected it of himself, if he had indeed got so far as to investigate his passing impulses. There was something pitiful in the contrast, perhaps, of the pure, fresh, exquisite blossoms, and the breath of sweet air he and they brought with them in their swift transit from the places where it blessed all things to the places where so much languished in the need of it, not knowing, even, the privation. The old, trodden, half-cleansed door-mat in her hands,—the just-created beauty in his. He stopped, and divided his handful.

"Here, Miss Bree,—you would like a piece of the country, I imagine, this morning! I couldn't have come in without it."

The voice rang blithe and bright into the room where Bel sat, basting machine work; the eyes went after the voice.

The light from the east window was full upon the shining hair, the young, unworn outlines, the fresh, pure color of the skin. Few city beauties could bear such morning light as that. Nothing but the morning in the face can meet it.

Morris Hewland lifted his hat, and bowed toward the young girl, silently. Then he passed on, up to his room. Bel heard his step, back and forth, overhead.

The tuberoses were put into a clear, plain tumbler. Bel would not have them in the broken vase; she would not have them in a *blue* vase, at all. She laid a white napkin over the red of the tablecloth, and set them on it. The perfume rose from them and spread all through the room.

"I am so glad we have work at home to-day," said Bel.

There had been nothing but little things like these; out into Bel's head, as she and Aunt Blin carried home the tea-blush silk, and laid it by with care in its white box upon the sofa-end, came that little wish, with a spring and a heart-beat,—"If she might have it on for a minute, and if in that minute he might happen to come by!"

She did not think she was planning for it; but when on the Tuesday evening the step went down the stairs at eight o'clock, while they sat busily working, each at a sleeve, by the drop-light over the white-covered table, a little involuntary calculation ran through her thoughts.

"He always comes back by eleven. We shall have two hours' work—or more,—on this, if we don't hurry; and it's miserable to hurry!"

They stitched on, comfortably enough; yet the sleeves were finished sooner than she expected. Before nine o'clock, Aunt Blin was sewing them in. Then Bel wanted a drink of water; then they could not both get at the waist together; there was no need.

"I'll do it," said Bel, out of her conscience, with a jump of fright as she said it, lest Aunt Blin should take her at her word, and begin gauging and plaiting the skirt.

"No, you rest. I shall want you by and by, for a figure."

"May I have it *all* on?" says Bel eagerly. "Do, Auntie! I should just like to be in such a dress once—a minute!"

"I don't see any reason why not. *You* couldn't do any hurt to it, if 'twas made for a queen," responded Aunt Blin.

"I'll do up my hair on the top of my head," said Bel.

And forthwith, at the far end of the room, away from the delicate robe and its scattered material, she got out her combs and brushes, and let down her gleaming brown hair.

It took different shades, from umber to almost golden, this "funny hair" of hers, as she called it. She thought it was because she had faded it, playing out in the sun when she was a child; but it was more like having got the shine into it. It did not curl, or wave; but it grew in lovely arches, with roots even set, around her temple and in the curves of her neck; and now, as she combed it up in a long, beautiful mass, over her grasping hand, raising it with each sweep higher toward the crown of her pretty head, all this vigorous, beautiful growth showed itself, and marked with its shadowy outline the dainty shapings. One twist at the top for the comb to go in, and then she parted it in two, and coiled it like a golden-bronze cable; and laid it round and round till the foremost turn rested like a wreath midway about her head. She pulled three fresh geranium leaves and a pink-white umbel of blossom from the plant in the window, and tucked the cluster among the soft front locks against the coil above the temple.

Then she took off the loose wrapping-sack she had thrown over her shoulders, washed her fingers at the basin, and came back to her seat under the lamp.

Aunt Blin looked up at her and smiled. It was like having it all herself,—this youth and beauty,—to have it belonging to her, and showing its charming ways and phases, in little Bel. Why shouldn't the child, with her fair, sweet freshness, and the deep-green, velvety leaves making her look already like a rose against which they leaned themselves, have on this delicate rose dress? If things stayed, or came, where they belonged, to whom should it more fittingly fall to wear it than to her?

Bel watched the clock and Aunt Blin's fingers.

It was ten when the plaits and gathers were laid, and the skirt basted to its band for the trying. Bel was dilatory one minute, and in a hurry the next.

"It would be done too soon; but he might come in early; and, O dear, they hadn't thought,—there was that puffing to put round the corsage, bertha-wise, with the blonde edging. 'It was all ready; give it to her.'"

"Now!"

The wonderful, glistening, aurora-like robe goes over her head; she stands in the midst, with the tender glowing color sweeping out from her upon the white sheet pinned down above the carpet.

Was that anybody coming?

Aunt Blin left her for an instant to put up the window-top that had been open to cool the lighted and heated room. Bel might catch cold, standing like this.

"O, it is *so* warm, Auntie! We can't have everything shut up!" And with this swift excuse instantly suggesting itself and making justification to her deceitful little heart that lay in wait for it, Bel sprang to the opposite corner where the doorway opened full toward her, diagonally commanding the room. She set it hastily just a hand's length ajar. "There is no wind in the entry, and nobody will come," she said.

When she was only excitedly afraid there wouldn't! I cannot justify little Bel. I do not try to.

"Now, see! isn't it beautiful?"

"It sags just a crumb, here at the left," said Aunt Blin, poking and stooping under Bel's elbow. "No; it is only a baste give way. You shouldn't have sprung so, child."

The bare neck and the dimpled arms showed from among the cream-pink tints like the high white lights upon the rose. Bel had not looked in the glass yet: Aunt Blin was busy, and she really had not thought of it; she was happy just in being in that beautiful raiment—in the heart of its color and shine; feeling its softly rustling length float away from her, and reach out radiantly behind. What is there about that sweeping and trailing that all women like, and that becomes them so? That even the little child pins a shawl about her waist and walks to and fro, looking over her shoulder, to get a sensation of?

The door *did* shut, below. A step did come up the stairs, with a few light springs.

Suddenly Bel was ashamed!

She did not want it, now that it had come! She had set a dreadful trap for herself!

"O, Aunt Blin, let me go! Put something over me!" she whispered.

But Aunt Blin was down on the floor, far behind her, drawing out and arranging the slope of the train, measuring from hem to band with her professional eye.

The footstep suddenly checked; then, as if with an as swift bethinking, it went by. But through that door ajar, in that bright light that revealed the room, Morris Hewland had been smitten with the vision; had seen little Bel Bree in all the possible flush of fair array, and marvelous blossom of consummate, adorned loveliness.

Somehow, it broke down the safeguard he had had.

In what was Bel Bree different, really, from women who wore such robes as that, with whom he had danced and chatted in drawing-rooms? Only in being a thousand times fresher and prettier.

After that, he began to make reasons for speaking to them. He brought Aunt Blin a lot of illustrated papers; he lent them a stereoscope, with Alpine and Italian views; he brought down a picture of his own, one day, to show them; before October was out, he had spent an evening in Aunt Blin's room, reading aloud to them "Mirèio."

Among the strange metaphysical doublings which human nature discovers in itself, there is such a fact, not seldom experienced, as the dreaming of a dream.

It is one thing to dream utterly, so that one believes one is awake; it is another to sleep in one's dream, and in a vision give way to vision. It is done in sleep, it is done also in life.

This was what Bel Bree—and it is with her side of the experience that I have business—was in danger now of doing.

It is done in life, as to many forms of living—as to religion, as to art. People are religious, not infrequently because they are in love with the idea of being so, not because they are simply and directly devoted to God. They are æsthetic, because "The Beautiful" is so beautiful, to see and to talk of, and they choose to affect artistic having and doing; but they have not come even into that sheepfold by the door, by the honest, inevitable pathway that their nature took because it must,—by the entrance that it found through a force of celestial urging and guidance that was behind them all the while, though they but half knew it or understood.

Women fall in love that way, so often! It is a lovely thing to be loved; there is new living, which seems to them rare and grand, into which it offers to lift them up. They fall into a dream about a dream; they do not lay them down to sleep and give the Lord their souls to keep, till He shall touch their trustful rest with a divine fire, and waken them into his apocalypse.

It was this atmosphere in which Morris Hewland lived, and which he brought about him to transfuse the heavier air of her lowly living, that bewildered Bel. And she knew that she was bewildered. She knew that it was the poetic side of her nature that was stirred, excited; not the real deep, woman's heart of her that found, suddenly, its satisfying. If women will look, they can see this.

She knew—she had found out—that she was a fair picture in the artist's eyes; that the perception keen to discover and test and analyze all harmonies of form and tint,—holding a hallowed, mysterious kinship in this power to the Power that had made and spoken by them,—turned its search upon her, and found her lovely in the study. It was as if a daisy bearing the pure message and meaning of the heavenly, could thrill with the consciousness of its transmission; could feel the exaltation of fulfilling to a human soul, grand in its far up mystery and waiting upon God,—one of his dear ideas.

There was something holy in the spirit with which she thus realized her possession of maidenly beauty; her gift of mental charm and fitness even; it was the countersign by which she entered into this realm of which Morris Hewland had the freedom; it belonged to her also,—she to it; she had received her first recognition. It was a look back into Paradise for this Eve's daughter, born to labor, but with a reminiscence in her nature out of which she had built all her sweetest notions of being, doing, abiding; from which came the-home-picture, so simple in its outlines, but so rich and gentle in all its significance, that she had drawn to herself as "her wish"; the thing she would give most, and do most, to have come true.

But all this was not necessarily love, even in its beginning,—though she might come for a while to fancy it so,—for this one man. It was a thing between her own life and the Maker of it; an unfolding of herself toward that which waited for her in Him, and which she should surely come to, whatever she might grasp at mistakenly and miss upon the way.

Morris Hewland—young, honest-hearted, but full of a young man's fire and impulse, of an artist's susceptibility to outward beauty, of the ready delight of educated taste in fresh, natural, responsive cleverness—was treading dangerous ground.

He, too, knew that he was bewildered; and that if he opened his eyes he should see no way out of it. Therefore he shut his eyes and drifted on.

Aunt Blin, with her simplicity,—her incapacity of believing, though there might be wrong and mischief in the world, that anybody she knew could ever do it, sat there between them, the most bewildered, the most inwardly and utterly befooled of the three.

CHAPTER XXII
BOX FIFTY-TWO

In the midst of it all, she went and caught a horrible cold.

Aunt Blin, I mean.

It was all by wearing her india-rubbers a week too long, a week after she had found the heels were split; and in that week there came a heavy rain-storm.

She had to stay at home now. Bel went to the rooms and brought back button-holes for her to make. She could not do much; she was feverish and languid, and her eyes suffered. But she liked to see something in the basket; she was always going to be "well enough to-morrow." When the work had to be returned, Bel hurried, and did the button-holes of an evening.

Mr. Hewland brought grapes and oranges and flowers to Miss Bree. Bel fetched home little presents of her own to her aunt, making a pet of her: ice-cream in a paper cone, horehound candy, once, a tumbler of black currant jelly. But that last was very dear. If Aunt Blin had eaten much of other things, they could not have afforded it, for there were only half earnings now.

To-morrow kept coming, but Miss Bree kept on not getting any better. "She didn't see the reason," she said; "she never had a cold hang on so. She believed she'd better go out and shake it off. If she could have rode down-town she would, but somehow she didn't seem to have the strength to walk."

The reason she "couldn't have rode," was because all the horses were sick. It was the singular epidemic of 1872. There were no cars, no teams; the queer sight was presented in a great city, of the driveways as clear as the sidewalks; of nobody needed to guard the crossings or unsnarl the "blocks;" of stillness like Sunday, day after day; of men harnessed into wagons,—eight human beings drawing, slowly and heavily, what any poor old prickle-ribs of a horse, that had life left in him at all, would have trotted cheerfully off with. A lady's trunk was a cartload; and a lady's trunk passing through the streets was a curiosity; you could scarcely get one carried for love or money.

Aunt Blin was a good deal excited; she always was by everything that befell "her Boston." She would sit by the window in her blanket shawl, and peer down the Place to see the mail-carts and express wagons creep slowly by, along Tremont Street, to and from the railways. She was proud for the men who turned to and did quadruped work with a will in the emergency, and so took hold of its sublimity; she was proud of the poor horses, standing in suffering but royal seclusion in their stables, with hostlers sitting up nights for them, and the world and all its business "seeing how it could get along without them;" she was proud of all this crowd of business that had, by hook or by crook (literally, now), to be done.

She wanted the evening paper the minute it came. She and the music mistress took the "Transcript" between them, and had the first reading weeks about. This was her week; she held herself lucky.

The epizootic was like the war: we should have to subside into common items that would not seem like news at all when that was over.

We all know, now, what the news was after the epizootic.

Meanwhile Aunt Blin believed, "on her conscience," she had got the epidemic herself.

Bel had worked hard at the rooms this week, and late at home in the evenings. Some of the girls lived out at the Highlands, and some in South Boston; there were days when they could not get in from these districts; for such as were on the spot there was double press and hurry. And it was right in the midst of fall and winter work. Bel earned twelve dollars in six days, and got her pay.

On Saturday night she brought home four Chater's crumpets, and a pint of oysters. She stewed the oysters in a porringer out of which everything came nicer than out of any other utensil. While they were stewing, she made a bit of butter up into a "pat," and stamped it with the star in the middle of the pressed glass saltcellar; she set the table near the fire, and laid it out in a specially dainty way; then she toasted the muffins, and it was past seven o'clock before all was done.

Aunt Blin sat by, and watched and smelled. She was in no hurry; two senses at a time were enough to have filled. She had finished the paper,—it was getting to be an old and much rehashed story, now,—and had sent it down to Miss Smalley. It would be hers first, now, for a week. Very well, the excitement was over. That was all she knew about it.

In the privacy and security of her own room, and with muffins and oysters for tea, Aunt Blin took out her upper teeth, that she might eat comfortably. Poor Aunt Blin! she showed her age and her thinness so. She had fallen away a good deal since she had been sick. But she was getting better. On Monday morning, she thought she would certainly be able to go out. All she had to do now was to be careful of her cough; and Bel had just bought her a new pair of rubbers.

Bartholomew had done his watching and smelling, likewise; he had made all he could be expected to of that limited enjoyment. Now he walked round the table with an air of consciousness that supper was served. He sat by his mistress's chair, lifted one paw with well-bred expressiveness, stretching out the digits of it as a dainty lady extends her lesser fingers when she lifts her cup, or breaks a bit of bread. It was a delicate suggestion of exquisite appreciation, and of most excellent manners. Once he began a whine, but recollected himself and suppressed it, as the dainty lady might a yawn.

Aunt Blin gave him two oysters, and three spoonfuls of broth in his own saucer, before she helped herself. After all, she ate in her turn very little more. It was hardly worth while to have made a business of being comfortable.

"I don't think they have such good oysters as they used to," she remarked, stepping over her s'es in a very carpeted and stocking-footed way.

"Perhaps I didn't put enough seasoning"—Bel began, but was interrupted in the middle of her reply.

The big bell two squares off clanged a heavy stroke caught up on the echo by others that sounded smaller farther and farther away, making their irregular, yet familiar phrase and cadence on the air.

It was the fire alarm.

"H—zh! Hark!" Aunt Blin changed the muffled but eager monosyllable to a sharper one; and being reminded, felt in her lap, under her napkin, for her "ornaments," as Bel called them.

But she counted the strokes before she put them in, nodding her head, and holding up her finger to Bel and Bartholomew for silence. Everything stopped where it was with Miss Bree when the fire alarm sounded.

One—two—three—four—five.

"In the city," said Aunt Blin, with a certain weird unconscious satisfaction; and whipped the porcelains into their places before the second tolling should begin. They were like Pleasant Riderhood's back hair: she was all twisted up, now, and ready.

One—two.

"That ain't fur off. Down Bedford Street way. Give me the fire-book, and my glasses."

She turned the folds of the card with one hand, and adjusted her spectacles with the other.

"Bedford and Lincoln. Why, that's close by where Miss Proddle boards!"

"That's the *box*, Auntie. You always forget the fire isn't in the box."

"Well, it will be if they don't get along with their steamers. I ain't heard one go by yet."

"They haven't any horses, you know."

"Hark! there's one now! O, *do* hush! There's the bell again!"

Bel was picking up the tea-things for washing. She set down the little pile which she had gathered, went to the window, and drew up the blind.

"My gracious! And there's the fire!"

It shone up, red, into the sky, from over the tall roofs.

Ten strokes from the deep, deliberate bells.

"There comes Miss Smalley, todillating up to see," said Bel, excitedly.

"And the people are just *rushing* along Tremont Street!"

"*Can* you see? asked Miss Smalley, bustling in like the last little belated hen at feeding-time, with a look on all sides at once to discover where the corn might be.

"*Isn't* it big, O?" And she stood up, tiptoe, by the window, as if that would make any comparative difference between her height and that of Hotel Devereux, across the square; or as if she could reach up farther with her eyes after the great flashes that streamed into the heavens.

Again the smiting clang,—repeated, solemn, exact. No flurry in those measured sounds, although their continuance tolled out a city's doom.

Twice twelve.

"There goes Mr. Sparrow," said the music mistress, as the watchmaker's light, unequal hop came over the stairs. "I suppose he can see from his window pretty near where it is."

A slight, dull color came up into the angles of the little lady's face, as she alluded to the upper lodger's room, for there was a tacit impression in the house—and she knew it—that if Miss Smalley and Mr. Sparrow had been thrown together earlier in life, it would have been very suitable; and that even now it might not be altogether too late.

Another step went springing down. Bel knew that, but she said nothing.

"Don't you think we might go out to the end of the street and see?" suggested Miss Smalley.

Bel had on hat and waterproof in a moment.

"Don't you stir, Auntie, to catch cold, now! We'll be back directly."

Miss Smalley was already in her room below, snatching up hood and shawl.

Down the Place they went, and on, out into the broad street. Everybody was running one way,—northward. They followed, hurrying toward the great light, glowing and flashing before them.

From every westward avenue came more men, speeding in ever thickening lines verging to one centre. Like streams into a river channel, they poured around the corners into Essex Street, at last, filling it from wall to wall,—a human torrent.

"This is as far as we can go," Miss Smalley said, stopping in one of the doorways of Boylston Market. A man in a blouse stood there, ordering the driver of a cart.

"Where is the fire, sir?" asked Miss Smalley, with a ladylike air of not being used to speak to men in the street, but of this being an emergency.

"Corner of Kingston and Summer; great granite warehouse, five stories high," said the man in the blouse, civilly, and proceeding to finish his order, which was his own business at the moment, though Boston was burning.

The two women turned round and went back. The heavy bells were striking three times twelve.

A boy rushed past them at the corner by the great florist's shop. He was going the other way from the fire, and was impatient to do his errand and get back. He had a basket of roses to carry; ordered for some one to whom it would come,—the last commission of that sort done that night perhaps,—as out of the very smoke and terror of the hour; a singular lovely message of peace, of the blessed thoughts that live between human hearts though a world were in ashes. All through the wild night, those exquisite buds would be silently unfolding their gracious petals. How strange the bloomed-out roses would look to-morrow!

All the house in Leicester Place was astir, and recklessly mixed up, when Miss Smalley and Bel Bree came back. The landlady and her servant were up in Mr. Sparrow's room, calling to Miss Bree below. The whole place was full of red fierce light.

Aunt Blin, faithful to Bel's parting order, stood in the spirit of an unrelieved sentinel, though the whole army had broken camp, keeping herself steadfastly safe, in her own doorway. To be sure, there was a draught there, but it was not her fault.

"I *must* go up and see it," she said eagerly, when Bel appeared. Bel drew her into the room, put her first into a gray hospital dressing-gown, then into a waterproof, and after all covered her up with a striped blue and white bed comforter. She knew she would keep dodging in and out, and she might as well go where she would stay quiet.

And so these three women went up-stairs, where they had never been before. The door of Mr. Hewland's room was open. A pair of slippers lay in the middle of the floor; a newspaper had fluttered into a light heap, like a broken roof, beside them; a dressing-gown was thrown over the back of a chair.

Bel came last, and shut that door softly as she passed, not letting her eyes intrude beyond the first involuntary glimpse. She was maidenly shy of the place she had never seen,—where she had heard the footsteps go in and out, over her head.

The five women crowded about and into Mr. Sparrow's little dormer window. Miss Smalley lingered to notice the little black teapot on the grate-bar, where a low fire was sinking lower,—the faded cloth on the table, and the empty cup upon it,—the pipe laid down hastily, with ashes falling out of it. She thought how lonesome Mr. Sparrow was living,—doing for himself.

All the square open space down through which the blue heavens looked between those great towering buildings, was filled with brightness as with a flood. The air was lurid crimson. Every stone and chip and fragment, lay revealed in the strange, transfiguring light. Away across the stable-roofs, they could read far-off signs painted in black letters upon brick walls. Church spires stood up, bathed in a wild glory, pointing as out of some day of doom, into the everlasting rest. The stars showed like points of clear, green, unearthly radiance, against that contrast of fierce red.

It surged up and up, as if it would over-boil the very stars themselves. It swayed to right,—to left; growing in an awful bulk and intensity, without changing much its place, to their eyes, where they stood. On the tops of the high Apartment Hotel, and all the flat-roofed houses in Hero and Pilgrim streets, were men and women gazing. Their faces, which could not have been discerned in the daylight, shone distinct in this preternatural illumination. Their voices sounded now and then, against the yet distant hum and crackle of the conflagration, upon the otherwise still air. The rush had, for a while, gone by. The streets in this quarter were empty.

Grand and terrible as the sight was to them in Leicester Place, they could know or imagine little of what the fire was really doing.

"It backs against the wind," they heard one man say upon the stable-roof.

They could not resist opening the window, just a little, now and then, to listen; though Bel would instantly pull Aunt Blin away, and then they would put it down. Poor Aunt Blin's nose grew very cold, though she did not know it. Her nose was little and sensitive. It is not the big noses that feel the cold the most. Aunt Blin took cold through her face and her feet; and these the dressing-gown, and the waterproof, and the comforter, did not protect.

"It must have spread among those crowded houses in Kingston and South streets," Aunt Blin said; and as she spoke, her poor old "ornaments" chattered.

"Aunt Blin, you *shall* come down, and take something hot, and go to bed!" exclaimed Bel, peremptorily. "We can't stay here all night. Mr. Sparrow will be back,—and everybody. I think the fire is going down. It's pretty still now. We've seen it all. Come!"

They had never a thought, any of them, of more than a block or so, burning. Of course the firemen would put it out. They always did.

"See! See!" cried the landlady. "O my sakes and sorrows!"

A huge, volcanic column of glittering sparks—of great flaming fragments—shot up and soared broad and terrible into the deep sky. A long, magnificent, shimmering, scintillant train—fire spangled with fire—swept southward like the tail of a comet, that had at last swooped down and wrapped the earth.

"The roofs have fallen in," said innocent old Miss Smalley.

"That will be the last. Now they will stop it," said Bel. "Come, Auntie!"

And after midnight, for an hour or more, the house, with the five women in it, hushed. Aunt Blin took some hot Jamaica ginger, and Bel filled a jug with boiling water, wrapped it in flannel, and tucked it into the bed at her feet. Then she gave her a spoonful of her cough-mixture, took off her own clothes, and lay down.

Still the great fire roared, and put out the stars. Still the room was red with the light of it. Aunt Blin fell asleep.

Bel lay and listened, and wondered. She would not move to get up and look again, lest she should rouse her aunt. Suddenly, she heard the boom of a great explosion. She started up.

Miss Smalley's voice sounded at the door.

"It's awful!" she whispered, through the keyhole, in a ghostly way. "I thought you ought to know. The cinders are flying everywhere. I heard an engine come up from the railroad. People are running along the streets, and teams are going, and everything,—*the other way*! They're blowing up houses! There, don't you hear that?"

It was another sullen, heavy roar.

Bel sprang out of bed; hurried into her garments; opened the door to Miss Smalley. They went and stood together in the entry-window.

"All Kingman's carriages are out; sick horses and all; they've trundled wheelbarrow loads of things down to the stable. There's a heap of furniture dumped down in the middle of the place. Women are going up Tremont Street with bundles and little children. Where *do* you s'pose it's got to?"

"See there!" said Bel, pointing across the square to the great, dark, public building. High up, in one of the windows, a gas-light glimmered. Two men were visible in the otherwise deserted place. They were putting up a step-ladder.

"Do you suppose they are there nights,—other nights?" Bel asked Miss Smalley.

"No. They're after books and things. They're going to pack up."

"The fire *can't* be coming here!"

Bel opened the window carefully, as she spoke. A man was standing in the livery-stable door. A hack came rapidly down, and the driver called out something as he jumped off.

"Where?" they heard the hostler ask.

"Most up to Temple Place."

"Do they mean the fire? They can't!"

They did; but they were, as we know, somewhat mistaken. Yet that great, surf-like flame, rushing up and on, was rioting at the very head of Summer Street, and plunging down Washington. Trinity Church was already a blazing wreck.

"Has it come up Summer Street, or how?" asked Bel, helplessly, of helpless Miss Smalley. "Do you suppose Fillmer & Bylles is burnt?"

"I *must* ask somebody!"

These women, with no man belonging to them to come and give them news,—restrained by force of habit from what would have been at another time strange to do, and not knowing even yet the utter exceptionality of this time,—while down among the hissing engines and before the face of the conflagration stood girls in delicate dress under evening wraps, come from gay visits with brothers and friends, and drawn irresistibly by the grand, awful magnetism of the spectacle,—while up on the aristocratic avenues, along Arlington Street, whose windows flashed like jewels in the far-shining flames, where the wonderful bronze Washington sat majestic and still against that sky of stormy fire as he sits in every change and beautiful surprise of whatever sky of cloud or color may stretch about him,—on Commonwealth Avenue, where splendid mansions stood with doors wide open, and drays unloading merchandise saved from the falling warehouses into their freely offered shelter,—ladies were walking to and fro, as if in their own halls and parlors, watching, and questioning whomsoever came, and saying to each other hushed and solemn or excited words,—when the whole city was but one great home upon which had fallen a mighty agony and wonder that drove its hearts to each other as the hearts of a household,—these two, Bel Bree and little Miss Smalley, knew scarcely anything that was definite, and had been waiting and wondering all night, thinking it would be improper to talk into the street!

A young lad came up the court at last; he lived next door; he was an errand-boy in some great store on Franklin Street. His mother spoke to him from her window.

"Bennie! how is it?"

"Mother! All Boston is gone up! Summer Street, High Street, Federal Street, Pearl Street, Franklin Street, Milk Street, Devonshire Street,—everything, clear through to the New Post Office. I've been on the Common all night, guarding goods. There's another fellow there now, and I've come home to get warm. I'm almost frozen."

His mother was at the door as he finished speaking, and took him in; and they heard no more.

The boy's words were heavy with heavy meaning. He said them without any boy-excitement; they carried their own excitement in the heart of them. In those eight hours he had lived like a man; in an experience that until of late few men have known.

They did not know how long they stood there after that, with scarcely a word to each other,—only now and then some utterance of sudden recollection of this and that which must have vanished away within that stricken territory,—taking in, slowly, the reality, the tremendousness of what had happened,—was happening.

It was five o'clock when Mr. Hewland came in, and up the stairs, and found them there. Aunt Blin had not awaked. There was a trace of morphine in her cough-drops, and Bel knew now, since she had slept so long, that she would doubtless sleep late into the morning. That was well. It would be time enough to tell her by and by. There would be all day,—all winter,—to tell it in.

Mr. Hewland told them, hastily, the main history of the fire.

"Is Trinity Church?"—asked poor Miss Smalley tremblingly.

She had not said anything about it to Bel Bree; she could not think of that great stone tower as having let the fire in,—as not having stood, cool and strong, against any flame. And Trinity Church was *her* tower. She had sat in one seat in its free gallery for fourteen years. If that were gone, she would hardly know where to go, to get near to heaven. Only nine days ago,—All Saints' Day,—she had sat there listening to beautiful words that laid hold upon the faith of all believers, back through the church, back before Christ to the prophets and patriarchs, and told how God was *her* God because He had been theirs. The old faith,—and the Old Church! "Was Trinity?"—She could not say,—"burned."

But Mr. Hewland answered in one word,—"Gone."

That word answered so many questions on which life and love hung, that fearful night!

Mr. Hewland was wet and cold. He went up to his room and changed his clothing. When the daylight, pale and scared, was creeping in, he came down again.

"Would you not like to go down and see?" he said to Bel.

"Can I?"

"Yes. There is no danger. The streets are comparatively clear. I will go with you."

Bel asked Miss Smalley.

"Will you come? Auntie will be sure to sleep, I think."

Miss Smalley had scarcely heart either to go or stay. Of the two, it was easier to go. To do—to see—something.

Mr. Sparrow came in. He met them at the door, and turned directly back with them.

He, too, was a free-seat worshipper at Old Trinity. He and the music-mistress—they were both of English birth, hence of the same national faith—had been used to go from the same dwelling, separately, to the same house of worship, and sit in opposite galleries. But their hearts had gone up together in the holy old words that their lips breathed in the murmur of the congregation. These links between them, of country and religion, which they had never spoken of, were the real links.

As they went forth this Sunday morning, in company for the first time, toward the church in which they should never kneel again, they felt another,—the link that Eve and Adam felt when the sword of flame swept Paradise.

Plain old souls!—Plain old bodies, I mean, hopping and "todillating"— as Bel expressed the little spinster's gait—along together; their souls walked in a sweet and gracious reality before the sight of God.

Bel and Mr. Hewland were beside each other. They had never walked together before, of course; but they hardly thought of the unusualness. The time broke down distinctions; nothing looked strange, when everything was so.

They went along by the Common fence. In the street, a continuous line of wagons passed them, moving southward. Gentlemen sat on cart-fronts beside the teamsters, accompanying their fragments of property to places of bestowal. Inside the inclosure, in the malls, along under the trees, upon the grass, away back to the pond, were heaps of merchandise. Boxes, bales, hastily collected and unpacked goods of all kinds, from carpets to cotton-spools, were thrown in piles, which men and boys were guarding, the police passing to and fro among them all. People were wrapped against the keen November cold, in whatsoever they could lay their hands on. A group of men pacing back and forth before a pyramid of cases, had thrown great soft white blankets about their shoulders, whose bright striped borders hung fantastically about them, and whose corners fell and dragged upon the muddy ground.

Down by Park Street corner, and at Winter Street, black columns of coal smoke went up from the steamers; the hose, like monstrous serpents, twisted and trailed along the pavements; water stood in pools and flowed in runnels, everywhere.

They went down Winter Street, stepping over the hose-coils, and across the leaking streams; they came to the crossing of Washington, where yesterday throngs of women passed, shopping from stately store to store.

Beyond, were smoke and ruin; swaying walls, heaps of fallen masonry, chevaux-de-frises of bristling gas and water-pipes, broken and protruding. A little way down, to the left, sheets of flame, golden in the gray daylight, were pouring from the face of the beautiful "Transcript" building.

They stood, fearful and watchful, under the broken granite walls opposite Trinity Church.

Windows and doors were gone from the grand old edifice; inside, the fire was shining; devouring at its dreadful ease, the sacred architecture and furnishings that it had swept down to the ground.

"See! There he is!" whispered Miss Smalley to Mr. Sparrow, as she gazed with unconscious tears falling fast down her pale old cheeks.

It was the Rector of Trinity, who thought to have stood this morning in the holy place to speak to his people. Down the middle of the street he came, and went up to the cumbered threshold and the open arch, within which a terrible angel was speaking in his stead.

"Do you think he remembers now, what he said about the God of Daniel, as he looks into the blazing fiery furnace?"

"I dare say he doesn't ever remember what he *said*; but he remembers always what *is*," answered the watch-maker.

CHAPTER XXIII
EVENING AND MORNING: THE SECOND DAY

The strange, sad Sunday wore along.

The teams rolled on, incessantly, through the streets; the blaze and smoke went up from the sixty acres of destruction; friends gathered together and talked of the one thing, that talk as they might, would not be put into any words. Men whose wealth had turned to ashes in a night went to and fro in the same coats they had worn yesterday, and hardly knew yet whether they themselves were the same or not. It seemed, so strangely, as if the clock might be set back somehow, and yesterday be again; it was so little way off!

Women who had received, perhaps, their last wages for the winter on Saturday night, sat in their rooms and wondered what would be on Monday.

Aunt Blin was excited; strong with excitement. She went down-stairs to see Miss Smalley, who was too tired to sit up.

Out of the fire, Bel Bree and Paulina Smalley had each brought something that remained by them secretly all this day.

When they had stopped there under those smoked and shattered walls, and Morris Hewland had drawn Bel's hand within his arm to keep her from any movement into danger, he had gently laid his own fingers, in care and caution, upon hers. A feeling had come to them both with the act, and for a moment, as if the world, with all its great built-up barriers of stone, had broken down around them, and lay at their feet in fragments, among which they two stood free together.

The music-mistress and the watchmaker, looking in upon their place of prayer, seeing it empty and eaten out by the yet lingering tongues of fire, had exchanged those words about the things that *are*. For a minute, through the emptiness, they reached into the eternal deep; for a minute their simple souls felt themselves, over the threshold of earthly ruin, in the spaces where there is no need of a temple any more; they forgot their worn and far-spent lives,—each other's old and year-marked faces; they were as two spirits, met without hindrance or incongruity, looking into each other's spiritual eyes.

Poor old Miss Smalley, when she came home and took off her hood before her little glass, and saw how pale she was with her night's watching and excitement, and how the thin gray hairs had straggled over her forehead, came back with a pang into the flesh, and was afraid she had been ridiculous; but lying tired upon her bed, in the long after hours of the day, she forgot once more what manner of outside woman she was, and remembered only, with a pervading peace, how the watchmaker had spoken.

Night came. The pillar of smoke that had gone up all day, turned again into a pillar of fire, and stood in the eastern heavens.

The time of safety, when there had been no flaming terror, was already so far off, that people, fearing this night to surrender themselves to sleep, wondered that in any nights they had ever dared,—wondered that there had ever been anything but fear and burning, in this great, crowded city.

The guards paced the streets; the roll of wagons quieted. The stricken town was like a fever patient seized yesterday with a sudden, devouring rage of agony,—to-day, calmed, put under care, a rule established, watchers set.

Miss Smalley went from window to window as the darkness—and the apparition of flame—came on. Rested by the day's surrender to exhaustion, she was alert and apprehensive and excited now.

"It will be sure to burst out again," she said; "it always does."

"Don't say so to Aunt Blin," whispered Bel. "Look at her cheeks, and her eyes. She is sick-abed this minute, and she *will* keep up!"

At nine o'clock, the very last thing, she spoke with the music-mistress again, at the door. Miss Smalley kept coming up into the passage to look out at that end window.

"I don't mean to get up if it does burn," Bel said, resolutely. "It won't come here. We ought to sleep. That's our business. There'll be enough to do, maybe, afterwards."

But for all that, in the dead of the night, she was roused again.

A sound of bells; a long alarm of which she lost the count; a great explosion. Then that horrible cataract of flame and sparks overhanging the stars as it did before, and paling them out.

It seemed as if it had always been so; as if there had never been a still, dark heaven under which to lie down tranquilly and sleep.

"The wind has changed, and the fire is awful, and I can't help it," sounded Miss Smalley's voice, meek and deprecating, through the keyhole, at which she had listened till she had heard Bel moving.

Bel lit the gas, and then went out into the passage.

Flakes of fire were coming down over the roofs into the Place itself.

The great rush and blaze were all this way, now. They were right under the storm of it.

Aunt Blin woke up.

"What is it?" she asked, excitedly. "Is it begun again? Is it coming?" And before Bel could stop her, she was out on the entry floor with her bare feet.

A floating cinder fell and struck the sash.

"We must be dressed! We must pack up! Make haste, Bel! Where's Bartholomew?"

Making a movement, hurriedly, to go back across her own room, Miss Bree turned faint and giddy, and fell headlong.

They got her into bed again, and brought her to. But with circulation and consciousness, came the rush of fever. In half an hour she was in a burning heat, wandering and crying out deliriously.

"O what shall we do? We must have a doctor. She'll die!" cried Bel.

"If I dared to go up and call Mr. Sparrow?" said the spinster, timidly.

Her thought reverted as instantly to Mr. Sparrow, and yet with the same conscious shyness, as if she had been eighteen, and the poor old watchmaker twenty-one. Because, you see, she was a woman; and she had but been a woman the longer, and her woman's heart grown tenderer and shyer, in its unlived life, that she was four and fifty, and not eighteen. There are three times eighteen in four and fifty.

"O, Mr. Sparrow isn't any good!" cried Bel, impetuously. "If you wouldn't mind seeing whether Mr. Hewland is up-stairs?"

Miss Smalley did not mind that at all; and though numbly aggrieved at the reflection upon Mr. Sparrow, went up and knocked.

Bel heard Morris Hewland's spring upon the floor, and his voice, as he asked the matter. Heavy with fatigue, he had not roused till now.

As he came down, five minutes later, and Bel Bree met him at the door, the gas suddenly went out, and they stood, except for the flame outside, in darkness.

In house and street it was the same. Miss Smalley called out that it was so. "The stable light is gone," she said. "Yes,—and the lights down Tremont Street."

Then that fearful robe of fire, thick sown with spangling cinders, seemed sweeping against the window panes.

Only that terrible light over all the town.

"O, what does it mean?" said Bel.

"It is Chicago over again," the young man answered her, with a grave dismay in his voice.

"See there,—and there!" said Miss Smalley, at the window. "People are up, lighting candles."

"But Aunt Blin is sick!" said Bel. "We must take care of her. What shall we do?"

"I'll go and send a doctor; and I'll bring you news. Have you a candle? Stop; I'll fetch you something."

He sprang up-stairs, and returned with a box of small wax tapers. They were only a couple of inches long, and the size of her little finger.

"I'll get you something better if I can; and don't be frightened."

The great glare, though it shed its light luridly upon all outside, was not enough to find things by within. Bel took courage at this, thinking the heart of it must still be far off. She gave one look into the depth of the street, shadowed by its buildings, and having a strange look of eerie gloom, even so little way beneath that upper glow. Then she drew down the painted shades, and shut the sky phantom out.

"Mr. Hewland will come and tell us," she said. "We must work."

She heated water and got a bath for Aunt Blin's feet. She put a cool, wet bandage on her head. She mixed some mustard and spread a cloth and laid it to her chest. Miss Bree breathed easier; but the bandage upon her head dried as though the flame had touched it.

"I'll tell you what," said good, inopportune Miss Smalley; "she's going to be dreadful sick, I'm afraid. It'll be head and lungs both. That's what my sister had."

"*Don't* tell me what!" cried Bel, irritatedly.

But the doctor told her what, when he came.

Not in words; doctors don't do that. But she read it in his grave carefulness; she detected it in the orders which he gave. People brought up in the country,—where neighbors take care of each other, and where every symptom is talked over, and the history of every fatal disorder turns into a tradition,—learn about sickness and the meanings of it; on its ghastly and ominous side, at any rate.

Mr. Hewland came back and brought two candles, which he had with difficulty procured from a hotel. He brought word, also, that the fire was under control; that they need feel no more alarm.

And so this second night of peril and disaster passed painfully and slowly by.

But on the Monday, the day in which Boston was like a city given over into the hands of a host,—when its streets were like slow-moving human glaciers, down the midst of which in a narrow channel the heavier flow of burdened teams passed scarcely faster forward than the hindered side streams,—Aunt Blin lay in the grasp and scorch of a fire that feeds on life; wasting under that which uplifts and frenzies, only to prostrate and destroy.

I shall not dwell upon it. It had to be told; the fire also had to be told; for it happened, and could not be ignored. It happened, intermingling with all these very things of which I write; precipitating, changing, determining much.

Before the end of that first week, in which the stun and shock were reacting in prompt, cheerful, benevolent organizing and providing,—in which, through wonderful, dreamlike ruins, like the ruins of the far-off past, people were wandering, amazed, seeing a sudden torch laid right upon the heart and centre of a living metropolis and turning it to a shadow and a decay,—in which human interests and experiences came to mingle that had never consciously approached each other before,—in which the little household of independent existences in Leicester Place was fused into an almost family relation all at once, after years of mere juxtaposition,—before the end of that week, Aunt Blin died.

It was as though the fiery thrust that had transpierced the heart of "her Boston," had smitten the centre of her own vitality in the self-same hour.

All her clothes hung in the closet; the very bend of her arm was in the sleeve of the well worn alpaca dress, the work-basket, with a cloth jacket-front upon it, in which was a half-made button-hole, left just at the stitch where all her labor ended, was on the round table; Cheeps was singing in the window; Bartholomew was winking on the hearth-rug; and little Bel, among these belongings that she knew not what to do with any more, was all alone.

CHAPTER XXIV
TEMPTATION

The Relief Committee was organizing in Park Street Vestry.

Women with help in their hands and sympathy in their hearts, came there to meet women who wanted both; came, many of them, straight from the first knowledge of the loss of almost all their own money, with word and act of fellowship ready for those upon whose very life the blow fell yet closer and harder. Over the separating lines of class and occupation a divine impulse reached, at least for the moment, both ways.

"Boffin's Bower" was all alert with aggressive, independent movement. Here, they did not believe in the divine impulse of the hour. They would stay on their own side of the line. They would help themselves and each other. They would stand by their own class, and cry "hands off!" to the rich women.

What was to be done, for lasting understanding and true relation, between these conflicting, yet mutually dependent elements?

In their own separate places sat solitary girls and women who sought neither yet.

Bel Bree was one.

The little room which had been home while Aunt Blin lived there with her, was suddenly become only a dreary, lonely lodging-room. Cheeps and Bartholomew were there, chirping and purring, the sun was shining in; the things were all hers, for Aunt Blin had written one broad, straggling, unsteady line upon a sheet of paper the last day she lived, when the fever and confusion had ebbed away out of her brain as life ebbed slowly back, beaten from its outworks by disease, toward her heart, and she lay feebly, but clearly, conscious.

"I give all I leave in the world to my niece Belinda Bree."

"Kellup" came down and buried his sister, and "looked into things;" concluded that "Bel was pretty comfortable, and with good folks,—Mrs. Pimminy and Miss Smalley; 'sposed she calc'lated to keep on, now; she could come back if she wanted to, though."

Bel did not want to. She would stay here a little while, at any rate, and think. So Kellup went back into New Hampshire.

There was a little money laid up since Miss Bree and Bel had been together; Bel could get along, she thought, till work began again. But it was no longer living; it would not be living then; it would be only work and solitude. She was like a great many others of them now; girls without tie or belonging,—holding on where they could. Elise Mokey had said to her,—"See if you could help yourself if you hadn't Aunt Blin!" and now she began to look forward against that great, dark "If."

Everything had come together. If work had kept on, there would have been these little savings to fall back upon when earnings did not quite meet outlay. But now she should use them up before work came. And what did it signify, anyhow? All the comfort—all the meaning of it—was gone.

They were all kind to her; Miss Smalley sat with her evenings, till Bel wished she would have the wiser kindness to go away and let her be miserable, just a little while.

Morris Hewland knocked at the door one afternoon when the music-mistress was out, giving her lessons.

Bel did not ask him in to sit down; she stood just within the doorway, and talked with him.

He made some friendly inquiries that led to conversation; he drew her to say something of her plans. He had not come on purpose; he hardly knew what he had come for. He had only knocked to say a word of kindness; to look in the poor, pretty little face that he felt such a tenderness for.

"I can't bear to give things up,—because they *were* pleasant," Bel said. "But I suppose I shall have to go away. It isn't home; there isn't anybody to make home *with* any more. I know what I *had* thought of, a while ago; I believe I know what there is that I might do; I am just waiting until the thoughts come back, and begin to look as they did. Nothing looks as it did yet."

"Nothing?" asked Morris Hewland, his eyes questioning of hers.

"Yes,—friends. But the friends are all outside, after all."

Hewland stood silent.

How beautiful it might be to make home for such a little heart as this! To surround her with comfort and prettiness, such as she loved and knew how to contrive out of so little! To say,—"Let us belong together. Make home with *me!*"

Satan, as an angel of light, entered into him. He knew he could not say this to her as he ought to say it; as he would say it to a girl of his own class whom father and mother would welcome. There was no girl of his own class he had ever cared to say it to. This was the first woman he had found, with whom the home thought joined itself. And this could not rightly be. If he took her, he would no longer have the things to give her. They would be cast out together. And all he could do was to make pictures, of which he had never sold one, or thought to sell one, in all his life. He would be just as poor as she was; and he felt that he did not know how to be poor. Besides, he wanted to be rich for her. He wanted to give her,—now, right off,—everything.

Why shouldn't he give? Why shouldn't she take? He had plenty of money; he was his father's only son. He meant right; so he said to himself; and what had the world to do with it?

"I wish I could take care of you, Bel! Would you let me? Would you go with me?"

The words seemed to have said themselves. The devil, whom he had let have his heart for a minute, had got his lips and spoken through them before he knew.

"Where?" asked Bel. "Home?"

"Yes,—home," said the young man, hesitating.

"Where your mother lives?"

Bel Bree's simplicity went nigh to being a stronger battery of defense than any bristling of alarmed knowledge.

"No," said Morris Hewland. "Not there. It would not do for you, or her either. But I could give you a little home. I could take care of you all your life; all *my* life. And I would. I will never make a home for anybody else. I will be true to you, if you will trust me,—always. So help me God!"

He meant it; there was no dark, deliberate sin in his heart, any more than in hers; he was tempted on the tenderest, truest side of his nature, as he was tempting her. He did not see why he should not choose the woman he would live with all his life, though he knew he could not choose her in the face of all the world, though he could not be married to her in the Church of the Holy Commandments, with bridesmaids and ushers, and music and flowers, and point lace and white satin, and fifty private carriages waiting at the door, and half a ton of gold and silver plate and verd antique piled up for them in his father's house.

His father was a hard, proud, unflinching man, who loved and indulged his son, after his fashion and possibility; but who would never love or indulge him again if he offended in such a thing as this. His mother was a woman who simply could not understand that a girl like Bel Bree was a creature made by God at all, as her daughters were, and her son's wife should be.

"Do you care enough for me?"

Bel stood utterly still. She had never been asked any such questions before, but she felt in some way, that this was not all; ought not to be all; that there was more he was to say, before she could answer him.

He came toward her. He put his hands on hers. He looked eagerly in her eyes. He did not hesitate now; the man's nature was roused in him. He must make her speak,—say that she cared.

"*Don't* you care? Bel—you do! You are my little wife; and the world has not anything to do with it!"

She broke away from him; she shrunk back.

"Don't do that," he said, imploringly. "I'm not bad, Bel. The world is bad. Let us be as good and loving as we can be in it. Don't think me bad."

There was not anything bad in his eyes; in his young, loving, handsome face. Bel was not sure enough,—strong enough,—to denounce the evil that was using the love; to say to that which was tempting him, and her by him, as Peter's passionate remonstrance tempted the Christ,—"Thou art Satan. Get thee behind me."

Yet she shrunk, bewildered.

"I don't know; I can't understand. Let me go now Mr. Hewland."

She turned away from him, into the chamber, and reached her hand to the door as she turned, putting her fingers on its edge to close it after him. She stood with her back to him; listening, not looking, for him to go.

He retreated, then, lingeringly, across the threshold, his eyes upon her still. She shut the door slowly, walking backward as she pushed it to. She had *left*, if not driven the devil behind her. Yet she did not know what she had done. She was still bewildered. I believe the worst she thought of what had happened was that he wanted to marry her secretly, and hide her away.

"Aunt Blin!" she cried, when she felt herself all alone. "Aunt Blin!—She *can't* have gone so very far away, quite yet!"

She went over to the closet, with her arms stretched out.

She went in, where Aunt Blin's clothes were hanging. She grasped the old, worn dress, that was almost warm with the wearing. She hid her face against the sleeve, curved with the shape of the arm that had bent to its tasks in it.

"Tell me, Aunt Blin! You can see clear, where you are. Is there any good—any right in it? Ought I to tell him that I care?"

She cried, and she waited; but she got no answer there. She came away, and sat down.

She was left all to herself in the hard, dreary world, with this doubt, this temptation to deal with. It was her wilderness; and she did not remember, yet, the Son of God who had been there before her.

"Why do they go off so far away in that new life, out of which they might help us?"

She did not know how close the angels were. She listened outside for them, when they were whispering already at her heart. We need to go *in*; not to reach painfully up, and away,—after that world in which we also, though blindly, dwell.

On the table lay Aunt Blin's great Bible; beside it her glasses.

Something that Miss Euphrasia had told them one day at the chapel, came suddenly into her mind.

"The angels are always near us when we are reading the Word, because they read, always, the living Word in heaven."

Was that the way? Might she enter so, and find them?

She moved slowly to the table.

It was growing dark. She struck a match and lit the gas, turning it low. She laid back the leaves of the large volume, to the latter portion. She opened it in Matthew,—to the nineteenth chapter.

When she had read that, she knew what she was to do.

She heard nothing more from Morris Hewland that night.

In the morning, early, she had her room bright and ready for the day. The light was calm and clear about her. The shadows were all gone.

She opened her door, and sat down, waiting, before the fire. Did she think of that night when she had had on the rose-colored silk, and had set the door ajar? Something in her had made her ashamed of that. She was not ashamed—she had no misgiving—of this that she was going to do now.

She was all alone; she had no other place to wait in she had no one to tell her anything. She was going to do a plain, right thing, whether it was just what anybody else would do, or not. She never even asked herself that question.

She heard Mr. Sparrow, with his hop and step, come down over the stairs. He always came down first of all. Then for another half hour, she sat still. At the end of that time, Morris Hewland's door unlatched and closed again.

Her heart beat quick. She stood up, with her face toward the open door. At the foot of that upper flight, she heard him pause. She could not see him till he passed; and he might pass without turning. Unless he turned, she would be out of his sight; for the door swung inward from the far corner. No matter.

He went by with a slow step. He could not help seeing the open door. But he did not stop or turn, until he reached the stairhead of the second flight; then he had to face this way again. And as he passed around the railing, he looked up; for Bel was standing where she had stood last night.

She had put herself in his way; but she had not done it lightly, with any half intent, to give *him* new opportunity for words. There was a pure, gentle quiet in her face; she had something herself to say. He saw it, and went back.

He colored, as he gave her his hand. Her face was pale.

"Come in a moment, Mr. Hewland," said the simple, girlish, voice.

He followed her in.

"You asked me questions last night, and I did not know how to answer them. I want to ask you one question, now."

She had brought him to the side of the round table, upon whose red cloth the large Bible lay. It was open at the place where she had read it.

She put her finger on the page, and made him look. She drew the finger slowly down from line to line, as if she were pointing for a little child to read; and his eye followed it.

"For this cause shall a man leave father and mother, and shall cleave to his wife; and they twain shall be one flesh.

"Wherefore, they are no more twain, but one flesh. What therefore God hath joined together, let not man put asunder."

"Is that the way you will make a home and give it to me, — before them all?" she said.

He forgot the sophistries he might have used; he forgot to say that it *was* to leave father and mother and join himself to her, that he had purposed; he forgot to tell her again that he would be true to her all his life, and that nothing should put them asunder. He did not take up those words, as men have done, and say that God had joined their hearts together and made them in his sight one. The angels were beside him, in his turn, as he read. Those sentences of the Christ, shining up at him from the page, were like the look turned back upon Peter, showing him his sin.

"One flesh:" to be seen and known as one. To have one body of living; to be outwardly joined before the face of men. None to set them asunder, or hold them separate by thought, or accident, or misunderstanding. This was the sacred acknowledgment of man and wife, and he knew that he had not meant to make it.

As he stood there, silent, she knew it too. She knew that she should not have been his wife before anybody.

Her young face grew paler, and turned stern.

His flushed: a slow, burning, relentless flush, that betrayed him, marking him like Cain. He lowered his eyes in the heat of it, and stood so before the child.

She looked steadfastly at him for one instant; then she shut the book, and turned away, delivering him from the condemning light of her presence.

"No: I will not go to that little home with you," she said with a grief and scorn mingled in her voice, as they might have been in the voice of an angel.

When she looked round again, he was gone. Their ways had parted.

An hour later, Bel Bree turned the key outside her door, and with a little leather bag in her hand, saying not a word to any one, went down into the street.

Across the Common, and over the great hill, she walked straight to Greenley Street, and to Miss Desire.

CHAPTER XXV
BEL BREE'S CRUSADE: THE PREACHING

Desire Ledwith had a great many secrets to keep. Everybody came and told her one.

All these girls whom she knew, had histories; troubles, perplexities, wrongs, temptations,—greater or less. Gradually, they all confessed to her. The wrong side of the world's patchwork looked ugly to her, sometimes.

Now, here came Bel Bree; with her story, and her little leather bag; her homelessness, her friendlessness. No, not that; for Desire Ledwith herself contradicted it; even Mrs. Pimminy and Miss Smalley were a great deal better than nothing. Not friendlessness, then, exactly; but *belonglessness*.

Desire sent down to Leicester Place for Bel's box; for Cheeps also. Bel wrote a note to Miss Smalley, asking her to take in Bartholomew. What came of that, I may as well tell here as anywhere; it will not take long. It is not really an integral part of our story, but I think you will like to know.

Miss Smalley herself answered the note. It was easy enough to evade any close questions on her part; she thought it was "a good deal more suitable for Bel not to stay at Mrs. Pimminy's alone, and she wasn't an atom surprised to know she had concluded so;" besides, Miss Smalley was very much preoccupied with her own concerns.

"There was the room," she said; "and there was the furniture. Now, would Bel Bree let the things to her, just as they stood, if she,—well, if Mr. Sparrow,—for she didn't mind telling Bel that she and Mr. Sparrow had made up their minds to look after each other's comfort as well as they could the rest of their lives, seeing how liable we all were to need comfort and company, at fires and things;—if Mr. Sparrow hired the room of Mrs. Pimminy? And as to Bartholomew, Mr. Sparrow wouldn't mind him, and she didn't think Bartholomew would object to Mr. Sparrow. Cats rather took to him, he thought. They would make the creature welcome, and make much of him; and not expect it to be considered at all."

Bel concluded the arrangement. She thought it would be a comfort to know that Aunt Blin's little place was not all broken up, but that somebody was happy there; that Bartholomew had his old corner of the rug, and his airings on the sunny window-sill; and Miss Smalley—Mrs. Sparrow that was to be—would pay her fifteen dollars a year for the things, and make them last.

"That carpet?" she had said; "why, it hadn't begun to pocket yet; and there hadn't been any breadths changed; and the mats saved the hearth-front and the doorway, and she could lay down more. And it would turn, when it came to that, and last on—as long as ever. There was six years in that carpet, without darning, if there was a single day; and Mr. Sparrow always took off his boots and put on his slippers, the minute ever he got in."

Desire's library was full on Wednesday evenings, now. The girls came for instruction, for social companionship, for comfort. On the table in the dining-room were almost always little parcels waiting, ready done up for one and another; little things Desire and Hazel "thought of" beforehand, as what they "might like and find convenient; and what they"—Desire and Hazel—"happened to have." Sometimes it was a paper of nice prunes for a delicate appetite that was kept too much to dry, economical food. Perhaps it was a jar of "Liebig's Extract" for Emma Hollen, that she might make beef-tea for herself; or a remnant of flannel that "would just do for a couple of undervests." It was sure to be something just right; something with a real thought in it.

And out here in the dining-room, as they took their little parcels,—or lingering in the hall aside from the others, or stopping in a corner of the library,—they would have their "words" with Desire and Hazel and Sylvie; always some confidence, or some question, or some telling of how this or that had gone on or turned out.

In these days after the Great Fire, no wonder that the dozen or fifteen became twenty, or even thirty; the very pigeons and sparrows tell each other where the people are who love and feed them; no wonder that all the chairs had to be brought in, and that the room was full; that the room in heart and brain, for sympathy and plan and counsel, was crowded also, or would have been, if heart and brain were not made to grow as fast as they take in tendernesses and thoughts. If, too, one need did not fit right in and help another; and if being "right in the midst of the work" did not continually give light and suggestion and opportunity.

Bel Bree came among them now, with her heart full.

"I know it better than ever," she said to Miss Desire. "I *know* that what ever so many of these girls want, most of all, is *home*. A place to work in where they can rest between whiles, if it is only for snatches; not to be out, and on their feet, and just *driving*, with the minutes at their heels, all day long. Girls want to work under cover; they can favor themselves then, and not slight the work either. And especially, they want to *belong* somewhere. They can't fling themselves about, separate, anywhere, without a great many getting spoiled, or lost. They want some signs of care over them; and I believe there are places where they could have it. If they can put twenty tucks into a white petticoat for a cent a piece, and work half a day at it, and find their own fire and bread and tea, why can't they do it for half a cent a tuck, even, in people's houses, where they can have fire and lodging and meals, and a name, at any rate, of being seen to?"

"Say so to them, Bel. Tell them yourself, what you mean to do, and find out who will do it with you. If this movement could come from the girls themselves,—if two or three would join together and begin,—I believe the leaven would work. I believe it is the next thing, and that somebody is to lead the way. Why not you?"

That night, the Read-and-Talk left off the reading. Miss Ledwith told them that there was so much to say,—so much she wanted a word from them about,—that they would give up the books for one evening. They would think about home, instead of far-off places; about themselves,—each other,—and things that were laid out for them to do, instead of people who had taken their turn at the world's work hundreds of years ago. They would try and talk it out,—this hard question of work, and place, and living; and see, if they could, what way was provided,—as in the nature of things there must be some way,—for everybody to be busy, and everybody to be better satisfied. She thought Bel Bree had got a notion of one way, that was open, or might be, to a good many, a way that it remained, perhaps, for themselves to open rightly.

"Now, Bel, just tell us all how you feel about it. There isn't any of us whom you wouldn't say it to alone; and every one of us is only listening separately. When you have finished, somebody else may have a word to answer."

"I don't know as I *could* finish," said Bel Bree, "except by going and living it out. And that is just what I think we have got to do. I've said it before; the girls know I have; but I'm surer than ever of it now. Why, where does all the work come from, but out of the homes? I know some kinds may always have to be done in the lump; but there's ever so much that might be done where it is wanted, and everybody be better off. We want homes; and we want real people to work for; those two things. I *know* we do. A lot of *stuff*, and miles of stitches, ain't *work*; it don't make real human beings, I think. It makes business, I suppose, and money; I don't know what it all comes round to, though, for anybody; more spending, perhaps, and more having, but not half so much being. At any rate, it don't come round in that to us; and we've got to look out for ourselves. If we get right, who knows but other folks may get righter in consequence? What I think is, that wherever there's a family,—a father and a mother and little children,—there's work to do, and a home to do it in; and we girls who haven't homes and little children, and perhaps sha'n't ever have,—ain't much likely to have as things are now,—could be happier and safer, and more used to what we ought to be used to in case we should,"—(Bel's sentences were getting to be very rambling and involved, but her thoughts urged her on, and everybody's in the room followed her),—"if we went right in where the things were wanted, and did them. The sewing,—and the cooking,—and the sweeping, too; everything; I mean, whatever we could; any of it. You call it 'living out,' and say you won't do it, but what you do *now* is the living out! We could *afford* to go and say to people who are worrying about poor help and awful wages,—'We'll come and do well by you for half the money. We know what homes are worth.' And wouldn't some of them think the millennium was come? *I* am going to try it."

Bel stopped. She did not think of such a thing as having made a speech; she had only said a little—just as it came—of what she was full of.

"You'll get packed in with a lot of dirty servants. You won't have the home. You'll only have the work of it."

"No, Kate Sencerbox. I sha'n't do that; because I'm going to persuade you to go with me. And we'll make the home, if they give us ever so little a corner of it. And as soon as they find out what we are, they'll treat us accordingly."

Kate Sencerbox shrugged her shoulders.

"The world isn't going to be made all over in a day,—nor Boston either; not if it *is* all burnt up to begin with."

"That is true, Kate," said Desire Ledwith. "You will have difficulties. But you have difficulties now. And wouldn't it be worth while to change these that are growing worse, for such as might grow better? Wouldn't it be grand to begin to make even a little piece of the world over?"

"We could start with new people," said Bel. "Young people. They are the very ones that have the hardest time with the old sort of servants. We could go out of town, where the old sort won't stay. You see it's *homes* we're after; real ones; and to help make them; and it's homes they hate!"

"Where did you find it all out, Bel?"

"I don't know. Talk; and newspapers. And it's in the air."

Bel was her old, quick, bright, earnest self, taking hold of this thing that she so truly meant. She turned round to it eagerly, escaping from the thoughts which she resolutely flung out of her mind. There was perhaps a slight impetus of this hurry of escape in her eagerness. But Bel was strong; strong in her purity; in her real poet-nature, that reached for and demanded the real soul of living; in her incapacity to care for the shadow or pretense,—far more the *sullied* sham,—of anything. Contempt of the evil had come swiftly to cure the sting of the evil. Satan would fain have had her, to sift her like wheat; but she had been prayed for; and now that she was saved, she was inspired to strengthen her sisters.

"I don't think I could do anything but sewing," said Emma Hollen, plaintively. "I'm not strong enough. And ladies won't see to their own sewing, now, in their houses. It's so much easier to go right into Feede & Treddle's, and buy ready-made, that we've done the stitching for at forty cents a day, hard work, and find ourselves!"

"I don't say that every girl in Boston can walk right into a nice good home, and be given something to do there. But I say there's no danger of too many trying it yet awhile; and by the time they do, maybe we'll have changed things a little for them. I'm willing to be the thin edge of the wedge," said Bel Bree.

"Right things have the power. God sees to that," said Desire. "The right cannot stop working. The life is in it."

"The thing I think of," said Elise Mokey, decidedly, "is suller kitchens. I ain't ready to be put underground,—not yet awhile. Not even by way of going to heaven, every night; or as near as four flights can carry me."

"In the country they don't have cellar kitchens. And anyway, there's always a window, and a fire; and with things clean and cheerful, and some green thing growing for Cheeps to sing to, I'll do," said Bel. "You've got to begin with what there is, as the Pilgrim Fathers did."

Ray Ingraham could have told them, if she had been there this Wednesday evening, how Dot had begun. Miss Ledwith said nothing about it, because she felt that it was an exceptional case. She would not put a falsely flattering precedent before these girls, to win them to an experiment which with them might prove a hard and disappointing one. Desire Ledwith was absolutely fair-minded in everything she did. The feeling on their part that she was so, was what gave them their trust in her. To bring a subject to her consideration and judgment, was to bring it into clear sunlight.

Dot had gone up to Z——, to live with the Kincaids, at the Horse Shoe.

Drops of quicksilver, if they are put anywise near together, will run into each other. And that is the law of the kingdom of good. Circumstances are far more fluid to the blessed magnetism than we think. The whole tendency of the right, neighborly life is to reach forth and draw together; to bring into one circle of communication people and plans of one spirit and purpose. Then, before we know how it is, we find them linking and fitting here and there, helping wonderfully to make a beautiful organism of result that we could not have planned or foreseen beforehand, any more than we could have planned our own bodies. It is the growing up into one body in Christ.

Hazel Ripwinkley said it all came of "knowing the Muffin Man:" and so it did. The Bread-Giver; the Provider. It is queer they should have made such an unconscious parable in that nonsense-play. But you can't help making parables, do what you will.

Rosamond Kincaid had her hands full now, she had her little Stephen.

He came like a little angel of delight, in one way; the real, heart way; but another,—the practical way of day's doing and ordering,—he came like a little Hun, overrunning and devastating everything.

While Rosamond had been up-stairs, and Mrs. Waters had been nursing her, and Miss Arabel coming in and out to see that all was straight below, it had been lovely; it was the peace of heaven.

But when Mrs. Waters—who was one of those born nurses whom everybody who has any sort of claim sends for in all emergency of sickness—had to pack up her valise and go to Portland, where her niece's son was taken with rheumatic fever, and her niece had another bleeding at the lungs; when the days grew short, and the nights long, and the baby *would* not settle his relations with the solar system, but having begun his earthly career in the night-time, kept a dead reckoning accordingly, and continued to make the midnight hours his hours of demand and enterprise,—the nice little systematic calculations by which the household had been regulated fell into hopeless uncertainties.

Dorris had so many music scholars now, that she was obliged to leave home at nine in the morning; and at night she was very tired. It was indispensable for her and for Kenneth that dinner should be punctual. Rosamond could not let Miss Arabel's labors of love grow into matter-of-course service.

And then there were all the sewing and mending to do; which had not been anything to think of when there had been plenty of time; but which, now that the baby devoured all the minutes, and made a houseful of work beside, began to grow threatening with inevitable procrastinations.

[Barbara Goldthwaite, who was at home at West Hill with *her* baby, averred that *these* were the angels who came to declare that time should be no longer.]

Rosamond would not have a nursery maid; she "would not give up her baby to anybody;" neither would she let a "kitchen girl" into her paradisiacal realm of shining tins, and top-over cups, and white, hemmed dishcloths.

"Let's have a companion!" said Dorris. "Let's afford her together."

When their "Christian Register" came, that very week, there was Dot Ingraham's advertisement.

Mr. Kincaid went into the city, and round to Pilgrim Street, and found her; and now, in this November when every machine girl in Boston was thrown back upon her savings, or her friends, or the public contribution, she was tucking up little short dresses for Stephen, whom Rosamond, according to the family tradition, called resolutely by his name, and whom she would, at five months old, put into the freedom of frocks, "in which he could begin to feel himself a little human being, and not a tadpole."

Dot helped in the kitchen, too; but this was a home kitchen. She became one of themselves, for whatever there was to be done. Especially she took triumphant care of Rosamond's stand of plants, which, under her quickly recognized touch and tending, rushed tumultuously into a green splendor, and even at this early winter time, showed eager little buds of bloom, of all that could bloom.

They had books and loud reading over their work. Everything got done, and there were leisure hours again. Dot earned four dollars a week, and once a fortnight went home and spent a Sunday with her mother.

All went blessedly at the Horse Shoe; but there is not a Horse Shoe everywhere. It is always a piece of luck to find one.

Desire Ledwith knew that; so she held her peace about it for a while, among these girls to whom Bel Bree was preaching her crusade. All they knew was that Dot Ingraham and her machine were gone away into a family eighteen miles from Boston.

"If *you* find anything for me to do, Miss Ledwith, I'll do it," said Kate Sencerbox. "But I won't go into one of those offices, nor off into the country for the winter. I want to keep something to hold on to,—not run out to sea without a rope."

Desire did not propose advertising, as she had done to Dot; she would let Kate wait a week. A week in the new condition of things might teach her a good deal.

CHAPTER XXVI
TROUBLE AT THE SCHERMANS'

There was trouble in Mrs. Frank Scherman's pretty little household.

The trouble was, it did not stay little. Baby Karen was only six weeks old, and Marmaduke was only three years; great, splendid fellow though he was at that, and "galumphing round,"—as his mother said, who read nonsense to Sinsie out of "Wonderland," and the "Looking Glass,"—upon a stick.

Of course she read nonsense, and talked nonsense,—the very happiest and most reckless kind,—in her nursery; this bright Sin Scherman, who "had lived on nonsense," she declared, "herself, until she was twenty years old; and it did her good." Therefore, on physiological principles, she fed it to her little ones. It agreed with the Saxon constitution. There was nothing like understanding your own family idiosyncrasies.

Everything quaint and odd came naturally to them; even their names.

Asenath: Marmaduke: Kerenhappuch.

"I didn't go about to seek or invent them," said Mrs. Scherman, with grave, innocent eyes and lifted brows. "I didn't name myself, in the first place; did I? Sinsie had to be Sinsie; and then—how *am* I accountable for the blessed luck that gave me for best friends dear old Marmaduke Wharne and Kerenhappuch Craydocke?"

But down in the kitchen, and up in the nursery, there was disapproval.

"It was bad enough," they said,—these orderers of household administration,—"when there was two. And no second nurse-girl, and no laundress!"

"If Mrs. Scherman thinks I'm going to put up with baby-clothes slopping about all days of the week, whenever a nurse can get time from tending, and the parlor girl havin' to accommodate and hold the child when she gets her meals, and nobody to fetch out the dishes and give me a chance to clear up, I can just tell her it's too thin!"

"Ye'r a fool to stay," was the expostulation of an outside friend, calling one day to see and condole with and exasperate the aforesaid nurse. "When ther's places yer might have three an' a half a week, an' a nurse for the baby separate, an' not a stitch to wash, not even yer own things! If they was any account at all, they'd keep a laundress!"

"I know there's places," said the aggrieved, but wary Agnes. "But the thing is to be sure an' git 'em. And what would I do, waitin' round?"

"Ad*vertiss*," returned the friend. "Yer'd have heaps of 'em after yer. It's fun to see the carriages rollin' along, one after the other, in a hurry, and the coachmen lookin' out for the number with ther noses turned up. An' then yer take it quite calm, yer see, an' send 'em off agin till yer find out how many more comes; an' yer *consider*. That's the time yer'll know yer value! I've got an ad*vertiss* out now; an' I've had twenty-three of 'em, beggin' and prayin', down on ther bare knees all but, since yesterday mornin'. I've been down to Pinyon's to-day, with my croshy-work, for a change. Norah Moyle's there, with the rest of 'em; doin' ther little sewin' work, an' hearin' the news, an' aggravatin' the ladies. Yer'll see 'em come in,—betune ten an' eleven's the time, when the cars arrives,—hot and flustered, an' not knowin' for their lives which way to turn; an' yer talks 'em all up and down, deliberate; an' makes 'em answer all the questions yer like, and then yer tells 'em, quite perlite, at the end, that yer don't think 'twould suit yer expectash'ns; it's not precisely what yer was lookin' for. Yer toss 'em over for all the world as they tosses goods on the counter. Ah, yer can see a deal of life, that way, of a mornin'!"

Agnes feels, naturally, after this, that she makes a very paltry and small appearance in the eyes of her friend, and betrays herself to be very much behindhand in the ways of the world, putting up meekly, as she is, with a new baby and no second nurse or laundress; and forgetting the day when she thought her fortune was made and she was a lady forever, coming from general housework in Aberdeen Street to be nursery-maid in Harrisburg Square, she begins the usual preliminaries of neglect, and sauciness, and staying out beyond hours, and general defiance,—takes sides in the kitchen against the family regime, and so helps on the evolution of things all and particular, that at the end of another fortnight the house is empty of servants, Mr. and Mrs. Scherman are gracefully removing their breakfast dishes from the dining-room to the kitchen, and Marmaduke, left to the sugar-bowl and his own further devices, comes tumbling down the stairs just in time to meet Mrs. M'Cormick, the washerwoman, arrived for the day. She, used to her own half dozen, picks him up as if she had expected him, shuts him up like an umbrella, hustles him under her big, strong arm, and bears him summarily to the cold-water faucet, which, without uttering a syllable, she turns upon his small, bewildered, and pitifully bumped head.

It will be always a confused and mysterious riddle to his childish recollection,—what strange gulf he fell into that day, and how the kitchen sink and those great, grabbing arms came to be at the end of it.

"How happened Dukie to tumble down-stairs?" asked Mrs. Scherman, in the way mothers do, when she had released him from Mrs. M'Cormick, carried him to the nursery, got him on her knee in a speechful condition, and was tenderly sopping the blue lump on his forehead with arnica water.

"I dicher tumber," said the little Saxon, stoutly, replacing all the consonant combinations that he couldn't skip, with the aspirated 'ch;' "I dicher tumber. I f'ied."

"You *what*?"

"F'ied. I icher pa'yow. On'y die tare too big!"

"Yes, indeed," said Sin, laughing. "The stairs are a great deal too big. And little sparrows don't fly—down-stairs. They hop round, and pick up crumbs."

"Ho I did," said Marmaduke, showing his white little front teeth in the midst of a surrounding shine of stickiness.

"Yes. I see. Sugar. But you didn't manage that much better, either. The trouble is, you haven't *quite* turned into a little bird, yet. You haven't any little beak to pick up clean with, nor any wings to fly with. You'll have to wait till you grow."

"I ta'h wa'he. I icher pa'yow now!"

"What shall I do with this child, Frank?" asked Sin, with her grave, funny lifting of her brows, as her husband came into the room. "He's got hypochondriasis. He thinks he's a sparrow, and he's determined to fly. We shall have him trying it off every possible—I mean impossible—place in the house."

"Put him in a cage," said Mr. Scherman, with equal gravity.

"Yes, of course. That's where little house-birds belong. Duke, see here! Little birds that live in houses *never* fly. And they never pick up crumbs, either, except what are put for them into their own little dishes. They live in tiny wire rooms, fixed so that they can't fly out. Like your nursery, with the bars across the windows, and the gate at the door. You and Sinsie are two little birds; mamma's sparrows. And you mustn't try to get out of your cage unless she takes you."

"Then you're the great sparrow," put in Sinsie, coming up beside her, laughing. "Whose sparrow are you?"

Asenath looked up at her husband.

"Yes; it's a true story, after all. You can't make up anything. It has been all told before. We're all sparrows, Sinsie,—God's sparrows."

"In cages?"

"Yes. Only we can't always see the wires. They are very fine. There! That's as far as you or I can understand. Now be good little birdies, and hop round here together till mamma comes back."

She went into her own room, to the tiniest little birdie of all, that was just waking.

Sinsie and Marmaduke had got a new play, now. They were quite contented to be sparrows, and chirp at each other, springing and lighting about, from one green spot to another in the pattern of the nursery carpet.

"I'll tell you what," said Sinsie, confidentially; "sparrows don't have girls to interfere, do they? They live in the cages and help themselves. I like it. I'm glad Agnes is gone."

Sinsie was four and a half; she had "talked plain" ever since she was one; and the nonsense that her mother had talked to her being always bright nonsense, such as she would talk to anybody on the same subject, there was something quaint in the child's fashion of speech and her unexpected use of words. Asenath Scherman did not keep two dictionaries, nor pare off an idea, as she would a bit of apple before she gave it to a child. It was noticeable how she sharpened their little wits continually against her own without straining them.

And there was a reflex action to this sharpening. She was fuller of graceful little whims, of quick and keen illustrations, than ever. Her friends who were admitted to nursery intimacies and nursery talk, said it was ever so much better than any grown-up dinner-tables and drawing-rooms.

"Well," she would answer, "I'm not much in the way of dinner-tables and drawing-rooms. I just have to live right along, and what there is of me comes out here. I rather think we'll save time and comfort by it in the end,—Sinsie and I. She won't want so much special taking into society by and by, before she can learn to tell one thing from another. Frank and I, with such friends as come here in our own fashion, will make a society for her from the beginning, as well as we can. She will get more from us in twenty years than she would from 'society' in two. And if I 'kept up' outside, now, for the sake of her future, that would be the alternative? I believe more in growing up than in coming out."

If there was a reflex action in the mental influence, how much more in the tender and spiritual! How many a word came back into her own heart like a dove, that she first thought of in giving it to her child!

She sat now in her chamber bathing and dressing baby Karen; and all the perplexities of the day,—the days or weeks, perhaps,—that had stretched out before her, melted into a sweetness, remembering that she herself was but one of God's sparrows, fed out of his hand; and that all her limitations, as well as her unsuspected safeties, were the fine wires with which He surrounded and held her in.

"He knows my cage," she thought. "He has put me here Himself, and He will not forget me."

Frank dined down town; Asenath had her lunch of bread and butter, and beef tea; and an egg beaten in a tumbler, with sugar and cream, for her dessert. The children, with their biscuit and milk and baked apple, were easily cared for. They played "sparrow" all day; Asenath put their little bowls and spoons on the low nursery table, and left them to "help themselves."

Honest, rough Mrs. M'Cormick fetched and carried for her, and "cleaned up" down-stairs. Then Asenath wrote a few lines to Desire Ledwith, told her strait, and asked if she could take a little trouble for her, and send her some one.

Mrs. M'Cormick went round to Greenley Street, and delivered the note.

"There!" said Desire, when she had read it, to Bel Bree who was in the room. "The Providence mail is in, early; and this is for you."

When Bel had seen what it was, she realized suddenly that Providence had taken her at her word. She was in for it now; here was this thing for her to do. Her breath shortened with the thought of it, as with a sudden plunge into water. Who could tell how it would turn out? She had been so brave in counseling and urging others; what if she should make a mistake of it, herself?

"She hasn't anybody; she would take Kate, maybe Kate must just go. It won't be half a chance to try it, if I can't try it my way."

"It is a clear stage," said Desire Ledwith. "If you can act out your little programme anywhere, you can act it at the Schermans'."

"Is it a cellar kitchen?"

Bel laughed as soon as she had asked the question. She caught herself turning catechetical at once, after the servant-girl fashion.

"I was thinking about Kate. But I don't wonder they inquire about things. It's a question of home."

"Of course it is. There ought to be questions,—on both parts. Every fair person knows *that* is fair. Neither side ought to assume the pure bestowal of a favor. But the one who has the home already may be supposed to consider at least as carefully whom she will take in, as she who comes to offer service as an equivalent. I believe it is a cellar kitchen; at least, a basement. The house is on the lower side; there must be good windows."

"I'll go right round for Kate, and we'll just call and see. I don't know in the least how to begin about it when I get there. I could do the *thing*, if I can make out the first understanding. I hope Kate won't be very Kate-y!"

She said so to Miss Sencerbox when she found her.

"You needn't be afraid. I'm bound to astonish somebody. Impertinence wouldn't do that. I shall strike out a new line. I'm the cook,—or the chambermaid,—which is it? that they haven't had any of before. I shall keep my sharp relishes for our own private table. You might discriminate, Bel! I know I've got a kind of a pert, snappy-sounding name,—just like the outside of me; but if you stop to look at it, it isn't *Saucebox*, but *Sensebox*! They're related, sometimes, and they ain't bad together; but yet, apart, they're different."

CHAPTER XXVII
BEL BREE'S CRUSADE: THE TAKING OF JERUSALEM

Mrs. Frank Scherman's front door-bell rang. Of course she had to go down and open it herself. When she did so, she let in two girls whose pretty faces, bright with a sort of curious expectation, met hers in a way by which she could hardly guess their station or errand.

She did not know them; they might be anybody's daughters, yet they hardly looked like *technical* "young ladies."

They stepped directly in without asking; they moved aside till she had closed the door against the keen November wind; then Bel said,—

"We came to see what help you wanted, Mrs. Scherman. Miss Ledwith told us."

How did Bel know so quickly that it was Mrs. Scherman? There was something in her instant conclusion and her bright directness that amused Asenath, while it bore its own letter of recommendation so far.

"Do you mean you wished to inquire for yourselves,—or for either of you?" she asked, as she led the way up-stairs.

"I must bring you up where the children are," she said. "I cannot leave them."

They were all in the large back room, with western windows, over the parlor. The doors through a closet passage stood open into Mrs. Scherman's own. There were blocks, and linen picture-books, and a red tin wagon full of small rag-dolls, about on the floor. Baby Karen was rolled up in a blanket on the middle of a bed.

"You see, this is the family,—except Mr. Scherman. I want two good, experienced girls for general work, and another to help me here in the nursery. I say two for general work, because I want some things equally divided, and others exchanged willingly upon occasion. Do you want places for yourselves?"

She paused to repeat the question, hardly sure of the possibility. These girls did not look much like it. There was no half-suspicious, half-aggressive expression on their faces even yet. It was time for it; time for her own cross-examination to begin, according to all precedent, if they were really looking out for themselves. Why didn't they sit up straight and firm, with their hands in their muffs and their eyes on hers, and say with a rising inflection and lips that moved as little as possible,—"What wages, mum?" or "What's the conveniences—or the privileges—mum?"

Bel Bree had got her arm round little Sinsie, who had crept up to her side inquisitively; and Kate was making a funny face over her shoulder at Marmaduke, alternately with the pleased attentive glance she gave to his pretty young mother and her speaking.

"Yes'm," Bel answered. "We want places. We are sewing-girls. We have lost our work by the fire, and we were getting tired of it before. We have made up our minds to try families. We want a real place to live, you see. And we want to go together, so as to make our own place. We mightn't like things just as they happened, where there was others."

Mrs. Scherman's own face lighted up afresh. This was something that did not happen every day. She grew cordial with a pleased surprise. "Do you think you could? Do you know about housework, about cooking?"

"It's very good of you to put it in that way," said Kate Sencerbox. "We just do know *about* it, and perhaps that's all, at present. But we're Yankees, and we *mean* to know."

"And you would like to experiment with me?"

"Well, it wouldn't be altogether experiment, from the very beginning," said Bel. "I'm sure I can make good bread, and tea, and toast, and broil chickens or steaks; I can stew up sauces, I can do oysters. I can make a *splendid* huckleberry pudding! We had one every Sunday all last August."

"Where?" asked Asenath, gravely.

"In our room; Aunt Blin and I. Aunt Blin died just after the fire," said Bel, simply.

Asenath's gravity grew sweeter and more real; the tremulous twinkle quieted in her eyes.

"I don't know what to answer you, exactly," she said, presently. "This is just what we housekeepers have been saying ought to happen: and now that it does happen, I feel afraid of taking you in. It is very odd; but the difficulties on your side begin to come to me. I have no doubt that on my side it would be lovely. But have you thought about this 'real place to live' that you want? what it would have to be? Do you think you would be contented in a kitchen? And the washing? Our washings are so large, with all these little children!"

Yes, it was odd. Without waiting to be catechised, or resenting beforehand the spirit of jealous inquiry, Asenath Scherman was frankly putting it in the heads of these unused applicants that there might be doubts as to her service suiting them.

"I suppose we could do anything reasonable," said Kate Sencerbox.

"I wonder if it is reasonable!" said Mrs. Scherman. "Mr. Scherman has six shirts a week, and the children's things count up fearfully, and the ironing is nice work. I'm afraid you wouldn't think you had any time left for living. The clothes hardly ever all come up before Thursday morning."

"And the cooking and all are just the same those days?" asked Kate.

"Why yes, pretty nearly, except just Mondays. Monday always has to be rather awful. But after that, we *do* expect to live. We couldn't hold our breaths till Thursday."

"I guess there's something that isn't quite reasonable, somewhere," said Kate. "But I don't think it's you, Mrs. Scherman, not meaningly. I wonder if two or three sensible people couldn't straighten it out? There ought to be a way. The nursery girl helps, doesn't she?"

"Yes. She does the baby's things. But while baby is so little, I can't spare her for much more. With doing them, and her own clothes, I don't seem to have her more than half the time, now."

Kate Sencerbox sat still, considering.

Bel Bree was afraid that was the last of it. In that one still minute she could almost feel her beautiful plan crumbling, by little bits, like a heap of sand in a minute-glass, away into the opposite end where things had been before, with nobody to turn them upside down again. Which *was* upside down, or right side up?

She had not thought a word about big, impossible washings.

Kate spoke out at last.

"Every one brings the work of one, you see," she said.

"What do you mean?"

"I wish there needn't be any nursery girl."

Mrs. Scherman lifted her eyebrows in utter amaze. The suggestion to the ordinary Irish mind would have been, as she had already experienced, another nurse; certainly not the dispensing with that official altogether.

"What wages do you pay, Mrs. Scherman?" was Kate's next question. It came, evidently in the process of a reasoning calculation; not, as usual, with the grasping of demand.

"Four dollars to the cook. Which *is* the cook?"

"I don't believe we know yet," answered Bel Bree, laughing in the glee of her recovering spirits. "But I think it would probably be me. Kate can make molasses candy, but she hasn't had the chance for much else. And I should like to have the kitchen in my charge. I feel responsible for the home-iness of it, for I started the plan."

With that covert suggestion and encouragement, she stopped, leaving the lead to Kate again.

Kate Sencerbox was as earnest as a judge.

"How much to the others?" said she.

"Three dollars each."

"That's ten dollars a week. Now, if you only had Bel and me, and paid us three or three and a half a piece, couldn't you put out—say, five dollars' worth of fine washing? Wouldn't the nurse's board and wages come to that? And I'd engage to help with the baby as much as you say you get helped now."

"But you would want some time to yourself?"

"Babies can't be awake all the time. I guess I should get it. I've never had anything but evenings, so far. The thing is, Mrs. Scherman, if I can try this anywhere, I can try it here. I don't suppose people have got things fixed just as they would have been if there'd always been a home all over the house. If we go to live with anybody, we mean to make it living *in*, not living *out*. And we shall find out ways as we go along,—all round. If you're willing, we are. It's Bel's idea, not mine; though she's let me take it to myself, and do the talking. I suppose because she thought I should be the hardest of the two to be suited. And so I am. I didn't believe in it at first. But I begin to see into it; and I've got interested. I'd like to work it out on this line, now. Then I shall know."

There were not many more words after that; there did not need to be. Mrs. Scherman engaged them to come, at once, for three dollars and a half a week each.

"It's a kind of a kitchen gospel," said Bel Bree, as they walked up Summit Street. "And it's got to come from the *girls*. What can the poor ladies do, up in their nurseries, with their big houses, full of everything, on their hands, and the servants dictating and clearing out? They can't say their souls are their own. They can't plan their work, or say how many they'll have to do it. The more they have, the more they'll have to have. It ain't Mr. and Mrs. Scherman, and those two little children,—or two and a half,—that makes all the to-do. Every girl they get makes the dinners more, and the Mondays heavier. Why, the family grows faster down-stairs than up, with a nurse for every baby! Think of the tracking and travelling, the wear and tear. Every one makes work for one, and dirt for two. It's taking in a regiment down below, and laying the trouble all off on to the poor little last baby up-stairs! And the ladies don't see through it. They just keep getting another parlor girl, or door girl, or nursery girl, and wondering that the things don't grow easier. It's like that queer rule in arithmetic about fractions,—where dividing and multiplying get all mixed up, and you can't hold on to the reason why, in your mind, long enough to look at it."

"Why didn't you go down and see the kitchen?"

"Because, how could she leave those tots to take care of themselves while she showed us? Our minds were made up. You said just the truth; if we can try it anywhere, we can try it there. And whatever the kitchen is, it's only our place to begin on. We'll have it all right, or something near it, before we've been there a fortnight. It's only a room we take, where the work is given in to do. If we had one anywhere else, we should expect to fix up and settle in it according to our own notions, and why not there? We're rent free, and paid for our work. I'm going to have things of my own; personal property. If I want a chandelier, I'll save up and get one; only I sha'n't want it. There's ways to contrive, Kate; and real fun doing it."

An hour afterward, they were on their way back, with their leather bags.

Baby Karen was asleep, and Mrs. Scherman came down-stairs to let them in again, with Marmaduke holding to her hand, and Sinsie hopping along behind. They all went into the kitchen together.

Mrs. McCormick had "cleared it up," so that there was at least a surface tidiness and cheerfulness. The floor was freshly scrubbed, the table-tops scoured down, the fire made, and the gas lighted. Mrs. McCormick had gone home, to be ready for her own husband and her two "boys" when they should come in from their work to their suppers.

The kitchen was in an L; there were two windows looking out upon a bricked yard. Bel Bree kept the points of the compass in her head.

"Those are south windows," said she. "We can have plants in them. And it's real nice their opening out on a level."

Forward, the house ran underground. They used the front basement for a store-room. Above the kitchen, in the L, was the dining-room. A short, separate flight of stairs led to it; also a dumb waiter ran up and down between china closet and kitchen pantry. Both kitchen and dining-room were small; the L had only the width of the hall and the additional space to where the first window opened in the western wall.

In one corner of the kitchen were set tubs; a long cover slid over them, and formed a sideboard. Opposite, beside the fire-place, were sink and boiler; between the windows, a white-topped table. There were four dark painted wooden chairs. A clock over the table, and a rolling-towel beside the sink; green Holland window-shades; these were the only adornments and drapery. There was a closet at each end of the room.

"Will you go up to your room now, or wait till after tea?" asked Mrs. Scherman.

"We might take up our things, now," said Bel, looking round at the four chairs. "They would be in the way here, perhaps."

Kate took up her bag from the table.

"We can find the room," she said, "if you will direct us."

"Up three flights; two from the dining-room; the back chamber. You can stop at my room as you come down, and we will think about tea. Mr. Scherman will soon be home; and I should like to surprise him with something very comfortable."

The girls found their way up-stairs.

The room, when they reached it, looked pleasant, though bare. The sun had gone below the horizon, beyond the river which they could not see; but the western light still shone in across the roofs. There were window-seats in the two windows, uncushioned. A square of clean, but faded carpet was laid down before the bed and reached to the table, — simple maple-stained pine, uncovered, — that stood beneath a looking-glass in a maple frame, between the windows. There were three maple-stained chairs in the room. A door into a good, deep closet stood open; there was a low grate in the chimney, unused of course, with no fire-irons about it, and some scraps of refuse thrown into it and left there; this was the only actual untidiness about the room, where there was not the first touch of cosiness or comfort. The only depth of color was in a heavy woven dark-blue and white counterpane upon the bed.

"Now, Kate Sencerbox, shut up!" said Bel Bree, turning round upon her, after the first comprehensive glance, as Kate came in last, and closed the door.

Kate put her muff down on the bed, folded her hands meekly, and looked at Bel with a mischievous air that said plainly enough "Ain't I?" and which she would not falsify by speech.

"Yes, I know you are; but—*stay* shut up! All this isn't as it is a going to be,—though it's *not* bad even now!"

Kate resolutely stayed shut up.

"You see that carpet is just put there; within this last hour, I dare say. Look at the clean ravel in the end. They've taken away the old, tramped one. That's a piece out of saved-up spare ends of breadths, left after some turn-round or make-over, I know! It's faded, and it's homely; but it's spandy clean! I sha'n't let it stay raveled long. And I've got things. Just wait till my trunk comes. My ottoman, I mean. That's what it turns into. Have you got a stuffed cover to your trunk, Katie?"

Kate lifted up her eyebrows for permission to break silence.

"Of course you can, when you're asked a question. You've had time now for second thoughts. I wasn't going to let you fly right out with discouragements."

"It is you that flies out with taking for granteds," said Kate Sencerbox, in a subdued monotone of quietness. "I was only going to remark that we had got neither cellar windows, nor attic skylights after all. I'm favorably surprised with the accommodations. I've paid four dollars a week for a great deal worse. And I wouldn't cast reflections by arguing objections that haven't been made, if I were the leader of this enterprise, Miss Bree."

"Kate! That's what I call real double lock-stitch pluck! That goes back of everything. You needn't shut up any more. Now let's come down and see about supper."

They had pinned on linen aprons, with three-cornered bibs; such as they wore at their machines. When they came down into Mrs. Scherman's room, that young matron said within herself,—"I wonder if it's real or if we're in a charade! At any rate, we'll have a real tea in the play. They do sometimes."

"What is the nicest, and quickest, and easiest thing to get, I wonder?" she asked of her waiting ministers. "Don't say toast. We're so tired of toast!"

"Do you like muffins and stewed oysters?" asked Bel Bree, drawing upon her best experience.

"Very much," Mrs. Scherman answered.

And Kate, looking sharply on, delighted herself with the guarded astonishment that widened the lady's beautiful eyes.

"Only we have neither muffins nor oysters in the house; and the grocery and the fish-market are down round the corner, in Selchar Street."

"I could go for them right off. What time do you have tea?"

Really, Asenath Scherman had never acted in a charade where her cues were so unexpected.

"I wonder if I'm getting mixed up again," she thought. "Which *is* the cook?"

Of course a cook never would have offered to go out and order muffins and oysters. Mrs. Scherman could not have *asked* it of the parlor-maid.

Kate Sencerbox relieved her.

"I'll go, Bel," she interposed. "I guess it's my place. That is, if you like, Mrs. Scherman."

"I like it exceedingly," said Asenath, congratulating herself upon the happy inspiration of her answer, which was not surprise nor thanks, but cordial and pleased enough for either. "The shops are next each other, just beyond Filbert Street. Have the things charged to Mrs. Francis Scherman. A quart of oysters,—and how many muffins? A dozen I think; then if there are two or three left, they'll be nice for breakfast. They will send them up. Say that we want them directly."

"I can bring the muffins. I suppose they'll want the oyster-can back."

It may be a little doubtful whether Kate's spirit of supererogatory doing would have gone so far, if it had not been for the deliciousness of piling up the wonder. She retreated, upon the word, magnanimously, remitting further reply; and Bel directly after descended to her kitchen, to make the needful investigations among saucepans and toasters.

"Don't be frightened at anything you may find," Mrs. Scherman said to her as she went. "I won't answer for the insides of cupboards and pans. But we will make it all right as fast as possible. You shall have help if you need it; and at the worst, we can throw away and get new, you know. Suppose, Bel," she added, with enchanting confidence and accustomedness, "we were to have a cup of coffee with the oysters? There is some real Mocha in the japanned canister in the china closet, and there are eggs in the pantry, to clear with; you know how? Mr. Scherman is so fond of coffee."

Bel knew how; and Bel assented. As the door closed after her, below stairs, Mrs. Scherman caught up Sinsie into her lap, and gave her a great congratulatory hug.

"Do you suppose it will last, little womanie? If it isn't all gone in the morning, what comfort we'll have in keeping house and taking care of baby!"

The daughter is so soon the "little womanie" to the mother's loving anticipation!

Marmaduke was lustily struggling with and shouting to a tin horse six inches long, and tipping up a cart filled with small pebbles on the carpet. He was outside already; the housekeeping was nothing to him, except as it had to do with the getting in of coals.

When Mr. Scherman opened the front door, the delicious aroma of oysters and coffee saluted his chilled and hungry senses. He wondered if there were unexpected company, and what Asenath could have done about it. He passed the parlor door cautiously, but there was no sound of voices. Up-stairs, all was still; the children were in crib and cradle, and Asenath was shaking and folding little garments,—shapes out of which the busy spirits had slidden.

He came up behind her, where she stood before the fire.

"All well, little mother?" he questioned. "Or tired to death? There are festive odors in the house. Has anybody repented and come back again?"

"Not a bit of it!" Sin exclaimed triumphantly, turning round and facing him, all rosy with the loving romp she had been having just a little while before with her babies. "Frank! I've got a pair of Abraham's angels down-stairs! Or Mrs. Abraham's,—if she ever had any. I don't remember that they used to send them to women much, now I think of it, after Eve demeaned herself to entertain the old serpent. Ah! the *babies* came instead; that was it! Well; there is a couple in the kitchen now, at any rate; and they're toasting and stewing in the most E—*ly*sian manner! That's what you smell."

"Angels? Babies? What terrible ambiguity! What, or who, is stewing, if you please, dear?"

"Muffins. No! oysters. There! you sha'n't know anything about it till you go down to tea. But the millennium's come, and it's begun in our house."

"I knew that, six years ago," said Frank Scherman. "There are exactly nine hundred and ninety-four left of it. I can wait till tea-time with the patience of the saints."

CHAPTER XXVIII
"LIVING IN"

Desire Ledwith went over to Leicester Place with Bel Bree, when she returned there for the first needful sorting and packing and removing. Bel could not go alone, to risk any meeting; to put herself, voluntarily and unprotected in the way again. Miss Ledwith took a carriage and called for her. In that manner they could bring away nearly all. What remained could be sent for.

Miss Smalley possessed some movables of her own, though the furnishings in her room had been mostly Mrs. Pimminy's. There were some things of her aunt's that Bel would like, and which she had asked leave to bring to Mrs. Scherman's.

The light, round table, with its old fashioned slender legs and claw feet, its red cloth, and the books and little ornaments, Bel wanted in her sleeping-room. "Because they were Aunt Blin's," she said, "and nothing else would seem so pleasant. She should like to take them with her wherever she went."

The two trunks—hers and Katy's—(Bel had Aunt Blin's great flat-topped one now, with its cushion and flounce of Turkey red; and Kate had speedily stitched up a cover for hers to match, of cloth that Mrs. Scherman gave her) stood one each side the chimney,—in the recesses. A red and white patchwork quilt, done in stars, Bel's own work before she ever came to Boston, lay folded across the foot of the bed, in patriotic contrast with the blue,—reversing the colors in stars and stripes. Bel had found in the attic a discarded stairway drugget, scarlet and black, of which, the centre was worn to threads, but the bright border still remained; and this she had asked for and sewed around the square of neutral tinted carpet, upon whose middle the round table stood, covering its dullness with red again, the color of the cloth. There was plenty of bordering left, of which she pieced a foot-mat for the floor before the dressing-glass, and in the open grate now lay a little unlighted pile of kindlings and coals, as carefully placed behind well blackened bars and a facing of paper, as that in the parlor below.

"It looks nice," Bel said to Mrs. Scherman, "and we don't expect to light it, unless one of us is sick, or something."

"Light it whenever you wish for it," Mrs. Scherman had replied. "I am perfectly willing to trust your reasonableness for that."

So on Sunday afternoons, or of a bitter cold morning, they had their own little blaze to sit or dress by; and it made the difference of a continual feeling of cheeriness and comfort to them, always possible when not immediately actual; and of a bushel or two of coal, perhaps, in the winter's supply of fuel.

"Where were the babies of a Sunday afternoon,—and how about the offered tending?"

This was one more place for them also; a treat and a change to Sinsie and Marmaduke, or a perfectly safe and sweet and comfortable resource in tending Baby Karen, who would lie content on the soft quilts by the half hour, feeling in the blind, ignorant way that little babies certainly do, the novelty and rest.

The household, you see, was melting into one; the spirit of home was above and below. It was home as much as wages, that these girls had come for; and they expected to help make it. Not that they parted with their own individual lives and interests, either; every one must have things that are separate; it is the way human souls and lives are made. It would have been so with daughters, or sisters. But in a true living, it is the individual interests that at once aggregate and specialize, it is a putting into the common stock that which must be distinct and real that it may be put in at all. It was not money and goods alone, that the early Christians had in common.

Instead of a part of their house being foreign and distasteful,—tolerated through necessity only, that the rest might be ministered to,—there was a region in it, now, of new, extended family pleasure. "It was as good as building out a conservatory, or a billiard-room," Asenath said. "It was just so much more to enjoy."

There was a little old rocking-chair, railed round till it was almost like a basket, with just a break in the front palings to sit into. It had a soft down cushion, covered with a damask patterned patch of wild and divaricating device; and its rockers were short, giving a jerk and thud if you leaned to and fro in it, like the trot an old nurse gives a child in an ordinary, four-legged, impracticable seat. All the better for that; the rockers were not in the way; and all Aunt Blin had wanted of it as a sewing chair, was to tip conveniently, as she might wish to bend and reach, to pick up scissors or spool, or draw to herself any of those surroundings of part, pattern, or material, which are sure, at the moment one wants them to be on the opposite side of the table.

Bel brought this away from Leicester Place, and had it in the kitchen. Mrs. Scherman, then seeing that there remained for Kate only the choice of the four wooden chairs, and pleased with the cosy expression they were causing to pervade their precincts, suggested their making space for a short, broad lounge that she would spare to them from an upper room which was hardly ever used. It was an old one that she had had sent from home among some other things that were reminiscences, when her father and mother, the second year after her marriage, had broken up their household in New York, and resolved on a holiday, late in life, in Europe. It was a comfortable, shabby old thing, that she had used to curl up on to learn her German, with the black kitten in her lap, and the tip of its tail for a pointer. She had always meant to cover it new, but had never had time. There was a large gray travelling shawl folded over it now, making extra padding for back and seat, and the thick fringe fell below, a garnishing along the front.

"Let it be," said Asenath. "I don't think you'll set the soup-kettle or the roasting-pan down on it; and you can always shake it out fresh and make it comfortable. It was only getting full of dust up-stairs. There's a square pillow in the trunk-room that you can have too, and cover with something. A five minutes' level rest is nice, between times, I know. I wonder I never thought of it before."

How would Bel or Kate have ever got a "five minutes' level rest," over their machine-driving at Fillmer & Bylles? Bel had said well, that girls and women need to work under cover; in a *home*, where they can "rest by snatches." A mere roof is not a cover; there may be driving afield in a great warehouse, as well as out upon a plantation.

The last touch and achievement was more of the dun-gray carpet, like that in their bedroom, and more of the scarlet and black stair-border, made into a rug, which was spread down when work was over, and rolled up under the table when dinner was to dish, or a wash was going on. They had been with Mrs. Scherman a month before they ventured upon that asking.

When it was finished, Sin brought her husband down after tea one night, to look at it.

"It is the most fascinating room in the house," she said.

There was a side gas-light over the white-topped table, burning brightly. Upon the table were work-baskets, and a volume from the Public Library. The lounge was just turned out from the wall a little, towards it, and opposite stood the round rocking-chair. Cheeps, in his cage at the farther window, was asleep in a yellow ball, his head under his wing. Bel was hanging the last dish-towel upon a little folding-horse in the chimney corner, and they could hear Kate singing up-stairs to a gentle clatter of the dishes that she was putting away from the dining-room use.

"It looks as a kitchen ought to," said Mr. Scherman. "As my grandmother's used to look; as if all the house-comfort came from it."

"It isn't a place to forbid children out of, is it?" asked Asenath.

"I should think the only condition would be their own best behavior," returned her husband.

"They're almost always good down here," said Bel. "Children like to be where things are doing. They always feel put away, out of the good times, I think, in a nursery."

"My housekeeping is all turning round on a new pivot," said Sin to Frank, after they were seated again up-stairs. "Don't take up the 'Skelligs' yet; I want to tell you. If I thought the pivot would really *stay*, there are two or three more things I should do. And one of them is,—I'd have the nursery—a day-nursery—down-stairs; that is, if I could coax you into it."

"It seems the new pivot is two very large 'ifs,'" said Frank, laughing. "And not much space to turn in, either. Would you take the cellar, or build out? And if so, where?"

"I'd take the dining-room, Frank; and eat in the back parlor."

"I wish you would. I don't like dining-rooms. I was brought up to a back parlor."

"You do? You don't? You were? Why, Frank, I thought you'd hate it," cried Asenath, pouring forth her exclamations all in a heap, and coming round to lean upon his shoulder. "I wish I'd told you before! Just think of those south dining-room windows that they'll have the good of all the forenoon, and that all we do with is to shade them down at dinner-time! And the horse-chestnut tree, and the grape-vines, making it green and pleasant, by and by! And the saving of going over the stairs, and the times one of the girls might help me when I *couldn't* ring her away up to my room; and the tending of table, with baby only to be looked after in here. Why, I should sit here, myself, mornings, always; and everything would be all together and the up-stairs work,—it would be better than two nurse-girls to have it so!"

"Then why not have it so right off? The more you turn on your pivot, the smoother it gets, you know. And the more nicely you balance and concentrate, the longer your machine will last."

Asenath lay awake late, and woke early, that night and the next morning, "planning."

When Frank saw a certain wide, intent, shining, "don't-speak-to-me" look in her eyes, he always knew that she was "planning." And he had found that out of her plans almost always resulted some charming novelty, at least, that gave one the feeling of beginning life over again; if it were only the putting of his bureau on the other side of the room, so that he started the wrong way for a few days, whenever he wanted to get a clean collar; or the setting the bedstead with side instead of head to the wall; issuing in delightful bewilderments of mind, when wakened suddenly and asked to find a match or turn up the dressing-room gas in the night, to meet some emergency of the baby's.

This time the development was a very busy Friday forenoon; in which the silver rubbing was omitted, and the dinner preparations put off,—the man who came for "chores" detained for heavy lifting,—the large dining-table turned up on edge and rolled into the back parlor, the sideboard brought in and put in the place of a sofa, which was wheeled to an obtuse angle with the fire-place,—nine square yards of gray drugget, with a black Etruscan border, sent up by Mr. Scherman from Lovejoy's, and tacked carefully down by seam and stripe, under Asenath's personal direction; cradle, rocking-horse, baby-house, tin carts and picture-books removed from the nursery and arranged in the new quarters,—the children themselves following back and forth untiringly with their one-foot-foremost hop over the stairs, and their hands clasping the rods of the balusters,—some little shabby treasure always hugged in the spare arm, chairs and crickets, and the low table suited to their baby-chairs, at which they played and ate, transferred also; until Asenath stood with a sudden sadness in the deserted chamber, reduced to the regular bedroom furnishings, and looking dead and bleak with the little life gone out of it.

But the warm south sun was beaming full into the pretty room below, where the small possessors of a whole new, beautiful world were chattering and dancing with delight; and up here, by and by, the western shine would come to meet them at their bedtime, and the new moon and the star-twinkle would peep in upon their sleep.

With her own hands, Asenath made the room as fresh and nice as could be; put little frilled covers over the pillows of the low bed, and on the half-high bureau top; brought in and set upon the middle of this last a slender vase from her own table, with a tea-rose in it, and said to herself when all was done,—

"How sweet and still it will be for them to come up to, after all! It *isn't* nice for children to be put to sleep in the midst of the whole day's muss!"

The final thing was done the next morning. The carpenter came and put a little gate across the head of the short stairway which would now only be used as required between play-room and kitchen; the back stairway of the main house giving equal access on the other side to the parlor dining-room. China closet and dumb waiter were luckily in that angle, also.

A second little railed gate barred baby trespass into the halls. The sparrows were caged again.

"What would you have done if they hadn't been?" asked Hazel Ripwinkley, speaking of the china closet and dumb waiter happening to be just as they were. She had come over one morning with Miss Craydocke, for a nursery visit and to see the new arrangements.

"What should we have done if anything hadn't been?" asked Asenath, in return. "Everything always has been, somehow, in my life. I don't believe we have anything to do with the 'ifs' way back, do you, Miss Hapsie? We couldn't stop short of the 'if' out of which we came into the world,—or the world came out of darkness! I think that's the very beauty of living."

"The very everlasting livingness," said Miss Hapsie. "We don't want to see the strings by which the earths and moons are hung up; nor, any more, the threads that hold our little daily possibilities."

Asenath had other visitors, sometimes, with whom it was not so easy to strike the key-note of things.

Glossy Megilp and her mother had come home from Europe. They and the Ledwiths were in apartments in one of the great "Babulous" hotels, as Sin called them, with a mingling of idea and etymology.

"Good places enough," she said, "for the prologue and the epilogue of life; but not for the blessed meanwhile; for the acting of all the dear heart and home parts."

The two families had managed very well by taking two small "suites" and making a common parlor; thus bestowing themselves in one room less than they could possibly have done apart. They were very comfortable and content, made economical breakfasts and teas together, dined at the café, and had long forenoons in which to run about and look in upon their friends.

Glossy had always "cultivated" Asenath Scherman for though that young dame lived at present a very retired and domestic life, Miss Megilp was quite aware that she *might* come out, and in precisely the right place, at any minute she chose; and meanwhile it was exceedingly suitable to know her well in this same intimate privilege of domesticity.

Glossy Megilp was very polite; but she did not believe in the new order of things; and her eyelids and the corners of her mouth showed it. Mrs. Megilp admired; thought it lovely for Asenath *just now*; but of course not a thing to count upon, or to expect generally. In short, they treated it all as a whim; a coincidence of whims. Asenath, although she would not trouble herself about the "ifs away back," had a spirit of looking forward which impelled her to argue against and clear away prospective ones.

"Bad things have lasted long enough," she said; "I don't see why the good ones should not, when once they have begun."

"They won't begin; one swallow never makes a summer. This has happened to you, but it is absolutely exceptional; it will never be pandemic," said Mrs. Megilp, who was fond of picking up little knowing terms of speech, and delivering herself of them at her earliest subsequent convenience.

"'Never' is the only really imposing word in the language," said Asenath, innocently. "I don't believe either you or I quite understand it. But I fancy everything begins with exceptions, and happens in spots,—from the settling of a continent to the doing up of back-hair in new fashions. I shouldn't wonder if it were an excellent way to take life, to make it as exceptional as you can, in all unexceptionable directions. To help to thicken up the good spots till the world gets confluent with them. I suppose that is what is meant by making one's mark in it, don't you?"

Mrs. Megilp headed about, as if in the turn the talk had taken she suddenly found no thoroughfare; and asked Asenath if she had been to hear Rubinstein.

Of course it was not in talk only, that—up-stairs or down-stairs—the exceptional household found its difficulties. It was not all pleasant arranging and contriving for an undeviating "living happy ever after."

There were days now and then when the baby fretted, or lost her nap, and somebody had to hold her nearly all the time; when the door-bell rang as if with a continuous and concerted intent of malice. Stormy Mondays happened when clothes would not dry, entailing Tuesdays and Wednesdays and Thursdays of interrupted and irregular service elsewhere.

If Asenath Scherman's real life had been anywhere but in her home and with her children,—if it had consisted in being dressed in train-skirt and panier, lace sleeves and bracelets, with hair in a result of hour-long elaboration, at twelve o'clock; or of being out making calls in high street toilet from that time until two; or if her strength had had to be reserved for and repaired after evening parties; if family care had been merely the constantly increasing friction which the whole study of the art of living must be to reduce and evade, that the real purpose and desire might sweep on unimpeded,—she would soon have given up her experiment in despair.

Or if, on the other part, there had been a household below, struggling continually to escape the necessity it was paid to meet, that it might get to its own separate interests and "privileges,"—if it had been utterly foreign and unsympathetic in idea and perception, only watchful that no "hand's turn" should be required of it beyond those set down in the bond,—resenting every occurrence, however unavoidable, which changed or modified the day's ordering,—there would speedily have come the old story of worry, discontent, unreliance, disruption.

But Asenath's heart was with her little ones; she went back into her own childhood with and for them, bringing out of it and living over again all its bright, blessed little ways.

"She would be grown up again," she said, "by and by, when they were."

She was keeping herself winsomely gay and fresh against the time,—laying up treasure in the kingdom of all sweet harmonies and divine intents, that need not be banished beyond the grave,—although of that she never thought. It would come by and by, for her reward.

She played with Sinsie in her baby-house; she did over again, with her, in little, the things she was doing on not so very much larger scale, for actual every day. She invented plays for Marmaduke which kept the little man in him busy and satisfied. She collected, eagerly, all treasures of small song and story and picture, to help build the world of imagination into which all child-life must open out.

As for Baby Karen, she was, for the most part, only manifest as one of those little embodiments that are but given and grown out of such loyal and happy motherhood. She was a real baby,—not a little interloping animal. She was never nursed or tended in a hurry. Babies blossom, as plants do, under the tender touch.

Kate Sencerbox, or Bel Bree, was glad to come into this nest-warm pleasantness, when the mother must leave it for a while. It was not an irksomeness flung by, like a tangled skein, for somebody else to tug at and unravel; it was a joy in running order.

When the hard Monday came, or the baby had her little tribulations, or it took a good tithe of the time to run and tell callers that Mrs. Scherman was "very much engaged"—(why can't it be the fashion to put those messages out upon the door-knob, or to tie it up with—a silk duster, or a knot of tape?)—Kate or Bel would look one at another and say, as they began with saying,—"Now, shut up!" It was an understood thing that they were not to "fly out with discouragements."

And nobody knows how many things would straighten themselves if that could only be made the law of the land.

On Wednesday evenings, Mrs. Scherman always managed it that they should both go to Desire Ledwith's, for the Read-and-Talk.

You may say Jerusalem is not taken yet, after all; there are plenty of "hard places," where girls like Kate Sencerbox and Bel Bree would not stay a week; there are hundreds of women, heads of houses, who would not be bothered with so much superfluous intelligence,—with refinements so nearly on a level with their own.

Granted: but it is the first steps that cost. Do you not think—do you not *know*—that a real good, planted in the world,—in social living,—*must* spread, from point to point where the circumstance is ready, where it is the "next thing?" If you do not believe this, you do not practically believe in the kingdom ever coming at all.

There is a rotation of crops in living and in communities, as well as in the order of vegetation of secret seeds that lie in the earth's bosom.

We shall not always be rank with noisome weeds and thistles; here and there, the better thought is swelling toward the germination; the cotyledons of a fairer hope are rising through the mould.

CHAPTER XXIX
WINTERGREEN

To tell of what has been happening with Sylvie Argenter's thread of our story, we must go back some weeks and pages to the time just after the great fire.

As it was with the spread of the conflagration itself, so it proved also with the results,—of loss, and deprivation, and change. Many seemed at first to stand safely away out on the margin, mere lookers-on, to whom presently, with more or less direct advance, the great red wave of ruin reached, touching, scorching, consuming.

It was a week afterward that Sylvie Argenter learned that the Manufacturers' Insurance Company, in which her mother had, at her persuasion, invested the little actual, tangible remnant of her property, had found itself swallowed up in its enormous debt; must reorganize, begin again, with fresh capital and new stockholders.

They had nothing to reinvest. The money in the Continental Bank would just about last through the winter, paying the seven dollars a week for Mrs. Argenter, and spending as nearly nothing for other things as possible. Unless something came from Mr. Farron Saftleigh before the spring, that would be the end.

Thus far they had heard nothing from these zealous friends since they had parted from them at Sharon, except one sentimental letter from Mrs. Farron Saftleigh to Mrs. Argenter, written from Newport in September.

Early in December, another just such missive came this time from Denver City. Not a word of business; a pure woman's letter, as Mrs. Farron Saftleigh chose to rank a woman's thought and sympathy; nothing practical, nothing that had to do with coarse topics of bond and scrip; taking the common essentials of life for granted, referring to the inignorable catastrophe of the fire as a grand elemental phenomenon and spectacle, and soaring easily away and beyond all fact and literalness, into the tender vague, the rare empyrean.

Mrs. Argenter read it over and over, and wished plaintively that she could go out to Denver, and be near her friend. She should like a new place; and such appreciation and affection were not be met with everywhere, or often in a lifetime.

Sylvie read the letter once, and had great necessity of self-restraint not to toss it contemptuously and indignantly into the fire.

She made up her mind to one thing, at least; that if, at the end of the six months, nothing were heard from Mr. Saftleigh himself, she would write to him upon her own responsibility, and demand some intelligence as to her mother's investments in the Latterend and Donnowhair road, the reason why a dividend was not forthcoming, and a statement in regard to actual or probable sales of land, which he had given them reason to expect would before that time have been made.

One afternoon she had gone down with Desire and Hazel among the shops; Desire and the Ripwinkleys were very busy about Christmas; they had ever so many "notches to fill in" in their rather mixed up and mutable memoranda. Sylvie only accompanied them as far as Winter Street corner, where she had to buy some peach-colored double-zephyr for her mother; then she bade them good-by, saying that two were bad enough dragging each other about with their two shopping lists, but that a third would extinguish fatally both time and space and taking her little parcel in her hand, and wondering how many more such she could ever buy, she returned home over the long hill alone. So it happened that on reaching Greenley Street, she had quite to herself a surprise and pleasure which she found there.

She went straight to the gray room first of all.

Mrs. Argenter was asleep on the low sofa near the fire, her crochet stripe-work fallen by her side upon the carpet, her book laid face down with open leaves upon the cushion.

Sylvie passed softly into her own chamber, took off her outside things, and returned with careful steps through her mother's room to the hall, and into the library, to find a book which she wanted.

On the table, at the side which had come of late to be considered hers, lay an express parcel directed to herself. She knew the writing, — the capital "S" made with a quick, upward, slanting line, and finished with a swell and curl upon itself like a portly figure "5" with the top-pennant left off; the round sweep after final letters, — the "t's" crossed backward from their roots, and the stroke stopped short like a little rocket just in poise of bursting. She knew it all by heart, though she had never received but one scrap of it before,—the card that had been tied to the ivy-plant, with Rodney Sherrett's name and compliments.

She had heard nothing now of Rodney for two months. She was glad to be alone to wonder at this, to open it with fingers that trembled, to see what he could possibly have put into it for her.

Within the brown wrapper was a square white box. Up in the corner of its cover was a line of writing in the same hand; the letters very small, and a delicate dash drawn under them. How neatly special it looked!

"A message from the woods for 'Sylvia.'"

She lifted it off, as if she were lifting it from over a thought that it concealed, a something within all, that waited for her to see, to know.

Inside,—well, the thought was lovely!

It was a mid-winter wreath; a wreath of things that wait in the heart of the woodland for the spring; over which the snows slowly gather, keeping them like a secret which must not yet be told, but which peeps green and fresh and full of life at every melting, in soft sunny weather, such as comes by spells beforehand; that must have been gathered by somebody who knew the hidden places and had marked them long ago.

It was made of clusters, here and there, of the glossy daphne-like wintergreen, and most delicate, tiny, feathery plumes of princess-pine; of stout, brave, constant little shield-ferns and spires of slender, fine-notched spleenwort, such as thrust themselves up from rough rock-crevices and tell what life is, that though the great stones are rolled against the doors of its sepulchre, yet finds its way from the heart of things, somehow, to the light. Mitchella vines, with thread-like, wandering stems, and here and there a gleaming scarlet berry among small, round, close-lying waxy leaves; breaths of silvery moss, like a frosty vapor; these flung a grace of lightness over the closer garlanding, and the whole lay upon a bed of exquisitely curled and laminated soft gray lichen.

A message. Yes, it was a simple thing, an unostentatious remembrance; no breaking, surely, of his father's conditions. Rodney loyally kept away and manfully stuck to his business, but every spire and frond and leaf of green in this winter wreath shed off the secret, magnetic meaning with which it was charged. Heart-light flowed from them, and touching the responsive sensitivity, made photographs that pictured the whole story. It was a fuller telling of what the star-leaved ferns had told before.

Rodney was not to "offer himself" to Sylvie Argenter till the two years were over; he was to let her have her life and its chances; he was to prove himself, and show that he could earn and keep a little money; he was to lay by two thousand dollars. This was what he had undertaken to do. His father thought he had a right to demand these two years, even extending beyond the term of legal freedom, to offset the half-dozen of boyish, heedless extravagance, before he should put money into his son's hands to begin responsible work with, or consent approvingly to his making of what might be only a youthful attraction, a tie to bind him solemnly and unalterably for life.

But the very stones cry out. The meaning that is repressed from speech intensifies in all that is permitted. You may keep two persons from being nominally "engaged," but you cannot keep two hearts, by any mere silence, from finding each other out; and the inward betrothal in which they trust and wait,—that is the most beautiful time of all. The blessedness of acknowledgment, when it comes, is the blessedness of owning and looking back together upon what has already been.

Sylvie made a space for the white box upon a broad old bureau-top in her room. She put its cover on again over the message in green cipher; she would only care to look at it on purpose, and once in a while; she would not keep it out to the fading light and soiling touch of every day. She spread across the cover itself and its written sentence her last remaining broidered and laced handkerchief. The wreath would dry, she knew; it must lose its first glossy freshness with which it had come from under the snows; but it should dry there where Rodney put it, and not a leaf should fall out of it and be lost.

She was happier in these subtle signs that revealed inward relation than she would have been just now in an outspokenness that demanded present, definite answer and acceptance of outward tie. It might come to be: who could tell? But if she had been asked now to let it be, there would have been her troubles to give, with her affection. How could she burden anybody doubly? How could she fling all her needs and anxieties into the life of one she cared for?

There was a great deal for Sylvie to do between now and any marriage. Her worry soon came back upon her with a dim fear, as the days passed on, touching the very secret hope and consciousness that she was happy in. What might come to be her plain duty, now, very shortly? Something, perhaps, that would change it all; that would make it seem strange and unsuitable for Rodney Sherrett ever to interpret that fair message into words. Something that would put social distance between them.

Her mother, above all, must be cared for; and her mother's money was so nearly gone!

Desire Ledwith was kind, but she must not live on anybody's kindness. As soon as she possibly could, she must find something to do. There must be no delay, no lingering, after the little need there was of her here now, should cease. Every day of willing waiting would be a day of dishonorable dependence.

It was now three months since Mrs. Froke had gone away; and letters from her brought the good tidings of successful surgical treatment and a rapid gaining of strength. She might soon be able to come back. Sylvie knew that Desire could either continue to contrive work for her a while longer, or spare her to other and more full employment, could such be found. She watched the "Transcript" list of "Wants," and wished there might be a "Want" made expressly for her.

How many anxious eyes scan those columns through with a like longing, every night!

If she could get copying to do,—if she could obtain a situation in the State House, that paradise of well paid female scribes! If she could even learn to set up type, and be employed in a printing-office? If there were any chance in a library? Even work of this sort would take her away from her mother in the daytime; she would have to provide some attendance for her. She must furnish her room nicely, wherever it was; that she could do from the remnants of their household possessions stored at Dorbury; and her mother must have a delicate little dinner every day. For breakfast and tea—she could see to those before and after work; and her own dinners could be anything,—anywhere. She must get a cheap rooms where some tidy lodging woman would do what was needful; and that would take,— oh, dear! she *couldn't* say less than six or seven dollars a week, and where were food and clothes to come from? At any rate, she must begin before their present resources were utterly exhausted, or what would become of her mother's cream, and fruit, and beef-tea?

Mingled with all her troubled and often-reviewed calculations, would intrude now and then the thought,—shouldn't she have to be willing to wear out and grow ugly, with hard work and insufficient nourishing? And she would have so liked to keep fresh and pretty for the time that might have come!

In the days when these things were keeping her anxious, the winter wreath was also slowly turning dry.

She found herself hemmed in and headed at every turn by the pitiless hedge and ditch of circumstance, at which girls and women in our time have to chafe and wait; and from which there seems to be no way out. Yet there are ways out from this, as from all things. One way—the way of thorough womanly home-helpfulness—was not clear to her; there are many to whom it is not clear. Yet if those to whom it is, or might be, would take it,—if those who might give it, in many forms, *would give,*—who knows what relief and loosening would come to others in the hard jostle and press?

There is another way out of all puzzle and perplexity and hardness; it is the Lord's special way for each one, that we cannot foresee, and that we never know until it comes. Then we discern that there has never been impossibility; that all things are open before his eyes; and that there is no temptation,—no trying of us,—to which He will not provide some end or escape.

In the first week of January, Sylvie acted upon her resolve of writing to Mr. Farron Saftleigh. She asked brief and direct questions; told him that she was obliged to request an answer without the least delay; and begged that he would render them a clear statement of all their affairs. She reminded him that he had *told* them that he would be responsible for their receiving a dividend of at least four per cent, at the end of the six months.

Mr. Farron Saftleigh "told" people a great many things in his genial, exhilarating business talks, which he was a great deal too wise ever to put down on paper.

Sylvie waited ten days; a fortnight; three weeks; no answer came. Mr. Farron Saftleigh had simply destroyed the letter, of no consequence at all as coming from a person not primarily concerned or authorized, and set off from Denver City the same day for a business visit to San Francisco.

Sylvie saw the plain fact; that they were penniless. And this could not be told to her mother.

She went to Desire Ledwith, and asked her what she could do.

"I would go into a household anywhere, as Dot Ingraham and Bel Bree have done, to earn board and wages, and spend my money for my mother; but I can't leave her. And there's no sewing work to get, even if I could do it at night and in honest spare time. I know, as it is, that my service isn't worth what you give me in return, and of course I cannot stay here any longer now."

"Of course you can stay where God puts you, dear," answered Desire Ledwith. "Let your side of it alone for a minute, and think of mine. If you were in my place,—trying to live as one of the *large household*, remember, and looking for your opportunities,—what would you say,—what would you plainly hear said to you,—about this?"

Sylvie was silent.

"Tell me truly, Sylvie. Put it into words. What would it be? What would you hear?"

"Just what you do, I suppose," said Sylvie, slowly "But I *don't* hear it on my side. My part doesn't seem to chord."

"Your part just pauses. There are no notes written just here, in your score. Your part is to wait. Think, and see if it isn't. The Dakie Thaynes are going out West again. Mr. Thayne knows about lands, and such things. He would do something, and let you know. A real business man would make this Saftleigh fellow afraid."

The Thaynes—Mrs. Dakie Thayne is our dear little old friend Ruth Holabird, you know—had been visiting in Boston; staying partly here, and partly at Mrs. Frank Scherman's. At Asenath's they were real "comfort-friends;" Asenath had the faculty of gathering only such about her. She felt no necessity, with them, for grand, late dinners, or any show; there was no trouble or complication in her household because of them. Ruth insisted upon the care of her own room; it was like the "coöperative times" at Westover. Mrs. Scherman said it was wonderful, when your links were with the right people, how simple you could make your art of living, you could actually be "quite Holabird-y," even in Boston! But this digresses.

"I shall speak to Mr. Thayne about it," said Desire. "And now, dear, if you could just mark these towels this morning?"

Sylvie sat marking the towels, and Desire passed to and fro, gathering things which were to go to Neighbor Street in the afternoon.

"Do you see," she said, stopping behind Sylvie a while after, and putting her fingers upon her hair with a caressing little touch,—"the sun has got round from the east to the south. It shines into this window now. And you have been keeping quiet, just doing your own little work of the moment. The world is all alive, and changing. Things are working—away up in the heavens—for us all. When people don't know which way to turn, it is very often good not to turn at all; if they are *driven,* they do know. Wait till you are driven, or see; you will be shown, one way or the other. It is almost always when things are all blocked up and impossible, that a happening comes. It has to. A dead block can't last, any more than a vacuum. If you are sure you are looking and ready, that is all you need. God is turning the world round all the time."

Desire did not say one word about the ninety-eight dollars which lay in one of the locked drawers of her writing desk, in precisely the shape in which every two or three weeks she had let Sylvie put the money into her hands. There would be a right time for that. She would force nothing. Sylvie would come near enough, yet, for that perfect understanding in which those bits of stamped paper would cease to be terrible between their hands, *either* way.

CHAPTER XXX
NEIGHBOR STREET AND GRAVES ALLEY

Rodney Sherrett had heard of the Argenters' losses by the fire; what would have been the good of his correspondence with Aunt Euphrasia, and how would she have expected to keep him pacified up in Arlesbury, if he could not get, regularly, all she knew? Of course he ferreted out of her, likewise, the rest of the business, as fast as she heard it.

"It's really a dreadful thing to be so confided in, all round!" she said to Desire Ledwith, when they had been talking one morning. "People don't know half the ways in which everything that gets poured into my mind concerns everything else. As an intelligent human being, to say nothing of sympathies, I *can't* act as if they weren't there. I feel like a kind of Judas with a bag of secrets to keep, and playing the traitor with every one of them!"

"What a nice world it would be if there were only plenty more just such Judases to carry the bags!" Desire answered, buttoning on her Astrachan collar, and picking up her muff to go.

Whereupon five minutes after, the amiable traitress was seated at her writing-desk replying to Rodney's last imperative inquiry, and telling him, under protest, as something he could not possibly help, or have to do with, the further misfortune of Sylvie and her mother.

Mr. Dakie Thayne had honestly expressed his conviction to Miss Kirkbright and Desire Ledwith, that the Donnowhair business was an irresponsible, loose speculation. He said that he had heard of this Farron Saftleigh and his schemes; that he might frighten him into some sort of small restitution, and that he would look into the title of the lands for Mrs. Argenter; but that the value of these fell of course, with the railroad shares; and the railroad was, at present, at any rate, mere moonshine; stopped short, probably, in the woods somewhere, waiting for the country to be settled up beyond Latterend.

"Am I bound by my promise against such a time as this?" Rodney wrote back to Aunt Euphrasia. "Can't I let Sylvie know, at least, that I am working for her, and that if she will say so, I will be her mother's son? I could get a little house here in Arlesbury, for a hundred dollars a year. I am earning fifteen hundred now, and I shall save my this year's thousand. I shall not need any larger putting into business. I don't care for it. I shall work my way up here. I believe I am better off with an income that I can clearly see through, than with one which sits loose enough around my imagination to let me take notions. Can't you stretch your discretionary power? Don't you see my father couldn't but consent?"

The motive had touched Rodney Sherrett's love and manliness, just as this fine manœuvrer,—pulling wires whose ends laid hold of character, not circumstance,—believed and meant. It had only added to the strength and loyalty of his purpose. She had looked deeper than a mere word-faithfulness in communicating to him what another might have deemed it wiser not to let him know. She thought he had a right to the motives that were made for him. But when a month would take this question of his abroad and bring back an answer, Miss Euphrasia would not force beyond the letter any interpretation of provisional authority which her brother-in-law had deputed. She would only draw herself closer to Sylvie in all possible confidence and friendliness. She would only move her to acquiescence yet a little longer in what her friends offered and urged. She represented to her that they must at least wait to hear from Mr. Thayne; there might be something coming from the West; and it would be cruel to hurry her mother into a life which could not but afflict her, until an absolute necessity should be upon them.

She bade Rodney be patient yet a few weeks more, and to leave it to her to write to his father. She did write: but she also put Rodney's letter in.

"Things which *are* might as well, and more truly, be taken into account, and put in their proper tense," she urged, to Mr. Sherrett. "There is a bond between these two lives which neither you nor I have the making or the timing of. It will assert itself; it will modify everything. This is just what the Lord has given Rodney to do. It is not your plan, or authority, but this in his heart, which has set him to work, and made him save his money. Why not let them begin to live the life while it is yet alive? It wears by waiting; it cannot help it. You must not expect a miracle of your boy; you must take the motive while it is fresh, and let it work in God's way. The power is there; but you must let the wheels be put in gear. Simply, I advise you to permit the engagement, and the marriage. If you do not, I think you will rob them of a part of their real history which they have a right to. Marriage is a making of life together; not a taking of it after it is made."

It was February when this letter was sent out.

One day in the middle of the month, Desire Ledwith, Hazel Ripwinkley, and Sylvie had business with Luclarion in Neighbor Street. There was work to carry; a little basket of things for the fine laundry; some bakery orders to give. There was always Luclarion herself to see. Just now, besides and especially, they were all interested in Ray Ingraham's rooms that were preparing in the next house to the Neighbors; a house which Mr. Geoffrey and others had bought, enlarged, and built up; fitting it in comfortable suites for housekeeping, at rents of from twenty-five to thirty dollars a month, each. They were as complete and substantial in all their appointments as apartments as the Commonwealth or the Berkeley; there was only no magnificence, and there was no "locality" to pay for. The locality was to be ministered to and redeemed, by the very presence of this growth of pure and pleasant and honorable living in its midst. For the most part, those who took up an abiding here had enough of the generous human sense in them to account it a satisfaction so to contribute themselves; for the rest, there was a sprinkling of decent people, who were glad to get good homes cheap in the heart of a dear city; and the public, Christian intent of the movement sheltered and countenanced them with its chivalrous respectability.

Frank Sunderline and Ray were to live here for a year; they were to be married the first of March. Frank had said that Ray would have to manage him and the Bakery too, and Ray was prepared to fulfill both obligations.

She was going to carry out here, with Luclarion Grapp, her idea of public supply for the chief staple of food. They were going to try a manufacture of breadstuffs and cakestuffs, on real home principles, by real domestic receipts. They were going to have sale shops in different quarters,—at the South and West ends. Already their laundry sustained itself by doing excellent work at moderate prices; why should they not, in still another way meet and play into the movement of the time for simplifying it, and making household routine more independent?

"Why shouldn't there be," Ray said, with appetizing emphasis, "a place to buy *cup* cake, and *composition* cake, and *sponge* cake, tender and rich, made with eggs instead of ammonia? Why shouldn't there be pies with sweet butter-crust crisp and good like mother's, and nice wholesome little puddings? Everybody knew that since the war, when the confectioners began to economize in their materials and double their prices at the same time, there was nothing fit to buy and call cake in the city. Why shouldn't somebody begin again, honest? And here, where they didn't count upon outrageous profits, why couldn't it be as well as not? When there was a good thing to be had in one place, other places would have to keep up. It would make a difference everywhere, sooner or later."

"And all these girls to be learning a business that they could set up anywhere!" said Hazel Ripwinkley. "Everybody eats! Just a new thing, if it's only new trash, sells for a while; and these new, old-fashioned, grandmother's cupboard things,—why, people would just *swarm* after them! Cooks never knew how, and ladies didn't have time. Don't forget, Luclarion, the bright yellow ginger pound-cake that we used to have up at Homesworth! Everything was so good at Homesworth—the place was named out of comforts! Why don't you call it the Homesworth Bakery? That would be double-an-tender,—eh, Lukey!"

Marion Kent made a beautiful silk quilt for Ray Ingraham, out of her sea-green and buff dresses, and had given it to her for a wedding-present. For the one only time as she did so, she spoke her heart out upon that which they had both perfectly understood, but had never alluded to.

"You know, Ray, just as I do, what might have been, and I want you to know that I'm contented, and there isn't a grudge in my heart. You and Frank have both been too much to me for that. I can see how it was, though. It was a hand's turn once. But I went my way and you kept quietly on. It was the real woman, not the sham one, that he wanted for a wife. It doesn't trouble me now; it's all right; and when it might have troubled me, it didn't add a straw's weight. It fell right off from me. You can't suffer *all through* with more than one thing; when you were engaged, I had my load to bear. I knew I had forfeited everything; what difference did one part make more than another? It was what I had let go *out of the world*, Ray, that made the whole world a prison and a punishment. I couldn't have taken a happiness, if it had come to me. All I wanted was work and forgiveness."

"Dear Marion, how certainly you must know you are forgiven, by the spirit that is in you! And for happiness, dear, there is a Forever that is full of it! I *don't* think it is any one thing,—not even any one marrying."

So the two kissed each other, and went down into the other house—Luclarion's.

That had been only a few days ago, and Ray had shown the quilt, so rich and lustrous, and delicate with beautiful shellwork stitchery,—to the young girls this afternoon.

She showed the quilt with loving pride and praise, but the story of it she kept in her heart, among her prayers. Frank Sunderline never knew more than the fair fabric and color, and the name of the giver, told him. Frank Sunderline scarcely knew so much as these two women did, of the unanalyzed secrets of his own life.

Luclarion waited till all this was over, and Desire Ledwith had come back from Ray Ingraham's rooms to hers, leaving Hazel and Sylvie among the fascinations of new crockery and bridal tin pans, before she said anything about a very sad and important thing she had to tell her and consult about. She took her into her own little sitting-room to hear the story, and then upstairs, to see the woman of whom the story had to be told.

"It was Mr. Tipps, the milkman, came to me yesterday with it all," said Luclarion. "He's a good soul, Tipps; as clever as ever was. He was just in on his early rounds, at four o'clock in the morning,—an awful blustering, cold night, night before last was,—and he was coming by Graves Alley, when he heard a queer kind of crazy howling down there out of sight. He wouldn't have minded it, I suppose, for there's always drunken noise enough about in those places, but it was a woman's voice, and a baby's crying was mixed up with it. So he just flung his reins down over his horse's back, and jumped off his wagon, and ran down. It was this girl,—Mary Moxall her name is, and Mocks-all it ought to be, sure enough, to finish up after that pure, blessed name so many of these miserables have got christened with; and she was holding the child by the heels, head down, swinging it back and for'ard, as you'd let a gold ring swing on a hair in a tumbler, to try your fortune by, waiting till it would hit and ring.

"It was all but striking the brick walls each side, and she was muttering and howling like a young she-devil over it, her eyes all crazy and wild, and her hair hanging down her shoulders. Tipps flew and grabbed the baby, and then she turned and clawed him like a tiger-cat. But he's a strong man, and cool; he held the child back with one hand, and with the other he got hold of one of her wrists and gave it a grip,—just twist enough to make the other hand come after his; and then he caught them both. She spit and kicked; it was all she could do; she was just a mad thing. She lost her balance, of course, and went down; he put his foot on her chest, just enough to show her he could master her; and then she went from howling to crying. 'Finish me, and I wouldn't care!' she said; and then lay still, all in a heap, moaning. 'I won't hurt ye,' says Tipps. 'I never hurt a woman yet, soul nor body. What was ye goin' to do with this 'ere little baby?' 'I was goin' to send it out of the hell it's born into,' she said, with an awful hate in the sound of her voice. 'Goin' to *kill* it! You wouldn't ha' done that?' 'Yes, I would. I'd 'a done it, if I was hanged for it the next minute. Isn't it my business that ever it was here?'

"'Now look here!' says Tipps. 'You're calmed down a little. If you'll stay calm, and come with me, I'll take you to a safe place. If you don't, I'll call a policeman, and you'll go to the lock-up. Which'll ye have?' 'You've got me,' she said, in a kind of a sulk. 'I s'pose you'll do what you like with me. That's the way of it. Anybody can be as bad and as miserable as they please, but they won't be let out of it. It's hell, I tell you,—this very world. And folks don't know they've got there.'

"Tipps says there's hopes of her from just that word bad. She wouldn't have put that in, otherways. Well, he brought her here, and the baby. And they're both up-stairs. She's as weak as water, now the drink is out of her. But it wasn't all drink. The desperation is in her eyes, though it's give way, and helpless. And what to do with 'em next, I *don't* know."

"I do," said Desire, with her eyes full. "She must be comforted up. And then, Mr. Vireo must know, the first thing. Afterwards, he will see."

Luclarion took Desire up-stairs.

The girl was lying, in a clean night-dress, in a clean, white bed. Her hair, dark and beautiful, was combed and braided away from her face, and lay back, in two long, heavy plaits, across the pillow. Her features were sharp, but delicate, and were meant to have been pretty. But her eyes! Out of them a suffering demon seemed to look, with a still, hopeless rage.

Desire came up to the bedside.

"What do you want?" the girl said, slowly, with a deep, hard, resentful scorn in her voice. "Have you come to see what it is all like? Do you want to feel how clean you are beside me? That's a part of it; the way they torment."

It was like the cry of the devil out of the man against the Son of God.

"No," said Desire, just as slowly, in her turn. "I can only feel the cleanness in you that is making you suffer against the sin. The badness doesn't belong to you. Let it go, and begin again."

It was the word of the Lord,—"Hold thy peace, and come out of him." Desire Ledwith spoke as she was that minute moved of the Spirit. The touch of power went down through all the misery and badness, to the woman's soul, that knew itself to be just clean enough for agony. She turned her eyes, with the fiery gloom in them, away, pressing her forehead down against the pillow.

"God sees it better than I do," said Desire, gently.

An arm flung itself out from under the bedclothes, thrusting them off. The head rolled itself over, with the face away.

"God! Pf!"

So far from Him; and yet so close, in the awful hold of his unrelaxing love!

Desire kept silence; she could not force upon her the thought, the Name: the Name for whose hallowing to pray, is to pray for the holiness in ourselves that alone can make it tender.

"What do you know about God?" the voice asked defiantly, the face still turned away.

"I know that his Living Spirit touches your thought and mine, this moment, and moves them to each other. As you and I are alive, He is alive beside us and between us. Your pain is his pain for you. You feel it just where you are joined to Him; in the quick of your soul. If it were not for that, you would be dead; you could not feel at all."

Was this the Desire Ledwith of the old time, with deep thoughts but half understood, and shrinking always from any recognizing word? She shrunk now, just as much, from any needless expression of herself; from any parade or talking over of sacred perception and experience; but the real life was all the stronger in her; all the surer to use her when its hour came. She had escaped out of all shams and contradictions. Unconsent to the divine impulse comes of incongruity. There was no incongruity now, to shame or to deter; no separate or double consciousness to stand apart in her soul, rebuked or repugnant. She gave herself quietly, simply, freely, to God's thought for this other child of his; the Thought that she knew was touching and stirring her own.

"I shall send somebody to you who can tell you more than I can, Mary," she said, presently. "You will find there is heart and help in the world that can only be God's own. Believe in that, and you will come to believe in Him. You have seen only the wrong, bad side, I am afraid. The *under* side; the side turned down toward" —

"Hell-fire," said Mary Moxall, filling Desire's hesitation with an utterance of hard, unrecking distinctness.

But Desire Ledwith knew that the hard unreckingness was only the reflex of a tenderness quick, not dead, which the Lord would not let go of to perish.

Sylvie and Hazel came in below, and she left Mary Moxall and went down to them. The three took leave, for it was after five o'clock.

When they got out from the street-car at Borden Square, Desire left them, to go round by Savin Street, and see Mr. Vireo. Hazel went home; Mrs. Ripwinkley expected her to-night; Miss Craydocke and some of the Beehive people were to come to tea. Sylvie hastened on to Greenley Street, anxious to return to her mother. She had rarely left her, lately, so long as this.

How would it be when they had heard from Mr. Thayne what she felt sure they must hear,—when they had to leave Greenley Street and go into that cheap little lodging-room, and she had to stay away from her mother all day long?

She remembered the time when she had thought it would be nice to have a "few things;" nice to earn her own living; to be one of the "Other Girls."

CHAPTER XXXI
CHOSEN: AND CALLED

Desire Ledwith found nobody at home at Mr. Vireo's. The maid-servant said that she could not tell when they would return. Mrs. Vireo was at her mother's, and she believed they would not come back to tea.

Desire knew that it was one of the minister's chapel nights. She went away, up Savin Street, disappointed; wishing that she could have sent instant help to Mary Moxall, who, she thought, could not withstand the evangel of Hilary Vireo's presence. It is so sure that nothing so instantly brings the heavenly power to bear upon a soul as contact with a humanity in which it already abides and rules. She wanted this girl to touch the hem of a garment of earthly living, with which it had clothed itself to do a work in the world. For the Christ still finds and puts such garments on to walk the earth; the seamless robes of undivided consecration to Himself.

As Desire crossed to Borden Street, and went on up the hill, there came suddenly to her mind recollection of the Sunday noon, years since, when she had walked over that same sidewalk with Kenneth Kincaid; when he had urged her to take up Mission work, and she had answered him with her girlish bluffness, that "she thought he did not approve of brokering business; it was all there, why should they not take it for themselves? Why should she set up to go between?" She thought how she had learned, since, the beautiful links of endless ministry; the prismatic law of mediation,—that there is no tint or shade of spiritual being, no angle at which any soul catches the Divine beam, that does not join and melt into the next above and the next below; that the farther apart in the spectrum of humanity the red of passion and the violet of peace, the more place and need for every subdivided ray, to help translate the whole story of the pure, whole whiteness.

She remembered what she had said another time about "seeing blue, and living red." She was thinking out by the type the mystery of difference,—the broken refractions that God lets his Spirit fall into,—when, looking up as she was about to pass some person, she met the face of Christopher Kirkbright.

He had not been at home of late; he had been busy up at Brickfield Farms.

For nearly four months past, Cone Hill and the Clay Pits had been his by purchase and legal transfer. He had lost no time in making his offer to his brother-in-law. Ten words by the Atlantic cable had done it, and the instructions had come back by the first mail steamer. Repairing and building had been at once begun; an odd, rambling wing, thrown out eastward, slanting off at a wholly unarchitectural angle from the main house, and climbing the terraced rock where it found best space and foothold, already made the quaint structure look more like a great two-story Chinese puzzle than ever, and covered in space for an ample, airy, sunny work-saloon above a range of smaller rooms calculated for individual and home occupancy.

But the details of the plan at Brickfields would make a long story within a story; we may have further glimpses of it, on beyond; we must not leave our friends now standing in the street.

Mr. Kirkbright held out his hand to Desire, as he stopped to speak with her.

"I am going down to Vireo's," he said. "I have come to a place in my work where I want him."

"So have I," said Desire. "But he is not at home. I was going next to Miss Euphrasia."

"And you and I are sent to stop each other. My sister is away, at Milton, for two days."

Desire turned round. "Then I must go home again," she said.

Mr. Kirkbright moved on, down the hill beside her.

"Can I do anything for you?" he inquired.

"Yes," returned Desire, pausing, and looking gravely up at him. "If you could go down to Luclarion Grapp's,—the Neighbors, you know,—and carry some kind of a promise to a poor thing who has just been brought there, and who thinks there is no promise in the world; a woman who tried to kill her baby to get him out of it, and who says that the world is hell, and people don't know they've got into it. Go and tell her some of the things you told me, that morning up at Brickfields."

"You have been to her? What have you told her yourself, already?"

"I told her that it was not all badness when one could feel the misery of the badness. That her pain at it was God's pain for her. That if He had done with her, she would be dead."

"Would she believe you? Did she seem to begin to believe?"

"I do not think she believes anything. She can't until the things to believe in come to her. Mr. Vireo—or you—would make her see. I told her I would send somebody who had more for her than I."

"You have told her the first message,—that the kingdom is at hand. The Christ-errand must be done next. The full errand of *help*. That was what was sent to the world, after the voice had cried in the wilderness. It isn't Mr. Vireo or I,—but the helping hand; the righting of condition; the giving of the new chance. We must not leave all that to death and the angels. Miss Desire, this woman must go to our mountain-refuge; to our sanatorium of souls. I have a good deal to tell you about that."

They had walked on again, as they talked; they had come to the foot of Borden Street. They must now turn two different ways.

They were standing a moment at the corner, as Mr. Kirkbright spoke. When he said "our refuge,—our sanatorium,"—Desire blushed again as she had blushed at Brickfields.

She was provoked at herself; why need personal pronouns come in at all? Why, if they did, need they remind her of herself and him, instead of merely the thoughts that they had had together, the intent of which was high above them both? Why need she be pleased and shy in her selfhood,— ashamed lest he should detect the thought of pleasure in her at his sharing with her his grand purpose, recognizing in her the echo of his inspiration? What made it so different that Christopher Kirkbright should discover and acknowledge such a sympathy between them, from her meeting it, as she had long done, in Miss Euphrasia?

She would not let it be different; she would not be such a fool.

It was twilight, and her little lace veil was down. She took courage behind it, and in her resolve,—for she knew that to be very determined would make her pale, not red; and the next time she would be on her guard, and very determined.

She gave him the hand he held out his own for, and bade him good evening, with her head lifted just imperceptibly higher than was its wont, and her face turned full toward him. Her eyes met his with an honest calmness; she had summoned herself back.

He saw strength and earnestness; a flush of feeling; the face of a woman made to look nobleness and enthusiasm into the soul of a man.

She sat in the library that evening at nine o'clock.

She had drawn up her large chair to the open fire; her feet were resting on the low fender; her eyes were watching shapes in the coals.

Mrs. Lewes's "Middlemarch" lay on her lap; she had just begun to read it. Her hands, crossed upon each other, had fallen upon the page; she had found something of herself in those first chapters. Something that reminded of her old longings and hindrances; of the shallowness and half-living that had been about her, and the chafe of her discontent in it.

She did not wonder that Dorothea was going to marry Mr. Casaubon. Into some dream-trap just such as that she might have fallen, had a Mr. Casaubon come in her way.

Instead, had come pain and mistake; a keen self-searching; a learning to bear with all her might, to work, and to wait.

She had not been waiting for any making good in God Providence of that special happiness which had passed her by. If she had, she would not have been doing the sort of work she had taken into her hands. When we wait for one particular hope, and will not be satisfied with any other, the whole force of ourselves bends toward it; we dictate to life, and wrest its tendencies at every turn.

The thing comes. Ask,—with the real might of whatever asking there is in you,—and it shall be given you. But when you have got it, it may not be the thing you thought it would be. Whosoever will have his life shall lose it.

No; Desire Ledwith had rather turned away from all special hope, thinking it was over for her. But she came to believe that all the good in God's long years was not over; that she had not been hindered from one thing, save to be kept for some other that He saw better. She was willing to wait for his better,—his best. When she paused to look at her life objectively, she rejoiced in it as the one thread—a thread of changing colors—in God's manifold work, that He was letting her follow alone with Him, and showing her the secret beauty of. Up and down, in and out, backward and forward, she wrought it after his pattern, and discerned continually where it fell into combinations that she had never planned,—made surprises for her of effects that were not her own. There is much ridicule of mere tapestry and broidery work, as a business for women's fingers; but I think the secret, uninterpreted charm of it, to the silliest sorters of colors and counters of stitches, is beyond the fact, as the beauty of children's plays is the parable they cannot help having in them. Patient and careful doing, after a law and rule,—and the gradual apparition of result, foreseen by the deviser of the law and rule; it is life measured out upon a canvas. Who knows how,—in this spiritual Kindergarten of a world,—the rudiments of all small human devices were set in human faculty and aptness for its own object-teaching toward a perfect heavenly enlightenment?

Desire was thinking to-night, how impossible it is, as the pattern of life grows, to help seeing a little of the shapes it may be taking; to refrain from a looking forward that becomes eager with a hint of possible unfolding.

Once, a while ago, she had thought that she discerned a green beauty springing out from the dull, half-filled background; tender leaves forming about a bare and awkward shoot; but suddenly there were no more stitches in that direction that she could set; the leaves stopped short in half-developed curves that never were completed. The pattern set before her—given but one bit at a time, as life patterns are, like part etchings of a picture in which you know not how the spaces are to be filled up and related—changed; the place, and the tint of the thread, changed also; she had to work on in a new part, and in a different way. She could not discover then, that these abortive leaves were the slender claspings of a calyx, in whose midst might sometime fit the rose-bloom of a wonderful joy. Was she discovering it now? For browns and grays,—generous and strong, tender and restful,—was a flush of blossom hues that she had not looked for, coming to be woven in? Was the empty calyx showing the first shadowy petal-shapes of a most perfect flower?

It might be the flower of a gracious friendship only a joining of hands in work for the kingdom-building; she did not let herself go farther than this. But it was a friendship across which there lay no bar and somehow, while she put from herself the thought that it might ever be so promised to her as to be hers of all the world and to the world's exclusion,—while she resented in herself that foolish girl's blush, and resolved that it should never come again,—she sat here to-night thinking how grand and perfect a thing for a woman a grand man's friendship is; how it is different from any, the most pure and sweet, of woman-tenderness; how the crossing of her path with such a path as Christopher Kirkbright's, if it were only once a day, or once a week, or once a month, would be a thing to reckon joy and courage from; to live on from, as she lived on from her prayers.

An hour had come in her life which gathered about her realities of heaven, whether the earthly correspondence should concur, or no. A noble influence which had met and moved her, seemed to come and abide about her,—a thought-presence.

And a thought-presence was precisely what it was. A thousand circumstances may stretch that hyphen which at once links and separates the sign-syllables of the wonderful fact; an impossibility, of physical conditions, may be between; but the fact subsists—and in rare moments we know it—when that which belongs to us comes invisibly and takes us to itself; when we feel the footsteps afar off which may or may not be feet of the flesh turned toward us. Yet even this conjunction does happen, now and again; the will—the blessed purpose—is accomplished at once on earth and in heaven.

When many minutes after the city bells had ceased to sound for nine o'clock, the bell of her own door rang with a clear, strong stroke, Desire Ledwith thought instantly of Mr. Kirkbright with a singular recall,—that was less a change than a transfer of the same perception,—from the inward to the actual. She had no reason to suppose it,—no ordinary reason why,—but she was suddenly persuaded that the friend who in the last hour had stood spiritually beside her, stood now, in reality, upon her door-stone.

She did not even wonder for what he could have come. She did not move from her chair; she did not lift her crossed hands from off her open book. She did not break the external conditions in which unseen forces had been acting. If she had moved,—pushed back her chair,—put by her book,—it would have begun to seem strange, she would have been back in a bond of circumstance which would have embarrassed her; she would have been receiving an evening call at an unusual hour. But to have the verity come in and fill the dream,—this was not strange. And yet Christopher Kirkbright had scarcely been in that house ten times before.

She heard him ask if Miss Ledwith were still below; if he might see her. She heard Frendely close the outer door, and precede him toward the door of the library. He entered, and she lifted her eyes.

"Don't move," he said quickly. "I have been seeing you sitting like that, all the evening. It is a reverie come true. Only I have walked out of my end of it, and into yours. May I stay a little while?"

Her face answered him in a very natural way. There was a wonder in her eyes, and in the smile that crept over her lips; there were wonder and waiting in the silence which she kept, answering in her face only, at the first, that peculiar greeting. Perhaps any woman, who had had no dream, would have found other response as difficult.

"I am going back to Brickfields to-morrow. I am more eager than ever to get the home finished there, for those who are waiting for its shelter. I have had a busy day,—a busy evening; it has not been a *still* reverie in which I have seen you. In this last half hour, I have been with Vireo. He has found a woman for me who can be a directress of work; can manage the sewing-room. A good woman, too, who will *mother*—not 'matron'—the girls. I have bought five machines. They will make their own garments first; then they will work for pay, some hours each day, or a day or two every week,—in turn. That money will be their own. The rest of the time will be due to the commonwealth. There will be a farm-kitchen, where they will cook—and learn to cook well—for the farm hands; they will wash and iron; they will take care of fruit and poultry. As they learn the various employments, they will take their place as teachers to new-comers; we shall keep them busy, and shall make a life around them, that will be worth their laboring for; as God makes all the beauty of the world for us to live in, in compensation for the little that He leaves it needful for us to do. There is where I think our privilege comes in, after the similitude of his; to supplement broadly that which shall not hinder honest and conditional exertion. I have been longing to tell you about it; I have had a vision of you in the midst of my work and talk; I have had a feeling of you this evening, waiting just so and there; I had to come. I went to see your Mary Moxall, Miss Desire."

"In the midst of all you had to do!"

"Was it not a part? 'All in the day's work' is a good proverb."

"What did you say to her?"

"I asked her if she would come up into the country with my sister, to a home among great, still, beautiful hills, and take care of her baby, and some flowers."

"It was like asking her to come home—to God!"

"Yes,—I think it was asking her God's way. How can we, standing among all the helps and harmonies of our lives, ask them to come straight up to Him,—His invisible unapproachable Self,—out of the terrible darkness and chaos of theirs? There are no steps."

"Tell me more about the steps you have been making—in the hills. You said 'flowers.'"

"Yes; there will be a conservatory. I must have them all the year through; the short summer gardening would not be ministry enough. Beyond the Chapel Rock runs back a large new wing, with sewing and living rooms; they only wait good weather for finishing. A dozen women can live and work there. As they grow fit and willing, and numerous enough to colonize off, there are little houses to be built that they can move into, set up homes, earn their machines, and at last, in cases where it proves safe and wise, their homes themselves. I shall provide a depot for their needlework in the city; and as the village grows it will create a little demand of its own. Mr. Thayne is going to build the cottages, and he and I have contracted for the seven miles of railroad to Tillington, as a private enterprise. The brickmaking is to begin at once; we shall do something for the building of the new, fire-proof Boston. Your thought is growing into a fact, Miss Desire; and I think

I have not forgotten any particular of it. Now, I have come back to you for more,—a great deal more, if I can get it. First, a name. We can't *call* it a City of Refuge, beautiful as such a city is—to *be*. Neither will I call it a Home, or an Asylum. The first thing Mary Moxall said to me was,—'I won't go to no Refuges nor Sile'ums. I don't want to be raked up, mud an' all, into a heap that everybody knows the name of. If the world was big enough for me to begin again,—in a clean place; but there ain't no clean places!' And then I asked her to come home with me and my sister."

"You mean, of course, a neighborhood name, for the settlement, as it grows?"

"Exactly. 'Brickfield Farms' belongs to the outlying husbandry and homesteads. And 'Clay Pits!' It is *out* of the pit and the miry clay that we want to bring them. The suggestion of that is too much like Mary Moxall's 'heap that everybody knows the name of.'"

"Why not call it 'Hill-hope'? 'The hills, whence cometh our strength;' 'the mountain of the height of Israel where the Lord will plant it, and the dry tree shall flourish'?"

"Thank you," said Mr. Kirkbright, heartily. "That is the right word. It is named."

Desire said nothing. She looked quietly into the fire with a flush of deep pleasure on her face. Mr. Kirkbright remained silent also for a few minutes.

He looked at her as she sat there, in this room that was her own; that was filled with home-feeling and association for her; where a solemnly tender commission and opportunity had been given her, and had centred, and he almost doubted whether the thing that was urging itself with him to be asked for last and greatest of all, were right to ask; whether it existed for him, and a way could be made for it to be given him. Yet the question was in him, strong and earnest; a question that had never been in him before to ask of any woman. Why had it been put there if it might not at least be spoken? If there were not possibly, in this woman's keeping, the ordained and perfect answer?

While he sat and scrupled about it, it sprang, with an impulse that he did not stop to scruple at, to his lips.

"I shall want to ask you questions every day, dear friend! What are we to do about it?"

Desire's eyes flashed up at him with a happiness in them that waited not to weigh anything; that he could not mistake. The color was bright upon her cheek; her lips were soft and tremulous. Then the eyes dropped gently away again; she answered nothing,—with words.

So far as he had spoken, she had answered.

"I want you there, by my side, to help me make a real human home around which other homes may grow. There ought to be a heart in it, and I cannot do it alone. Could you—*will* you—come? Will you be to me the one woman of the world, and out of your purity and strength help me to help your sisters?"

He had risen and walked the few steps across the distance that was between them. He stopped before her, and bending toward her, held out his hands.

Desire stood up and laid hers in them.

"It must be right. You have come for me. I cannot possibly do otherwise than this."

The deep, gracious, divine fact had asserted itself. A house here, or a house there could not change or bind it. They belonged together. There was a new love in the world, and the world would have to arrange itself around it. Around it and the Will that it was to be wedded to do.

They stood together, hands in hands. Christopher Kirkbright leaned over and laid his lips against her forehead.

He whispered her name, set in other syllables that were only for him to say to her. I shall not say them over on this page to you.

But there is a line in the blessed Scripture that we all know, and God had fulfilled it to his heart.

Strangely—more strangely than any story can contrive—are the happenings of life put side by side.

As they sat there a little longer in the quiet library, forgetting the late evening hour, because it was morning all at once to them; forgetting Sylvie Argenter and her mother as they were at just this moment in the next room; only remembering them among those whom this new relation and joining of purpose must make surer and safer, not less carefully provided for in the changes that would occur,—the door of the gray parlor opened; a quick step fell along the passage, and Sylvie unlatched the library door, and stood in the entrance wide-eyed and pale.

"Desire! Come!"

"Sylvie! *What*, dear?" cried Desire, quickly, as she sprang to meet her, her voice chording responsive to Sylvie's own, catching in it the indescribable tone that tells so much more than words. She did not need the further revelation of her face to know that something deep and strange had happened.

Sylvie said not a syllable more, but turned and hurried back along the hall.

Desire and Mr. Kirkbright followed her.

Mrs. Argenter was sitting in the deep corner of her broad, low sofa, against the two large pillows.

"A minute ago," said Sylvie, in the same changed voice, that spoke out of a different world from the world of five minutes before, "she was *here*! She gave me her plate to put away on the sideboard, and *now*,—when I turned round,"—

She was *There*.

The plate, with its bits of orange-rind, and an untasted section of the fruit, stood upon the sideboard. The book she had been reading fifteen minutes since lay, with her eye-glasses inside it, at the page where she had stopped, upon the couch; her left hand had fallen, palm upward, upon the cushioned seat; her life had gone instantly and without a sign, out from her mortal body.

Mrs. Argenter had died of that disease which lets the spirit free like the uncaging of a bird.

Hypertrophy of the heart. The gradual thickening and hardening of those mysterious little gates of life and the walls in which they are set; the slower moving of them on their palpitating hinges, till a moment comes when they open or close for the last time, and in that pause ajar the soul flits out, like some curious, unwary thing, over a threshold it may pass no more again, forever.

CHAPTER XXXII
EASTER LILIES

Bright, soft days began to come; days in which windows stood open, and pots of plants were set out on the window-sills; days alternating as in the long, New England spring they always do, with bleak intervals of sharp winds and cold sea-storms; yet giving sweet anticipation tenderly, as a mother gives beforehand that which she cannot find in her heart to keep back till the birthday. That is the charm of Nature with us; the motherliness in her that offsets, and breaks through with loving impulse, her rule of rigidness. The year comes slowly to its growth, but she relaxes toward it with a kind of pity, and says, "There, take this! It isn't time for it, but you needn't wait for everything till you're grown up!"

People feel happy, in advance of all their hopes and realizations, on such days; the ripeness of the year, in whatever good it may be making for them, touches them like the soft air that blows up from the south. There is a new look on men's and women's faces as you meet them in the street; a New Jerusalem sort of look; the heavens are opened upon them, and the divineness of sunshine flows in through sense and spirit.

Sylvie Argenter was very peaceful. She told Desire that she never would be afraid again in all her life; she *knew* how things were measured, now. She was "so glad the money had almost all been spent while mother lived; that not a dollar that could buy her a comfort had been kept back."

She was quite content to stay now; at least till Rachel Froke should come; she was busily helping Desire with her wedding outfit. She was willing to receive from her the fair wages of a seamstress, now that she could freely give her time, and there was no one to accept and use an invalid's expensive luxuries.

Desire would not have thought it needful that hundreds of extra yards of cambric and linen should be made up for her, simply because she was going to be married, if it had not been that her marriage was to be so especially a beginning of new life and work, in which she did not wish to be crippled by any present care for self.

"I see the sense of it now, so far as concerns quantity; as for quality, I will have nothing different from what I have always had."

There was no trousseau to exhibit; there were only trunks-full of good plenishing that would last for years.

Sylvie cut out, and parceled. Elise Mokey, and one or two other girls who had had only precarious employment and Committee "relief" since the fire, had the stitching given them to do; and every tuck and hem was justly paid for. When the work came back from their hands, Sylvie finished and marked delicately.

She had the sunny little room, now, over the gray parlor, adjoining Desire's own. The white box lay upon a round, damask-covered-stand in the corner, under her mother's picture painted in the graceful days of the gray silks and llama laces; and around this, drooping and trailing till they touched the little table and veiled the box that held the beautiful secret,— seeming to say, "We know it too, for we are a part,"—wreathed the shining sprays of blossomy fern.

In these sunny days of early spring, Sylvie could not help being happy. The snows were gone now, except in deep, dark places, out of the woods; the ferns and vines and grasses were alive and eager for a new summer's grace and fullness; their far-off presence made the air different, already, from the airs of winter.

Yet Rodney Sherrett had kept silence.

All these weeks had gone by, and Miss Euphrasia had had no answer from over the water. Of all the letters that went safely into mail bags, and of all the mail bags that went as they were bound, and of all the white messages that were scattered like doves when those bags were opened,— somehow—it can never be told how,—that particular little white, folded sheet got mishandled, mislaid, or missent, and failed of its errand; and at the time when Miss Euphrasia began to be convinced that it must be so, there came a letter from Mr. Sherrett to herself, written from London, where he had just arrived after a visit to Berlin.

"I have had no family news," he wrote, "of later date than January 20th. Trust all is well. Shall sail from Liverpool on the 9th."

The date of that was March 20th.

The fourteenth of April, Easter Monday, was fixed for Desire Ledwith's marriage.

Rachel Froke came back on the Friday previous. Desire would have her in time, but not for any fatigues.

The gray parlor was all ready; everything just as it had been before she left it. The ivies had been carefully tended, and the golden and brown canary was singing in his cage. There was nothing to remind of the different life to which, the place had been lent, making its last hours restful and pleasant, or of the death that had stepped so noiselessly and solemnly in.

Desire had formally made over this house to her cousin and co-heiress, Hazel Ripwinkley.

"It must never be left waiting, a mere possible convenience, for anybody," she said. "There must be a real life in it, as long as we can order it so."

The Ripwinkleys were to leave Aspen Street, and come here with Hazel. Miss Craydocke, who never had half room enough in Orchard Street, was to "spill over" from the Bee-hive into the Mile-hill house. "She knew just whom to put there; people who would take care and comfort. Them shouldn't be any hurt, and there would be lots of help."

There was a widow with three daughters, to begin with; "just as neat as a row of pins;" but who had had less and less to be neat with for seven years past; one of the daughters had just got a situation as compositor, and another as a book-keeper; between them, they could earn twelve hundred dollars a year. The youngest had to stay at home and help her mother do the work, that they might all keep together. They could pay three hundred dollars for four rooms; but of course they could not get decent ones, in a decent neighborhood, for that. That was what Bee-hives were for; houses that other people could do without.

Hazel had her wish; it came to pass that they also should make a bee-hive.

"And whenever I marry," Hazel said, "I hope he won't be building a town of his own to take me to; for I shall *have* to bring him here. I'm the last of the line."

"That will all be taken care of as the rest has been. There isn't half as much left for us to manage as we think," said Desire, putting back into the desk the copy of Uncle Titus's will which they had been reading over together. "He knew the executorship into which he gave it."

Shall I stop here with them until the Easter tide, and finish telling you how it all was?

There is a little bit about Bel Bree and Kate Sencerbox and the Schermans, which belongs somewhat earlier than that,—in those few pleasant days when March was beguiling us to believe in the more engaging of his double moods, and in the possibility of his behaving sweetly at the end, and going out after all like a lamb.

We can turn back afterwards for that. I think you would like to hear about the wedding.

Does it never occur to you that this "going back and living up" in a story-book is a sign of a possibility that may be laid by in the divine story-telling, for the things we have to hurry away from, and miss of, now? It does to me. I know that *That* can manage at least as well as mine can.

Christopher Kirkbright and Desire Ledwith were married in the library, where they had betrothed themselves; where Desire had felt all the sacredness of her life laid upon her; where she took up now another trust, that was only an outgrowth and expansion of the first, and for which she laid down nothing of its spirit and intent.

Mrs. Ledwith and the sisters—Mrs. Megilp and Glossy—were there, of course.

Mrs. Megilp had said over to herself little imaginary speeches about the homestead and old associations, and "Daisy's great love and reverence for all that touched the memory of her uncle, to whom she certainly owed everything;" about the journey to New York, and the few days they had to give there to Mr. Oldway's life-long friend and Desire's adviser, Mr. Marmaduke Wharne ("*Sir* Marmaduke he would be, everybody knew, if he had chosen to claim the English title that belonged to him"),—who was too infirm to come on to the wedding; and the necessity there was for them to go as fast as possible to their estate in the country,—Hill-hope,—where Mr. Kirkbright was building "mills and a village and a perfect castle of a house, and a private railroad and heaven knows what,"—all this to account, indirectly, for the quiet little ordinary ceremony, which of course would otherwise have been at the Church of the Holy Commandments; or at least up-stairs in the long, stately old drawing-room which was hardly ever used.

But none of the people were there to whom any such little speeches had to be made; nobody who needed any accounting to for its oddity was present at Desire Ledwith's wedding.

Mr. Vireo officiated; there was something in his method and manner which Mrs. Megilp decidedly objected to.

It was "everyday," she thought. "It didn't give you a feeling of sanctity. It was just as if he was used to the Almighty, and didn't mind! It seemed as if he were just mentioning things, in a quiet way, to somebody who was right at his elbow. For her part, she liked a little lifting up."

Hazel Ripwinkley heard her, and told Sylvie and Diana that "that came of having all your ideas of home in the seventh story; of course you wanted an elevator to go up in."

Desire Ledwith looked what she was, to-day; a grand, pure woman; a fit woman to stand up beside a man like Christopher Kirkbright, in fair white garments, and say the words that made her his wife. There was a beautiful, sweet majesty in her giving of herself.

She did not disdain rich robes to-day,—she would give herself at her very best, with all generous and gracious outward sign.

She wore a dress of heavy silk, long-trained; the cream-white folds, unspoiled by any frippery of lace, took, as they dropped around her, the shade and convolutions of a lily. Upon her bosom, and fastening her veil, were deep green leaves that gave the contrast against which a lily rests itself. Around her throat were links of frosted silver, from which hung a pure plain silver cross; these were the gift of Hazel. The veil, of point, and rarely beautiful, fell back from her head,—lovely in its shape, and the simple wreathing of the dark, soft hair,—like a drift of water spray; not covering or misting her all over,—only lending a touch of delicate suggestion to the pure, cool, graceful, flower-like unity of her whole air and apparel.

"Desire is beautiful!" said Hazel Ripwinkley to her mother. "She never *stopped* to be *pretty!*"

White calla-lilies, with their tall stems and great shadowy leaves, were in the Pompeiian vases on the mantel; in the India jars in the corners below; in a large Oriental china bowl that was set upon the closed desk on the library table, wheeled back for the first time that anybody there had seen it so, against the wall.

Hazel had hung a lily-wreath upon the carved back of Uncle Titus's chair, that no one might sit down in it, and placed it in the recess at Desire's left hand, as she should stand up to be married.

"Will you two take each other, to love and dwell together, and to do God's work, as He shall show and help you, so long as He keeps you both in this his world? Will you, Desire Ledwith, take Christopher Kirkbright to be your wedded husband; will you, Christopher Kirkbright, take Desire Ledwith to be your wedded wife; and do you thereto mutually make your vows in the sight of God and before this company?"

And they answered together, "We do."

It was a promise for more than each other; it was a life-consecration. It was a gathering up and renewal of all that had been holy in the resolves of either while they had lived apart; a joining of two souls in the Lord.

Hilary Vireo would not have dared to lead to perjury, by such words, a common man and woman. It was enough for such to ask if they would take, and keep to, each other.

Mrs. Megilp thought it was "so jumbled!" "If it was *her* daughter, she should not think she was half married."

Mrs. Megilp put it more shrewdly than she had intended.

Desire and Christopher Kirkbright were very sure they had *not* been "half married." It was not the world's half marriage that they had stood up there together for.

CHAPTER XXXIII
KITCHEN CRAMBO

Elise Mokey and Mary Pinfall came in one evening to see Bel Bree and Kate.

There had been company to tea up-stairs, and the dishes were more than usual, and the hour was a little later.

Kate was putting up the last of the cooking utensils, and scalding down the big tin dish-pan and the sink. Bel was up-stairs.

A table with a fresh brown linen cloth upon it, two white plates and cups, and two white *napkins*, stood out on the kitchen floor under the gas-light. The dumb-waiter came rumbling down, with toast dish, tea and coffee pots, oyster dish and muffin plate. Several slices of cream toast were left, and there was a generous remnant of nicely browned scalloped oysters. The half muffins, buttered hot, looked tender and tempting still.

Kate removed the dishes, sent up the waiter, and producing some nice little stone-ware nappies hot from the hot closet, transferred the food from the china to these, laying it neatly together, and replaced them in the closet, to wait till Bel should come. The tea and coffee she poured into small white pitchers, also hot in readiness, and set them on the range corner. Then she washed the porcelain and silver in fresh-drawn scalding water, wiped and set them safely on the long, white sideboard. There they gleamed in the gas-light, and lent their beauty to the brightness of the room, just as much as they would have done in actual using.

"But what a lot of trouble!" said Elise Mokey.

"Half a dozen dishes?" returned Kate. "Just three minutes' work; and a warm, fresh supper to make it worth while. Besides rubbing the silver once in four weeks, instead of every Friday. A Yankee kitchen is a labor-saving institution, Mrs. Scherman says."

Down came the waiter again, and down the stairs came Bel. Kate brought two more cups and plates and napkins.

"Now, girls, come and take some tea," she said, drawing up the chairs.

Mrs. Scherman was not strict about "kitchen company." She gave the girls freely to understand that a friend or two happening in now and then to see them, were as welcome to their down-stairs table as her own happeners in were to hers. "I know it is just the cosiness and the worth-while of home and living," she said. "And I'll trust the 'now and then' of it to you."

The hint of reasonable limit, and the word of trust, were better than lock and law.

"How nice this is!" said Mary Pinfall, as Bel put a hot muffin, mellow with sweet butter, upon her plate.

"If Matilda Meane only knew which side—and where—bread *was* buttered! She's living on 'relief,' yet; and she buys cream-cakes for dinner, and peanuts for tea! But, Bel, what were you up-stairs for? I thought you was queen o' the kitchen!"

"Kate gives me her chance, sometimes. We change about, to make things even. The best of it is in the up-stairs work, and waiting at table is the first-best chance of all. You see, you 'take it in at the pores,' as the man says in the play."

"Tea and oysters?" said Elise, with an exclamatory interrogation.

"You know better. See here, Elise. You don't half believe in this experiment, though you appreciate the muffins. But it isn't just loaves and fishes. There's a *living* in the world, and a way to earn it, besides clothes, and bread and butter. If you want it, you can choose your work nearest to where the living is. And wherever else it may or mayn't be, it *is* in houses, and round tea-tables like this."

"Other people's living,—for you to look at and wait on," said Elise. "I like to be independent."

"They can't keep it back from us, if they wanted to," said Bel. "And you *can't* be independent; there's no such thing in the world. It's all give and take."

"How about 'other folks' dust,' Kate? Do you remember?"

"There's only one place, I guess, after all," said Kate, "where you can be shut up with nothing but your own dust!"

"Sharper than ever, Kate Sencerbox! I guess you *do* get rubbed up!"

"Mr. Stalworth is there to-night," said Bel. "He tells as good stories as he writes. And they've been talking about Tyndall's Essays, and the spectroscope. Mrs. Scherman asked questions that I don't believe she'd any particular need of answers to, herself; and she stopped me once when I was going out of the room for something. I knew by her look that she wanted me to hear."

"If they want you to hear, why don't they ask you to sit down and hear comfortably?" said Elise Mokey, who had got her social science—with a *little* warp in it—from Boffin's Bower.

"Because it's my place to stand, at that time," said Bel, stoutly; "and I shouldn't be comfortable out of my place. I haven't earned a place like Mrs. Scherman's yet, or married a man that has earned it for me. There are proper things for everybody. It isn't always proper for Mrs. Scherman to sit down herself; or for Mr. Scherman to keep his hat on. It's the knowing what's proper that sets people really up; it *never* puts them down!"

"There's one thing," said Kate Sencerbox. "You might be parlor people all your days, and not get into everybody's parlor, either. There's an up-side and a down-side, all the way through, from top to bottom. The very best chance, for some people, if they only knew it, into some houses, would be up through the kitchen."

"Never mind," said Bel, putting sugar into Mary Pinfall's second cup of coffee. "I've got the notion of those lines, Kate,—I was going to tell you,—into my head at last, I do believe. Red-hot iron makes a rainbow through a prism, like any light; but iron-*steam* stops a stripe of the color; and every burning thing does the same way,—stops its own color when it shines through its own vapor; there! Let's hold on to that, and we'll go all over it another time. There's a piece about it in last month's Scribner."

"What *are* you talking about?" said Elise Mokey.

"The way they've been finding out what the sun is made of. By the black lines across the rainbow colors. It's a telegraph; they've just learned to read it."

"But what do *you* care?"

"I guess it's put there as much, for me as anybody," said Bel. "I don't think we should ever pick up such things, though, among the basting threads at Fillmer & Bylles'. They're lying round here, loose; in books and talk, and everything. They're going to have Crambo this evening, Kate. After these dishes are washed, I mean to try my hand at it. They were laughing about one Mrs. Scherman made last time; they couldn't quite remember it. I've got it. I picked it up among the sweepings. I shall take it in to her by and by."

Bel went to her work-basket as she spoke, and lifting up some calico pieces that lay upon it, drew from underneath two or three folded bits of paper.

"This is it," she said, selecting one, and coming back and reading.

(Do you see, let me ask in a hurried parenthesis, — how the tone of this household might easily have been a different one, and pervaded differently its auxiliary department? How, in that case, it might have been nothing better than a surreptitious scrap of silk or velvet, that would have lain in Bel Bree's work-basket, with a story about it of how, and for what gayety, it had been made; a scrap out of a life that these girls could only gossip and wonder about, — not participate, and with self-same human privilege and faculty delight in; and yet the only scrap that — "out of the sweepings" — they could have picked up? *There* is where, if you know it, dear parlor people, the up-side, by just living, can so graciously and generously be always helping the down.)

Bel read: —

"'What of that second great fire that was prophesied to come before Christmas?' — 'Peaches.'"

"You've got to get that word into the answer, you see and it hasn't the very least thing to do with it! Now see: —

'A prophet, after the event,

No startling wisdom teaches;

A second fire would scarce be sent

To gratify the morbid bent

That for fresh horror reaches.

But, friend, do tell me why you went

And mixed it up with *peaches!*'

It's great fun! And sometimes it's lovely, real poetry. Kate, you've got to give me some words and questions, I'm going to take to Crambo."

"You'll have to mix it up with dish-washing," said Elise. "Dish-washing and dust, — you can't get rid of them!"

"We do, though!" said Kate, alertly, jumping up and beginning to fetch the plates and cups from the dumb-waiter. "Here, Bel!" And she tossed three or four long, soft, clean towels over to her from the shelf beside the china.

"And about that dusting," she went on, after the noise of the hot water rushing from the faucet was over, and she began dropping the things carefully down through the cloud of steam into the great pan full of suds, and fishing them up again with a fork and a little mop,—"about the dusting, I didn't finish. It's a work of art to dust Mrs. Scherman's parlor. Don't you think there's a pleasure in handling and touching up and setting out all those pretty things? Don't they get to be a part of our having, too? Don't I take as much comfort in her fernery as she does? I know every little green and woolly loop that comes up in it. It's the only sense there is in things. There's a picture there, of cows coming home, down a green lane, and the sun striking through, and lighting up the gravel, and a patch of green grass, and the red hair on the cows' necks. You think you just catch it *coming*, suddenly, through the trees, when you first look up at it. And you go right into a little piece of the country, and stand there. Mr. Scherman doesn't own that lane, or those cows, though he bought the picture. All he owns is what he gets by the signs; and I get that, every day, for the dusting! There are things to be earned and shared where people *live*, that you can't earn in the sewing-shops."

"That's what Bel said. Well, I'm glad you like it. Sha'n't I wipe up some of those cups?"

"They're all done now," said Bel, piling them together.

In fifteen minutes after their own tea was ended, the kitchen was in order again; the dumb-waiter, with its freight, sent up to the china closet; the brown linen cloth and the napkins folded away in the drawer, and the white-topped table ready for evening use. Bel Bree had not been brought up in a New England farm-house, and seen her capable stepmother "whew round," to be hard put to it, now, over half a dozen cups and tumblers more or less.

"We must go," said Elise Mokey. "I've got the buttons to sew on to those last night-gowns of Miss Ledwith's. I want to carry them back to-morrow."

"You're lucky to sew for her," said Bel. "But you see we all have to do for somebody, and I'd as lief it would be teacups, for my part, as buttons."

Bel Bree's old tricks of rhyming were running in her head. This game of Crambo—a favorite one with the Schermans and their bright little intimate circle—stirred up her wits with a challenge. And under the wits,—under the quick mechanic action of the serving brain,—thoughts had been daily crowding and growing, for which these mere mental facilities were waiting, the ready instruments.

I have said that Bel Bree was a born reformer and a born poet; and that the two things go together. To see freshly and clearly,—to discern new meaning in old living,—living as old as the world is; to find by instinct new and better ways of doing, the finding of which is often only returning to the heart and simplicity of the old living before it *was* old with social circumventions and needed to be fresh interpreted; these are the very heavenly gift and office of illumination and leadership. Just as she had been made, and just where she had been put,—a girl with the questions of woman-life before her in these days of restless asking and uncertain reply,—with her lot cast here, in this very crowding, fermenting, aspiring, great New England metropolis, in the hour of its most changeful and involved experience,—she brought the divine talisman of her nature to bear upon the nearest, most practical point of the wide tangle with which it came in contact. And around her in this right place that she had found and taken, gathered and wrought already, by effluence and influence, forces and results that gather and work about any nucleus of life, however deep hidden it may be in a surrounding deadness. All things,—creation itself,—as Asenath had said, must begin in spots; and she and Bel Bree had begun a fair new spot, in which was a vitality that tends to organic completeness, to full establishment, and triumphant growth.

Upon Bel herself reflected quickly and surely the beneficent action of this life. She was taking in truly, at every pore. How long would it have been before, out of the hard coarse limits in which her one line of labor and association had first placed her, she would have come up into such an atmosphere as was here, ready made for her to breathe and abide in? To help make also; to stand at its practical mainspring, and keep it possible that it should move on.

The talk, the ideas of the day, were in her ears; the books, the periodicals of the day were at hand, and free for her to avail herself of. The very fun at Mrs, Scherman's tea-table was the sort of fun that can only sparkle out of culture. There was a grace that her aptness caught, and that was making a lady of her.

"I'll give in," said Elise Mokey, "that you're getting *style*; though I can't tell how it is either. It ain't in your calico dresses, nor the doing up of your hair."

Perhaps it was a good deal in the very simplifying of these from the exaggerated imitations of the shop and street, as well as in the tone of all the rest with which these inevitably fell into harmony.

But I want to tell you about Bel's kitchen Crambo. I want to show you how what is in a woman, in heart and mind, springs up and shows itself, and may grow to whatever is meant for it, out of the quietest background of homely use.

She brought out pencil and paper, and made Kate write question slips and detached words.

"I feel just tingling to try," she said. "There's a kind of dancing in my head, of things that have been there ever so long. I believe I shall make a poem to-night. It's catching, when you're predisposed; and it's partly the spring weather, and the sap coming up. 'Put a name to it,' Katie! Almost anything will set me off."

Kate wrote, on half a dozen scraps; then tossed them up, and pushed them over for Bel to draw.

"How do you like the city in the spring?" was the question; and the word, suggested by Kate's work at the moment, was,—"Hem."

Bel put her elbows on the table, and her hands up against her ears. Her eyes shone, as they rested intent upon the two penciled bits. The link between them suggested itself quickly and faintly; she was grasping at an elusive something with all the fine little quivering brain-tentacles that lay hold of spiritual apprehension.

Just at that moment the parlor bell rang.

"I'll go," she said. "You keep to your sewing. It's for the nursery, I guess, and I'll do my poem up there."

She caught up pencil and paper, and the other fragment also,—Mrs. Scherman's own rhyme about the "peaches."

Mrs. Scherman met her at the parlor door.

"I'm sorry to interrupt you," she said; "but the baby is stirring. Could you, or Kate, go up and try to hush her off again? If I go, she'll keep me."

"I will," said Bel. "Here is that 'Crambo' you were talking of at tea, Mrs. Scherman. I kept it. Kate picked it up with the scraps."

"O, thank you! Why, Bel, how your face shines!"

Bel hurried off, for Baby Karen "stirred" more emphatically at this moment. Asenath went back into the parlor.

"Here is that rhyme of mine, Frank, that you were asking for. Bel found it in the dust-pan. I believe she's writing rhymes herself. She tries out every idea she picks up among us. She had a pencil in her hand, and her face was brimful of something. Mr. Stalworth, if *I* find anything in the dust-pan, I shall turn it over to you. 'First and Last' is bound to act up to its title, and transpose itself freely, according to Scripture."

"'First and Last' will receive, under either head, whatever you will indorse, Mrs. Scherman,—and the last not least,"—returned the benign and brilliant editor.

Bel had a knack with a baby. She knew enough to understand that small human beings have a good many feelings and experiences precisely like those of large ones. She knew that if *she* woke up in the night, she should not be likely to fall asleep again if pulled up out of her bed into the cold; nor if she were very much patted and talked to. So she just took gently hold of the upper edge of the small, fine blanket in which Baby Karen was wrapped, and by it drew her quietly over upon her other side. The little limbs fell into a new place and sensation of rest, as larger limbs do; little Karen put off waking up and crying for one delicious instant, as anybody would; and in that instant sleep laid hold of her again. She was safe, now, for another hour or two, at least.

Mrs. Scherman said she had really never had so little trouble with a baby as with this one, who had nobody especially appointed to make out her own necessity by constant "tending."

Bel did not go down-stairs again. She could do better here than with Kate sitting opposite, aware of all her scratches and poetical predicaments.

An hour went by. Bel was hardly equal yet to five-minute Crambo; and besides, she was doing her best; trying to put something clearly into syllables that said itself, unsyllabled, to her.

She did not hear Mrs. Scherman when she came up the stairs. She had just read over to herself the five completed stanzas of her poem.

It had really come. It was as if a violet had been born to actual bloom from the thought, the intangible vision of one. She wondered at the phrasing, marveling how those particular words had come and ranged themselves at her call. She did not know how she had done it, or whether she herself had done it at all. She began almost to think she must have read it before somewhere. Had she just picked it up out of her memory? Was it a borrowing, a mimicry, a patchwork?

But it was very pretty, very sweet! It told her own feelings over to her, with more that she had not known she had felt or perceived. She read it again from beginning to end in a whisper. Her mouth was bright with a smile and her eyes with tears when she had ended.

Asenath Scherman with her light step came in and stood beside her.

"Won't you tell *me*?" the sweet, gracious voice demanded.

Bel Bree looked up.

"I thought I'd try, in fun," she said, "and it came in real earnest."

Asenath forgot that the face turned up to hers, with the smile and the tears and the color in it, was the face of her hired servant. A lovely soul, all alight with thought and gladness, met her through it.

She bent down and touched Bel's forehead with her lady-lips.

Bel put the little scribbled paper in her hand, and ran away, up-stairs.

"Will you give it to me, Bel, and let me do what I please with it?"—Mrs. Scherman went to Bel and asked next day.

Bel blushed. She had been a little frightened in the morning to think of what had happened over night. She could not quite recollect all the words of her verses, and she wondered if they were really as pretty as she had fancied in the moment of making them.

All she could answer was that Mrs. Scherman was "very kind."

"Then you'll trust me?"

And Bel, wondering very much, but too shy to question, said she would.

A few days after that, Asenath called her up-stairs. The postman had rung five minutes before, and Kate had carried up a note.

"We were just in time with our little spring song," she said. "*Blue*birds have to sing early; at least a month beforehand. See here! Is this all right?" and she put into Bel's hand a little roughish slip of paper, upon which was printed:—

"THE CITY IN SPRING.

"It is not much that makes me glad:
I hold more than I ever had.
The empty hand may farther reach,
And small, sweet signs all beauty teach.

"I like the city in the spring,
It has a hint of everything.
Down in the yard I like to see
The budding of that single tree.

"The little sparrows on the shed;
The scrap of soft sky overhead;
The cat upon the sunny wall;
There's so much *meant* among them all.

"The dandelion in the cleft
A broken pavement may have left,
Is like the star that, still and sweet,
Shines where the house-tops almost meet.

"I like a little; all the rest
Is somewhere; and our Lord knows best
How the whole robe hath grace for them
Who only touch the garment's hem."

At the bottom, in small capitals, was the signature,—Bel Bree.

"I don't understand," said Bel, bewildered. "What is it? Who did it?"

"It is a proof," said Mrs. Scherman. "A proof-sheet. And here is another kind of proof that came with it. Your spring song is going into the May number of 'First and Last.'"

Mrs. Scherman reached out a slip of paper, printed and filled in.

It was a publisher's check for fifteen dollars.

"You see I'm very unselfish, Bel," she said. "I'm going to work the very way to lose you."

Bel's eyes flashed up wide at her.

The way to lose her! Why, nobody had ever got such a hold upon her before! The printed verses and the money were wonderful surprises, but they were not the surprise that had gone straight into her heart, and dropped a grapple there. Mrs. Scherman had believed in her; and she had *kissed* her. Bel Bree would never forget that, though she should live to sing songs of all the years.

"When you can earn money like this, of course I cannot expect to keep you in my kitchen," said Mrs. Scherman, answering her look.

"I might never do it again in all my life," sensible Bel replied. "And I hope you'll keep me somewhere. It wouldn't be any reason, I think, because one little green leaf has budded out, for a plant to say that it would not be kept growing in the ground any longer. I couldn't go and set up a poem-factory, without a home and a living for the poems to grow up out of. I'm pleased I can write!" she exclaimed, brimming up suddenly with the pleasure she had but half stopped to realize. "I *thought* I could. But I know very well that the best and brightest things I've ever thought have come into my head over the ironing-board or the bread-making. Even at home. And *here*,—why, Mrs. Scherman, it's *living* in a poem here! And if you can be in the very foundation part of such living, you're in the realest place of all, I think. I don't believe poetry can be skimmed off the top, till it has risen up from the bottom!"

"But you *ought* to come into my parlor, among my friends! People would be glad to get you into their parlors, by and by, when you have made the name you can make. I've no business to keep you down. And you don't know yourself. You won't stay."

"Just please wait and see," said Bel. "I haven't a great deal of experience in going about in parlors; but I don't think I should much like it,—*that* way. I'd rather keep on being the woman that made the name, than to run round airing it. I guess it would keep better."

"I see I can't advise you. I shouldn't dare to meddle with inspirations. But I'm proud, and glad, Bel; and you're my friend! The rest will all work out right, somehow."

"Thank you, dear Mrs. Scherman," said Bel, her voice full of feeling. "And—if you please—will you have the grouse broiled to-day, or roasted with bread-sauce?"

At that, the two young women laughed out, in each other's faces.

Bel stopped first.

"It isn't half so funny as it sounds," she said. "It's part of the poetry; the rhyme's inside; it is to everything. We're human people: that's the way we get it."

And Bel went away, and stuffed the grouse, and grated her bread-crumbs, and sang over her work,—not out loud with her lips, but over and over to a merry measure in her mind,—

"Everything comes to its luck some day:

I've got chickens! What will folks say?"

"I'm solving more than I set out to do," Sin Scherman said to her husband. "Westover was nothing to it. I know one thing, though, that I'll do next."

"*One* thing is reasonable," said Frank. "What is it?"

"Take her to York with us, this summer. Row out on the river with her. Sit on the rocks, and read and sew, and play with the children. Show her the ocean. She never saw it in all her life."

"How wonderful is 'one thing' in the mind of a woman! It is a germ-cell, that holds all things."

"Thank you, my dear. If I weren't helping you to soup, I'd get up and make you a courtesy. But what a grand privilege it is for a man to live with a woman, after he has found that out! And how cosmical a woman feels herself when her capacity is recognized!"

Mrs. Scherman has told her plan to Bel. Kate also has a plan for the two summer months in which the household must be broken up.

"I mean to see the mountains myself," she said, boldly. "I don't see why I shouldn't go to the country. There are homes there that want help, as well as here. I can get my living where the living goes. That's just where it fays in, different from other work. Bel knows places where I could get two dollars a week just for a little helping round; or I could even afford to pay board, and buy a little time for resting. I shall have clothes to make, and fix over. It always took all I could earn, before, to keep me from hand to mouth. I never saw six months' wages all together, in my life. I feel real rich."

"I will pay you half wages for the two months," said Mrs. Scherman, "if you will come back to me in September. And next year, if we all keep together, it will be your turn, if you like, to go with me."

Kate feels the spring in her heart, knowing that she is to have a piece of the summer. The horse-chestnut tree in the yard is not a mockery to her. She has a property in every promise that its great brown buds are making.

"The pleasant weather used to be like the spring-suits," she said. "Something making up for other people. Nothing to me, except more work, with a little difference. Now, somewhere, the hills are getting green for me! I'm one of the meek, that inherit the earth!"

"You are earning a *whole* living," Bel said, reverting to her favorite and comprehensive conclusion.

"And yet,—*somebody* has got to run machines," said Kate.

"But *all* the bodies haven't. That is the mistake we have been making. That keeps the pay low, and makes it horrid. There's a *little* more room now, where you and I were. Anyhow, we Yankee girls have a right to our turn at the home-wheels. If we had been as cute as we thought we were, we should have found it out before."

Bel Bree has written half a dozen little poems at odd times, since the rhyme that began her fortune. Mr. Stalworth says they are stamped with her own name, every one; breezy, and freshly delicious. For that very reason, of course, people will not believe, when they see the name in print, that it is a real name. It is so much easier to believe in little tricks of invention, than in things that simply come to pass by a wonderful, beautiful determination, because they belong so. They think the poem is a trick of invention, too. They think that of almost everything that they see in print. Their incredulity is marvelously credulous! There is no end to that which mortals may contrive; but the limit is such a measurable one to that which can really be! We slip our human leash so easily, and get outside of all creation, and the "Divinity that shapes our ends," to shape and to create, ourselves!

For my part, the more stories I write out, the more I learn how, even in fiction, things happen and take relation according to some hidden reality; that we have only to stand by, and see the shiftings and combinings, and with what care and honesty we may, to put them down.

If there is anything in this story that you cannot credit,—if you cannot believe in such a relation, and such a friendship, and such a mutual service, as Asenath Scherman's and Bel Bree's,—if you cannot believe that Bel Bree may at this moment be ironing Mrs. Scherman's damask table-cloths, and as the ivy leaf or morning-glory pattern comes out under the polish, some beautiful thought in her takes line and shade under the very rub of labor, and shows itself as it would have done no other way, and that by and by it will shine on a printed page, made substantive in words,—then, perhaps, you have only not lived quite long—or deep—enough. There is a more real and perfect architecture than any that has ever got worked out in stone, or even sketched on paper.

Neither Boston, nor the world, is "finished" yet. There may be many a burning and rebuilding, first. Meanwhile, we will tell what we can see.

And that word sends me back to Bel herself, of whom this present seeing and telling can read and recite no further.

Are you dissatisfied to leave her here? Is it a pity, you think, that the little glimmer of romance in Leicester Place meant nothing, after all? There are blind turns in the labyrinth of life. Would you have our Bel lost in a blind turn?

The *right and the wrong* settled it, as they settle all things. The right and the wrong are the reins with which we are guided into the very best, sooner or later; yes,—sooner *and* later. If we will go God's way, we shall have manifold more in this present world, and in the world to come life everlasting.

CHAPTER XXXIV
WHAT NOBODY COULD HELP

Mr. and Mrs. Kirkbright went away to New York on the afternoon of their marriage.

Miss Euphrasia went up to Brickfields. Sylvie Argenter was to follow her on Thursday. It had been settled that she should remain with Desire, who, with her husband, would reach home on Saturday.

It was a sweet, pleasant spring day, when Sylvie Argenter, with some last boxes and packages, took the northward train for Tillington.

She was going to a life of use and service. She was going into a home; a home that not only made a fitting place for her in it, and was perfect in itself, but that, with noble plan and enlargement, found way to reach its safety and benediction, and the contagion of its spirit, over souls that would turn toward it, come under its rule, and receive from it, as their only shelter and salvation; over a neighborhood that was to be a planting of Hope,—a heavenly feudality.

Sylvie's own dreams of a possible future for herself were only purple lights upon a far horizon.

It seemed a very great way off, any bringing to speech and result the mute, infrequent signs of what was yet the very real, secret strength and joy and hope of her girl's heart.

She had a thought of Rodney Sherrett that she was sure she had a right to. That was all she wanted, yet. Of course, Rodney was not ready to marry; he was too young; he was not much older than she was, and that was very young for a man. She did not even think about it; she recognized the whole position without thinking.

She remembered vividly the little way-station in Middlesex, where he had bought the ferns, that day in last October; she thought of him as the train ran slowly alongside the platform at East Keaton. She wondered if he would not sometimes come up for a Sunday; to spend it with his uncle and his Aunt Euphrasia. It was a secret gladness to her that she was to be where he partly, and very affectionately, belonged. She was sure she should see him, now and then. Her life looked pleasant to her, its current setting alongside one current, certainly, of his.

She sat thinking how he had come up behind her that day in the drawing-room car, and of all the happy nonsense they had begun to talk, in such a hurry, together. She was lost in the imagination of that old surprise, living it over again, remembering how it had seemed when she suddenly knew that it was he who touched her shoulder. Her thought of him was a backward thought, with a sense in it of his presence just behind her again, perhaps, if she should turn her head,—which she would not do, for all the world, to break the spell,—when suddenly,—face to face,—through the car-window, she awoke to his eyes and smile.

"How did you know?" she asked, as he came in and took the seat beside her. Then she blushed to think what she had taken for granted.

"I didn't," he answered; "except as a Yankee always knows things, and a cat comes down upon her feet. I am taking a week's holiday, and I began it two days sooner, that I might run up to see Aunt Effie before I go down to Boston to meet my father. The steamer will be due by Saturday. It is my first holiday since I went to Arlesbury. I'm turning into a regular old Gradgrind, Miss Sylvie."

Sylvie smiled at him, as if a regular old Gradgrind were just the most beautiful and praiseworthy creature a bright, hearty young fellow could turn into.

"You'd better not encourage me," he said, shaking his head. "It would be a dreadful thing if I should get sordid, you know. I'm not apt to stop half way in anything; and I'm awfully in earnest now about saving up money."

He had to stop there. He was coming close to motives, and these he could say nothing about.

But a sudden stop, in speech as in music, is sometimes more significant than any stricken note.

Sylvie did not speak at once, either. She was thinking what different reasons there might be, for spending or saving; how there might be hardest self-denial in most uncalculating extravagance.

When she found that they were growing awkwardly quiet, she said,—"I suppose the right thing is to remember that there is neither virtue nor blame in just saving or not saving."

"My father lost a good deal by the fire," said Rodney. "More than he thought, at first. He is coming home sooner, in consequence. I'm very glad I did not go abroad. I should have been just whirled out of everything, if I had. As it is, I'm in a place; I've got a lever planted. It's no time now for a fellow to look round for a foothold."

"You like Arlesbury?" asked Sylvie. "I think it must be a lovely place."

"Why?" said Rodney, taken by surprise.

"From the piece of it you sent me in the winter."

"Oh! those ferns? I'm glad you liked them. There's something nice and plucky about those little things, isn't there?"

It was every word he could think of to reply. He had a provoked perception that was not altogether nice and plucky, of himself, just then. But that was because the snow was still unlifted from him. He was under a burden of coldness and constraint. Somebody ought to come and take it away. It was time. The spring, that would not be kept back, was here.

He had not said a word to Sylvie about her mother. How could he speak of what had left her alone in the world, and not say that he wanted to make a new world for her? That he had longed for it through all her troubles, and that this, and nothing else, was what he was keeping his probation for?

So they came to Tillington at last, and there had been between them only little drifting talk of the moment, that told nothing.

After all, do we not, for a great part, drift through life so, giving each other crumbs off the loaf that will only seem to break in that paltry way? And by and by, when the journey is over, do we not wonder that we could not have given better and more at a time? Yet the crumbs have the leaven and the sweetness of the loaf in them; the commonest little wayside things are charged full of whatever is really within us. God's own love is broken small for us. "This is my Body, broken for you."

If life were nothing but what gets phrased and substanced, the world might as well be rolled up and laid away again in darkness.

Sylvie had a handful of checks; Rodney took them from her, and went out to the end of the platform to find the boxes. Two vehicles had been driven over from Hill-hope to meet her; an open spring-wagon for the luggage, and a chaise-top buggy to convey herself.

Trunks, boxes, and the great padlocked basket were speedily piled upon the wagon; then the two men who had come jumped up together to the front seat of the same, and Sylvie saw that it was left for her and Rodney to proceed together for the seven-mile drive.

Rodney came back to her with an alert and felicitous air. How could he help the falling out of this? Of course he could not ride upon the wagon and leave a farm-boy to charioteer Sylvie.

"Shall you be afraid of me?" he asked, as he tossed in his valise for a footstool, and carefully bestowed Sylvie's shawl against the back, to cushion her more comfortably. "Do you suppose we can manage to get over there without running down a bake-shop?"

"Or a cider-mill," said Sylvie, laughing. "You will have to adapt your exploits to circumstances."

Up and down, through that beautiful, wild hill-country, the brown country roadway wound; now going straight up a pitch that looked as perpendicular as you approached it as the side of a barn; then flinging itself down such a steep as seemed at every turn to come to a blank end, and to lead off with a plunge, into air; the water-bars, ridged across at rough intervals, girding it to the bosom of the mountain, and breaking the accelerated velocity of the descending wheels. Sylvie caught her breath, more than once; but she did it behind shut lips, with only a dilatation of her nostrils. She was so afraid that Rodney might think she doubted his driving.

The woods were growing tender with fretwork of swelling buds, and beautiful with bright, young hemlock-tips; there was a twittering and calling of birds all through the air; the first little breaths and ripples of spring music before the whole gay, summer burst of song gushed forth.

The fields lay rich in brown seams, where the plough had newly furrowed them. Farmers were throwing in seed of barley and spring wheat. The cattle were standing in the low sunshine, in barn-doors and milking-yards. Sheep were browsing the little buds on the pasture bushes.

The April day would soon be over. To-morrow might bring a cold wind, perhaps; but the winter had been long and hard; and after such, we believe in the spring pleasantness when it comes.

"What a little way brings us into a different world!" said Sylvie as they rode along. "Just back there in the city, you can hardly believe in these hills."

Her own words reminded her.

"I suppose we shall find, sometime," she said gently, "that the other world is only a little way out."

"I've been very sorry for you, Sylvie," said Rodney. "I hope you know that."

His slight abruptness told her how the thought had been ready and pressing for speech, underneath all their casual talk.

And he had dropped the prefix from her name.

He had not meant to, but he could not go back and put it on. It was another little falling out that he could not help. The things he could not help were the most comfortable.

"Mother would have had a very hard time if she had lived," said Sylvie. "I am glad for her. It was a great deal better. And it came so tenderly! I had dreaded sickness and pain for her."

"It has been all hard for you. I hope it will be easier now. I hope it will always be easier."

"I am going to live with Mrs. Kirkbright," said Sylvie.

"Tell me about my new aunt," said Rodney.

Sylvie was glad to go on about Desire, about the wedding, about Hillhope, and the plans for living there.

"I think it will be almost like heaven," she said. "It will be home and happiness; all that people look forward to for themselves. And yet, right alongside, there will be the work and the help. It will open right out into it, as heaven does into earth. Mr. Kirkbright is a grand man."

"Yes. He's one of the ten-talent people. But I suppose we can all do something. It is good to have some little one-horse teams for the light jobs."

"I never could *be* Desire," said Sylvie. "But I am glad, to work with her. I am glad to live one of the little lives."

There would always be a boy and girl simpleness between these two, and in their taking of the world together. And that is good for the world, as well. It cannot be all made of mountains. If all were high and grand, it would be as if nothing were. Heaven itself is not built like that.

"There goes some of Uncle Christopher's stuff, I suppose," said Rodney, a while afterward, as they came to the top of a long ascent. He pointed to a great loaded wain that stood with its three powerful horses on the crest of a forward hill. It was piled high up with tiling and drain-pipe, packed with straw. The long cylinders showed their round mouths behind, like the mouths of cannon.

"A nice cargo for these hills, I should think."

"They have brakes on the wheels, of course," said Sylvie. "And the horses are strong. That must be for the new houses. They will soon make all those things here. Mr. Kirkbright has large contracts for brick, already. He has been sending down specimens. They say the clay is of remarkably fine quality."

"We shall have to get by that thing, presently," said Rodney. "I hope the horse will take it well."

"Are you trying to frighten me?" asked Sylvie, smiling. "I'm used to these roads. I have spent half a summer here, you know."

But Rodney knew that it was the "being used" that would be the question with the horse. He doubted if the little country beast had ever seen drain-pipe before. He had once driven Red Squirrel past a steam boiler that was being transported on a truck. He remembered the writhe with which the animal had doubled himself, and the side spring he had made. It was growing dusk, now, also. They were not more than a mile from Brickfield Basin, and the sun was dropping behind the hills.

"I shall take you out, and lead him by," he said. "I've no wish to give you another spill. We won't go on through life in that way."

It was quite as well that they had only another mile to go. Rodney was keeping his promise, but the thread of it was wearing very thin.

They rode slowly up the opposite slope, then waited, in their turn, on the top, to give the team time to reach the next level.

They heard it creak and grind as it wore heavily down, taking up the whole track with careful zigzag tackings; they could see, as it turned, how the pole stood sharp up between the shoulders of the straining wheel horses, as their haunches pressed out either way, and their backs hollowed, and their noses came together, and the driver touched them dexterously right and left upon their flanks to bring them in again.

"Uncle Kit has a good teamster there," said Rodney.

Just against the foot of the next rise, they overtook him. The gray nag that Rodney drove pricked his ears and stretched his head up, and began to take short, cringing steps, as they drew near the formidable, moving mass.

Rodney jumped out, and keeping eye and hand upon him, helped down Sylvie also. Then he threw the long reins over his arm, and took the horse by the bridle.

The animal made a half parenthesis of himself, curving skittishly, and watching jealously, as he went by the frightsome pile.

"You see it was as well not to risk it," Rodney said, as Sylvie came up with him beyond. "He would have had us down there among the blackberry vines. He's all right now. Will you get in?"

"Let us walk on to the top," said Sylvie. "It is so pleasant to feel one's feet upon the ground."

They kept on, accordingly; the slow team rumbling behind them. At the top, was a wide, beautiful level; oak-trees and maples grew along the roadside, and fields stretched out along a table land to right and left. Before them, lying in the golden mist of twilight, was a sea of distant hill-tops, —

purple and shadow-black and gray. The sky bent down its tender, mellow sphere, and touched them softly.

Sylvie stood still, with folded hands, and Rodney stopped the horse. A rod or two back, just at the edge of the level, the loaded wagon had stopped also.

"Hills,—and the sunset,—and stillness," said Sylvie. "They always seem like heaven."

Rodney stood with his right hand, from which fell the looped reins, reached up and resting on the saddle.

"I never saw a sight like that before," he said.

While they looked, the evening star trembled out through the clear saffron, above the floating mist that hung among the hills.

"O, they never can help it!" exclaimed Sylvie, suddenly.

"Help it? Who?" asked Rodney, wondering.

"Beginning again. Growing good. Those people who are coming up to Hill-hope. There's a man coming, with his wife; a young man, who got into bad ways, and took to drinking. Mr. Vireo has been watching and advising him so long! He married them, five years ago, and they have two little children. The wife is delicate; she has worried through everything. She has taken in working-men's washing, to earn the rent; and he had a good trade, too; he was a plasterer. He has really tried; but it was no use in the city; it was all around him. And he lost character and chances; the bosses wouldn't have him, he said. When he was trying most, sometimes, they wouldn't believe in him; and then there would come idle days, and he would meet old companions, and get led off, and then there would be weeks of misery. Now he is coming away from it all. There is a little cottage ready, with a garden; the little wife is so happy! He *can't* get it here; and he will have work at his trade, and will learn brickmaking. Do you know, I think a place like this, where such work is doing, is almost better than heaven, where it is all done, Rodney!"

She spoke his name, as he had hers a little while ago, without thinking. He turned his face toward her with a look which kindled into sudden light at that last word, but which had warmed all through before with the generous pathos of what she told him, and the earnest, simple way of it.

"I've found out that even in our own affairs, *making* is better than ready-made," he said. "This last year has been the best year of my life. If my father had given me fifty thousand dollars, and told me I might—have all my own way with it,—I shouldn't have thanked him as much to-day, as I do. But I wish that steamer were in, and he were here! He has got something which belongs to me, and I want him to give it back."

After enunciating this little riddle, Rodney changed hands with his reins, and faced about toward the vehicle, reaching his other to Sylvie.

"You had better jump in," he said; and there was a tone and an inflection at the pause, as if another word, that would have been tenderly spoken, hung refrained upon it. "We must get well ahead of that old catapult."

They drove on rapidly along the level; then they came to the long, gradual slope that brought them down into Brickfields.

To the right, just before reaching the Basin, a turn struck off that skirted round, partly ascending again until it fell into the Cone Hill road and so led direct to Hill-hope.

They could see the buildings, grouped picturesquely against rocks and pines and down against the root of the green hill. They had all been painted of a light gray or slate color, with red roofs.

They passed on, down into the shadows, where trees were thick and dark. A damp, rich smell of the woods was about them,—a different atmosphere from the breath of the hill-top. They heard the tinkle of little unseen streams, and the far-off, foaming plunge of the cascades.

Suddenly, there came a sound behind them like the rush of an avalanche; a noise that seemed to fill up all the space of the air, and to gather itself down toward them on every side alike.

"O, Rodney, turn!" cried Sylvie.

But there was a horrible second in which he could not know how to turn.

He did not stop to look, even. He sprang, with one leap, he knew not how,—over step or dasher,—to the horse's head. He seized him by the bridle, and pulled him off the road, into a thicket of bush-branches, in a hollow rough with stones.

The wheels caught fast; Rodney clung to the horse, who tried to rear; Sylvie sat still on the seat sloped with the sharp cant of the half-overturned vehicle.

There was only a single instant. Down, with the awful roar of an earthquake, came crashing swift and headlong, passing within a hand's breadth of their wheel, the enormous, toppling, loaded team; its three strong horses in a wild, plunging gallop; heels, heads, haunches, one dark, frantic, struggling tumble and rush. An instant more, of paralyzed breathlessness, and then a thundering fall, that made the ground quiver under their feet; then a stillness more suddenly dreadful than the noise. A great cloud of dust rose slowly up into the air, and showed dimly in the dusky light.

The gray horse quieted, cowed by the very terror and the hush. Sylvie slipped down from the tilting buggy, and found her feet upon a stone.

Rodney reached out one hand, and she came to his side. He put his arm around her, and drew her close.

"My darling little Sylvie!" he said.

She turned her face, and leaned it down upon his shoulder.

"O, Rodney, the poor man is killed!"

But as they stood so, a figure came toward them, over the high water-bar below which they had stopped.

"For God's sake, is anybody hurt?" asked a strange, hoarse voice with a tremble in it.

"Nobody!"

"O, are you the driver? I thought you must be killed! How thankful!" — And Sylvie sobbed on Rodney's shoulder.

"Can I help you?" asked the man.

"No, look after your horses." And the man went on, down into the dust, where the wreck was.

"We'll go, and send help to you," shouted Rodney.

Then he backed the gray horse carefully out upon the road again.

"Will you dare get in?" he asked of Sylvie.

"I do not think we had better. How can we tell how it is down there? We may not be able to pass."

"It is below the turn, I think. But come, — we'll walk."

He took the bridle again, and gave his other hand to Sylvie. Holding each other so, they went along.

When they came to the turn, they could see, just beyond the mass of ruin; the great wagon, three wheels in the air, — one rolled away into the ditch; the broken freight, flung all across the road, and lying piled about the wagon. One horse was dead, — buried underneath. Another lay motionless, making horrid moans. The teamster was freeing the third — the leader, which stood safe — from chains and harness.

Leading him, the man came up with Rodney and Sylvie, as they turned into the side road.

"I knew you were just ahead, when it happened. I thought you were gone for certain."

"There was a Mercy over us all!" said Sylvie, with sweet, tremulous intenseness.

The rough man lifted his hand to his bare head. Rodney clasped tighter the little fingers that lay within his own.

"What did happen?" he asked.

"The brake-rod broke; the pole-strap gave way; it was all in a heap in a minute. I saw it was no use; I had to jump. And then I thought of you. I'm glad you saw me, sir. You know I was sober."

"I know you were sober, and managing most skillfully. I had been saying that."

"Thank you, sir. It's an awful job."

"Hark!" said Sylvie. "There's the man with the trunks."

"I forgot all about him," said Rodney.

"That's a fact," said the teamster. "Turn down here, to let him by. Hallo!"

"Hallo! Come to grief?"

"We just have, then. Go ahead, will you, and bring back—*something to shoot with*," he added, in a lower tone, and coming close,—remembering Sylvie. "I had a crow-bar, but it's lost in the jumble. I'll stay here, now."

The wagon drove by, rapidly. The man led his horse down by the wall, to wait there. Sylvie and Rodney, hand in hand, walked on.

Sylvie shivered with the horrible excitement; her teeth chattered; a nervous trembling was taking hold of her.

Rodney put his arm round her again. "Don't tremble, dear," he said.

"O, Rodney! What were we kept alive for?"

"For each other," whispered Rodney.

CHAPTER XXXV
HILL-HOPE

They were sitting together, the next day, on the rock below the cascade, in the warm sunshine.

Aunt Euphrasia knew all about it; Aunt Euphrasia had let them go down there together. She was as content as Rodney in the thing that could not now be helped.

"I've broken my promise," said Rodney to Sylvie. "I agreed with my father that I wouldn't be engaged for two years."

"Why, we aren't engaged,—yet,—are we?" asked Sylvie, with bewitching surprise.

"I don't know," said Rodney, his old, merry, mischievous twinkle coming in the corners of his eyes, as he flashed them up at her. "I think we've got the refusal of each other!"

"Well. We'll keep it so. We'll wait. You shall not break any promise for me," said Sylvie, still sweetly obtuse.

"I'm satisfied with that way of looking at it," said Rodney, laughing out. "Unless—you mean to be as cunning about everything else, Sylvie. In that case, I don't know; I'm afraid you'd be dangerous."

"I wonder if I'm always going to be dangerous to you," said Sylvie, gravely, taking up the word. "I always get you into an accident."

"When we take matters quietly, the way they were meant to go, we shall leave off being hustled, I suppose," said Rodney, just as gravely. "There has certainly been intent in the way we have been—thrown together!"

"I don't believe you ought to say such things, Rodney,—yet! You are talking just as if"—

"We weren't waiting. O, yes! I'm glad you invented that little temporary arrangement. But it's a difficult one to carry out. I shall be gladder when my father comes. I'm tired of being Casabianca. I don't see how we can talk at all. Mayn't I tell you about a little house there is at Arlesbury, with a square porch and a three-windowed room over it, where anybody could sit and sew—among plants and things—and see all up and down the road, to and from the mills? A little brown house, with turf up to the door-stone, and only a hundred dollars a year? Mayn't I tell you how much I've saved up, and how I like being a real working man with a salary, just as you liked being one of the Other Girls?"

"Yes; you may tell me that; that last," said Sylvie, softly. "You may tell me anything you like about yourself."

"Then I must tell you that I never should have been good for anything if it hadn't been for you."

"O, dear!" said Sylvie. "I don't see how we *can* talk. It keeps coming back again. I've had all those plants kept safe that you sent me, Rodney," she began, briskly, upon a fresh tack.

"Those very ivies? Ah, the little three-windowed room!"

"Rodney! I didn't think you were so unprincipled!" said Sylvie, getting up. "I wouldn't have come down here, if I had known there was a promise! I shall certainly help you keep it. I shall go away."

She turned round, and met a gentleman coming down along the slope of the smooth, broad rock.

"Mr. Sherrett!—Rodney!"

Rodney sprang to his feet.

"My boy! How are you?"

"Father! When—how—did you come?"

"I came to Tillington by the late train last night, and have just driven over. I went to Arlesbury yesterday."

"But the steamer! She wasn't due till Sunday. You sailed the *ninth*?"

"No. I exchanged passages with a friend who was detained in London. I came by the Palmyra. But you don't let me speak to Sylvie."

He pronounced her name with a kind emphasis; he had turned and taken her hand, after the first grasp of Rodney's.

"Father, I've broken my promise; but I don't think anybody could have helped it. You couldn't have helped it yourself."

"I've seen Aunt Euphrasia. I've been here almost an hour. I have thanked God that nothing is broken *but* the promise, Rodney; and I think the term of that was broken only because the intent had been so faithfully kept. I'm satisfied with *one* year. I believe all the rest of your years will be safer and better for having this little lady to promise to, and to help you keep your word."

And he bent down his splendid gray head, with the dark eyes looking softly at her, and kissed Sylvie on the forehead.

Sylvie stood still a moment, with a very lovely, happy, shy look upon her downcast face; then she lifted it up quickly, with a clear, earnest expression.

"I hope you think, Mr. Sherrett,—I hope you feel sure,"—she said, "that I wouldn't have been engaged to Rodney while there was a promise?"

"Not more than you could possibly help," said Mr. Sherrett, smiling.

"Not the very least little bit!" said Sylvie, emphatically; and then they all three laughed together.

I don't know why everything should have happened as it did, just in these few days; except—that this book was to be all printed by the twenty-third of April, and it all had to go in.

That very afternoon there came a letter to Miss Euphrasia from Mr. Dakie Thayne.

He had found Mr. Farron Saftleigh in Dubuque; he had pressed him close upon the matter of his transactions with Mrs. Argenter; he had obtained a hold upon him in some other business that had come to his knowledge in the course of his inquiries at Denver: and the result had been that Mr. Farron Saftleigh had repurchased of him the railroad bonds and the deeds of Donnowhair land, to the amount of five thousand dollars; which sum he inclosed in his own cheek payable to the order of Sylvia Argenter.

Knowing, morally, some things that I have not had opportunity to investigate in detail, and cannot therefore set down as verities,—I am privately convinced that this little business agency on the part of Dakie Thayne, was—in some proportion at least,—a piece of a horse-shoe!

If you have not happened to read "Real Folks," you will not know what that means. If you have, you will now get a glimpse of how it had come to Ruth and Dakie that their horse-shoe,—their little section of the world's great magnet of loving relation,—might be made. Indeed, I do know, and can tell you, the very words Ruth said to Dakie one day when they had been married just three weeks.

"I've always thought, Dakie, that if ever I had money,—or if ever I came to advise or help anybody who had, and who wanted to do good with it,—that there would be one special way I should like to take. I should like to sit up in the branches, and shake down fruit into the laps of some people who never would know where it came from, and wouldn't take it if they did; though they couldn't reach a single bough to pick for themselves. I mean nice, unlucky people; people who always have a hard time, and need to have a good one; and are obliged in many things to pretend they do. There are a good many who are willing and anxious to help the very poor, but I think there's a mission waiting for somebody among the pinched-and-smiling people. I've been a Ruth Pinch myself, you see; and I know all about it, Mr. John Westlock!"

So I know they looked about for crafty little chances to piece out and supplement small ways and means; to put little traps of good luck in the way for people to stumble upon,—and to act the part generally of a human limited providence, which is a better thing than fairy godmothers, or enchanted cats, or frogs under the bridge at the world's end, in which guise the gentle charities clothed themselves in the old elf fables, that were told, I truly believe, to be lived out in real doing, as much as the New Testament Parables were. And a great deal of the manifold responsibility that Mr. Dakie Thayne undertakes, as broker or agent in the concerns of others, is undertaken with a deliberate ulterior design of this sort. I think Mr. Farron Saftleigh probably was made to pay about three thousand dollars of the sum he had wheedled Mrs. Argenter out of. Dakie Thayne makes things yield of themselves as far as they will; he brings capacity and character to bear upon his ends as well as money; he knows his money would not last forever if he did not.

Mr. Sherrett and Rodney stayed at Hill-hope over the Sunday. Mr. and Mrs. Kirkbright arrived on Saturday morning.

There was a first home-service in the Chapel-Room that looked out upon the Rock, and into which the conservatory already gave its greenness and sweetness, that first Sunday after Easter.

Christopher Kirkbright read the Collect, Epistle, and Gospel for the day; the Prayer, that God "who had given his only Son to die for our sins, and to rise again for our justification, would grant them so to put away the leaven of malice and wickedness, that they might always serve Him in pureness and truth"; the Assurance of "the victory that overcometh the world, even our faith in the Son of God," who came "not by water only, but by water and blood"; and that "the spirit and the water and the blood agree in one,"—in our redemption; the Story of that First Day of the week, when Jesus came back to his disciples, after his resurrection, and said, "Peace be unto you," *showing them his hands and his side.*

He spoke to them of the Blood of Christ, which is the Pain of God for every one of us; which touches the quick of our own souls where their life is joined to his or else is dead. Of how, when we feel it, we know that this Divine Pain comes down that we may die by it to sin and live again to justification, in pureness and truth, that the Lord shows us his wounds for us, and waits to pronounce his peace upon us; because *He suffers* till we are at peace. That so his goodness leads us to repentance; that the blood of suffering, and the water of cleansing, and the spirit of life renewed, agree in one, that if we receive the one,—if we bear the pain with which He touches us,—we shall also receive the other.

"Bear, therefore, whatever crucifixion you have to bear, because of your wrong-doing. We, indeed, suffer justly; but He, who hath done nothing amiss, suffers at our side. 'If we are planted together in the likeness of his death, we shall also be in the likeness of his resurrection;' our old life is crucified with Him, that the body of sin might be destroyed. 'We are dead unto sin, but alive unto God, through Jesus Christ our Lord.'"

Mary Moxall was there, clothed and in her right mind; her baby on her lap. Good Mrs. Crumford, the mother-matron, sat beside her. Andrew Dorray, the plasterer, and his wife, Annie, were there. Men and women from the farmhouse and the cottages, dressed in their Sabbath best; and little children, looking in with steadfast, wondering eyes, at the open conservatory door, upon the vines and blooms steeped in sunshine, and mingling their sweet odors with the scent of the warm, moist earth in which they grew.

They would all have pinks and rosebuds to carry away with them, to remember the Sunday by, and to be forever linked, in their tender color and fragrance, with the dim apprehension of somewhat holy. There would be an association for them of the heavenly things unseen with the heavenliest things that are seen.

Mr. Kirkbright had given especial pains and foresight to the filling of this little greenhouse. He meant that there should be a summer pleasantness at Hill-hope from the very first.

After dinner he and Desire walked up and down the long front upper gallery upon which their own rooms and their guest-rooms opened, and whence the many windows on the other hand gave the whole outlook upon

Farm and Basin, the smoking kilns, the tidy little homes already established, and the buildings that were making ready for more.

Christopher Kirkbright told his wife of many things he hoped to accomplish. He pointed out here and there what might be done. Over there was a maple wood where they would have sugar-makings in the spring. There was a quarry in yonder hill. Down here, through that left hand hollow and ravine, would run their bit of railroad.

"A little world of itself might almost grow up here on these two hundred acres," he said.

"And for the home,—you must make that large and beautiful, Desire! We are not shut up here to guard and rule a penitentiary; we are to bring the best and sweetest and most beautiful life possible to us, close to the life we want to help. There is room for them and us; there is opportunity for their world and ours to touch each other and grow toward one. We must have friends here, Daisy"; (she let *him* call her "Daisy"; had he not the right to give her a new name for her new life?) "friends to enjoy the delicious summers, and to make the long winters full of holiday times. You must invent delights as well as uses: delights that will be uses. It must be so for *your* sake; I must have my Desire satisfied,—content, in ways that perhaps she herself would not find out her need in."

"*Is* not your Desire satisfied?"

"What a blessed little double name you have! Yes, Daisy, the very Desire of my heart has come to me!"

Rodney and Sylvie walked down again to the Cascade Rock, and finished their talk together,—this April number of it, I mean,—about the brown house and the three-windowed, sunny room, and the grass plot where they would play croquet, and the road to the mills that was shaded all the way down, so that she could walk with her bonnet off to meet him when he was coming up to tea. About the ivies that the "good Miss Goodwyns" had kept safe and thriving at Dorbury, and the furniture that Sylvie had stored in a loft in the Bank Block. How pretty the white frilled curtains would be in the porch room!

"And the interest of the five thousand dollars will be all I shall ever want to spend for anything!"

"We shall be quite rich people, Sylvie. We must take care not to grow proud and snobbish."

"We had much better walk than ride, Rodney. I think that is the riddle that all our spills have been meant to read us."